JOHNNY RODRIGUEZ

Desperado

A piece of my soul

A memoir

JOHNNY RODRIGUEZ

DESPERADO

A PIECE OF MY SOUL

by

JOHNNY RODRIGUEZ

with Austin Teutsch

"Johnny is my hero and owns every song he sings, and if he didn't write it, he might as well have." – Dennis Quaid, actor and singer-songwriter.

"I first met Johnny Rodriguez in 1974 while touring together. We had matching Lincoln Continentals, and we must have played every juke joint in Texas. Now, over 40 years later, I'm proud to say we just recorded our first duet together. He is one of our greatest singers and my buddy!" – Tanya Tucker, two-time Grammy Award winner and Country Music Hall of Fame Inductee, 2023.

Johnny Rodriguez
Desperado: A Piece of My Soul

Published by:
Vega Publishing House, LLC
P.O. Box 81262
Bakersfield, CA 93380

vegapublishinghousellc@gmail.com
https://johnnyrodriguezofficial.com

ISBN: 979-8394959226
Editor: Jordan Gonzales

Front and back cover photos: Patrice Ash
Back cover photo: Earl Nottingham/Texas Parks and Wildlife Department

Cover Design: Mantera Advertising Agency

Library of Congress Control Number: 2021938827

Printed in the United States of America

Best Wishes...Vaya con Dios!

Johnny Rodriguez

Dedication

"And he will restore the hearts of fathers to their children and the hearts of the children to their fathers."
– Malachi 4:6

To my two beloved daughters:
Aubry Rae
Teresa Ann

And godchildren:
Blanca and Blake

This book is also dedicated to my late father, Andres Sr., for his acts of integrity and courage. It is further dedicated to my beloved late mother, Isabel, for her unwavering love, support, and faith in me. Thank you for encouraging me to follow my heart's desire, pursue my dreams, and reach for the stars to become a singer. Your memory lives forever in my heart.

Table of Contents

* * * * *

Prologue

"Give Your Hands to serve and your hearts to love."
– Mother Teresa

December 10, 1951
Rodriguez Home
Sabinal, Texas
My First Recording

In a tiny four-room house in the small town of Sabinal, Texas, a petite, biracial woman named Isabel Davis Rodriguez starts her day like any other. But this day will be eventful, as she will deliver a beloved son by nightfall. She is adored by her loving husband, Andres Rodriguez, a hard-working man, and is already a mother to eight children. These are sons Andres Jr., Manual Jesus "Jesse," Valeriano "Vale," Reynaldo, and Raul (deceased), and three daughters, Ofelia, Antonia, and Eloisa.

Well-known as a woman of substance, she makes visible her faith in God and the Blessed Virgin Mary, mother of Jesus, with a cross and saints that surround and sustain her. Her family knows her as a woman of song, humor, kindness, humility, and strength.

As the increasing labor pains near and the doctor is summoned, this God-fearing and devout Catholic Christian is leaving the delivery in His hands. Anxiously awaiting the birth of her child, one can only imagine the silent prayer going through her mind: "By the grace of God, I'll have this child with the help of the doctor." Isabel's only concern is that her newborn baby be healthy, be that child, son, or daughter.

When the white doctor in another town accepted a late call to travel 60 miles away to deliver another routine pregnancy, he arrived on time. He tended to his familiar patient, Isabel. During delivery, he notices the ten o'clock news is on and can't resist eyeing the television. He knows the drill of delivery that has brought many babies into the world. Mother Isabel notices that her doctor has his eyes focused on the nightly news and can't help feeling uneasy. She fears he is not entirely focused on her delivery.

A healthy baby boy named Juan Raul Davis-Rodriguez was recorded as being born at home in Sabinal, Texas, on December 11, 1951. It was early the next day that the doctor made the long trip back home.

That doctor was exhausted when, the next day, he completed the birth paperwork. He incorrectly recorded the date on Johnny's birth certificate as the 11th rather than the 10th. This incident gave Johnny a complex that would affect the rest of his young life. Is it any wonder, growing up, that he felt a sense of insignificance? The doctor could not even record the correct day he was born.

Perhaps it was an oversight. Perhaps it did not concern his ethnicity or being born in poverty. Nonetheless, it created a feeling of inadequacy in Johnny. One could also speculate that it made a young boy more determined to prove to himself and others that he was just as important as those around him.

"All I know is this one recording error affected my self-worth throughout my upbringing and adult years," Johnny said. "It would take years before my mindset knew the truth and reality of what transpired… it was an unintentional mistake."

Everyone knows a father may forget the date and time of his child's birth, but a mother never forgets the details of her child's delivery. Johnny's mother, Isabel, was asked if she could remember what time of day her son was born. She replied: "I clearly remember what day and time my son, Raul, was born: December 10th. He was then, as he is to me today, God's gift and blessing."

Johnny's first language was Spanish. He admits he did not speak English until pre-kindergarten. Regardless of his language limitation, he didn't know that his ability to speak two languages would be an asset. It would define his distinctive voice and signature style in country music, ultimately making him a superstar overnight. His musical ability as a singer and master guitarist made him a formidable force in his impressive and lucrative career. It leveled the playing field.

Johnny would go on to move adoring fans through his music in country, mariachi, rancheros, and Tejano genres for generations.

"I must have been listening in my mother's womb," he explained, "because I am an avid news viewer today who listens to the news wherever I am. I turn the TV on when I'm traveling from hotel to hotel and will opt to tune in to the news, even at home. I like staying abreast of the news while traveling because it keeps my mind fresh, and I like staying informed about what's going on in the world. The news makes for an interesting conversation and breaks the ice as well. It also allows me to know who's who and who's doing what in the world, including local news. Many times, in an empty, sterile, and lonely hotel room, I will turn the TV on to keep me company. It gives me an edge and enlightens me. I feel a sense of connection to a city, big or small. They say an unborn child can pick up on vibrations and sounds coming from the mother's womb. In my case, it's true… the good doctor and I both were tuned in to the same channel."

Little did the doctor know that he would be delivering a baby who would grow to impact and capture the hearts of millions on channels and stages around the world. Juan Raul Davis-Rodriguez, better known as "Johnny," was that child.

This is his story.

* * * * *

Introduction

By Austin Teutsch

I first met Johnny Rodriguez in Pleasanton, Texas, in 1973, during the summer before my freshman year at the University of Arkansas, just after Johnny released his first number-one record. I believed I knew a little bit about music, quality, and what it takes to become a superstar. After all, I had been playing in country bands in South Texas since age 15. As I was beginning a new chapter in my life, Johnny was about to begin a new chapter in the story of the country music industry as the first Mexican American country music star.

It was clear to see the raw talent Johnny possessed, as song after song, the crowd became more mesmerized by this young man's unique voice. It was a very pleasant night in Pleasanton.

From the moment Johnny stepped on stage with his guitar, I knew he was bound for stardom. I knew he was going to shine brighter than the stage lights that propelled him into the galaxy of greatness. In fact, that sweltering summer night, Johnny proved he wasn't, isn't, and never will be a one-hit wonder. He sizzled as hot as the other great musicians sharing the bill with him that night. I'm talking about major hitmakers such as Tanya Tucker, a woman with a big voice who launched her career when she was still a young girl opening and touring with Johnny Rodriguez. Today, Johnny is still filling dance halls and venues. I believe he always will.

Let's face it: Music is a universal language. But most people speak it merely by listening. If making music was easy, we'd all be doing it. It is, in fact, very difficult to "make it."

Johnny covered all the necessary factors from day one. He had the looks, the guitar-playing ability, the voice of a natural-born singer, and the intangible humility that saw him in good stead before the powers that be in Nashville. These qualities served him well with his country music peers, too.

He was and is just a good old Texas boy with a Texas-size talent admired by the best. From Johnny Cash and Merle

Haggard to Marty Robbins, Roger Miller, and Willie Nelson, he's a star. And then there are Dolly, Loretta Lynn, Connie Smith, Tammy, and Charley McClain. Johnny has played with and has been admired by them all. I guess what makes Johnny so incredibly good is that he never lets anything go to his head. He lets his music do his talking for him.

Shy to a fault, Johnny wears his music and smile well because it is genuine and straight from his heart. People love him as much as they love his work.

Like many country music musicians, part of the success came from his sincerity to live every moment in life — even when that lifestyle sometimes allowed things to get in the way. I guess the fact that Johnny became so famous and earned so much money while still so young and vulnerable caused him to falter occasionally.

Johnny, however, always came back to living his passion and purpose of playing music in time to save himself. His fans have never left his side no matter how life unfolded in the ballad of his life's song.

While he's famous for his clear, smooth, flowing, and unique sound, Johnny's life was not always smooth and easy. He came from a hard-scrabble background in South Texas. He stumbled along the way as many country music musicians have, but like many who falter, Johnny picked himself up. He showed resilience, took responsibility, played again, and let life unfold.

Johnny's fans have remained loyal. They continue to travel for miles around, proving the potency of hard-core country music is still very much a cultural experience. It is an experience that helped shape the mindset of a nation. Johnny and his fans have a special connection that keeps this popular art form alive and well today despite a pandemic or the constant changes country music endures.

Now comes this book, of which I'm so proud to be a part. I am fortunate to have worked with Johnny to co-write and record his life on paper for posterity, dispelling rumors accompanying his truth.

One thing about Johnny Rodriguez: He is a man of integrity. He wants things to be *right*. He works at that in every show he does today. At 70, Johnny still wants to deliver quality. He refuses to let his fans down.

Johnny poured out his heart as we worked to get things right for this book. He shared his story so you will see beyond his musical talent and the pedestal upon which misguided fans have put him on. It is his hope that you will view him as the man he is, one who is more human and relatable than we might at first think.

Perfect? Johnny Rodriguez is far from that. Sincere? Johnny is that, without a doubt. Relevant and resilient? He's always that. Why is there a book and a new CD after all these years? Because it's time.

There will never be a lineup of country music stars such as those who shined between 1945 and 1995. Johnny Rodriguez is one of the last of those great country stars. This book substantiates that he is anything but a remnant of a dying breed. Throughout his career, Johnny charted 14 country number-one hits as he became a country music superstar and achieved international stardom. He released 36 albums and charted 45 singles. Music is in his veins. He isn't going to slow down his Rodriguez Run anytime soon.

It was time for Johnny to tell his life story. All the old guards of what true country music was — Buck Owens, Merle Haggard, George Jones, Johnny Cash, Johnny Bush, Gary Stewart, Tammy Wynette, and Loretta Lynn — are gone now. Johnny Rodriguez is a living legend. Through that legacy, country music fans… the young, the old, the rich, the poor, and the unemployed… are reminded of what true country music was and should be. When a talented star such as Johnny performs, there is no need for rock guitarists, double-bass drum kits, pyrotechnics, and other toots and whistles. These gimmicks have infiltrated the industry during the past 25 years to appeal to the buying power of the 14- to 35-year-old fan base.

There's nothing wrong with making money. After all, country music is big business. Fortunately, Johnny has remained true to himself and the genre. His intention is to give fans what they deserve: good, quality music. The big payoff is for Johnny's fans, who appreciate talent in pure form. That's where Johnny focuses his energy rather than on the power of a dollar. That's just his style. He is the most beloved singer in country music history for a reason.

Coming from a small four-room house shared with nine brothers and sisters in Sabinal, Texas, Johnny is my neighbor of sorts. That's just down the road a way — or within spitting distance — from where I grew up.

Before I heard him live on that summer night in 1973, Johnny was one of my favorite country music singers. He still is. I'm proud, finally, to be a part of presenting his legendary life in this book. I hope you enjoy this inspiring look at how the luck of the draw combined with pure talent, passion, purpose, and love can turn a young Mexican boy into one of the most appreciated entertainers of all time.

I am also confident that you are going to fall in love all over again with the man and his music as you discover what is myth and what is truth. These lie behind the legend whose light will shine if there are still country stars in the galaxy of American music.

Be inspired by one of the most beloved country music singers in history. Let him tell you his compelling story.

– Austin Teutsch

* * * * *

Chapter 1 Deep in the Heart of Texas

"A reader lives a thousand lives before he dies. The man who never reads lives only one."
– George R.R. Martin

It's an honor to share the most heartfelt stories that I have experienced in my life as a singer in the arena of country music. Hopefully, they will encourage you to pursue your goals and never give up, no matter the odds. My message is simple. My life's journey shows people who are struggling that if I could break barriers, achieve success, and overcome challenges, they can too.

I firmly believe Texas is the greatest state in the union, with its breathtaking flowers, athletes, BBQ, history, longhorns, food, people, places, and its music. I've visited a lot of places in the world. One thing is certain: there is no place on Earth where I would rather live than right here. Texas is and will always be in my blood and in my heart. I am also a proud patriot supporting our veterans at home and overseas.

If there's one thing I can say before I begin, it is that my profession has been a blessing to me. I have learned invaluable life lessons that I carry with me today. Do I have regrets? I have some, but I wouldn't be the man I am today if it weren't for my past.

If I have learned anything in life, it is not to live or dwell in the past. I hold no grudges. I choose to keep looking forward *siempre adelante* because I am a better person today. I refuse to distance myself from people for mistakes I made. I have evolved and am enjoying my life doing what I do best, singing to my heart's content. I still perform on stage and entertain fans with my music. I am very grateful for God's blessings. I don't want to take anything for granted, lest I be cursed.

I look forward to new beginnings and have a purpose in life to serve others for the higher good. I enjoy helping others overcome barriers by offering hope in sharing my personal experiences. These range from the beginning of my life to where I am today.

To be honest, I never thought I would make it long enough to write a book about my life. When I look back on my life, when I see how many people have passed, it feels unreal to me. How am I still here? Who would have believed it? I am here to stay.

Frankly, I had thought of writing a book one day, but did not take that step or take the time to put it all down. That was not until Austin Teutsch kept nudging me about it. In 2012, he contacted me and kept after me, saying I was one of the last country music singers left to inspire the up-and-coming country artists.

When the documentary filmmaker Ken Burns did his 2019 exposé on the History of Country Music on PBS, my life was given a few minutes of airtime with the likes of Willie Nelson, Buck Owens, Merle Haggard, Johnny Cash, George and Tammy, Loretta Lynn, and Dolly. I was in good company, so I got to think seriously about my book.

So here it is, all of it. When you are a poor Mexican American kid from a small town deep in the heart of South Texas, you are not supposed to dream of becoming a famous *anything*, let alone a country music singer. During those times, it was unheard of. Those were pipe dreams. Lying in a four-room house with my nine brothers and sisters and my mother and father, Isabell Davis-Rodriguez, and Andres Rodriguez Sr., I was just another Mexican boy destined to work the crops in the fields. Maybe I'd end up on the derrick of an oil rig, or maybe I'd get some menial job around town. They say you have got to dream big! But for me, I had to dream within what was reality. Anything else was a lost cause that would lead nowhere, I was told.

When I talk about my life, it's going to sound like I'm bragging, but I'm not. I thank God for my life's experiences and opportunities. Today, my heart is full of gratitude. I have been doing this for a long time — about 50 years — feeling blessed to be doing things out of the ordinary.

One thing that I will say up front is that I give a lot of credit to the generation (Baby Boomers) into which I was born. It seems that in the generation before mine, there was a lot more prejudice expressed in opinions, politics, and values. Luckily, times were changing gradually.

When I was in the first grade, most of the time the Mexican kids kept to themselves in the Barrio and the white kids stayed with their own kind. That's just the way it was in my hometown. Making friends at school just opened a whole different experience. It opened my ears to country music, for one thing, because I had been listening to mariachi music before that. I started playing the guitar when I was six years old. I remember I got a guitar on Easter Day.

Between 6 and 12 years old, I went to Bible School every day. I was an altar boy and went to catechism and made my first Holy Communion and Confirmation. I just stayed close to the church because I lived right across the street from it. Obviously, I was raised and rooted in tradition at St. Patrick's. Any function that came through town, that's where it happened — at the Catholic Church to make money.

They had fiestas called *Jamaica* and we had Cinco De Mayo, which was a big day, and all the La Junto dances next door would be right there. We celebrated every kind of festival theme at the church; there was a lot going on several times a year where I lived. It's where our social life revolved. I started hanging out with both white kids and Mexican kids.

When I got to sixth grade, my friends and I entered a junior high talent show in school. I started playing more music. I'd hang out and get in a truck with just guys and some old ranchers. I always had an old soul because I was taught to respect elders. I'd get in a car with just guys playing my guitar singing away, going down a country road, out in the boonies where nobody could bother us and where we'd drink beer. Every now and then we'd run into a carload of girls who would show up. We'd hang out with them making small talk. We'd have a lot of fun out in the country in that small town, Sabinal.

For some reason, God gave me a voice. I didn't know it until I got a guitar from my older brother, Andres Jr., at 8. He was like a father to me, while my actual father was busy trying to make money for all of us to be able to eat. In my adult years, when I was accepted in the entertainment industry, I remember sitting down one day with a friend, Dolly Parton. We were trying to figure out how poor people like us ever get out of being poor. We both came from large families—she had 12 brothers and sisters, and I had 9. We both asked one another why it was us who God picked for fame instead of someone else. We figured out there really was no rhyme or reason to it all. It is the luck of the draw or God's blessing who filled the slot.

In the arena of my life, there are countless crazy ups and downs. I am a father, brother, grandfather, godfather, and uncle of many nephews and nieces. I have first-hand experience in the music business industry and with the disastrous results of relationships of every kind. Like many families, we have our problems, but we also have a lot of love. You know the saying: Blood is thicker than water. When someone needs prayer or help, we are each there for one another. No matter how much time has gone by, we can always pick up the phone and talk like it was yesterday. We love one another, and I am always available to my daughters, Aubry and Teresa, and no less to my siblings.

There is not a thing I would not do for my children. My daughters especially are the beat of my heart and bloodline… your blood in my body (*tu sangre en mi cuerpo*). They are my reason and "why" I do what I do. I love them with every fiber of my being, body, mind, and soul. They give me strength more than anyone every day of my life since the day they were born. Any expression of love given to them is felt and received by me because when they hurt, I hurt. My love for them is unconditional and immeasurable.

It is well known that drugs and alcohol in America have affected many households. These issues followed me in my career. It was always a choice I made and a decision that cost me dearly, even to this day. Luckily, I have forgiven myself for all the hardship and bad decisions I made that affected others. I have also let go, in turn, of those who wronged me. I can now move forward in my life with some degree of self-respect and functionality. God's grace made it possible for me to have faith in Him.

I would not be the man I am today if it were not for my family, as well as the relationships of friends and lovers who journeyed with me through my life. I helped individuals both personally, and professionally, because there were many who gave me a hand up and helped me in my growth to evolve.

During my lifetime, I have met many people and visited different countries worldwide, but I am happy and proud to say that I keep in touch with the same friends in my youth as I do today.

In a nutshell, some could call me the prodigal son. I went out in search of adventure, sowing my wild oats, living in the streets, and living off the land. I tried and gave my hand in marriage, (4 times). I've been in and out of relationships only to end up alone, sometimes by choice, sadly, sometimes not.

What I discovered while I was living my crazy and wild life was, I was in search of finding and loving myself. It took me a lifetime to learn that self-love is key to any relationship. I found this out just in time, so I know there is still hope for me — and for others — to choose love and life, whether you see or feel it. You only need to believe it. Everything else is irrelevant.

Law Enforcement and My Father's Ways: Head Honcho

I have always had respect for law enforcement and been secretly attracted to the profession. My father was a sheriff for San Antonio Sheriff's Department. He did not hold back on what he expected from his children. That was to toe the line and be respectful and law-abiding. My dad was a disciplinarian, but a gentle giant of a man. He raised his family to be hard-working, kind, and close. All us kids knew we could always depend on our dad and each other, but my dad expected more from each of us and he was unapologetic about his strict ways.

I continued to make mistakes that threw me back in a jail cell when I was a kid. It would end up being like a disappearing act for me while I did my time (and no one was any wiser for it). Little did I know that later in my life I would be faced with much more than merely stealing goats. It would be the most serious thing of which I had ever been a part… and it scared the hell out of me. I did not have to ask God to be by my side. The only way I got out of it was in the name of justice and by His grace and unconditional love for me.

Overall, I had a good life growing up. We were not rich, but my father worked hard, first as a San Antonio policeman and then in a civil service job at Kelly Air Force Field. San Antonio had 5 military bases. They always said if the Russians were going to hit the United States, San Antonio would be one of the first targets. We sure learned how to jump under our desks during those old drills in grade school should war come to town again.

For fun we used to go camping. It was cheap, fun, and there were usually a few girls hanging around. Now, if you know anything about the part of Texas Hill country I grew up in, you know it really is God's country, beautiful and serene.

When you were poor and not working, there was little to do in those days. For me, it was strumming a guitar and trying to get my voice up to sing. I hung around a lot of white boys, but I had some Mexican friends who liked country music, too. There were not many Mexicans in those days who listened to country music. As a matter of fact, back then, I do not remember any Mexican singers playing country music.

Freddie Fender had a minor hit in 1959 with some songs he sung in both Spanish and English, but that was about it. His hit song was "Wasted Days And Wasted Nights." He'd pull that one back out in the '70s and run it up the pop charts again in 1975. Then there was the late Ritchie Valens, who was a legitimate rockstar in the '50s… until the day the music died in a plane crash with Buddy Holly and The Big Bopper. Fender and Valens were the only acts that had chart success back then as Mexicans, well, until I came along.

After my success, the door was always open to anyone of any race to become a musical star of any genre. There are white boys and girls singing bilingual country music today… It's the sign of the times and culture that's always been a part of our history, so it's no surprise there. Little did I know a South Texas rancher, a stint in jail, a Texas Ranger, and a silly goat would set me on that trail to stardom.

Memories of My Mother

As a child, I marveled at how my mother knew how to keep our family together. My father worked hard and supported nine children, so he often worked two jobs and was far away. In the meantime, mom held down the fort at home, cooking, cleaning, raising my siblings and me.

My mother's wisdom and ability to get along with others was extraordinary. She was loving, caring, honest, and funny. My mother was a teacher to many. She could cook like no one and made the best Mexican food, especially enchiladas. I learned to cook from my mother. She put her whole heart and soul into cooking for her family and friends. Everyone loved her personality, too. She was easy to talk with and she loved people. I miss her every day of my life. She was my best cheerleader, a blessing who supported me throughout my life.

In every sense of the word, I was my mother's son and proud of it. I admired, respected, and paid attention to my mom, especially her cooking skills.

The Music and My Childhood

I guess if it was not for music, I would not have known what to do as a kid. It opened doors for me in many ways, helping me socially, emotionally, physically, and spiritually. And I am sure glad my fame came at a young age, preventing me from getting into more trouble out of boredom or heartache. Losing my father, then a much-loved brother who meant the world to me, then landing in jail for this or that… It was a life with no end to it unless you got out. I thank God I got out when I did.

It would take a world of unbelievable events for it to happen for me. It would also take a few people who believed in me when I started getting rather good at picking and singing country music. I always felt God's hand on my shoulder, gently getting my attention and reminding me He was with me. Who else could it have been?

From my days as an altar server at St. Patrick's, then getting out of high school with a diploma, I knew right from wrong, but I did not always apply it to my own life. I found myself fudging or manipulating things in life to get by. I had a "survival of the fittest" mentality. I learned to fend for myself.

To a certain extent, I am still doing a little growing up every day. As I write this book, I keep thinking back to my days as a kid in high school and then my days of learning how to be a country music performer.

I ran long-distance track and played on the varsity football and basketball teams for the Sabinal Yellowjackets. Participating in sports really helped give me confidence, although that is not why I joined. I signed up because sports were a great outlet for me, giving me something positive to do.

I tried out for the annual Ford Punt, Pass, and Kick football contest and I was a runner-up to Tommy Smith in a talent contest I entered with my guitar. When I first walked up to the stage to sing, I could hear a pin drop. Then it happened: I got a big applause. It was the sweetest sound ever, holding and standing in front of a microphone. I was doing whatever I could to keep focused on getting out of high school in one piece. I was frustrated with how slow getting into a real band was taking. I wanted to get this music thing started here and now, especially since I decided I wanted to sing and play country music as my life's work and dream.

In 1970, when it was time for me to leave Sabinal, Texas and break out into wherever it is I was supposed to be… I did not know where I was supposed to be! All I did know was that I wanted my music to be a part of it. Little did I know that getting in trouble again would start a chain of events that would take me to heights those crazy dreams of my childhood could never equal. Unfortunately, as fate would have it, I had to take a detour along the way.

* * * * *

Chapter 2 Stories in My Youth

"My family has always been an inspiration to me, and I will never be able to repay them for what they've done."
– Johnny Rodriguez

My father possessed a strong work ethic that I inherited from him, my mother, and my entire family. Both my parents taught me how to treat people and how to have respect for others around me. They also taught me about God and the Bible. I am not religious, but I strongly believe in my Catholic faith. It has kept my family close. To this day, we love and care about one another very much.

My dad was a strong and dignified man. I looked up to and respected him above others my entire life. I started singing at the age of six. My dad played guitar, but he was no genius with it, nor did he play professionally. He knew how to play chords enough to play music. He and my brother, Andres, inspired me to sing and play guitar. He was my dad, my hero, and I was his biggest fan.

I lost my dad to cancer. It is an insidious disease and his death caused me deep grief and sorrow in both my personal and professional career. The pain of loss never goes away. It was a turning point in my life to continue to numb myself or somehow find the courage to move forward in my life.

On the day he entered the hospital, he had come directly from work. He was a man who had a high tolerance for pain to continue working despite feeling unbearable discomfort. My grieving mother emptied the hospital closet where she found my dad's work uniform still hanging in the closet. He worked on the job until his frail body could go no more.

It was hard to shake thinking all the time how cancer robbed me of my dad. I always felt paralyzed and stuck because of it. It felt as if my life stood still, and I stopped growing emotionally. I could not face that death came knocking at my door so early in my life. It didn't seem fair to feel such deep pain and loss.

My poor mother. My biggest "Aha" moment was that I had to become a man quickly. I was in desperate need of both a personal and professional plan because I sure as hell had my "why." When my father died in my late teens, I started thinking about what I was going to do with my life to help my mother. It was a lot of weight on my shoulders.

I can remember my brothers and my mom working to get paid, pitching in to make sure we would make it. . . paying our bills on time and putting food on the table. We all did what we could to make things easier for the family. I never wanted to be a burden to my mother, so I did what I could to earn a little money to pay my way. That is where my trusty guitar and voice came in handy for the rest of my life.

Family Mi Familia

I come from a very close and loving family of educators. I am just as proud of each of my siblings as I think they are of me. I was the only singer in the bunch, although my brother Andres, my hero, was a huge influence in my life. He cowboyed and loved music. Andres sang both Spanish and country music, mostly around the house and with friends. My family is where I inherited my love to sing in Spanish and had the greatest impact and growing popularity with the masses.

I would like to mention that I have a nephew named Vale who is a good country music singer and I think his singing and audio voice comes as close to mine as anyone. He also has a daughter, Alyssa Rae, who sings.

I always felt my mother's tongue (Spanish) was an asset for me because there was more ground to cover in terms of an audience and relatability with music listeners everywhere. I felt like Mariachi music and country music were myriad of sorts.

We all have contributed something of ourselves that is greater than ourselves to reach and teach others through words, and in my case, songs. Some family members went into public service, and some dedicated their lives in the education profession. My youngest brother, Ricky, is a compassionate and caring high school Special Education teacher. He recently retired from the school system in our hometown of Sabinal, Texas. I've always admired and respected my younger brother for his intelligence, desire, and dedication to teaching. My brother would often return to teaching after retiring. He loved his profession and kids that much. My two remaining sisters, Antonia and Eloisa, both worked for the school system as well. They were always self-sufficient, good moms who had very fine and respectable professions as well.

My Mother's Son

"A mother is a son's first true love... a son especially that first son, is a mother's last true love."
– Denzel Washington

My mother would sing Mariachi songs at the Catholic church, St. Patrick's, across the street. I loved that church and intended to someday step foot into it again. They called my mom "El Charra," and, like me, she loved to sing, mostly around the house.

The first time I ever stood on stage I was standing next to my mother while she sang. I was only four years old. Someone handed me the maracas to play. I loved the jovial feeling of it all: happy faces, cheering, dancing, and applauding. I was attracted to performing on stage hook, line, and sinker from that day on.

In my mother's memory, my newest upcoming CD release is why I sing the mariachi songs of my mother or Canciones de Mi Madre. *Building Bridges*: *A Beyond the Interview Box Set*" is the name of my bilingual album. In my singing career and in relationships, I am most proud my songs were mostly about building and mending burning bridges — connecting the dots and bridging gaps, if you will, where cultures sometimes collided and were once divided.

As our family would gather around the dinner table, conversations going all at once, I can still hear my mother say, "Eat and shut up," or "Come y callese." After slaving over a hot stove, mom knew best, and she wanted her food to be enjoyed while it was piping hot. I miss my mother daily. The songs of my mother remain in my heart today as they did in my youth

My Brothers: Mis Hermanos

I miss my eldest brother, Andres, and my parents, every day of my life. Andres worked hard in different jobs. Once he sheared sheep with eight other guys in that nasty, hot, and oily job, but he did it. He was a hard worker and provider like my dad. I always felt protected around him.

Bullies left me alone because Andres was my brother. He made me feel proud. Of all my brothers, I followed Andres around the most, observing him mostly in silence. My eyes would ask questions that only he could read.

I'd go hunting and fishing with my brothers all the time. I was 12 years old when I got my first shotgun. We played games around the house and always had something to occupy us. One brother taught me one thing or another: to be better at sports, ride a horse, how to work or learn a new skill. I was blessed with their love and support, never feeling alone. I miss my brothers dearly. We learned to live off the land, improvising tools or items to get by. In our big family, it was never about "things." It was about the company and the memories we made of being together. It is who I am today, appreciating family and being in the moment.

I was close to all my brothers, and we did a lot of cool things together, especially driving around in a car or gathering for holidays and visits in my mother's home. I have one brother left, Ricky. He's a kind and great guy. Smart, too. Everyone loves him.

When we were younger, my brother Jesse's wife, Cory, would make bunuelos (fried pastry sprinkled with sugar/cinnamon), but my brother Ricky and I could not get enough of them. We also enjoyed going on errands for her and family members, too, especially when we were told to get ourselves a soda pop.

I have always been attracted to the cowboy and rodeo ways of life. It all started with Andres. Some say he was a little rough around the edges, but as I said, he worked hard for his family. He liked his beer and the bars, but he had a dang good heart and he watched out for me. I had just lost my dad, and he died. It was then that I knew how cruel and unfair life can be.

My grieving seemed endless, so I put pen to paper and wrote a song about my brother in remembrance *recuerdo*. It was my way of expressing my love while missing him.

The song is "Jimmy Was A Drinking Kind of Man," released in 1973 on my *All I Ever Meant To Do Was Sing* album. The lyrics begin, "Jimmy was a drinking kind of man... He loved to hear a good hillbilly band, the scar across his face was Jimmy's brand cause Jimmy was a drinking kind of a man."

My Sisters: *Mis Hermanas*

My sisters, *mis hermanas*, played a big part in my life. My oldest sister, Ofelia (who has since passed), practically raised me because my mother had so many kids vying for her love and attention. There were so many of us kids scattered throughout the whole house. God bless her... she tried her best to keep up with all of us.

Ofelia would always make me feel special by bringing me something for my birthday or special occasions for this or that. She also bought me a real guitar on Easter. I carried and played it everywhere I'd go and kept it for a long time.

I learned a lot from my brothers, too, of course, things that men like to do... work and sports, mostly. But my sisters taught me different things, like grooming and what I looked like if I was combing my hair wrong, or what clothes looked best on me. They had good eyes and would forever advise me as sisters honestly do, mostly about how to do the right thing. Both my sisters, Antonia and Eloisa, were educators who taught in schools.

My middle sister, Antonia, was level-headed and never afraid to speak her truth with me. I remember when I first got the idea to go to Nashville. I didn't know what to do. She said, "well, at least you could say you've been there if you go." Her words of encouragement helped me a lot at that time. Little did she know that her advice gave me the confidence I needed to step out of my comfort zone and pursue my dream. I could always count on and turn to Antonia and Eloisa to give me sound advice, as only sisters can do.

My sisters also taught me how to cook. I cook well, too. I know how to do domestic chores because of my sisters. Among the people I'd met years later, my family helped me get through everything and would make it all feel worth it.

To Wish Upon a Star

At the tender age of six or seven, I remember squeezing in with family around the television on Sunday to watch Disney's opening theme song, where Jiminy Cricket sang, "When You Wish Upon A Star." Its melody enthralled me to no end then, as it mesmerizes me today whenever I look up to Texas's most beautiful star-lit skies in search of the brightest "star" among them all. Nostalgia always sets in and makes me smile as I think back to the same song stuck in my head. I remember the dreams I imagined back then and the ones I wish for today.

Life is funny that way! Some things remain hidden in our hearts as they did in childhood yet resurface at times in our adulthood when we least expect them. They give us hope.

In my youth, it was easier for me to take care of me and keep my eyes on the prize, up towards the heavenly skies and to believe in myself, lest I hit my target or risk my fairytale coming true as I became a country music singer. If you want to make your wishes come true, my advice is to work hard, network, and connect heart-to-heart with others. Keep on dreaming.

As a young boy looking up at the Texas sky, my wish would be then, as it remains today... to sing to the world.

Dreamin' About a Nomad's Life

I remember reading about the nomads in *National Geographic Magazine*—I found their lifestyle fascinating because I've always loved adventure and travel. What I learned in life is exercising the power of visualization could make it come true. First, by setting off rockets of desire and seeing what materializes. In other words, dream on, but you must be careful what you wish for bccausc I've been to every state in the United States, in doing so. Not bad for a South Texas country boy.

In the Still of the Night

There was an important and scary time in my life that happened at home when I was six or seven years old. It's a vivid memory that I think about today, which sends a shiver down my spine when I do. Andres and my mother were in a heavy conversation in which he was frantically telling her that he had just beat the hell out of a rival *Lucio,* or a brother of his in the hood ***barrio***. Soon, a Mexican gang member in a car pulled up in front of the house. Before I knew what was happening, a bullet flew across my brother's back. It upset and scared me. I can only imagine what fear my mother felt when she saw it before her own eyes.

I understand that later, the matter got all ironed out. It really did. One thing about my brother Andres is that he would never back down from a fight. He stood tall, slim, and confident. He wouldn't start a fight, but he was sure to finish one. The machismo in the Rodriguez men got the best of us at times.

Crocodile Story: A Boy's Pet

Not your everyday pet . . . but a conversation piece for a young kid making friends. Guess you could say my fascination with animals was out of the ordinary. At seven years old, my brother Andres brought home a souvenir of sorts just for me. It was a 6" long crocodile that he found while picking vegetables up north in the fields. He had a funny-looking bunt nose and pudgy stubby little legs.

As you can guess, an animal like that can't be tamed. Truth is he's dangerous and unpredictable and has its own place in the wild.

My mother warned me, "Son, I'm going to warn you one time only about that crocodile, so you better keep an eye on him. There will be no second chances." It was my responsibility to care for and keep tabs of its whereabouts, which meant out of everyone's way.

My sisters hated that thing. .....They were scared to death of him. I guess because he had ugly-looking teeth. I was just a kid, but I loved taking care of my little buddy, but it drove the girls crazy. I thought it was cool and my twenty friends coming over to see him, did too. No one had a crocodile as a pet in their house, let alone in their room. Yeah, I guess you could say, I was unique or strange, but I felt an obligation to protect the species and not the other way around. After all, the pet was small and seemingly harmless, but that's not what my family thought. I had him for four months and the little sucker would bite the hand that fed him.

At first, I would grab him by his tail to move him around and let him craw up my arm to my elbow. You might ask, what does a crocodile sound like when crawling up my arm? Well, he makes his clack, clack, clack sound with his teeth . . . it sounds like a laser gun sound . . . pew pew pew chirps with some squeaking and grunting. I kept him in a box, for a while, but he started to grow. Oh! and they do bite. I didn't trust that MF anymore.

Soon, I had to put him in a 5' x 8' deep pit in the backyard where I threw in water, rocks, and vegetation and stuff for him to crawl around.

Again, my friends couldn't believe I had a crocodile as a pet. All he did was try to bite people. That sucker grew way too fast to about 1 ½ ft long. I remember coming home from school one day, excited to see my buddy (no name crocodile), but I found it mysteriously disappeared. To my surprise, he was gone, just like that! I know who did it too. It was one of my sisters and that's all I'm going to say. You can only imagine why. Screeching girls don't care much for critters, let alone a dangerous and creepy-lookin' crocodile. Still, he was my crocodile; nobody else wanted him. I had a tarantula, too.

Grammar School: Bartering At Its Best

In grammar school, everyone knew me as Raul. I was shy because English was my second language 'til grade school. What was helpful to me and broke the ice-making friends was in the first grade, when classmate Bobby Wall shared half of his peanut butter and jelly sandwich with me. I gave him part of my taco because I wanted half of his lunch. I didn't like eating tacos for lunch in a paper bag because too many kids made fun of it not looking like a plain Balogna sandwich, I guess. It was a nice change and a delicious, sweet treat. This small exchange was helpful for me because I could make a friend this way. It was a friendship that lasted a lifetime for doing things that kids do when life was not complicated. It was the best of times to have the heart of a child where innocence was the norm and not prejudice. I am still friends with all the guys I knew back then, and we all still stay in touch despite the years and distance between us.

When I was six years old, I would play baseball in the muddy puddles. I had a sling shot too and a tarantula, and Horny toad. I broke my arm playing around like I was Tarzan… "Me Tarzan, You Jane." Wasn't Tarzan everyone's hero? Oh, and let's not forget Zorro with Anita Cabrillo portrayed by Mouseketeer favorite, "Annette, Annette, Annette" Funicello.

Since I was the second to the youngest of the nine kids, some of my older brothers and sisters had left home to marry and do their own thing by the time I was a freshman in high school, and sports was my way of trying to stand out from the pack. I ran track, played on the starting line in football, and loved playing Little League baseball. I tried out for the annual Ford Punt, Pass & Kick competition. I was a skinny or mean and lean little thing, not much bigger than 5'7" and 135 pounds soaking wet, but I had an asset—I could run, making it hard to catch me on the football field. To this day, I haven't gained much weight since. I can eat like a horse, drink buckets of beer, and not gain an ounce. I guess I'm blessed more than most. I should start the Johnny Rodriguez Liquid Diet.

Boy Scouts of America

A bunch of my buddies, about four of us, joined up with the Boys Scouts of America, where we started out as Cub Scouts to Eagle Scouts. It was cool, too, because we engaged in a lot of outdoor activities in sports and in nature. We earned our scout badges, too, for the good deeds we did in the community and organization. Seems like we were always raising money to pay for our adventures and outings. Our Scout Master providing coaching and support was Scout Leader Glenn Mayfield.

Church Influences

In my late teens, I was in a little gang in Uvalde called the Moses. One day, Tony and I were drinking wine at St. Patrick's Catholic Church. We thought we were cool.

George was driving and giving a Catholic priest a ride to Hondo, Texas. They had a festival going on, and we walked around to check out the pretty girls. It was a blast visiting the kissing booths at the church's fiesta *Jamaica*, where a kiss only cost 10 cents — for the benefit of the church, of course. A memory that stands out in my mind that is not too cool was when the Nuns would twist and pull on my ears for one reason or another. Yes, they knew how to get their point across. The sisters were no-nonsense, super strict, and they meant business.

Branding Cattle

The first time I worked branding cattle, I was about 14 years old. It was fun, but it was serious work, too, cooperating with other men and a hot iron rod. Everyone has a job to do. You want to get in there and earmark your calf (20 to 24 seconds) or earmark your cow (25 to 30 seconds) while watching yourself with the animal and staying out of harm's way. You need to get in there and get it done deliberately, all while taking care of the animal. While cutting the steers, I ate tasty bull nuts for the first time. The gathering and food after are always nice. Today, alternative techniques are used other than hot branding.

Running Around in the Streets

In high school, I played music and sports and kept up with my schoolwork while running around with my friends most of the time. Then, I began to put aside my schoolwork and sports and think of being a singer. I excelled in sports at Sabinal High School in little old Sabinal, Texas, where the Yellowjackets always struggled in football, track, and basketball. I managed to be one of the go-to guys in the sports I played. I loved sports — any kid would love sports if they were half good at it. Going out for sports builds self-esteem, especially when you are one of the smallest in your family, and getting a place at the supper table could be a game within itself.

Once in Sabinal, I rode in an SUV with 4 or 5 guys. We were all drinking and whatnot. I guess that's why I'm this way today; I started drinking very young. Well, I got into a disagreement with my girlfriend, so she insisted I drop her off at Sanderson and Alpine. I had a little too much to drink, and I was acting like a jerk to her, as some guys do. The next day, I'd remember and regret it. The song that comes to mind is "Lawless Avenue" by Jackson Browne. It brings back memories and makes me reflect on my life.

Close Graduation Call

Another time, my friend Ernest and I thought we were slick. We played hooky, and we were seen... caught red-handed. I think I saw my brother, the youngest of all four of us, but I wasn't sure. We didn't get a ride, but we crossed each other's paths. I knew he was okay, and he knew I was okay. Normally, I was home by three o'clock.

The story goes that Mason Ranch Malley and I were hanging out at the peaceful Sabinal River, just having a good ol' time, enjoying being with nature and throwing rocks. Suddenly, we heard someone yell, "Mason Ernest!" It was the sound of being in trouble and busted. I commented about his name, which I hadn't heard before, and my buddy replied, "Yeah, that's my second name and I just ripped my pants."

The next thing I knew, all eyes watched us march up the school steps for our punishment. We were told that we had to stay two hours a day for the whole semester, taking typing classes. We weren't told if we were going to graduate. Most students were getting fitted for their caps and gowns, but not Mason and me. They were making us sweat it out, not telling us anything. What were we to say to our parents?

They made us paint the tennis courts and do whatever other chores they wanted done. We didn't know if we were going to graduate up until the very last minute. Finally, they told us we would be. To that point, it was pure torture.

Jukebox

I loved going to my aunt Ofilia's house. She had a jukebox, and I loved checking it out. I used to stand outside too, and watch the girls walk or drive by. In front of her yard, there was a drug store that I'd hang out at too, doing nothing but passing time . . . you know, doing typical guy stuff.

Car Wrecks

My brother wrecked and ruined my car when I was 18 years old. It was an accident close to my house. I remember that car always had a doughnut on it. I also witnessed a bad car accident when I was just 12 years old. My coach went to check out the accident and came back asking me to interpret in Spanish for the frightened child inside the vehicle. His parents were injured badly, and he was scared to move. In Spanish, I persuaded the young boy to trust me and let me get him out of the car safely.

Another time, I was sitting in the car when we had a small wreck in the Barrio. When I look back, I had close encounters of so many kinds. Seems the red flags were there.

Lost & Found

My family and I loved to pack up and go for a ride, sometimes inviting nephews, nieces, and cousins to go along with us. We would go to the park, or river, or visit a relative who lived across or out of town. When we went out of town, we would stop at the store to gas up and get some snacks and sodas, then we were on our way.

After driving about halfway home one of the kids noticed my nephew wasn't in the car. Everyone had a horrid and "big eye" look on their face. He was missing. We all realized we left him behind and circled back to get our little nephew. When we got there, he was in the same spot we left him with the track of tears running down his face. He looked heartbroken, worried, and scared. Once we got him in the car, we assured him we loved him and told him we were sorry, telling him everything was fine, and it would never happen again. He was always the first one in the car after that.

Saxophone Give-away

I wanted to play the saxophone so bad in the school band, but my parents couldn't afford to rent me one to play in the band. They had this great big bass saxophone (baritone) to play, but it was bigger than me. They got me to play that thing, so I'd messed with it for a while but everyone kinda made fun of me, so I quit the band and that's when I started working with my guitar more. I was in the sixth grade then. Later, when I started to make money and had a couple of hits . . . I bought myself a saxophone. A nice one, too. I ended up giving it away to this kid who needed a saxophone, and he could play the hell out of it, so I just gave it to him. Didn't know what his name was, but it was a fine saxophone. I just wanted my saxophone to go to someone who could play and would appreciate the gift. I chose the kid.

* * * * *

Chapter 3 Garner State Park

"I believe luck is preparation meeting the opportunity. If you hadn't been prepared when the opportunity came along, you wouldn't have been lucky."
– Oprah Winfrey

"Garner in the headlights, Missouri City in the taillights."

I first met Randy Willis at Garner State Park. He was sitting on a park bench with several friends. "They say you can sing, sing one, please," he said. I lifted my guitar and sang "You Gave Me A Mountain" by Marty Robbins. Randy said, "Yeah, you can sing." Larry Holden with Country Weekly took us back to that same park bench 25 years later for a photo shoot and an article on our return to Garner State Park and the Bob Davis Ranch. That's where the infamous goat was stolen.

Randy was producing the 75th anniversary of the Texas Parks and Wildlife celebration to be held at Garner in a month at the request of the head of the park service, Andrew Sansom, and Governor George W. Bush. Texas Parks & Wildlife produced a video of us to promote the event, which is still on YouTube.

There's something to be said of long-time friends. The ones you bonded with in your youth go way back. A silent bond (blood oath) binds you with humility, respect, and patience. You are like brothers; it's just not blood-related. I have a circle of friends I would do anything for, and I know they would do the same for me. I trust these guys, and they are protective of me because I know they have my back. I have always felt more comfortable in their presence back in the day or at one of my shows. I never told them, but I felt safer having them around me. I've experienced a lot in my lifetime, but I can count my true friends on the one hand. We consider ourselves strong men, so we are free to express our feelings (without fear) in good and bad times.

Of course, I'm not going to chop off a finger of mine to make the point, nor would they, but it's nice knowing we always make time for one another every chance we can, even if it's through song. My way of staying in touch with my closest friends is to send them a song that relates to me and my memories of our time together.

This includes my Houston football buddies, who sometimes hitchhike to Garner Park. It's not something I would advise anyone to do today because it's just not safe. A stranger is not a friend until a bridge and trust are built. A lot has changed since those days, and there's much to be said about keeping safety first.

Allure of Garner State Park

Garner State Park is near the community of Concan, close to my hometown, Sabinal, Uvalde County, and beautiful hill country. It's a popular camping park where the Frio River flows. The park usually filled up quickly during the day, and we would walk to check out its visitors. It was a place we loved to go during the summers because it was like a fantastic vacation and retreat. It wasn't like work at all. We met many people, and l made many friends I have now whom I met at that beautiful park. We had to stay outside the gate a lot due to being underage. That's because you had to be 21 to be sponsored at the park to stay overnight and the reason Texas Ranger Joaquin Jackson would find me sleeping on the side of the road.

It's a great place to enjoy a relaxing weekend for a swim, dance, or chillin' on the cool FrioRiver. The scenery is beautiful and breath-taking . . . Nature's best. Our favorite saying was *Let's meet at Garner Park or be there or be square*. It's where you could dance on the Pavilion grounds to your favorite jukebox song, always with the pretty and young girls to shake a leg with. Back then, we would do anything to improve our game, so we gave dancing lessons to anyone who wanted them. It was so much fun. Today, I went there to relax and be in the company of longtime friends. Besides, it's free to the public and I like the change of pace it provides.

In the beginning, at Garner State Park, when I was just a little guy, I was working among grownups, getting what needed to be cleaned and cleared. Once I made friends, I got invited to work on some of their ranches, where we would hunt and have fun. My friends and I worked wherever we could to make extra money, but it was usually on Nick Finley's ranch in Uvalde for a couple of summers. About six to eight of us would bale hay in the middle of nowhere—Knippa, Texas. We would do just about any kind of work to make some money. In that order, it was our spending money for beer, gas, food, and clothes.

My Buddy Bullit

This is a story about my friend, Bullit. In the summer, we drove by to see him at his job as a lifeguard and we persuaded him to come with us, we were headed to Garner. He told us, "Listen guys, I can't go I've got a job and I need to be responsible." Well, we didn't let up and kept nudging him and finally he gave in. His boss, Mr. Wools, didn't like it one bit. He was the local grade school teacher who oversaw the municipal pool in Hondo. We heard his boss yell, "You'll never get a job in this town, again." I told his boss, "That's ok . . . Bullit was looking for a job when he found this one." We all laughed at that one while we made our great escape, feeling giddy with alluring anticipations of summer wonders to come. Bullit told us, "You knuckleheads are crazy, I was making $1.00 per hour. I can't believe I gave it up."

Bullit was always someone fun and easy to be around. He was an Eagle Scout and had a lifeguard merit badge. I liked him because he liked my singing. That made him a cool guy to me.

We usually were in Bullit's dad's '54 Chevy, which had been given to him by Bullet's grandpa who had passed away. We thought it was cool that he had access to a car, especially the first time we saw him pull up on the side of the road. Our friend, Donald Sweat had a beat-up Pontiac, and Vicky Green had a cool El Camino, too that we'd ride around in. I mentioned most of the time, we hitch-hiked to wherever we were going.

At Garner, we would walk around with a can opener with cat and dog food pretending that's all we had to eat when the young gullible girls inquired. They showed sympathy to us and invited us to meet their moms who'd share a sandwich or hamburger with us. If it was a real protective and wise mom, we'd get nothing, but usually, the moms took pity on us, and I'd play my guitar and music for them, too.

We did not discriminate when it came to girls; we liked them in all shapes and sizes. We enjoyed getting to know them and their parents, who took pity on us, letting us hang around till closing time. We met a lot of nice girls with beautiful personalities, and they got to know us, too, allowing us to be helpful during their camp stay.

In the evening, we would all meet at the Pavilion (concrete), where there would be a jukebox playing and a concession stand. Earlier in the day, we would dance and teach country and western dances like the Cotton Eye Joe, Texas two-step, and the whip. We always had a great time on the dance floor. Some kept in touch and remained lifelong friends today.

We were always in chasing mode with girls and always had a great time on the dance floor with lots of them. Sometimes, we wouldn't recognize the girls because, in the daytime, they'd be sun tanning in their bikinis with their hair under wraps or with huge juice cans/rollers on their heads. Come evening at the dance, they'd be all dolled up with their pretty curled, beehive or straight hair and lipstick and makeup on.

Marines, The Few, The Proud

Duty came knocking when I was 18 years old, along with a friend. We were determined to go fight for our country because people were dying for sure. I met a Marine Officer named Prine in Uvalde who wore the proud uniform of *The Few, The Proud*, who I would run into a year later. By then, they had come out with the first draft lottery experiment (December 1, 1969), which gave us guys a random number corresponding to our birthday for active duty sent to the Vietnam War. I was 1A, which is prime meat. They said they were going to call me that year later to show me where to go. Well, as fate would have it, they came up with the lottery system – I drew a high number that year, so I didn't get to go. The next year, my number was even higher, so I ended up in the music business. The date of the last lottery was on March 12, 1975, and suspended in 1976.

Some of my friends, "Bullit" Bob Naegelin, Tito Vann, and Billy Ray McNair, went to fight in Vietnam. Another friend of mine, Gary Gravell of Hondo, enlisted in the Navy. I went with Billy to meet his bus in Franklin on his way to boot camp and gave him a ten-commandment bracelet for good luck. I wanted my buddies to come back alive and thought of them often while they were away.

Bullit and Tito were the two guys who helped me out in Queens when 8 or 10 guys were harassing me. They were all big in statue too. Another guy who helped me out in Queens was Joey Fender, and Freddie Fletcher who all remain my friends today. Both Bullit, Tito, and Billy retired from the Marines with Honorable Discharges. That's probably why I'm still alive and I'm thankful to them for their service. Somehow, God helped me dodge a bullet on that one because it wasn't in the cards for me to go away and fight.

Later, the war became known as an unpopular and escalating protest war. Sadly, our soldiers were not welcomed home with open arms as they are met today. God bless our Veterans . . . I tip my hat to them, like in the song I sing, "You're a Hero To Me."

Reunion Between Friends

I was happy to attend a gathering with my fellow grade school classmates, and I had a wonderful time. We had lunch at Neil's Restaurant in Concan overlooking the scenic Frio River in the hill country. We all reminisced and told stories of old times where we swam, listened, and danced to playing the jukebox on 8 tracks and cassettes. This gathering brought back a flood of memories that were some of the best days of my life.

It was a reunion of the sort where we came together for the pure fun of it and the relief of the social distance that has kept most of us apart. Some are possibly plagued by tragedies, death, sorrow, and grief due to circumstances and life experiences that you wouldn't have known. But, for one afternoon, we connected and were captured in one another's presence in bliss with a peace that only true friendship could bridge.

My friends included: Austin "Hot Shot" Schaefer Jr., Susan Buchanon-Stone, Susan-Johnson Bailey, Danny Kincaid, Judy Mctheny-Kincaid, Jackie Obrien-Chaney, Neil Calvert, Terry Welch, Elizabeth Fence-Massey, and Lisa Oaks. I couldn't stop smiling the whole time and caught myself smiling long past our gathering that evening and the next..

As the Garner State Park song goes, "I'll be back again next year."

Frio River Therapy Road Trip

The last reunion at Garner State Park was in May 2022, where my daughter, Teresa, and husband, Karl Parker; and my friends . . . Corky Parker, Charles Gammill, Thomas "Twig" Phillips, Bethany Brandon, and Bob "Bullit" Naegelin, and Don Sweat.

We just had to get away and looked forward to gathering at the Pavilion to reminisce. We took in the beauty of nature and wildlife; the water, the food and enjoyed each other's camaraderie. Lots of laughs, fun, and good company. We had a great time swapping stories and catching up on each other's lives...enjoying plenty of river therapy. Some of us even got in the refreshing Frio River, including me.

We danced at the Pavilion, where people from all over Texas came with the same thoughts. The park was crowded but we all expected it would be. I'm just glad it didn't stop us from going nor did the pandemic. Nature and fresh air did us all good.

My friend Corky drove me a distance away so I could have better reception with my cell phone to do a radio interview with the one and only DJ Kenny Graves of Willy 1550 & 98.7 (Houston) to promote my upcoming CD and book, *Johnny Rodriguez Desperado: A Piece of My Soul.* I enjoyed my interview with Kenny very much. He brought back memories for me talking about the Houston area where I reminisced about my high school football buddies and the blast, we all had.

"Johnny is a humble and kind guy . . .cool too, always has been. He's strong minded, polite, and honest, but you don't want to mistake his kindness for weakness."
– Corky Parker

"The first time I met Johnny was at Garner State Park in the '60s sitting on a picnic table. I liked him off the bat. That's where I heard him sing and knew in my heart, right then and there, he was destined to be a country music star. We became fast friends and still have a bond to this day. I love him like a brother."
– Charles Gammill

"Johnny is one of a kind. He's the most thoughtful person I've ever met. I first met him at age 15 and he blew me away hearing him sing *Cocaine Blues*, by Johnny Cash. Over the years, in good times and bad, we've bonded over camaraderie, comfort, and strength that deepened our friendship. Congratulations, my brother."
– Thomas "Twig" Phillips

"Johnny is the kinda guy who puts friendship before the music. After the goat rustling incident, we went our different ways and reunited years later and it felt like yesterday." "Success didn't change him; he hasn't forgotten his old friends. He's a cool guy and a fantastic singer and musician. I'm happy to call him my friend."
– Donald Sweat

"Johnny is a special guy with a golden voice, but I see him beyond his extraordinary talent. What I like best about my friend is his ability to make me feel good after being out of contact for years. And whenever we do connect, he makes me feel like there's never been a separation. We just pick up and relate like it was only yesterday."
– Bullit Naegelin

"But seek first the kingdom of God and His righteousness, and all thcsc things shall bc addcd to you."
– Randy Willis

* * * * *

Chapter 4 The Goat Story: Leader of the Pack

"Throw me to the wolves and I will return leading the pack." – Suzanne Collins

Have you ever had something happen in your life that everyone keeps bringing back up every time they see you? Well, that crazy goat story is my ball and chain and has been ever since it happened. It's a story where the legend became bigger than the truth.

Hell, I was a kid partying with all my friends when it happened, but, in every interview and in every show I was to do, someone would bring up that poor goat. So, for the last time, I am going to tell my story and put it to rest once and for all. Then if you or your friends want to hear it again, you can recite and tell the tale you read here in my first-ever memoir, co-written in my own words. At least the lies will end where the truth begins.

When you are poor in South Texas, you fudge things a little to get by. You also learn to do without living in the country. That's called survival. It was well known that you did not mess with people's livestock because there is still a hanging clause in Texas law for it.

I believe Texas is and always will be the best and greatest state to live in, but our laws are strict and unforgiving in some instances. Stealing candy and the occasional watermelon or pack of meat in the local grocery store or a sack of corn stalks from the field was overlooked by most farmers and ranchers if you did not steal too much. However, messing with a person's livestock was not something anyone would overlook.

Livestock and oil are the lifeblood of Texas. If you got caught stealing livestock, no one would care much if you got shot. That was the deterrent... zero tolerance. You knew it and so did everyone else.

We loved going to Garner State Park during the summers because there were girls who came from various parts of the state. We met many people and made many friends and memories to go with them to that beautiful park.

Now my buddies and I did not mean any harm when we stole any goat at any time. I think a few times we were under the spell of Lone Star beer or some other spirits. The chance came about when we saw this goat in a pen near our campsite in Garner State Park one night.

At the old Garner Park entry, we were just out having a little get-together. There were 15 of us at the roadside park that night, having a great time partying outside the gate. Some surfer kids from Florida, California-bound, also wanted to hang out. Hey, why not? They had credit cards — we were thinking, there's our gas and food supply. Usually, none of us had any money, but we were always hungry. We were always unchaperoned, too, but we worked, even helping the campers set up camp, tending to the concession stand, and picking up trash.

So that goat was fat and looking mighty good and my friends were all hungry and half in the bag. To us, a goat is a goat is a goat, right? Anyway, a goat was stolen and thrown onto the barbecue fire. Again, it was dark. The goat I got caught with I was basting it with grape jelly ad mayonnaise.

About that time, Constable J.R. Jackson of Utopia rolled in with his headlights shining on the hanging goat strung up, cut up, and gutted up.

To be honest, I was guilty of barbecuing a goat or two in the past with my three friends, and I did know better than the out-of-town guys who also got caught that night.

I yelled, "Run! There's only one of them!" We had an escape route that went down to the river that no one could get down to except for us. They all took off running and I was left holding the bag, That was the beginning of my reputation as an outlaw and desperado-type guy.

Constable Jackson wanted to get all the names out of me, but I wouldn't give them to him, so he told me I was going to go to jail for stealing goats and other livestock. I said, okay, so he took me to jail, questioned me, and released me.

A few days later, the constable came by the Pavilion "Prom Dance," where my friends Corky, Donald, and Bullit were, and they had a conversation.

The constable instructed them to report to Sheriff Kenneth Kelley at the jail in the morning at 8 a.m. for questioning. My friends told him they couldn't go, but he warned them there would be a warrant issued if they didn't show up. I was taken to jail and held for questioning, too.

We figured the other guys got caught, so we would deny anything they said. It would be their word against ours. Our stories were solid, airtight, and ready to be told.

A week later, the other guys got called in and showed up at the jail. Can you imagine the scenario of questions these guys were asked; well, I can because they interrogated me good and made me feel like they got me red-handed. I think the interrogation went something like this for the other guys . . .

We know you boys aren't local and aren't familiar with our laws against goat rustling. What we want is the ringleader who knows better. How did you know and where to steal a goat? Tell us, and you can go free . . . we're willing to let you go if you tell us. Set yourself free.

At the time, I was 18 years old at Garner State Park and I didn't know stealing a goat was a felony. I was acting cool in front of the guys, yet I was shaking in my boots. It was a big deal being called in to report to the Sheriff's office. I mean for young teenagers like we were, it was a scary thing.

We each got interrogated (one at a time) in separate rooms. That felt intimidating, though none of us talked about it to one another.

No one would own up to stealing the goat outright, so like an idiot, guess who confessed? There were no parents, no attorney, no counsel. It was just me and the lawman. Sheriff Kelley and his deputy walked me out and I told the guys that I took the rap. It wasn't because I wanted to go back to jail again and disappoint my mother, but because I thought I would be the hero, thinking we were all going to be charged anyway.

I was wrong. Everyone else stayed tight-lipped as planned and confessed nothing. Besides that, in the lawman's eyes, I was the culprit and happened to be the one to share with the other guys where, when, and how to "get a goat." The guys knew it, I knew it, and the Ranger knew it. They felt I knew better than the out-of-town guys who committed the actual theft.

Guess you could say I was the scapegoat because I had prior offenses. With my priors I was facing some jail time. I was becoming the kid, I never wanted to be. I had read about Johnny Cash doing jail time. Merle Haggard had done jail time and prison for all sorts of crimes they did and still became country music stars. If I ever had the kind of mark against me as Cash and Haggard had against them, then I thought I would still have a chance at playing country music in my own life.

It was a stupid way to justify stealing goats, but as it turned out, ironically, it was one of the avenues to my becoming a successful country music singer. No one wants to be branded a thief, but I did have a backstory and rap sheet.

The only thing I could think of was getting my guitar so I could pass time while I was sitting in that cold and lonely county jail. I did not care how long it took to find me guilty and either put me on probation or maybe I'd have to do some county time for theft. I just did not want to be without my guitar because it was my safe place and security. I used my guitar as a diversion. I was a kid, so I felt if I had my guitar with me, I could get through doing time if I had to.

Later, in my life, Merle Haggard and I would talk about his time in prison out in California, where he saw the Johnny Cash Show in prison. That changed his life forever. He said he began to work on his voice while doing time in San Quentin so, by the time he was freed, he hit the ground running on his way to become one of country music's greatest stars. Talk about turning a bad situation into something positive! In the back of my mind, I praised Merle for his mindset. I was thinking that very same thing as I lay on that bunk in the Uvalde County Jail for taking the blame for stealing that goat.

As I laid there, I thought about my deceased brother who thought I was a good singer and how I was on the path of shaming my family pulling stunts like this. He bought me my first guitar and here I was screwing everything up stealing silly Billy goats.

I'd been in that jail before and I got along with the other prisoners because my older brother Andres had friends that spent time there, too. Everything was going all right in jail... as good as it could be.

The Truth and Nothing but The Truth

The moral of the story…remember the movie "The Man Who Shot Liberty Valance?" It was produced by John Ford in 1979. *When the myth is bigger than the truth, print the myth.* The story becomes engrained in the mind of a romanticist, which begs the question: why did one imaginative person, promoter Happy Shahan, mold the tale for a young Johnny Rodriguez to take the rap? Well, as the saying goes, "if it ain't broke, don't fix it! But is it the truth? More importantly, is their value in truth? For some, they cannot handle the truth.

Well, I got into the entertainment world in the most unconventional way, one which dumbfounded me still, today. It all began, believe it or not, when my musical talent was recognized because of a championed prized Angora goat. It's a funny story really, but not at the time it went down. I hated the thought of my hometown or anyone else for that matter calling me a goat rustler, but Happy was my boss and he knew how to promote, so I went along with the convoluted story, even if it meant everyone laughing at my expense. I had to hide the fact that I always felt embarrassed about being branded a thief.

This is a true story. On the night of the goat story in question, my friends Corky, Donald, Bullit, and I were swimming and came up from the swimming hole soaking wet when we walked up to some 15 guys (mostly surfers from Florida, California-bound; not locals). They were at the scene drinking and partying and were the ones who stole, barbecued, and basted the goat with grape jelly. The four of us looked at each other and knew we didn't want to have anything to do with them. We decided to leave them basking in the glory of their hunt and go back to the swimming hole. We made that decision to turn back before any lawmen showed up.

Apparently, the goat that we killed at a roadside in a ditch got called in by a citizen reporting a theft at the Bob Davis Ranch on Cherry Creek. I was guilty of a crime in the past, but not on the night in question.

The Sheriff of Uvalde County who summoned me to come in for questioning was Kenneth Kelley. He worked closely with the 6-ft 5-inch, Texas Ranger, Joaquin Jackson. It was the

Sheriff who heard me singing an old Merle Haggard song. He came back into the cell block and stood there and listened to me for a while, wondering who the hell was singing in his jailhouse.

While I was sitting in the jail cell thinking about my predicament, I had another visitor, a familiar face. Texas Ranger Joaquin Jackson arrived and walked over to my cell. The first thing he said to me was, "Kid, what are you doing here?" He said he recognized me hanging around and working at Garner State Park. Eventually, he came to my cell and said he wanted to talk to me. He took me downstairs. While talking, he mentioned he wanted to give me a guitar, so he handed me a Gibson guitar that he retrieved from his house and said he wanted me to sing to the Sheriff, the Game warden, and two highway patrolmen. I didn't mind entertaining them at all. I sang to them for three hours.

The Ranger and Sheriff interrogated us guys in separate rooms. No telling what was told to each one to coax them to confess. No one wanted to go to jail and have a record or stigma following them. I get that! I'm sure they asked my friends and the non-locals how and who showed you how to "get a goat?"

Admittedly, I rustled up goats many times with a few friends of mine, in search of having a good time at the expense of a farmer's livelihood. Consequently, I was looking at being charged with a Felony. It sounds glamorous for a poor kid, but it's not exactly a true story of that fated night.

Thinking I did not sign up for this class is an understatement and one I lived to regret. To be honest, it was hard to live down the blame and shame.

I was cited for Misdemeanors for unpaid prior tickets ($250.00), Minor in Possession, and Public Drinking. I had no money for bail. Ranger Joaquin Jackson was instrumental in helping me get out of jail on probation to get a real job and pay restitution. I was hoping some of my friends would help me out because they ate the tasty goat *cabrieto,* too. Nope. That did not happen.

Lucky for me, Ranger Jackson liked me and my singing enough to vouch for me and recommend me to his friend, Happy Shahan. I was sentenced to three to seven years but ended up getting three to four months on probation and paying restitution.

I was not charged for goat thieving and didn't realize how serious that could have been.

The goat story was fabricated from a press agent's pen and paper that was sent to United Press International (UPI) and Associated Press. You know how that sort of thing goes; anything for a story.

Let it be a cautionary tale to not be so quick to confess when you don't have all the facts. And know who your friends are. I knew about my three close ones, but not the others. Well, I never held any grudges against anyone, and besides, I was the uninformed one who confessed. Over a period, I finally paid off the fines and the only good that came out of it was my release from probation. That stigma stayed with me forever, so I had mixed emotions that were bittersweet about the whole ordeal.

In a way, that goat story was a blessing in disguise, no matter how you look at it. I imagine today, my buddies think back and sigh with relief, "Man that was a close one." All I can say about that is…it sure was.

Now came the chain of events that would change my life. After I got out, Ranger Jackson encouraged me to continue playing and singing. He said that he had a friend who might be able to help me out in the country music world. That person was promoter Happy Shahan, and things for me would be different after that moment.

So that is my goat story in the beginning, the middle, and the end, and I'm sticking to it. Yes, I was arrested for goat thieving. No, I was not charged for goat thieving. And yes, thanks to being in jail and being asked to sing, thanks to the Texas Ranger and the Sheriff and to Happy Shahan, my life was forever changed.

Please don't ask me to tell the goat story if you see me.

* * * * *

Chapter 5 Alamo Village

"Nothing was ever created by a human that was not first conceived in the imagination through desire and then transformed into reality through concentration."
– Napoleon Hill

When we went through the gate at Alamo Amusement Park Village near Brackettville, Texas, there was a booth beside it. Inside the booth was a ticket taker as the entertainment season was in full swing. The landscape was as far as you could see because there were no trees and a whole lot of brush and cactus. It looked like a Western movie set and soon I would learn the attractions and history behind it. I would also learn while telling my story to my co-writer, Austin, that he, too, had spent time playing a couple of years later after I had moved to Nashville. It looks like every musician who ever played Texas spent time on the range at the Village, as it was affectionately called. It was a great way to perfect your craft in more ways than one.

Brackettville, Texas, was a small town down the road from Alamo Village. Near the town was the old army post, where I also wrangled, called Fort Clark Springs, a fort built in the mid-1800s to keep the peace between the US and Mexico. It was also set up to stop the Indian raids of the day and to protect the road from San Antonio to El Paso from marauders and the like. Fort Clark was like a utopia in the brush country. It had a little river fed from a cool underground spring with trees all around it. The fort served troops as a stopover along a dusty trail. After a while, it, too, became a tourist location set up for weddings and parties in the late 1900s. To me the whole place was way out in the middle of nowhere. I had never seen so much dead land in my life. No one lived there! But that is where my future seemed to be, so I did not complain. I was ready to go to the ends of the Earth to get a chance at singing and playing country music on a professional level. Guess you could say I had blind faith it would eventually happen, throwing caution to the wind . . . I took a chancc on mc.

Alamo Village was owned by Virginia (a singer) and promoter/rancher James T. "Happy" Shahan. At the height of the ranch, Happy owned 22,000 acres. He fashioned himself as a movie buff and entrepreneur, ready to make a buck at the right opportunity. Happy was a man who I loved like a father, and I appreciated all he ever did for me. He cared enough to share a piece of his soul. He managed me for about five to six years. What you saw is what you got. He never held back and never minced his words. I learned that trait from him. In other words, you knew where you stood with him. He would talk to you like a man and at times, he talked to me like a son.

Shortly before Happy died in 1996, Governor George W. Bush named "Happy" the Father of Texas Movie Makers. He sure had the goods to back it up when actor/icon John Wayne came calling in 1959 looking for a set for his epic Western, "The Alamo." I was this little Mexican singer coming to Alamo Village looking for a chance to see if I could make something of myself.

The story of Happy's Alamo Village and John Wayne's filming of the 1960 movie *The Alamo* was legendary in the halls of Hollywood. Wayne was looking all over the United States for an authentic locale for his take on the Alamo siege in 1836 but the real Alamo still located in San Antonio some 120 miles east of Brackettville, Texas where Alamo Village was located and the daughters of the Republic of Texas who cared for the old fort would not grant Wayne use it for his movie. To this day, the Alamo is a sacred place to all Texans and the daughters of the Republic of Texas take great care in protecting it. So, Wayne found Happy had a similar terrain of San Antonio circa 1836 perfect for the shoot and since he was financing the movie, he decided to just build an entire replica of the Alamo fort church with surrounding walls and grounds.

The reason I know so much about all this is it was part of my job at Alamo Village when I joined in 1970. All of us workers had to tell the story to the tourists when asked while we worked the tourist attraction seven days a week. Happy told Wayne that together they could build a replica of the Alamo fort on his property, but that Happy wanted the actual buildings to be real buildings, not just Hollywood facades. Wayne lost funding from his backers, so entrepreneur, Happy, said he would help finance the set if he could own it after filming which John Wayne agreed to. Construction began and actual buildings were formed for the movie set and then when filming wrapped, Happy would have himself a complete working tourist attraction ready for thousands of lovers of the Texas West and all things cowboys.

So, they filmed the movie there with John Wayne and Richard Widmark and a host of old Western-style actors to do the siege of the Alamo justice, historically. Although the movie barely broke even, it did get an Academy Award for sound and after it wrapped and John Wayne left, Happy had his tourist attraction, Alamo Village.

This is where I came some ten years later. Everyone who worked at Alamo Village had to do everything. No job was too big or small. You either had a work ethic or you did not and Happy would find out soon enough if you made the cut or not. There were no spoken lines of "that's not in my job description." The Village had a Cantina Lonesome Dove stage where we musicians would play and sing and act in gunfights in between waiting tables, driving the stagecoach, shoveling horse manure in the streets, and cleaning the restrooms. If that was not enough to humble a guy or run you off, the pay would. Not me though, because I needed a J.O.B. and this was a steppingstone to where I was hoping to eventually go. Since the Village was so far from anywhere, you had to live in the bunkhouse on the property. The remote location made you homesick because if you were not working, you were not doing much of anything else either. That made for a long and boring day. It sure took some sacrifice for any musician to spend time at Alamo Village. You really had to see the big picture to survive and thrive.

As I mentioned, Happy demanded all us workers to be versatile. Our jobs demanded it. I had to provide trail rides, tours, and stage shootouts to the cheers of the tourists, and then shovel horse manure and break and ride horses in an escape scene.

I rode a stagecoach at the age of 18. I would drive the stagecoach in scenes where tourists could ride into town as they did in the old days. The tourists loved it and didn't seem to mind the dust and dirt. It was the thrill of the west that they were after. And it was our job to deliver the whole kit and caboodle and put a smile on their face.

The horse I rode was a wrangler, *Mike,* who was stubborn and wanted to turn and jerk his head. Ron Curry, the Sheriff couldn't straighten him out either when he turned and got drugged into the dirt in front of the cantina. The tourists went crazy, clapping and excited as if they were in a real scene of a Western movie.

Turns out I was at the reins that day and it was top-heavy anyway and came around the corner way too fast and turned the damn stagecoach over. You had to watch your speed even though the tourists were yelling at you to go faster and faster. Everyone said they were ok including the horses, but Happy was fit to be tied. I could see his veins popping out at his temple, but he let me slide, barely. I think because I was a good draw singing in the Cantina. I remember him saying, "If we couldn't ride a horse, he'd get some real cowboys to get the job done." In my mind, I was waiting for him to kick me out of the Village and make me walk those 120 miles back home! I thought he was going to drop his ice cream cone, too. Happy loved his ice cream. A meal at the Alamo—a cheeseburger, chili, and salad—cost $8.00.

There were also girl acts, gunfights with a short script as Ortho with a mustache in the streets, and me on stage with other up-and-coming singers in that old *Lonesome Dove* stage Cantina, singing western songs for our supper to a full house every day and night. During the tourist season, the days were filled with people who had never seen a horse or a stagecoach or dust in their mouths outside of watching *Gunsmoke* or *Bonanza* on TV. It could get busy and as I perfected my act, I was beginning to get attention for my singing style. This is when it happened! And I could not believe my beginner's luck when success came calling.

This dusty old place was very isolated in "timbuktu." My job duties included anything and everything. I drove a stagecoach, broke and trained horses, and sang in the cantina, the Lonesome Dove stage. It was where I grew up quickly and was during the happiest days of my life. I learned my strengths and weaknesses and grew to evolve as a man. Most of the guests who visited had money to spend their vacation time with family at the park. There was even a Dude Ranch where ranchers and rich cats could participate in games to fish and hunt. Usually, there were always three cowboys working afternoon to end as there was not much business going on. You were counted on to never slack off on the job as there was always something to do.

One of my friends working at the Alamo with me came to me flustered, saying these ladies aged 28 and 29 in a fancy Jaguar asked him, "Do you want to see my p....? I'll be right here?" I replied, "Get back over there, stupid!" Yeah, it was a big bad pussy cat, alright! A pet bobcat. Those ladies knew we were easy pickens. I worked there for three years, including two summers, and saw about everything out in the wild.

You're Fired!

My boss, Happy, fired me when I didn't show up for work because I drove a Mexican family that needed a ride back to Mexico. I dropped them off and headed back to Brackettville, Texas. He was sore at me big time, but I went back to talk to him after a while and apologized. He hired me back, but I was watching my p's and q's thereafter.

Lifelong Friends

Those were great times for me, and I will always think of the crew as my college Alumni because of the experiences and personal growth that took place among us. It's where I met Linda Davis (mother of Lady Antebellum, *Lady A)*, who sang a duet with Reba McEntire *Does He Love You*, and Dottsy Dwyer, who sang *I'll Be Your San Antone Rose*. Both went on to become great singers. I'm proud to know them and was able to share a friendship and common interest in music and be of any help.

Texas Ranger Turn Friend

My Texas Ranger and friend Joaquin and I would hunt deer and eat quail. It tastes just like a rabbit to me. Delicious. He was a good hunter and was good at target practicing, too. The two of us would go hunting and sometimes he'd bring his sons, Joaquin, Jr, and Don or his other buddies. We'd always have a good time laughing, cutting up and sharing stories. And, if I was driving too fast, the lawman that he was, would order me to "slow down, Rodriguez." There was no greater feeling than being out in the hill country hunting game, doing what men do best for the love of hunting, fishing, drinking, and enjoying life.

Love Is in The Air

Another blessing happened to me while I spent time at Alamo Village. Between the shootouts and the singing in the Cantina, all of us workers would take breaks in the old jail on the movie set. Girls would come around and flirt, and some would ask for autographs. Some would ask about our lives and why we were there. A little redhead, "gringa" came up to me one day, she was about my age, and we began to talk. We'd talk with one another, and it just seemed natural and easy. We connected on an emotional level. I told her I was going to Nashville one day and trying to make it as a singer, but she said her dream was to be a flight attendant. Little did I know that some four years later I would meet her again after my first hit record, "Pass Me By" and we would begin dating. Her name was Linda Patterson, and she would become my first wife. Talk about a small world. She was working for Southern Airways as her dream came true; just as mine had come true singing in Nashville. To make a long story short, Linda and I were to meet again on a flight I took to a show. That is where our life together would begin.

On The Road Again by Dottsy Dwyer

Long before Johnny and I had Number 1 Country Hits, we became acquainted while working at the "Alamo" Village in Brackettville, Texas, where we worked hard for our money and our days were long. "Happy" Shahan, owner of the amusement park, managed us both. All in all, it was still fun because we loved what we were doing, and it paved the way for our lifelong friendship and success.I am grateful to Johnny in many ways as few people know that he not only helped me when he became a success, but he also helped me when we were both struggling to make something of ourselves.

He and I reviewed 500 songs from various Nashville songwriters that Johnny introduced me to meet. Together, we picked five pieces that allowed me to open shows and secure a record deal because of his persistence and guidance.

He accompanied me to sign a record deal and helped me learn the ropes when he did not have to once he became a country music star. In my eyes, he was my friend, protector, and gentleman, sweet and business savvy.

When he became a marquee name, he toured and was booked with stars like Asleep at The Wheel, Tammy Wynette, and me, who opened for him during intermission, the second half of the show. This opportunity helped my career beyond measure.

My first and most extended trip with Johnny was on the road, touring California, Denver, Phoenix, and Tucson for 21 dates. There were 36 of us crammed on the bus, but it worked, and it was a lot of fun. Most of the time, I kept the bus driver company because he was busy driving us safely to our next show.

There were times when Johnny and I would kill time talking to the Transportation industry, our truck-driving friends on the road. Since we were often on the CB radio channels, we often played guitar and sang harmony, entertaining them with our songs. And, sometimes, we would even take requests. We had loads of laughs accommodating these hard-working men making an honest living for their families at home and in America. We enjoyed exchanging our CB handles and entertaining them as much as they wanted, listening to our songs. CB radio was equivalent to today's social media platform and just as famous and influential in staying connected. I will forever be grateful to Johnny Rodriguez as I see him not only as a legend in country music but also as a good friend.

Once, I was booked to perform in Sequin, Texas, my hometown, where promoter Tracy Pitcox booked Johnny and me to sing. Johnny did a great show, but he was going through a rough patch and disappeared after his performance. Better known as the

"Rodriguez Run." Tracy was looking for him but could not find him anywhere to sign autographs. I told Tracy, "I will find him."

Well, I found him all right under a bus, hiding. I decided there and then to be a friend and give him a dose of tough love, sharing, "Hey, dude! You need to gain weight, get a haircut, and buy a new shirt because you look like crap!" He replied, "Well, you're not nice!" I replied, "Well if your best friend can't tell you, who can?" He responded, "Yeah, you're right . . . thank you!" To this day, I am beholding Johnny, who's been a vital part of my early career. My friend has amazing talent and a golden voice that is still alive today.

My old boss, Happy, used to allow wealthy lawyers, doctors, and professionals to hunt on the vast dude ranch. Mule deer was the prize, and these rich cats would spend big bucks to hunt early in the morning and get drunk in the afternoon. Some would bring their families, and they would live the dream of the Western life for a weekend, much like in that old movie "Westworld" starring Yul Brynner and countless other Western cowboy movie stars.

Meeting Tom T. Hall

On Labor Day, I met country singer/songwriter great and late Tom T. Hall and singer Bobby Bare at Alamo Village near Breckenridge, Texas. They both came to hunt, drink, and crash the place for relaxation.

I am sure glad Happy had set it all up because Happy believed in me. Again, someone in my life used their sphere of influence to give me a hand to help myself. I have always felt grateful to those I was blessed to call my friends. Happy thought I was worth a shot in Nashville, and if I were good enough, Tom T. and Bobby B. would know it. But Happy had me on his blacklist at the time for turning over the stagecoach earlier in the month. Luckily, no one got hurt or complained. I learned fast that safety first will keep you alive at your job.

I remember clearly that I was up on stage during my set, and Tom T. and Bobby B. were out in the audience. Double table-take when I saw them in the audience because I knew who they were. It was my first time seeing a sure-fire country music star in the flesh. And they were in the audience to listen to me! What a feeling! Happy had talked to them about me and they wanted to see if it was true, that a little Mexican kid could sing country music. I did not mind piquing their curiosity and being a nuance of sort. Well, one thing is for sure, I did not want to disappoint them, so I gave it my all and put my whole heart and soul into it. My goal was to sing to impress them, hook, line, and sinker. I would not hold back. I could tell it worked, too, when I added a verse or two in Spanish mixed into the lyrics of an old Don Gibson classic, "I Can't Stop Loving You." It worked like a charm, and both Tom T. Hall and Bobby Bare were impressed with my singing style.

Tom and Bobby approached me near the stage which made me feel good. Tom especially commented that he loved my singing in Spanish and asked if I could translate it for him. It was a Don Gibson song, "I Can't Stop Loving You." I politely obliged.

I do not suppose they had ever heard anything like me. The two men thought I was an original. The First Mexican American to sing (bilingual) Country Music. I was proud of myself, too. It had been a long time since I felt I contributed something of worth.

Bobby Bare gave me some words of encouragement, He handed me his business card and told me 'Kid, you sing pretty good; if you're ever in Nashville, look me up." Let me know if I can help you with some bread or in any way, I can." At the time, I lacked confidence and did not take either of them seriously and shrugged it off. Well, I wasn't looking for a handout or anything, but I was looking for a way to get into the music business.

Happy arranged for me to meet up with Tom T. and sing a couple of songs for him. He said, "hey man you'd be good in my band, some time." But I thought he was just being nice.

After meeting Tom T. and Bobby B., Tom added he thought I had what it took to make it in Nashville. He said that if a Black man can make it singing country music (Charley Pride), so could a Mexican singing country music. Then he offered to help me out with a label, Mercury Records, and if I could ever get myself up his way as he lived in Nashville at the time, to look him up when I hit the town. He said he might even have a spot in his band. My mind was blown away. Yeah, it almost sounded too good to be true and I didn't want to get ahead of myself. It was not supposed to happen this fast or easily, I thought. I had not paid my dues yet. Still, I did not care. All I cared about while talking to this legend was how in the world was, I was going to get my scrawny self-up all the way to Nashville, and Tennessee, a place I had only heard about. Nashville was over 1,000 miles away and I wondered how much money it would take to get there. It may as well have been on the moon. It seemed too laborious to think about. I needed a J.O.B. and I knew I had to start saving money if I wanted to take Tom T. up on his offer.

In a way, I didn't take it seriously, yet at the same time, I went to work with my brother, Jesse, who was working construction that year. For the first time, I had a plan to go to Nashville. It was my "why" and reason I was doing math in my head.

Well, I appreciated their kind words, but I wouldn't be interested in going to Nashville to get any bread or money or anything like that. I just wanted to get up there and get into the music business d I was willing to work hard for it.

It took me a year later when I started to think more seriously about my life and pursue it. That's when I saved enough money to take a plane to Nashville with only $14.00 in my pocket, two pairs of pants and three shirts, and my mother's blessing.

For those who do not know or remember either one, Tom T. Hall was the great Nashville songwriter who wrote the classic hit "Harper Valley P.T.A." for Jeannie C. Riley. And

Bobby Bare was this Garth Brooks-type singer of the day who had many hits, most notably "Detroit City" written by the also great, Mel Tillis. When I met them, they were at the height of their careers in the 1970s. A dream of mine was to be able to write like Tom T. (the storyteller) and a few years later, we would write a few of my hits together. I could not believe how God was aligning all these blessings up with me meeting Tom T. and later writing with him. Dreams do come true! I guess it's the hard part- digging in the trenches, having faith, and waiting for those dreams to come true.

Soon after Tom T. and Bobby B. left, Happy offered to manage me. I did not even know what a manager was supposed to do for you. He convinced me there were a lot of "snakes" in the music business world and that I needed to be on the lookout for them. I knew I could use some guidance. I told him that whatever he thought was alright by me if I could find my way to Nashville. I was excited to be Happy's protégé.

As the summer tourist season was starting to wind down, all I could think of was getting a plane ticket to Nashville and let us get this career started. I was on the right track for sure with Tom T's invitation, but I knew I could blow my chance if I did not focus on a plan to get me to Nashville. You know how Benjamin Franklin says, "If you fail to plan, you are planning to fail." I needed a game plan, and I needed one quick. I was always doing my arithmetic in my head, figuring out how much and how long it would take to get to A to Z. First, I needed money and all I could do was think of ways to get some to give myself a chance to get to Nashville. Nashville is where country music lived and thrived. This is when I began visualizing again my plan of action.

My career would have never come about had that goat story not been part of my publicity story in the beginning. If it were not for the sheriff of Uvalde County with Joaquin Jackson's nudging him to hear me sing in the jail, I would probably never have made it as big as I did. It was a chain of events that started with that jail time I did for those tickets and that infamous goat. It was a Godsend at the time, but you never feel that way when you are lying in a jail cell—staring at four walls—feeling ashamed of what you have done in your past. When you're raised like how I was raised with decent parents, no one wants to go to jail, especially a kid in high school from a small town where everybody would hear about it the next day. You would be labeled the rebel or worst "bad boy" of the town and at school. I felt I would be crucified to the hilt by the town and tortured myself for the longest time imagining families would make it their mission to drive the devil out of me for committing a crime against killing a goat and going to jail. That is how I felt I would be branded amongst the elder generation. Only my trusty guitar and my voice could save me, paving the way for me to be accepted enough to hold my head up once again. I was up for the task of redeeming myself, perfecting my craft and character.

We all understand bad things happen to good people, but at the same time I couldn't help but feel like an imposter . . . a phony. I was living a lie and foolin' people that I was this bad boy in exchange for some notoriety press attention; and in the back of my mind wondering how long I would have to keep up the charade.

When you grow up in a small town of 1,700 people, everyone knows your underwear size. But I would not have it any other way today. My hometown, Sabinal, Texas molded me into the man, I am today. Sure, it was tough being a poor kid, but then again, most of my friends were poor, too. Poor enough to steal a goat for a BBQ when you were partying and stealing watermelons at the same time. Could we have done worse? Absolutely, not undermining our behavior, but we were still good kids. Not out to hurt or cause any trouble with others. The bad thing about it all is that it would not be the last time I would see the inside of a jail cell.

Later, in my life, when my fame was dwindling, jail would become a pothole in the roads of my life. It seemed I just could not get it right, stumbling along the way to stardom and fame and back again as if I were starting all over again. If I've learned anything, it is that fame and fortune are fleeting. Much like beauty and appearance. You can get it all and you can lose it all. And if you think for one minute, you are not going to be affected by any of it, that your career will survive the downs when they get down, think again.

And, Happy told me he wanted to help me get to Nashville, but I didn't think it was happening fast enough. So, after my dad died, I took the initiative and got my paycheck and got a one-way plane ticket to Nashville at night with $14.00 at the most on me with 3 pairs of pants: 3 shirts, and my guitar in a cellophane bag. I flew up with Braniff International.

My friend, Jaimie Coston, and I lived in Brackettville, Texas, where we got plenty of work; we would throw out saddles and rigs in the back of his old white pick-up truck with chewing tobacco stains on the look for cowboy work at 19 years old. Also, Jack Boultinghouse, "Plunker" Schuede, Jay Kerr, worked too.

I was sad to hear later the story of how Alamo Village became a thing of the past. After Happy died in 1996, his wife, Virginia, and his only daughter, Tulisa ran the attraction for the next 10 years, but Virginia was getting up in years and the crowds were getting smaller even though a few movies and music videos were still being shot there. When that died out, as the movie industry did not have to shoot on location with the invention of all the new technology going on, it looked bleak. Location shooting was dying out as the movie industry was changing almost daily. When Virginia died at age 93, two months later, Tulisa, her daughter, died at 67. An investor from Corpus Christi bought the ranch and the attraction to try to revive it, but it failed.

Later, in 2010, that was the end of the road for what was once the first great Western movie set in Texas. Today, I heard that the only thing left was the tumbleweed, dust, and dilapidated buildings of the Alamo set. If it were not for Alamo Village, I would not have become what I am today. I owe Happy, Tom T., and Bobby Bare a prayer every day for helping a kid like me. He and John Wayne had a dream of a great movie on a classic movie set and it came true in the brush country of deep Southwest Texas. I will be eternally grateful for what he did for me while I worked for him at Alamo Village.

On the day of the stagecoach mishap, one lady did get a cracked elbow. I would discover years later that she turned out to be the sister of a good buddy of mine, Kelly Kenning's dad, and the late Ray Koenning's sister, Delora "Chipper" Koenning.

* * * * *

Chapter 6 Nashville

"Well, one thing you could say about Johnny is that he really had a lot of nerve. You know, he used to work in Texas at Alamo Village at one of those gunfighters' places where he shoots it out with the tourists, and then, if he was lucky, he'd get to sing a little bit. And, one day, Bobby Bear and I happened to hear him singing, and he was good, as you know. And, anyway after the show, I told Johnny that if you ever get to Tennessee, you ought to look me up and a couple of years he took me up and showed up in Nashville with $8.00 in his pocket. That kind of meager beginning from a fella who soon became my lead Guitar player, got a record contract, and had a number-one record with his first song out. Johnny had a lot of nerve."

– Tom T. Hall

As I flew on that plane for the first time in my life, to get control of my fears, I began to think of how I was going to sing my songs to whoever would listen to me. Where was I going to stay? How was I going to get around? Who would really help me once I got there? I had a thousand questions flying around in my head as that plane touched down in Nashville in 1971. I knew I'd have to be different, and I'd have to have a style of my own to stick out from the crowd of newcomers. And there were hundreds of bright-eyed newcomers like me coming into Nashville every day. The competition was heavy, and the stages were full of wannabe country music singing stars in all shapes and colors and styles.

When I first arrived in Nashville, I had a cloak of hope. I would not have made it in a new city if I didn't have my faith in God. To be honest, I had a kiss harry, which means I didn't know if they were going to welcome me with a kiss or tie me up. I know it sounds horrible and unfair, but when people are in your ear you have your doubts and fears convincing you otherwise, it's not easy.

It's an eerie feeling not knowing how folks will welcome you or not when you're new in town. Slowly but surely, the anxiety, confusion, and fear set in. These kinds of feelings are menacing and brutal to shake no matter how hard you try. First, I was a Mexican in town with an "I can" attitude, but I was determined to overcome insecurities that were setting in and adopt a "fake it until you make it" mentality instead. I was feeling a little discriminated against, too.

When I first got to Nashville, in about 3-4 weeks, I wrote my mother a letter to reassure her everything was great (I didn't want her to worry) even though I didn't know where I was going to stay or where my next meal would be coming. I had no money at all. To this day, I remember writing that letter to her and what I was feeling while writing it. To be honest I was scared, but I was hopeful. I prayed a lot and tried my best to follow His path. I'm smart enough to know that He doesn't listen to me when I get in my own way.

My mantra is to live every day in the present. I can live and feel in the moment and that is enough for me to handle. I can deal with what's in front of me because it's real, whereas what's out of sight, in the future, I would rather not worry or think about. In Nashville, I was focused on working hard and perfecting my craft. I was always down to listening to a local band. Sometimes, I'd go hunting or fishing, but music was always my main attraction.

Reflections of Nashville

Like a man in a boat set out to sea, I was alone all in Nashville. I was down to $3.00, a bag of clothes, and my trusted guitar.

I called Bobby Bare, but he was out of town. My next call would be to Tom, but he wasn't in, either. I left word with his secretary. Tom returned my call and told me to meet him on his bus, where he was doing a gig on WSM radio with Ralph Emery.

I caught a taxi and hightailed over to the radio station, where I was greeted by Tom's drummer, Gus Barba, who answered the door when I knocked on Tom's bus. The guys were having lunch (boxes) and I mostly kept quiet and observed.

I finally got to see Tom, who asked, "Do you have any money or a job, or do you know anybody here?" He took me to his house and let me stay with him for a week. He said I could play in his band if I could learn his music. I took the music sheet, and I studied it earnestly, learning everything in no time.

Early Opportunities Onstage

Opportunity knocked and I answered, following my instincts. Tom explained to me that his lead guitar player, Pete Bleu, had left the group, and I could replace him with his band, Tom T Hall, and the Storytellers. I took the job. I was happy and tried to be useful and continued to study my craft. At times, I served as kind of a secretary for Tom while he and I were traveling on the bus between shows. Tom would get a title or idea for a song and utter the lyrics while I wrote them down on a piece of paper so his idea wouldn't be forgotten. He really had a knack for songwriting and ideas came easily. He knew how to build a song.

Then the next thing I knew, I was on the road. Gus Barba, the drummer in the band, was to be my first real friend in Nashville. He told me I could stay with him for a while, as did piano player, Alan Base, who let me stay with him, too. They both gave me a hand up and gave me a place to stay. We'd go to work and come back. I'd sing 2 to 3 songs; when Tom came out, I'd introduce him. I was getting out of my comfort zone and shell faster than I thought.

Gus was a super cool dude, married to a sweet girl named Kathy. He had a little one-bedroom apartment down on Broadway Street and said I could stay on his couch while I was getting on my feet on Nashville stages or on the road with Tom.

Now this couch at Gus's apartment could be occupied by anyone — and it often was. Whoever got to it first got to sleep on it. There was another musician Gus was helping; I think his name was Chuck Stewart. There were a few nights I had beat Chuck home and got the couch, and then there were some nights he beat me home. The loser had to sleep on the floor on a pallet that Kathy had thoughtfully made up. I will never forget Gus and Kathy's hospitality and kindness. Gus would become Tom T.'s road manager when Tom hired another drummer. Gus was ahead of the time, sporting long hair while riding his Harley around Nashville like a California biker.

Mexicans were becoming mainstream when I became well-known, and to this day, all forms of Mexican music enjoy fame and fortune all by themselves. The early '70s was the beginning of how it all started for all of us Hispanic musicians helping each other. I say that with pride. While I was at the top of my game, as I had been helped, it was my privilege to help other Hispanics (and non-Hispanics, too) of all genres of music. If I ever have any musical legacy, I want it to be that of helping others to open doors to their own success.

When I started performing with Tom and the Storytellers, it was all anyone could talk about: the singing Mexican kid from Texas who steals goats to eat. I was the Mexican goat thief who sure knew how to sing country music. The press and the public ate it up as fast as we ate any poor goats. They say even bad publicity is good publicity on the road to stardom. I guess.

A few years later, Loretta Lynn's husband, Moonie Lynn, stepped out of a black limo holding a black goat with a red ribbon around its neck as a wedding gift. It was a long time ago. Enough already. I took the goat in stride and politely handed it to Tom T. I was getting used to being the brunt of the goat joke.

Grand Ole Opry

As long as I live, I will never forget the grandeur of the first time I stepped on stage at the Grand Ole Opry. I was tuning my guitar in the green room when Tom T. approached me and said, "You're on in three minutes."

I was only 20 years old, and I felt petrified and paralyzed. I can't describe it. My guitar string busted to boot. I didn't know what to do. I did not have an acoustic guitar with me because I had been playing electric lead guitar for Tom.
Guy Willis of Willis Brothers said, "Son, you can use my guitar." I grabbed it and ran with it and headed toward the stage. It was twice as big as me, but it was my only choice.

God, I prayed I would not drop it or bust a string. I used to listen to Don Gibson all the time and now I am on the Grand

Old Opry stage playing in front of a couple of thousand people. I was so scared to perform in front of a full house.

Minnie Pearl, Roy Acuff, and Little Jimmy Dickens were standing in the wings, and here was this little Mexican kid singing on stage like he belonged there. Give me a break! Singer Announcer, Roy Acuff, introduced me saying, "I don't know where this young kid is from, Johnny Rodgers quez. They just gave this piece of paper to me — here he is, Johnny Rodgers quez."

I made the sign of the cross for God's blessing and good luck. I did not know what song to sing, so I decided to be bold and give the audience my best shot and sing an old Don Gibson song. I did "I Can't Stop Loving You" in English and in Spanish.

The audience went crazy, giving me two encores and my life was changed forever. I managed to give the audience something new and fresh: a country love song in Español, the universal language of love.

Since I was the new kid in town, I was assigned to wake Mr. Tex Ritter up before he was to go on stage. He'd always fall asleep, and my job was to serve him a cup of coffee. The only thing I didn't like about that old man was that he always called me "Pissant," a name that insulted me and stuck out so much I was afraid others would hear and start doing the same.

Well, one day, I thought I'd get even with him and sing his song, "Jealous Heart," with some Spanish in it. The crowd loved it and ate it up, even giving me two encores, again. It sure made me feel good!

After my performance, he and I met up face to face. He said, "Pissant, what the hell did you do to my song? You sure screwed up my song singing it in Spanish."

I replied with, "Well, Mr. Ritter, old Pissant didn't do too bad because my song went to Number one." And, yes, I admit, I said it with a big old grin on my face. I was being vindictive in a good way, and it paid off for the greater good. It's true what they say that *success is sweet revenge* and that's a win-win situation.

Tom T. Hall was good to me. He was a great boss and a good friend, overlooking some of my early flops and miscues. He knew I was naïve and a scared kid from Texas, but he also knew I was teachable and a student of business. This made him like me and want to help.

Isn't it strange that way too many of us country music artists stumble and fall and find ourselves getting back up again? Some of us do and some of us do not. Some steal goats and some of us get sewed up in a bed sheet. Some get tied up to something or another to keep us from going out and drinking.

I continued to make mistakes that put my scrawny self-back in jail, even after being well-known. Little did I know that later in my life, I would be faced with way more than just stealing a goat or not paying for some old tickets.

Stage Fright

I still get stage fright before performing on stage... I always did, from the beginning of my musical career. It begins with feelings of jittery, tingles in the finger and sometimes a panic attack. Sitting alone, doing breathing exercises, and clearing my mind helps me most. There are always so many personalities in the audience that you never know what kind of mood the people will be in.

Hecklers take a shot on a whim. Unpredictability is a funny thing, especially when you throw alcohol in the mix; it's the uncertainty stemming even from my own psychic. I believe I can be even harder on myself. An artist always wants to come across as confident and courteous, and concentrating too hard to convey those traits can bring about the opposite outcome. Feeling anxious and too conscientious about ourselves does that.

I usually like to be alone before going on stage. Too, an artist does not want to hear bad news before a performance. You would be surprised how some people thinking you might want to know, will take the liberty to do just that. I never blame the person who makes this error, but it has affected my show in the past. To this day, before going on stage I make the sign of the cross in the name of the Father, Son, and Holy Spirit. Amen.

Hindsight is 20/20

When I was in Tom T.'s band, we opened in Spokane, Washington. It was early before playing a fair gig, and we ran into Dale Robertson, the actor who starred in *Return of The Texan*, achieving first-billing status in 1952. I didn't have anything to do after the show, so we let him know we were playing a beer joint with Tom T. Hall and the Storytellers and invited him. We played the gig and went to the beer joint. Where some waitresses and bartenders kept the drinks coming. There was this one drop-dead gorgeous girl I was attracted to and hitting on when I finally got the nerve to ask her to dance. I thought I was slick, too. She was sitting close to my friends, and as I walked the lady back to our seats, the guys were laughing and slapping their knees as if they knew something I didn't. I chalked it up to envy, and I told them y'all were just jealous because I always get to dance with the pretty ones.

I was walking like a peacock, feeling pretty sure of myself, when they yelled, "Yeah, she's pretty all right, but you danced with a dude, man." My face was beet red. That was the first time that ever happened to me. Anyway, I got over it, but Dale and the others were still laughing their asses off at my expense. I resented that they didn't give me the heads up about that one…some friends. That was the last time I saw Dale.

Girls Will Be Girls

One day, we played a gig, and I was wearing a diamond ring that my mother had given me when some little girl pulled it right off my left-hand finger. I had let go of the microphone to shake a fan's hand. Just like that, it was stolen. I've learned not to get attached to jewelry or material things after that mishap, especially since it had sentimental value to me. I sure would like that one back…no questions asked.

After the show, I turned to Gus and said, "The little girl got my ring right off my finger." We just laughed thinking about it. Easy come, easy go.

Another disappointing incident happened in 1972 when we were walking around the airport just window shopping and killing time. I wanted to make a purchase for a friend's birthday. To the retail staff, I guess we just looked like two Mexican guys with a Golden American Express card at a Dallas airport up to no good. It was a souvenir store that had this unique looking commode seat with coins made of fiberglass mounted inside. I wanted it inscribed for Tom T. to read "Happy Birthday to your money-making ass."

Without warning, the salesperson called security on us. I guess we looked suspicious or something, but you'd call it racial profiling today. They couldn't figure out how I had Golden American Express cards in my possession. Gus immediately found himself second guessing himself and apologizing for nothing. He pulled out his guitar case, which he used as a makeshift briefcase, to show my concert contracts and credentials with proof of identification.

When I went out on my own and formed a new band, Gus went on his own, too. He went from drumming to being my road manager. I could not have selected a better road manager, first because we were friends and we liked and respected one another. We were both given lessons from Frank Mull, the promotion manager for Statler Brothers and Jerry Lee Lewis. He was in the business of promotions and marketing; record distributions in Texas and was very good at what he did.

During downtime, we would share a gallon of vodka with Tom T. Hall, playing cards. We really would carry on and have too much to drink. I often think about and cherish Tom's memory, celebrating his life and legacy. He had a huge impact on my life as one of the greatest singer-songwriters and story tellers of all time. I could not have picked a better mentor, boss, or friend.

All Good Things Must Come to An End

One day, Tom T. said, "Look, Rodriguez, I'm tired of following you in Texas. You're going to have to get you a job. I didn't want to quit the band. I felt like I still needed to learn the ropes and he was the best mentor I knew to teach me. He'd fired me twice before that.

If you know anything about Nashville from the late '60s and early '70s, it was like a family. There were some egos, but it seems they set them aside when it came to helping new talent and being true to the genre of Country music. They had come out in droves to help an ailing artist who had cancer or a car wreck or a star whose light was beginning to dim and needed money.

In December of 2015, I suffered a health issue where I could not play at a show for promoters Barbara and Tim Worthy at Coupland Dance Hall. My band and musician friends and fans gathered around to play and support me. I can't tell you what that meant to me. I never felt more grateful to just be alive and see how my dire situation benefited all for the greater good. I was thankful to my musician friends and colleagues, the fans, friends, and promoters.

An even bigger surprise, if that wasn't enough, I received recognition and a proclamation from the county of Kern, Board of Supervisor, David Couch of Bakersfield, California for my contributions to supporting Veterans and country music. It was a beautiful gesture, and I was happy to have my daughter, Aubry, perform with me, along with having my band and close friends on stage...Kelly Kenning, Richie and Kim Allbright,

Back to what I was saying... there was a lot of love in Nashville in those old days, before the corporations bought everything out and changed the rules. It seems there was a lot of cut-throating going on after that. Even the great stars like Johnny Cash, Merle Haggard, and George Jones were being treated like second-class singers when the moneymen forgot the music and only cared for the bottom line. It was hard to know who to trust. Few could blame those great stars for being bitter, at that time. Changes were happening fast to the music business world, as we knew it and it wasn't pretty or as profitable. Entertainers could not get their music played on the radio anymore and they let the powers that be know just how upset they were about it. As for me, I was just praying for a record deal!

So, there I was, playing guitar and singing backup for Tom T. Hall. On top of that, I met so many huge Country music stars. I met George Jones, and he gave me all those custom-made stage clothes. Now I knew all about Willie Nelson and the songs he had written. Willie was in the same boat as Tom T. Hall. He was known more as a great songwriter with the songs he sold to Patsy Cline and Faron Young. In the early '60s they had Willie wearing turtlenecks and suits and looking like a Pop singer to market him as a solo singer. I had met him a few times in my early days in Nashville, but I never dreamt I would get to know him as a friend, too. Then I got to know Willie well... so much so that later, I would marry his talented daughter, Lana.

I would also get to know some fantastic studio musicians. Now these people were and are a special breed. Music is a job to them. Every once and a while a studio musician would dream of getting out on their own, taking the stage and becoming a star. Reba McIntyre, Faith Hill, Ronnie Milsap, and Janie Fricke were great studio musicians who emerged from behind the recording booths to become huge stars. And I have been blessed to know them all at one time or another.

Over the 50 years of my career, I have shared a stage with them all, either live or on TV. When it came time for me to hit the road on my own, I gathered up some great studio musicians who wanted to try the road out. One of those early musicians who I had the pleasure of being in my band playing keyboards and working as my band leader was Rick Durrett. Rick had been playing in the Pop band Coven ("One Tin Soldier" from the Billy Jack movies). He was such a great player and as it turns out, a great party brother, too.

Oh, the stories I could tell you that could put me in or under the jail, so I will digress. Safe to say Rick was my right-hand man when I hit the road on my own. As I write this book, I learned that my pal, Rick had died at the age of 75. I sent flowers in remembrance of a true friend and band member I will never forget. I guess we are all passing on when it is our time to go, so that is the way it goes.

I am getting a little ahead of myself, but I just wanted you to know how much Rick Durrett meant to me and my career before I forget to tell you.

Now back in those days, racism was on the table. You did not have to look for it; it was right out there. Charley Pride saw it firsthand. Still, through it all, Charley and I would resign ourselves to being ourselves and break the racial barriers that stood in our way, one by one.

For starters, getting out of a poverty mindset was my biggest challenge. I had decided to just pretend I was just as good as anyone else, no better, no worse. Charley and I knew we both had talent, so that was our God-given gift, and we would use it. Charley's story is well known. When he started out in the business, his first album did not even have his picture on the cover for fear the Country music world would shun him for being Black. He was the first, but he was ill-advised.

When Charley hit the charts like a freight train hitting a mountain, only then was he "allowed" to come out. Sure, was sad a great man and singer like Charley Pride had to be treated like that. And there were some hotels that would not allow him to stay in one of their rooms because of his skin color! I know your young whippersnappers will not believe that, but it is true. I was wondering if I would have the same fate.

In my early years my voice showed richness and thin tenor. I was at a perfect pitch. By the time I was 20 years old, I had approximately 11 to 12 hit songs to my credit. In 1979, I was having personal relationship problems and from that time on I never sang sober or from my diagram for six months in a row. I was in and out of detox over the years trying to save myself and get it right. Life is one hell of a road and it's a battlefield trying to stay out of the road with chicken shits who will mess you up every time, if you let them. I was going through the emotional and grieving stages of a divorce, and it wasn't pretty. I didn't want to deal with the pain, so I did it my way and self-meditated. Singer, Tammy Wynette sang her controversial number-one hit song, D I V O R C E, best.

Not that I'm trying to pass the buck for my mistakes but heed my advice. Be wary of smiling faces. Learn to let others earn your trust because not everyone is your friend no matter what city or state you reside in. We are all responsible for ourselves; it's our sole responsibility to protect our hearts and mental health. People who give you free stuff (drugs and alcohol) with their fake smiles aren't always your friend and, within time, you will learn this lesson the hard way. In business or otherwise, it's always wise to observe and listen; you may discover an ulterior motive that's not in your best interest.

* * * * *

Chapter 7 Pass Me By with a Jealous Heart

"The bravest sight in the world is to see a great man struggling against adversity."
– Seneca

One day, Tom told me he had to make a pit stop at Mercury Studio to talk to producers Roy Dea and Jerry Kennedy.

I went along and thought how cool it would be to meet these producers. Roy and Jerry were some of Nashville's top record men back in the day. It wasn't long until I stepped into the studio that Roy asked me to sing something. I sang a Don Gibson song, "I Can't Stop Loving You" in English and in Spanish, then followed it up with Merle's song, "If I'd Left It Up to You."

I could not believe my ears. He said, "I'll sign you up!" It all happened so fast that it was surreal. They signed me up immediately to their record label. I could not believe my luck that day. I was off and running! My first album, "Introducing Johnny Rodriguez" for Mercury, was a hit! I shot to stardom like a bullet from a gun. My head was spinning, and my nerves were shot at how fast it all skyrocketed. I found myself pinching myself as if it were all a dream... a dream that felt too good to be true. Jerry Kennedy and my childhood friend, Randy Willis, were cousins.

By this time, I had kept my ears open for how to craft a song, not just write words. There is a flow to a hit song, with chords that blend and complement the words being sung. I took the best songwriter's advice on how to write a Country song. For instance, when I sat down with Tom T. Hall, we wrote "You Always Come Back to Hurting Me." That song and my signature song, "Riding My Thumb to Mexico," were written in the first couple of years I was in Nashville. When I found out I had a little talent in songwriting well, I was writing down songs and ideas on cafe napkins and matchbooks. I had creative and deliberate intentions going on, and I did not want to forget an idea that would come to me. My desire was to get a piece of the pie that paid handsomely. I learned fast from the head honcho how the music and publishing business worked and what made it profitable. I got it, too, because it took more than passion to sing; it took a business mind.

The perfect Country hit has yet to be written, but there have been some that are close. "Stand By Your Man," written by Tammy Wynette and Billy Sherrill, is as close to perfection as it gets. But there have been others, too. If the melody and the "hook" of the song are in line, you have a good chance of your song being a hit. If it is a song that is relatable and sticks in people's minds as they go about their day, then you have a hit.

Johnny Cash's "A Boy Named Sue" comes to mind as such a song that will not go away when you hear it. Tom T. Hall's "Harper Valley P.T.A." is such a song, too. It tells a story that you keep at the back of your mind, and you never get tired of hearing it. Story songs like Bobby Goldsboro's "Honey" or Bobbi Gentry's "Ode to Billy Joe" come to mind as some great story songs. I began to try to write some story songs of my own in hopes of them becoming legendary hits.

When my first two songs ran up the charts, I felt that my singing style was etched in stone. They were hits. Now comes the hard part: Finding more hits to back up those hits and finding enough of them to fill an entire album. Jerry and Roy and I decided that the best way to introduce Johnny Rodriguez was to name the album *Introducing Johnny Rodriguez*. We kept it simple. We agreed to use those three songs that Tom T. and I had written while on tour in those Storyteller days. They were good songs with good hooks and solid lyrics. They would become hits later for me.

What happened next blew my mind. You see when you not only sing the songs on an album CD, but you also own the publishing rights if that's part of the deal, which usually is the way it works because if you write the song, you own the song. In those old days, many great singers wound up as poor as rabid cockroaches because she or he did not have publishing rights to the songs they had sung. Tom T. Hall, being the solid businessman he was then, made sure we had a piece of the publishing pie. "The squeaky wheel really does get the grease," if you speak up.

Now, there are a lot of rich, famous singers who hardly ever wrote their own songs, but their record deals gave them part of the publishing rights if the contract dictated it. Elvis comes to mind as do a lot of Las Vegas singers who own part of the publishing rights to the songs they sing. Every deal is different, but when you have a great Manager like Elvis did with Colonel Parker or George Strait with Erv Woolsey working on your behalf, you learn the dos and don'ts early. In the old days, many a singer or a band got screwed, blued, and tattooed-over deals that ripped them off and they wound up poor as a church mouse. The countless stories you hear are sad but true. I have to say, I always had my ears open listening to the lesson's others learned the hard way, and it stuck with me. Fortunately, Jerry Kennedy and Tom T. Hall made sure I was not taken advantage of in the deals I made at Mercury.

Regrets happen, but they really are avoidable when you are knowledgeable about the music business industry. I recommend reading the book, "All You Need to Know About the Music Business: Definitive Guide to the Music Industry" 10th Edition. Written by M. William Krasilovsky and Sidney Shemel. It will help you have a better understanding of the dos and don'ts in the music business. It's the musician's bible and I can't stress it enough. It's true what they say, the devil is in the detail.

As we sat down to put that first album out for a recording session to back up the great sales of my first 45, we picked what I thought were some great songs. One of them, written by another young Texas singer, Billy Joe Shaver, was "Easy Come, Easy Go." Talk about karma! Later, old Billy Joe and I would cross paths many, many times over a beer bottle and even later than that, we would both have some serious legal problems that could have landed us in jail for a long, long time. Billy Joe and I were to live out the words of our songs for the rest of our collective lives. I will bring all that back up a little later because it must be truthfully told to you the right way.

Jerry and Roy worked closely with me and Tom T. Hall in putting that first album out. Tom was happy for me but glad to be losing me to stardom. You see I had become his opening act and his lead guitar player. There was little doubt I would be leaving the Storytellers and putting my own band together soon to hit the road in promotion of the album. Now I had never hit the road doing anything but riding my thumb back home from Garner State Park after a drunk fest with my high school buddies. On this album, I would be pushing it on the stages of America and later, I'd be singing my songs all around the world and on the airwaves. Within one year of my first album, my name would become a household name in country music and my songs would hit the top of the charts. I could feel that I was well on my way.

Tom gave me up on my own devices. I was 21 and in a whirlwind of lights and stages. And the real stars I had come to meet in those early years made my head spin. Merle Haggard, Lefty Frizzell, Willie Nelson, The Wilburn Brothers, and stars you may have forgotten now but were no less huge stars back then. I had played the Opry with Tom but when it came time for me to play it by myself, well, that is a guitar of a different color for sure. Playing the Grand Ole Opry is the top of the ladder in country music and to be invited to play on that sacred stage is an honor. When it was my turn to play. I knew that I had arrived in Nashville as a rising country music star. And it sure felt good to a 22-year-old Mexican boy from Texas. Today, I am still a member.

The Country Music Association voted me on the nominees for awards in 1973. I was up for Male Vocalist of the Year and Newcomer of the Year awards. Jerry and Roy could not have been happier about my newfound success. They knew I might be a golden goose and by hitting Nashville as hard as I had done, they saw many more albums and songs and Opry dates in my future. I was like a sponge soaking it all up... teachings and lessons from the very best who knew what they were doing. Naturally, my success became their success in Nashville's elite and the phones began ringing off the wall! The trick was to keep it going, strike while the iron was hot, and never let it cool down. I learned from the best how to calibrate, collaborate, and let the momentum flow. Having a work ethic like my father taught me and helped big time. I was no stranger to work.

There were a lot of young studio musicians who wanted to hit thc road with mc by then. If you know anything about why musicians go to Nashville or New York or Los Angeles to "make it" and then they wind up as studio musicians, they learn just being a great musician at your instrument will not cut it if you wanted to take it to the next level of stardom. You must have something extra that sets you apart from all the others. I guess I had it, but I did not know it. When you hit it big, some studio musicians secretly long to ride that bus with you in hopes of getting noticed on their own if that is their bag.

Don Rich was forever Buck Owens main sideman, a great singer and guitar player in his own right. He did not care for the limelight. You could tell he was happy where he was supporting and singing with Buck. Then others like Ronnie Milsap or Charlie Rich were sidemen for years and paid their dues for all those years only to finally get discovered from backing stars on the road.

Ronnie backed Charley Pride while Charlie was the house piano player in the '50s for Sun, where he played with Elvis, Jerry Lee Lewis, Carl Perkins, and Johnny Cash. All studio musicians have the talent, they just do not have the connections... yet! And again, some are simply happy being out of the spotlight, they just love to play good music and get paid decent for doing it.

As I talked about Rick Durrett, my keyboard player and band leader who died just this month, I remember putting my band together and the name we used. I called us *The Music City Band*; it was a take on Nashville being called Music City. And as Tom T. had taught me, I wore a nice set of clothes while my band wore matching suits of a different color. We used to laugh as we wore those "monkey suits" like football players hitting the field. Later, Willie Nelson and Waylon Jennings would break that mold and wear whatever was in the closet, living up to their outlaw brand in country music.

I do not think any country band wears the same outfits today as we did back then. We all felt that to be taken seriously and get paid right in a band, you had to look the part. It was called showmanship, and we were doing it to look professional for the fans who expected to see a country music star perform on stage. Even the Beatles put away their mop tops and matching collarless suits and Beatle boots to become hippies, a new brand they would later become.

Being on the road is hell. There is a song by Bob Seger called "Turn the Page" that says it all. You hit the road to back the hits and after a while you do not know where and who you are. Plane or bus. Hotel. Stage. Party and then do it all over again. It's like being on an automatic pilot. Then there are the girls, girls, and girls and it's no secret I love women.

But when you have some throwing themselves at you, well, for a young kid like me back in those days, it's all consuming. I was not raised around girls like that. Sure, the female attention feeds the ego, and it's cool and fun for a while, but try doing 50 years of that and see how empty and messed up your mind becomes. It gets old quick. It becomes shallow, mechanical, and boring as hell. Not to mention, not all girls are impressed with stardom or any title; to think otherwise is plain foolish and a rude awakening.

My song "You Always Comes Back To Hurting Me" hit Number One. The whirlwind continued when I was named a finalist for "Male Vocalist Of The Year" by the Country Music Association. The album was a huge hit with songs hitting the charts and running up to the top or near the top. It sold millions and the money started rolling into my pocket like there was no tomorrow. Shortly after, in 1976, I was honored to win Billboard's Trend Setter Award for being the First Mexican American country singer to capture a national audience, and that meant a lot to me. My name was being spoken by people in other entertainment industries, too.

By this time, I had a handful of "handlers." By that, I mean agents, promoters, and publicity people working overtime to market and capitalize on this young kid from Texas. I was hitting the stages of America as a headliner with the best of them; at the same time these people were talking television and movies! Only in America! Movies? Me? No way. I was a singer, not a movie star. But I did as I was told, and by the time I got off the road after three months, Jerry and Roy were already putting together studio time for my next album! In my first year as a "star" in country music, I had done three months of a sweep of America and two albums. Burnout was on the horizon if I did not slow it all down a bit. In Nashville, they never let you do that. There will be time for failure later!

One thing that helped keep me grounded was Jerry and Roy at Mercury and Tom T. Hall. They had seen how young kids come and go, burn out, and die off. Another thing that happened to me in that first year was that I was paired with another young star from Seminole, Texas, named Tanya Tucker. When I say young, I mean young! She had a hit record at the age of 12 called "Delta Dawn" and then backed that up with "What's Your Mama's Name."

It was a collaboration at its best, but if it were not for having her father, Beau Tucker, standing guard by the stages we shared that first year, there is no telling what might have happened to us. Beau was not only a father figure to Tanya but also to me during that time. He was a gruff man who had tried everything in his life to make money to support his family. He was a good man, too. I heard he had once sold the family car to go to Las Vegas for a gig that left the entire family on the side of the road. He did not always make the right decisions, but he sure made the right one (sacrificing) by seeing his little girl's talent long enough to see her become a worldwide Country music star.

Tanya and I became fast friends. We were so young and blinded by fame and all. In those days, kids getting famous was a good thing. But as we have all learned, it really could be a not so good thing, too. Very few have themselves grounded enough to survive it. Michael Jackson and even Elvis proved that becoming famous at a young age can lead to an early death. Tanya and I were in that same boat in 1973 and 1974.

Do not get me wrong; there are some stars who are grounded because they have a huge family support base. Ricky Nelson, Debbie Boone, and sports stars like the Manning brothers come to mind who reached the very top and lived to tell the tale by having wonderful families of their own despite all their fame. Those families became the foundation of their living long and successful lives. Tanya had it to a certain extent, but I was on my own! I do know that her father, Beau protected and helped keep me grounded during that first tour Tanya and I worked on it in 1973. To this day she is someone I admire, respect, and love.

For me, I had lost my family, one by one. That hurt me bad, to the core. If it were not for guys like Tom T. Hall and Beau Tucker and my producers Roy Dea and Jerry Kennedy, well, I might be in my grave right now. For some reason, despite all my setbacks and self-sabotaging behavior, I have outlived it all. I had the focus of this music business down. I understand it all now, I was camouflaging my grief and pain by working non-stop, but at least it was constructive and productive, so I thought at the time.

I wanted to know if I had what it took to sustain it all and live to tell my tale of surviving fame and fortune. I did have the love of my family back in Texas but the fame of hitting the road and the craziness of it all sure was a test to separate the men from the boys. I had counsel on business affairs and all, but emotionally and mentally, I really was on my own. I may have come to Nashville as a boy, but I learned the music business and how to fend for myself and be a man, quick!

* * * * *

Chapter 8 My Shot at Mercury

"To thine own self, be true."
– William Shakespeare

As I've already explained, Tom T. Hall played a huge part in my life. His father was a preacher, and Tom was raised with values. He came across as plain-spoken, but he was highly literate. I admired those qualities in his upbringing as a country boy, like me.

I was the lead guitar player and only 20 years old when I went on the road with Tom T. I had to learn his songs fast—good thing I have a good memory. I was promoted to lead guitar in the band. Momentum was in motion and moving fast for me in the right direction.

My first trip was to John Wayne Theater in Hollywood, California, and we played at the Palomino Club on the same trip. John Wayne Theater freaked me out because it had a water curtain, and I had never seen anything like that. It was just a filter. That's where my whole dream started.

I wrote one song, but flat-out asked Tom for songwriting tips on how to write a song. He replied, "Keep it simple."

I really liked writing songs with Tom T. Hall, the storyteller in those early days of my career. Tom taught me about what sells and what does not sell. After all, selling records is the name of the game in any form or genre of music. At Mercury Records, I had put together that first album with the two songs that would define my career in country music. "Pass Me By" and "Jealous Heart" were great songs, but the instrumentation and arrangements made them great. Also, the recording techniques had advanced too. Not so you would notice today because today's studios look like spaceships. Nowadays, a person can make an entire CD by himself, thanks to Pro Tools and competent engineers. Welcome to the digital world... a new era.

While traveling with Tom, I was always a student of the business. In other words, I observed and took everything in like a sponge. He was the best and I knew it. I knew then and there that if I was going to copy anyone, it might as well be the right cat. Tom fit the bill and was good at writing songs too. He wrote a favorite "Old Dogs and Watermelon Wine." I continued to observe him in all he did and wherever we went. I acted as his secretary and would write for him while he came up with words for a new song. I was learning his style and pattern of how a song should sound and be concise.

In 1973, I felt like the luckiest guy in the world to begin a tour with Tom & The Story Tellers at the Houston Rodeo. I felt once again I landed on my feet. Every now and then, I just wanted to pinch myself. I do not think my friends would have believed me if I had told them what Raul Rodriguez of Sabinal, Texas, would be doing in less than five years after high school. I was happy with my life.

I learned a lot from the man who got me my first start in the music industry, especially the art of writing songs. He sure did know how to craft them. Another best lesson I learned from him, too, was that of using attorneys. I was incredibly young and green. Tom had an attorney named John Lentz, and they both gave me lessons about the inside and outs ranging from publishing rights to royalties and making percentages off songs and performances. For me, it was all about the music... loving what I do, but for others it's strictly business. I've learned in life it's smarter to have balance and strive to have both to be profitable moving forward.

After I left Tom's band, I borrowed his bus and played my first gig at the Farmer's Daughter concert in San Antonio, Texas. After paying for gas, I was in the hole for $400.00. When I complained to Tom T. Hall, his reply was "Welcome to show business." For me, that was a hard pill to swallow. Down the road, three years later, I ended up selling my bus, Silver Eagle.

I never wanted to venture out on my own when I was in T's band, but he insisted I could do it. He mentioned to me I had to go because his management company was getting calls wanting to book me and that was causing conflict of interest. I really did not want to leave. I liked the security of playing on stage with the band and having a boss without the pressure and responsibility to do it on my own and carrying a band.

I never tried to compete with or out sing anyone on stage, let alone my boss. But I did make a point to sing my ass off for the audience. I never wanted to be labeled the "one-hit wonder," either. I felt content and secure playing in a band vs. solo. It was the highest expression of myself I could give. I never competed against anyone. It's not who I am, but I will compete to be the best that I can be any day. In a nutshell, I compete against myself and try to have fun doing it, and I believe it comes across on stage. At least, that's what my audience tells me.

Tom T. Hall nicknamed Rick Wayne "LD," which stuck with him his entire life. He was the best guitar player I've ever known, and I was lucky to have him. LD discovered Randy Travis, who was working as a dishwasher in a restaurant. Randy ended up giving LD a demo on a tape, and LD turned around and gave it to Tom T. LD would play guitar for Travis after that, and the rest was history.

Roy and Jerry brought in some solid musicians, guys like Keyboard Player Hargus "Pig" Robbins, pianist Floyd Cramer of "Last Date" fame, and Jimmy Day or Buddy Emmons on pedal steel or fiddling masters such as Pete Drake, Johnny Gimble, then throw in guitarists like Jerry Kennedy. You had the best of the best. These top musicians were on that first album, and I would cross paths with all of them in the studio one day. I believe that if it were not for Jerry Kennedy and Roy Dea and their knowledge of the ever-changing country music stylings in the late '60s and early '70s, "Pass Me By" and "Jealous Heart" would not have hit the charts as hard as they did. There is one thing a good producer must do: know the trends.

When I came to Nashville, it was changing again after the lush recordings of Patsy Cline and Jim Reeves. In the early 1960s, say 1963, country music had gotten cosmopolitan and was losing its twang, stating it was too country. Can you believe that! The studios were bringing in drums, Stratocaster, and Gibson guitars with a huge array of backup singers, some of them entire choirs! Stand-up basses were a thing of the past, and musicians were using more electronic keyboards, like a Fender Rhodes piano. No venue fought this harder than the Grand Ole Opry.

The Opry was old school to the maximum. Drums were not allowed in the early days of singing acts on stage. Stand-up basses, fiddles, pedal steel guitars or dobroes, and a lone microphone center stage was the format. By the time The Carter Family gave way to Hank Williams Sr., all hell broke loose as any instrument that would sell seats was the name of the game. Money. Nothing cures the common cold like money. To this day, the Grand Ole Opry tries to hold onto those early rules of the road even after they moved out to Opryland when the old Ryman Auditorium closed in 1974. I am sure glad it has reopened because I get nostalgic when I think of this historic music venue that has changed with the times.

I had a manager when I started out who told me to play anywhere at any time for any reason if I wanted to stay one step ahead of failure. Thank God, I was given sound advice to survive in the ever-competing music business. I played the strip in Nashville where Tootsie's Orchid Lounge and Ernest Tubb's Record Shop had small stages set up for any artist who came in the door to showcase their talents or introduce some new songs from their latest CD. Even if you had a hit record, you would want to pay homage by visiting or playing in reverence to country music itself.

I remember Tootsie Bess, owner of Tootsies thought the Mexican Calvary had taken over her bar when I began singing in Spanish. I liked her sweet disposition and kindness, but mostly her no nonsense, matter-of-fact demeanor. She knew how to run her business, but knew how to keep her customers happy, too.

That old bar had been around since the end of World War I. I heard the story of how it got started, how when Tootsie had just enough money to buy the first round of beer to sell and she found a bucket of horrible purple paint to touch up the old building. To this day, it is the same color and with all the pictures and knick-knacks on the bar and tables. Any musician worth his or her salt must play that old stage if they want to have any credibility and forget that horrible purple paint that just keeps on peeling year after year.

Now for the Ryman Auditorium. The Ryman was a church in the beginning of the nineteenth century. My dream was to play the Ryman and when I did, I was impressed by the overwhelming feel of the place. I was with Tom T. Hall and The Storytellers back then. The old red brick building was in bad shape. By the time it finally closed, pigeons were living in the rafters, and the windows were all knocked out by kids shooting BB guns at them. When the old stars who had played it during its heyday thought of refurbishing it, they discovered the costs would be prohibitive.

In the 1990s, someone with some serious money poured into a restoration worthy of its legendary status. And with the help and blessing of the Nashville Historical Society, the Ryman lives again. They spent 10 million dollars insulating it, re-working the woodwork, and adding air conditioning to appease the tourist crowd.

So that was the way Nashville was when I got there in the early '70s. It really was run-down and country. Only now have you seen the changes made to turn it into a worldwide tourist attraction when country music became as famous as the stars that sang the songs? When I first hit town, country music was not as big as it is now. But to us old hats, Nashville lost its feel when it allowed Rock 'n Roll to become a part of it all. The lines got blurred, and what you hear today came in.

When those lines get blurred, a new sound comes with new singers, and according to marketing and popular statistics, it will lean to popular ages in terms of supply and demand for what sells. With all the ways to listen to country music today, it is no wonder why it has changed so much since I was having hit records. With the internet, country music has reached an audience it might not have ever found or survived.

After "Pass Me By" and "Jealous Heart" hit the charts, I got off the road promoting them long enough to get back in the studio for my second album. I was told what I must do to keep "it" going. I was set to do another studio album and the powers that be had me set up for another tour to promote myself. Back then, stars would do what was called "package" shows. Patsy Cline and Loretta Lynn wrote the book on these package shows where you would find yourself playing ballroom one night and then a county fair the next. I played dates with Dolly Parton, Loretta Lynn, and Charley Pride in those early days.

Again, I was calibrating and collaborating at its best because it was smart to do so. I didn't have an ego... I had an eager desire to work. I was a kid standing on the same stage with these great singers and performers that I had idolized as a youngster back in Sabinal, Texas. What struck me was how down to Earth they were and still are. They were grounded to a fault. They were unpretentious and kind to me. I was starting to feel comfortable and at home.

By the time I did these shows with Charley Pride, he had finally been given the respect he deserved from the get-go. Charley is an incredibly talented man; what you see is what you get. He was as fine a man as you'd ever want to meet, and we all knew how great a singer he was. Mr. Pride surely deserved his recognition in the Country Music Association for all his career achievements. I sure was saddened to hear of his death while writing this book. As I watched these older stars, I knew if I wanted to have a career like theirs, I would have to follow in their footsteps to get where I wanted to go. There would be no shortcuts taken because they were not slackers, in the least. I would have to check whatever ego I had long enough to see any longevity to my career.

Ego would never be my Amigo. All singers have egos as it comes with the territory to confidently deliver a song, especially when women are pawing all over you. But you can never let it get into your head or your career will be short-lived. People can see right through a prima donna. It is unattractive and a deal breaker with fans once they see it, and usually, they do. Confidence is one thing but being conceited does not work in any business.

America's priorities have been all screwed up when we all know it is the First Responders (those who take care of us) who are the true American heroes who deserve to be exalted to a pedestal of any kind. The teachers, the firemen, the policemen, the nurses, you know, those people with real courage and substance some entertainers do not.

I have got to tell this story of my life on the road in those early days. As I said earlier, Rick Durrett and I and the rest of my band, The Music City Band, went on the road for a string of shows in some nice places and some not-so-nice places. Rick

Another band member named Bill Bolling and I were on one of those dates with the late Waylon Jennings, who used to be the bass player for the great Buddy Holly. Back then, we all had long hair which was frowned on by the real die-hard country fans expecting slick-backed pompadours and Nudie suits. We were the new wave of country music artists, and we did not give any thought to what people said about our long hair or our partying.

The wild things Rick and I and other band members did back then could have put us in jail! I remember hearing of Rick's continued success with Crystal Gayle when he played on Burt Sugarman's Midnight Special. He was one of the best keyboard players I ever worked with.

As I was writing this book, Rick gave my co-writer, Austin, some stories, and unfortunately, he also died in 2020. Boy, was 2020 a Twilight Zone year to be alive! It hurts my heart thinking about the loss and death we are experiencing never seeing any of it coming our way.

I was blessed to have two major hit records at the same time and a number one selling album. All the ducks had to be lined up for me to continue to be successful. Because of Producers like Jerry Kennedy and Roy Dea and some outstanding managers who steered me in the right direction and venues on the road, I was set to become a country music singer for a long time.

Now it was time to see how far I could take this fame and fortune before I burned out. Truth be told, I did not know if I would ever tire of performing on the stage. To this day, I still don't know because I just won't quit. They say you cannot stop a man or woman who will not quit. I say this with passion because I love picking and singing so I guess I will just die with a guitar in my hands or at least with my boots on my feet. If you ask me, that's not a bad way to go.

* * * * *

Chapter 9 My Band

"Don't die with your music still in you."
– Wayne W. A. Dyer

I feel fortunate to say that I have always had the best guys performing in my band who loved playing music just as much as me. Each one of them was handpicked for a reason. Pure competence. I always appreciated having good musicians to play for me. That is why I paid them a comparable wage. I wanted to keep them.

There were times I was asked to play for a buddy at an event of some kind or another, and it was always hard for me to say no, especially at the beginning of my career. With that being said, I learned to respond with, I'll do it, but you'll have to pay my band. They always respected my answer and agreed. It always seemed fair to me.

Gary Goss, my keyboard player, was both band and road manager for 34 years. Sometimes, we'd room together for the night while traveling on the road. I suspect he was the right man for the job since he didn't drink nor do drugs, so he could keep me focused and on schedule better than anyone could. Plus, I enjoyed his company, sense of humor and common sense.

I attributed it to him, and I lasted this long when other bands didn't because he knew how to communicate with me better than most. I've been told by others that I'm unmanageable and I can be moody and impulsive, but Gary always knew how and what to say to me. Gary was a minimalist before his time and its popularity, which made him easy to get along with on the road.

He recorded with Mercy River Boys that was inducted in the Texas Gospel Music Hall of Fame, 2015. He also played for a gospel group for 12 years and is a Christian, so he has a lot of patience. Gary overlapped and played with Louisiana, Governor Jimmy Davis country and gospel music for 26 years. Jimmie co-wrote and sang, "You Are My Sunshine." Gary is a retired schoolteacher by profession. The fact that we are both nonjudgmental in our personalities and we understand a man code between the two of us who practice the line, "What happens in Vegas stays in Vegas."

I remember a cool time we experienced in Branson, Missouri performing and surviving the 30-year plague when we were banned there for one reason or another. Once, for a near drug overdose and another no show during a regretful incident that prevented me from performing. TG Sheppard and Ronnie Milsap appeared onstage with me one evening. When Bill Medley of the Righteous Brothers passed through the hall and chimed in my dressing room singing a song. That was pure magic for me because I'm a fan too. What a voice!

Another thing Gary would do for me was call out the catalog and he never mind queuing me on stage. The crowd loved the way he'd kid around with me on stage from time to time. It was funny, too, because I was his boss, but he had his way of getting away with it making the audience play a long and laugh, which made me laugh, too.

The late, Rick Durrett was one of the best piano/keyboard players to play for me, in my band called the Music City Band. Whether music came easy to him or not, I know for a fact that he worked tirelessly at his craft writing charts, studying, and practicing at every chance he could.

First Solo Tour

The first band I formed was Johnny Rodriguez and the Music City Band, but for one solid year, I played with Billy Gray and the Cow Towners, Sponsored by Pearl Beer (1972 – 1973). They were a bunch of great guys living out our dream playing music, some even following and performing for me in another band. All-Star band members included: Texan, Billy Gray (Band leader/rhythm guitar) Rip Willis (drums) Leon Rausch (vocals and rhythm guitar), Curtis Potter (base/vocal), Merle Counts (fiddle), Tommy Pyle (steel guitar) Bands would come and go in the years to come, but with band member each came with experience, talent, and a lifelong friendship that would last through the years.

Tom T. Hall & The Storytellers (1972–1972)

Band members included: Gus Barba, drummer; Johnny Rodriguez (lead guitar); Alan Pace, piano; Rick "LD" Wayne-Money, guitar; Glen "Gato" McGurt, steel guitar of Florida.

Johnny Rodriguez and The Music City Band (1973–1975)

Band leader Rick Durrett, piano; Johnny Cobb, electric bass; Rip Willis, drums & former Billy Gray and Cow towners; David "Rojo" Burns, pedal steel; the late Merle Counts, fiddle & former Billy Gray and Cow towners.

Hole In The Wall Gang (1976–1994)

Mike Solee, manager; Rick "LD" Wayne, guitar; the late Rick Durrett, keyboard; Merle Counts, fiddle; Jody Maphis, guitar; Dale Maphis, guitar (children of the late Joe and Rose Lee Maphis, Nashville, Tennessee—may they rest in peace); Bill Donuhue, piano; Charlie Anderson, Andy Terrant, Nick Destafano, drums/vocals; Joe Stephenson, fiddle; Richie Albright "Okie", drums; Gordon Payne, guitar/vocalist; Larry Gadler, base/vocalist; Don White, guitar/vocalist; Hank Singer, fiddle.

Johnny Rodriguez Band (1996–2021)

In the last 10-15 years Bruce Carter, Manager and drums, Houston, Texas, Gary Goss, keyboard, Nacogdoches, Texas (Retired; 12 years in a Gospel group; 35 years JR); Kenny Penny, fiddle/guitar; Don Sowersby, steel guitar; and Mike Hammock, steel guitar joining in 1989, Waxahachie, Texas; the late Randy Reinhard, steel guitar, San Antonio, Texas (last 10–15 years). Judy Newby was the band manager.

I was fortunate to have a wonderful band to back me up for so many years. We met a lot of phenomenal people and played at a lot of places. The memories are priceless.

In 2021, amid COVID-19, the Johnny Rodriguez Sound existing and new bandmembers included Bruce Carter,

(Manager, Drums) Kenny Penny (fiddle) Mike Hammock (guitar), David Reynolds (keyboard) and Billy McCoy (guitar). We were happy to play at venues despite the unforeseen pandemic interruption that hurt many businesses and musicians.

Joey Garcia: That's What Friends Are For

I have a good friend, a *compadre* of mine, named Joey from San Antonio. He and I have spent a lot of good times together. I've known him for 35 years and consider him more like my cousin *primo* and family than anything else. We've spent some Thanksgiving and Christmas holidays together and always have a great time. He manages David Garcia Y Los Musicales and others, so we have a lot in common. He also helped me with the production of my C*oming home* album, which was all in Spanish, except one bilingual song, *Wind Beneath My Wings*.

Joey is hard-working and he and I have music in common. We help each other when we can. My amigo was with me for the Miller Lite Tour where seven groups appeared such as George Strait, me, Darrell, Kid Rock, Brownsville McAllen, Los Sanbra, John Oats, John Hall Oats, and Darrell Rock. We ate at a Mexican Restaurant; 20 group walked across the border.

Now and then, Joey picks me up and takes me out for a ride where I can escape for the weekend. He always guarantees me fun having a good time and I do.

Regional Bandmembers

Again, I have been lucky to have some great band members play in my band. These include the likes of Dee Murray, a base guitar player who played with me for three years. Dee, formerly played for Elton John until his band broke up. We were lucky to have him on our team. Other talented musicians included Nick De Stefano, vocalists, and percussions who played for the rock band, *Toto*. Jim Aulthouse, John David Aultman, Kelly Kenning, Tony Ramey, Richie Allbright, Gabe *Bubba* Garcia, Phillip Fajardo, and the late Bill Boling. Also, Award-winning fiddle player, David Varnado, of Nederland, Texas;

Mario Carboni; Ralph Mooney, steel guitar player, Kyle Appleton, Ernie Lewis, Vern Monnette, and shout out to Mayf Nutter all of Bakersfield, California; the late Richie Albright, drummer (formerly from Waylon Jennings band) and the late music legend Bobby Flores, who received the 2017 American Fiddler Association's Legend Award and the 2018 Johnny Gimble Fiddler of the Year Award and inducted into Texas Western Swing Hall of Fame and in the Country Music Association Hall of Fame. Rest in peace, my friend.

In my opinion, there are a few best pickers around: Mike Solee, fiddle, and Jody Maphis guitarists. Late, Rick Durrett; all of Nashville, Tennessee. These guys are the cream of the crop, in high demand; and I'm happy to call them friends.

Managers

James T. "*Happy*" Shahan of Brackettville, Texas, was my first boss and manager to give me the break I needed before getting up my confidence and heading off to Nashville. He was more like a father to me as well as a disciplinarian and teacher, but I cherished him more as a friend.

Judy Newby was my manager between 1985 and 1990 when I was with Epic Records company, and she signed me on to Capital Records. We traveled and toured in the UK decades ago. My band members at the time with the Music City band in Fruitigen, Scotland, Poland, and Switzerland were Hugh Bennett, and late, Rick Durrett, Tony Barber, and Gary Goss. Ginger Anderson accompanied us as well.

Erv Woosley, the Master and a Full-Service Arts and Brand Management company, was my manager from 1991 to 1992. It was the best of time learning and working with him and his phenomenal team. I have nothing but gratitude and treasured memories during those times in my career with singer/songwriter and friend, The King of Country," *El Rey*, George Strait, whose talent and career Erv manages so successfully.

Road Managers

In the mid-1970s, my first Road Manager was Gus Barba; Phil Jones (NFL Football player) RB Kramer, a Bass guitarist (1986) Randy Doyle, Randy Jackson, Hugh Bennett, Jim Brown, Billy Mitchell of Oklahoma City, Oklahoma, Forrest Davis, Mike Solee, Road Manager, Sonny Foster, Mel Merrill, Gary Goss, keyboard & vocal, and Bruce Carter, "Drummer of the Year" Award, of CMA of Texas, 2021.

One For The Boys... My Band

The first time I went to New Orleans with Dolly Parton and her friend, Judy Ogle, along with my friend, Randy Willis, I had the time of my life. A little too much fun if you know what I mean, but it's a memory I wanted to revisit. I couldn't stop thinking about the drinks, soul-satisfying food, and its flavors; the people, and overall atmosphere and culture that I found nothing short of amazing. So, about three months later, I performed a Chilupia show in Mobile, Alabama where I was going to get paid big bucks and have money to burn.

In 1975, I wanted to revisit New Orleans and treat my entire band to have the same fun and great experience that I had while in New Orleans being with my friends. So, I made it happen and took a second trip to the French Quarters. Manager, Phil Jones hopped on a bus with Bill Bolling, LD Wayne-Money, Rojo Burns, and Merle Counts.

I bought several rounds of drinks for everyone, and we partied hardy, all night long with beautiful-looking girls, galore. I'd say it was a night like in Vegas where "What happens in New Orleans, stays in New Orleans." Yeah, the boys and I had a great time partying where there was no concept of time and where everything goes in New Orleans.

Too Cold For Comfort

Once my bus generator wasn't working and the bus got freezing cold. Too cold for me because I'm not much on cold weather, especially being from Texas. Well, anyway, I bought this waterbed for one. They were popular for a while and comfortable to sleep on feeling like you're floating on water without a splash. And too, I was told they remove pressure from the spine and provide relief to those with back pain. Plus, they were easy to clean. If you've never been on one, you won't know if you like it if you don't try it! Well, after a show, I was looking forward to lying on my bed when I plopped myself down and just about killed myself. The water in the bed froze and just almost darn stabbed me with an ice cycle. I got rid of it after that! The popularity wasn't worth the risk for me plus no one wants to sleep in a cold bed. No thank you.

Elvis's Big Orange Bus

In 1974, I had my first tour bus, but it broke down because the engine burnt up. We used a motor home, but we were able to rent Elvis's Road crew bus, the TCB (Taking Care of Business). It was this God ugly orange and black color that stood out like a sore thumb, including the loud orange wheels. One thing is for sure, the bus ran like a charm, though. Elvis had a singer named Larry Strickland, who performed with us at times. He had the deepest base voice and could sing gospel, too. He and Naomi Judd married and lived in Tennessee until her unfortunate death.

Stuck Out In The Boonies

Once, my good friend and band member, Mike Solee and I drove in a rented car, from Tennessee to Virginia. It was a long stretch and a lonesome drive where we drove to the end of Virginia. It was so dark we couldn't see anything, and we were driving in the wilderness. Mike drove off the road to get some much-needed coffee for us.

We were in a Pennsylvania town where there was no sign of life. It looked like a ghost town or *The Twilight Zone*, so we turned back on the freeway. We saw a bunch of people, but they reminded me of the Korn people... dead quiet. We drove easily for the next 2 hours and later, we came to town at 4:30 a.m. It was a dark spot with absolutely no houses that gave me the weirdest feeling that I will never forget. People were dressed like zombies...not sure if they were having some kind of party or what? To this day, Mike and I can't figure out that strange, trip.

Last, we viewed a pink neon sign that read, "Home of Sweet Dreams Patsy Cline." Winchester, Virginia. Honestly, we couldn't get out of that town fast enough.

Out of State

I performed a show in lower Manhattan, New York city where I took a date to a quaint Italian restaurant, *Little Italy*. My date was good company as was the romantic atmosphere which was world famous with its authentic and delicious pasta dishes.

A magical moment for me tattooed in my memory was when I performed at Carnegie Hall, and I could see my mother sitting in the front row. I can't tell you how proud I was of her as she no doubt was of her own son performing. My father never got to see my success, but oh! how I was filled with pride to have my mother there before me. Whenever I knew my mother would be at one of my shows...it was her and her alone that I sang to and gave my attention to the entire night.

Concert Challenges

We were on our way to a show when found ourselves running late in freezing weather. It was at 11 p.m. at night and we really had no time to spare. We decided to pull over the gravel road and change our clothes in the freezing weather. Luckily, there was no traffic or passersby's when we pulled over to change. Sometimes, unexpected times like these happen on the road. The next day we listened to the Super Bowl on the radio while driving to an interview. We barely did the interview in Pittsburg in 20-degree weather. Again, that was a close one that my faith got us through it. Sometimes, I found myself praying every day, all day long because I got myself in some dilemma or another, but luckily, I'd always land on my feet. Getting to a show on time made me happy.

Taking A Detour

On December 10, 2006, Ellen and Ezra Owens drove me to my shows. They were good friends to me, and many times went beyond the call of duty granting a request at the drop of a hat. I could always trust them, too, and confided in them often. Once the two were driving me to a New Mexico gig where I was going to open for pal, David Frizzell.

I was running late. Truth be told we made a pit stop. I called a friend, Ann Straughan, to tell David Frizzell (the show's headliner) that I was running late. She was hesitant to do so thinking she couldn't possibly get a message to him, but I told her I trusted she could. She gave the message to Ida Belle, who already had a sneaking suspicion, I stopped along the way to visit a casino, saying, "Ann, we all know where he really is…we know he stopped by one of the casinos along the way and

David's response didn't surprise me either saying "Oh, Johnny don't bother me none…he's just like my brother, Lefty was. I love him." I understand before the show there was even a birthday cake for me. My birthday is on December 10. We were sorry we got there late. Steve Parks was my Road Manager. And sweet Jo, David's wife, was selling merchandise as she always did for him. Both of my friends were always sweet and friendly to my fans at the shows. They are loved by many.

Highlight of My Life The White House

I performed at some historic venues such as the Ryman Auditorium, best known as the Grand Ole Opry (Nashville, Tennessee) and the present, The Opry House, and Carnegie Hall in New York City. I felt honored when I was recognized and performed at the White House for President, George H.W. Inaugural Ball. I had never seen so many Secret Service at one place in my life. It was an incredible and memorable experience.

Touring Overseas Poland & Germany

I traveled to a lot of places that I am grateful to have done, such as Alaska, Belgium, Canada, England, Germany (East and West), Guam, Mexico, Monte Carlo, Poland, Switzerland, and South Korea.

When we went to Poland the iron curtain had just come down. That was a huge deal and a whole new world for us. The audience was especially welcoming, and we were excited to be there. For the first time, the people danced, clapped, applauded, and expressed themselves like never before. It's hard to believe they couldn't applaud before. I met some great musicians who I think about and wonder what they are doing today. We went on tours in Poland and did that with every country we visited.

One of the funniest things I observed being overseas was that the musicians we met were not only creative and smart, but they were funny too. We were now walking along a trail with nine other guys and saw an escort with his dog in snow on the ground. One guy nonchalantly said, "hey what's this?" Another said, "that's your basic polish dog." I thought it was funny, especially the way he said it with dry humor.

We Americans can take our freedom for granted sometimes, not thinking twice what other liberties we have, while those in other parts of the world don't. This is a part of my history that I'm educated enough to know that our history changes constantly through cultures and science evolving over time. Hugh Bennett and Ginger Anderson went, too.

We decided not to take any weed there because we were afraid to get busted... we knew that wouldn't be a good thing and we didn't want to ruin anything. That just opened all the other places, like Canada. We played up there, too and loved it.

Traveling to another country expanded my horizons and cultural experiences. I felt like I didn't have a care in the world. Traveling inspired my creativity and acceptance of others that would last a lifetime. If I could, I would travel more. Southern Europe is a dream of mine to see the bullfights held in Madrid,

Seville, and Ronda, Spain. Madrid is one of the epicenters to watch Bullfighting in the arena called, the *Plaza de Toros*. By the way, I probably will wear a red handkerchief, not out of defiance as myths dictate, but because red does not make a bull mad, after all. They are partially color blind.

Golf Trail

I had the opportunity to perform in Germany and was beside myself thanks to Third Coast Talent Agency, the Moore sisters, and Country duo singers Carrie and Debbie. Along with Richie Albright, my drummer, my entire band was there with me. My road manager had to sign a *release to drive* form before taking in the scenery. We were transported in a military van. As you can imagine, the traffic seemed confusing since they moved in the opposite direction, to the left side.

On this one road, we were facing head-on traffic with people yelling, "Get off the golf course!" and waving crazy at us. I told the driver, "Let's stop and see what they want." Yep, you guessed it. We were driving the wrong way and on a golf course and bike trail, to boot. What did we know? We were guilty *Looky-loos* and we weren't in America, but we were high on life to be enjoying the sights and people in another country.

We visited every capital in Germany/England Buckingham Palace, Crown Jewels, Tower of London. I got a kick knowing I was flying in the same plane the Beatles flew into the U.S. In Germany, we drank vodka together and noticed they'd drink that liquor like it was water. Also, there is a drink I discovered called *blue wine*. It was the absolute best wine I tried there. I highly recommend it and the food is amazing, too.

Misbehavin'

An eventual trip to Germany and another funny story I have is when a couple of the guys in my band got kicked out of a brothel. I was in front of the place laughing so hard at some of the guys that I was literally rolling around on the ground. That did it. The guy working security put us in a taxi and we never looked back. The name of that place was called "Okie" and most of them came from Oklahoma. Imagine that. The establishment complained we were making the place look bad the way we were behaving. I guess we were causing a nuisance outside laughing and carrying on too much. Excuse Us!

Rock of Gibraltar

I saw the Rock of Gibraltar, which is located in the British territory of Gibraltar, near the southwestern tip of Europe on the Iberian Peninsula and near the entrance to the Mediterranean.

Eiger Mountain

Eiger Mountain is 3,967 meters tall, located in Switzerland of the Burmese Alps, overlooking Grindelwald and Lauterbrunnen in the Bernese Oberland of Switzerland. Many tragedies involving climbing expeditions have been publicized.

The Eiger sanction reads you can only climb this mountain as far as they let you. We stayed up all night in the good old days, but we don't do that anymore, but we did it then.

Voodoo Abroad

I visited Haiti and was surprised to learn how common *Hoodoo* and *Voodoo*; a powerful form of folk magic was practiced. Whatever you want to call it "*witchcraft,*" it's enough to scare the heebie-jeebies out of me. All I'm saying is you best know who your friends are (beware of the *evil eye*) because those people got lotion and potion for everything from lottery to love spells. It reminds me of a song playing in my head now…country song, "Marie Laveau." Song by Bobby Bare. Written by Baxter Taylor and Shel Silverstein.

I found this a funny coincidence, because a former U.S. war veteran and friend named "Chicoc" almost talked me into going into business with him raising chickens. And, for a minute, I gave it some serious consideration, but the thought of what I learned in Haiti and its taboo *Voodoo* practice and the song playing in my head, *Marie LeVeau* made me reconsider and pass.

I decided the chicken business was not for me. On the other side of the coin, we all know Curanderos...Mexican practitioners and traditional healers use Yerbedro, or herbalist remedies that both Mexican and Native Americans *Shamans* the Medicine man, also use teas and plants for smudging and burning.

United Kingdom – London, England

In 1974, wealthy British music promoter, Mervyn Conn (aka, Mr. Music Man) from Wimbledon sponsored a spectacular event called the International Festival of Country Music Show, otherwise known affectionately as Wembley Festival.

It was during a warmup in the dressing room where I met the Oak Ridge Boys in the same building where all of us were waiting to sing in the room next door that the BBC set up for a "live" radio show in London, England. Everyone was feeling jazzed because we were meeting so many performers from all over the world and the people were kind and receptive to us visiting their country.

Also, there to perform was George Jones and Tammy Wynette, Whispering Bill Anderson, Bill Monroe, and Kitty Wells. The event lasted for 23 consecutive years (1961–1991) and it was the first country music event of great magnitude to be held in Britain. For me, it was the experience of a lifetime.

Meryn worked with the Beatles, Johnny Cash, Dolly Parton, and Tom Jones who used his fame to promote worldwide country music concerts that gave him notoriety.

He was well-known for bringing American and local country music artists together, overseas. He was quite successful bringing top-notch entertainment to the United Kingdom and made many foreigners happy to see popular country singers.

As any fame happens quickly, it can come down just as fast. It can happen to unsuspecting promoters, singers, and in every genre or industry.

On the other side of the coin, it can also affect adoring fans the same way if they aren't prudent protecting their hearts. There is something called LSD and singers are acquainted with this term and it doesn't stand for any drug. It stands for *Lead*

Singer Disease. It's basically a case of mistaken identity or where emotions and egos go to the head. It's more about losing your ability to think. Having a lapse of judgement and being too much in your heart or too obsessed with success when you should be in your head. Some call it a lack of emotional intelligence where some people never grow up.

In the music and movie industry, this is a common occurrence and we read about it all the time. On the other hand, whose responsibility is it to protect the vulnerable and young girls who lose their minds and hearts when they need protection from themselves? I have a younger daughter and as her father, I will always want to protect her precious heart. It is the reason why I took the time to set her aside and shared my thoughts about how some musicians or influencers in the entertainment industry can operate and why she should keep a level head and always protect her heart. It was my duty as her father to have the tough talks. Mothers do a great job juggling all they do; raising children, managing the home and job, but dads can make a difference too in this sensitive conversation when it comes to the subject of guys.

When a fan becomes infatuated with a celebrity where she or he loses themselves, they sometimes do not make the best choices. There isn't anyone nearby to help them to distinguish right from wrong. It's like an addict being under the influence of drugs. In this case the most unsuspecting drug of all... is love or infatuation. It can happen to the best of them. Mostly, this influences young girls with tender hearts whose emotions are out of whack.

Young Girl's Tender Heart

A young fan named Tammy Spurgeon-Barker shared her story with me explaining that when she was just a young girl (13) her heart was touched by her favorite country singer. She revealed that I was her first crush, and explained to me that anyone who met her could see her bedroom screamed the innocent adoration she felt for me. She had posters and photos of me plastered everywhere on her wall.

On August 21, 1976, my band member, LD Money, invited her to be escorted backstage to see and meet her favorite performer, but first, she asked her father's permission. Her daddy looked at her with tender eyes that only a father can but with mixed emotions. Jimmy turned to his wife, Virginia asking, "Can she go, can she not…mother, what is your answer?" "Yes," "Father, what is your answer?" says the mother. Tammy waits impatiently, giving her dad a stare of death that speaks volumes if he disapproves and denies her the opportunity.

Tammy mentioned to me that her mother gently pulled her aside to give her the most loving heart-to-heart advice she could give her daughter. "Tammy, there is a responsibility for you to visit a singer backstage. You must remember to always be a lady in the presence of young musicians and singer, Mr. Johnny. Johnny has a job to do so you must respect him, his band members, and his crew. They will respect and treat you as you treat yourself." Tammy explained to me that she remembered her mother's astounding words from the moment she stepped onto my bus and for the rest of her life.

LD Money may have escorted Miss Tammy on my bus, but it was Tammy who would teach others how to treat her as her parents insisted. LD kept his promise to keep their minor daughter safe, but it is Tammy who abided by her parent's wishes to always be a lady. Tammy concluded she could not have made it in life without her mother guiding her into womanhood. She confided in me saying, "Johnny, my mother's words of wisdom live in my heart and soul today as does your friendship live in mine. I'm happy I listened to my mama and y'all abided by her wishes."

Security: Help When You Need It

When I first started out, security was not with me everywhere I went, but my friends were. They were always careful not to overstep their boundary and their mere presence spoke volume. No telling what could have happened if they would not have been there with me.

I'm talking about some women fans who were aggressive and clever, making their way to my bus or behind the stage. I never underestimate a woman's creativity and strength to go after what she wants, but heaven helps the girl who crosses the line and acts uncharacteristically to get what she wants come hell or high water. She does so at the expense of annoying others, and at the risk of losing self-respect.

Luckily, my driver and, sometimes, fans and friends would step in to bail me out, removing me from a strange woman's clutch. I remember my Manager, Randy Doyle, bringing to my attention that some obsessed fans were making their own lanyards to sneak all-access to the shows and backstage. Once these fake IDs were recognized and we were made aware, we'd warn the venue and their security to be on the lookout for such offenders.

There were a few times I can remember when my bus driver, Curtis Webb, took on the role of security & safety more times than he could count. He was an ex-drill Instructor on Self-Defense in the proud Marines and had an eagle eye for catching what looked out of place. Fortunately, he took his job seriously, watching out for me. He made it his business to ensure I was on that bus when I needed to and kept the distractions (girls, girls, girls) at bay. At times, I wished he wouldn't have, but no he did. Another team member I was fortunate to have on my team during that incident was Road Manager Randy Doyle. He was previously trained at Calcasieu Parish Police, Sheriff's Department in Louisiana, as a reserve officer in Investigations (burglary and robbery). Calcasieu means "crying eagle."

In my latest band, my road manager, Bruce Carter, a retired Houston Police Officer was just the guy to keep everyone above board ensuring our protection and safety. My family, band, and fan members have always been my number one priority to stay safe at any of my concerts. Fans flirting is innocent enough, but kissing and distracting us while we're working on stage with physical touch is overstepping boundaries and becomes alarming. It only worked for Elvis.

When the COVID-19 Pandemic hit, that safety priority did not shift... health guidelines and protection and safety were an extended concern for all, including my fans.

We were on a Cherokee Indian Reservation near Muskogee, Oklahoma, an isolated area where we were getting ready to unload our instruments onto a pickup truck to be closer to the stage. We were not prepared for what would happen next. Suddenly, our front door flew wide open, and this big-boned gal came running in out of nowhere catching us off guard knocking down my bus driver and road manager. All I could do was run to the nearest room and lock myself in. She started beating on the door, yelling "Johnny, Johnny!" She was not a happy camper when my guys restrained her and escorted her out of the bus.

That was a close call. I offer my thanks to the guys, road manager, Randy Doyle and bus driver, Curtis Webb. I'm telling you security have their jobs cut out for them sometimes, putting themselves in harm's way, especially during these times. You not only have to keep your eyes in the front and watchful in the back of you, but also on both sides of you because fanatical fans will come for you any which way. I do believe it is why I have a trained eagle eye and peripheral vision today because I keep myself keenly aware of my environment and the people in it.

Danger Zone

In Denton, Texas, I was the opening act at a Texas nightclub where singer Hank Williams Jr. was the closing act. In the night, there was this guy who got thrown out for drinking too much, fighting, and causing a commotion of one thing or another. Well, it didn't sit right with him, so he got in his vehicle and started circling around the club shooting randomly at everything. He shot at my bus, too, and could have hit my base player, Andy Tarrant, and Road Manager, Randy Doyle, who were both sitting on the couch.

We could hear disturbances from the bus of people outside running around and screaming. It was not until the next day that we discovered a bullet on the outside of the bus near the frame around the window where Andy was sitting.

I figured that is exactly what happens when you mix alcohol, emotions, and a person's unstable mental health. It is the reason why musicians and artists are leery of unsuspected fans. You never know what will trigger a fan, male or female, and it's the reason why I'm grateful to have selected friends nearby to keep a watchful eye. In the past, these trusted friends who always have my back and are like family to me include: Kelly Kenning, Corky Parker, Charles Gammill, Thomas Twig Phillips, Albert Castillo, brothers Alex and Allen Fox, and the late Steve Harrison.

Connecting with Native Americans at Wounded Knee

"The soul would have no rainbow if the eyes had no tears."
– Guy A. Zona

I can't tell you how much I enjoy playing at Indian casinos and reservations. I have immense respect for the Native American people…always did, and always will.

On one memorable evening that sticks out in my mind, I was at Wounded Knee on the Pine Ridge Reservation in Oglala Lakota County, South Dakota, in 1990. Before the gig, my band was hanging out in the casino during band rehearsal, where some local Natives were harassing some white guys, including my band, and everybody was more annoyed than scared. I heard about what was going on, so I asked staff if I could see Russell Means, an Oglala Lakota activist for the right of Native Americans who was at a concert where I would perform for the Sioux Indians. I didn't know much about Russell, but I found him to be a smart and good man. I had only seen him on TV before, but heard he was a radical guy. The next thing I knew he came on the bus. He made known his presence, slamming his fist on the bus and yelling, "I just want all you whities (non-Natives) to know that you can get back on the Mayflower and go back where you came from."

First off, I did not want to judge the man and I get the fact that he's resentful of whites after all these years and secondly, I've always understood a fact that hurt people hurt. So, there we were sitting across from each other on a table on my bus. I replied to him saying, Russell, let me speak my truth. He said, "No, we're kin."

I said, "Alright, man but let's just cool it on talking rude with my band, okay? Hell, we just came here to play music. I hope you understand."

Russell said, "I'll be back after the show." I spoke these words to him out of respect because I am very protective of my band, as they are of me. I was taught to be this way by many artists who I looked up to. So, after the show he came back, true to his word. He said he wanted to take me for a walk in the pale moonlight.

I said, "Yes, hell yeah!" I was feeling confident. It was just he and I so we took off walking in the bush out there in the middle of nowhere. One on one. Seemed harmless enough to me. We must have walked a good 1 ½ miles, but it really seemed like 100 ½ miles. It was just him and me walking. We seldom said anything—I did not know where the hell we were going.

Next thing we knew a little kid shows up in the dark and he speaks. "Tell him I've got Johnny Rodriguez." Truth is, it was an eerie feeling; I did not know if I was going to be abducted or what. We came up to this hill and I saw this light out of nowhere. I looked down and it was the most colorful thing you have ever seen in your life. It was a real council pow-wow where all the chiefs were dancing around the fire; Russell asked me to join him to dance where all the chiefs were dancing. I happily did.

Picture the scene—I didn't dance with wolves, I danced with chiefs. It was strong and a spiritual thing and I will never forget it, especially how they turned lose all these horses in the middle of the night. And, in front of the fire, they looked so magnificent. Next thing I know we walked back, and I got back on the bus. On the way out it was just like on the way back, I guess Russell put out the word to leave us alone because everybody was waving at us and saying goodbye to us. It was totally like night and day; an experience I will never forget.

That is my story playing up in Rosewood, South Dakota.

Don't Mess with the Indigenous

In the fall of 2006 in Durant, Oklahoma, I was to perform at a Choctaw casino in a small town. My mistake was I messed up with the wrong people. For some reason, I felt the sound was horrible even though my band and audience strongly disagreed. I felt strongly that I was being set up and sabotaged with the sound not being of quality. I won't say who I was suspicious of, but I had my reasons. The audience was insistent saying the sound was okay. On stage, I explained to the audience that I had been in the music business for 40 plus years and I know a bad sound when I hear it… so I performed three songs on stage and cut the show.

What I know about myself is I have keen senses and superb hearing where I can detect a singer or musician off key, even from a distance. I'm like Yoda, a master of sorts in my craft. It has a lot to do with my success as an artist. Having perfect pitch is vital to me. I can hear off key instruments too, often better than a sound man. Feeling dissatisfied, I walked off stage and headed to my hotel room to change clothes. Next thing I knew, I was being kicked out of the hotel room and asked to leave the premises without pay.

My band was dumbfounded but stayed behind to finish the rest of the show to get paid. Me, I was left high and dry for my own doings not letting it go. I walked into the casino to gamble, but in the lobby, I was stopped dead in my tracks by a Native American who was twice the height of me. He escorted me out of the casino without any expression except to give me the cold feeling he meant business.

My drivers, Ezra and Ellen, were paged on the intercom to come to the lobby. It is the worst and most humiliating feeling in the world to be kicked out of your hotel room. First, Ezra came, and then Ellen met us. Their faces looked bewildered. I had my suitcase in my hand. Ann Straughan came by and stood next to me. She asked me if I was okay, and I quietly replied. "I never wanted to hit an Indian as much as I wanted to hit him." Today, I use self-control and I have learned over the years to chill and let it go because my behavior back then hurt my band, my ego, and most importantly my fans.

Not only was I escorted out by one of the tallest Native Americans I've ever seen, but I also wasn't going to put up a fight…Black belt or no black belt. I knew when to call 'em and this was one of them. One thing I know about the indigenous people is they know who they are…they are proud people, and they don't take to nonsense when it comes to business. They don't play, and they won't put up with rubbish from anyone.

That night I drank a fifth of whiskey. You might ask, "Did it help?" Nope!

Memories of Special Friends

I have lots of memories of influential Native people from all walks of life, including the following:

Some of the Native Americans I proudly got to know well were Joe Running Fox, he was an Indian Dandy. John Means and I are good buddies, "Kola" which means we're like brothers, Sioux Indian of Pine Ridge So. Dakota (Wounded Knee). Little Bear is an Apache.

Russell Means I had the best time and spiritual experience dancing, singing, and carousing with those Native Americans. Yeah, we all got gassed (drunk) too.

Crazy Indian, Little Bear who was a side kick. He was an Apache where we'd go elk hunting, eagle, and game. He was good people who drank a lot but was just a great guy.

Chief Chataw mostly had a great time working for the Oklahoma Hope Indians, and Navajo Cherokee. In Carolina, I walked a lot on Indian reservations.

I turned around one time and came face-to-face with Hank Williams, Sr., and today I made a point to always have a Hank Williams song in my set. He sure could write and sing a great country song.

At an Austin Theater, in the middle of my performance, I was playing Jambalaya and suddenly the crowd went crazy. I thought dang these people really like this song, but the audience was looking over to my left. I turned around and it was Slim Pickens surprising me on stage dancing while I was singing my song.

After the show, we visited on the bus with each other some. I never saw him again, but God bless him.

Fans: Fanning the Flame

Celebrities undergo unknown personal sacrifices on their road to success; one of which being privacy. My reminder to the public is to be mindful of who you are and to be mindful of who celebrities really are. We are just people and humans like everyone else; we have strengths and weaknesses and share similarities and differences that make us more alike than not. No need to be star-struck because it's just a job to us, and we do it to the best of our ability.

What an artist appreciates most is number one... applause, eye contact, show up and to buy our merchandise. Please put your phone on silent, vibrate, or turn it off. This makes for an incredible audience showing the artist appreciation and respect.

The thing about my fans is I really appreciate them all; always have, always will. It's the extreme that some people will go to get in front of a celebrity that can be worrisome. Some fans will do anything to collect a souvenir or have physical contact.

Once, I was selected Grand Marshall in a parade, and I threw out my cigarette butt, and someone in the crowd rushed in to pick it up. I could go on and on about the stories; some are ridiculous, and you wouldn't believe me if I told you.

Opposite of those mentioned above, another time that stands out in my mind was when I was performing at a venue and took off in my truck to do another show—when a Latina fan caught up with me at my show sweetly saying, "Johnny you left your boots behind on the ground." I was so happy to get them back, I thanked her and took a picture with her. The Good Samaritan was Bernice Santos. She did not want anything from me, but I was happy to oblige to take a photo with her, autograph her daughter's deceased husband's guitar, and dedicate a song to her on stage; it was her favorite and one of mine to sing, "The Gypsy." Her kindness, humility, and honesty touched my soul.

It's our job to smile and appear charming and most of us feel fortunate and thankful to God because we love doing what we do for a living. It hardly feels like work at all. I go out on stage in front of an audience and do my best. I deeply appreciate and praise the fans who also show up to see my show; sometimes come rain or shine.

My fans have always been important to me. I care about their feelings and always want to give them a good show. Whenever I went on stage, I made a conscious effort to give them their money's worth and play their request, no matter the age, young or old. There were times I'd sing my heart out just for them and I couldn't always do a meet and greet like I used to in the past.

My primary reason for that was due to self-preservation and most recently, COVID-19 pandemic and safety. I exhausted myself on stage to the point that I didn't always have the energy to always give more and, I never want to give my fans less than what they deserve. Any artist worth their weight in gold feels the same way.

Performing on stage is not just about the paycheck. My reward comes when my fans share their appreciation to me with their applause and touching words about how much they like my music saying, "I wouldn't be the person I am today if it wasn't for your music" or "Your music got me through a hard time and changed my life giving me hope." Hearing these comments is music to my ears.

The show must go on for the fans! In Branson, Missouri, the stage monitor was down on the floor, and I tripped and almost fell because the mic was not placed where spotlights fell in a hole. I did not miss a beat and kept playing. Yes, in show business, you better get used to expecting the unexpected. Most of the time, it makes life interesting and makes me feel like a boy again, filled with wonder, and that is the best feeling to have.

Success Tips: Artist Guide 101

In business, I make it a best practice to be accountable. I have learned the hard way and have made enough mistakes, but I am wise enough now to learn from others who are more astute. I make the ultimate decisions that concern me, but I seek counsel on important decisions. Time is going to go by anyway, so you may as well as use your time wisely. It will pay off in the long run paying dividends if you do it long and good enough. I'm asked a lot what the secret is to fame and success, especially from upcoming artists. My answer is always the same... what you don't know could hurt and cost you.

The secret to success for me is using the expertise and techniques that I know best. I know the tips and tricks of the trade that give you a competitive edge. Knowing how to put your weaknesses to work for you will allow you to grow and expand your life. Everyone must pay their dues and put in the hard work, and with a little bit of luck and help from the good Lord, a musician can make some money playing and singing. In other words, believe in the possibilities and focus on what you want. Let go of thoughts, people, places, and things that don't serve you, especially if they don't support or believe in you. No one needs anyone to steal their joy and limelight.

If I have learned anything in my lifetime, I've learned that accolades and success do not define you; it's the life you live in between the dash—from birth to death and the amount of gifted time you put into it. Sure, folks will remember your talent and gifts, but in the end, the memories and the music will all be gone, but your real-life goals worth anything meaningful will be relationships. So, it is with caution to remind you to balance enjoying the journey on your way to success, not the destination, but remembering success is a feeling of joy and happiness that lives in your heart. It sure will make the journey more endurable and pleasant along the way. More accessible to feel the feelings, emotions, and moods when you're on your way to achieving your dreams.

Boosting and finding your talents and motivation takes effort and time to find your style and way. The key is consistency to learn good habits as time goes by anyway. You may also be disciplined and productive with who and how you spend your time. My voice and guitar have served me well in more ways than one, both economically and socially. Few know, I was shy as a youth, and every now and then, it comes back, and I must work through it. As an at-risk youth, singing and playing guitar helped me make friends because everyone liked music. Having my handy guitar was a sure way to make tips, too, almost everywhere I went. Here are my seven success tips that have guided me throughout my career.

In the end, run your marathon in your mind visualizing your goal and enjoying the journey. Don't run amuck and don't get story stuck; or star-struck with anyone or anything. Run through the good, the bad, and the ugly thoughts in your mind and run your own race. Connect with your heart that gets your

body to run to win. Be in it to win it. I could never get on stage to sing if I stayed amidst the chaos and disorder that goes on in my head,
and in my life. Rise above it and take control of your mind. It's the secret to success; best-kept secret and the law of attraction at its best.

Since COVID-19, self-reflecting is what I've spent a lot of time in isolation practicing and asking what would I tell my younger 18-year-old self? To be honest, the one thing I would tell my younger self would be, "straighten up!" In other words, what do I know now that I didn't know then, that I wish I would have or at least care enough to share with others now. Simple... I was good enough then as I am today.

Promoters

To be treated fairly in business with hospitality from the promoter down to their staff is something one never takes for granted but appreciates. I sure had fun performing in their dance halls, and my band did too. You always look forward to returning, playing music, and working for establishments like that because you always have a great time.

I've dealt with a lot of promoters and venues and for the most part they were upright and decent people but every now and then I met some not so honest. Some could say the same about me when I did not show up for a show or studio recording due to alcohol and drug abuse back in the day. That is fair to say.

Sometimes, a promoter would offer to pay for the door and to keep it honest, my manager would go in and scout the place counting the tables and chairs in the joint and approximate the pay owed. In business, it's all about a win-win situation to keep it above board. Everybody's trying to stay in business and make a living. COVID-19 pandemic certainly made that rule hard for everyone.

Promoter Tracy Pitcox and wife Charla, owner of Heart of Texas Records (Brady, Texas), are great people and professionals to do business with. He and his staff were always hospitable, upfront, and credible. I enjoyed the shows he put together for other artists as well and consider him a great friend to this day. I always appreciate him extending an open invitation to perform for him in Brady or in general, Texas.

Other Promoters that easily come to mind are my friends in the entertainment music business: Jack Teeler of JMT Entertainment; Barbara and Tim Worthy, formerly of Coupland Dance Hall, Coupland, Texas; Tony Talanco of Texas Pride BBQ, Atkins, Texas; Jerry Gomez, R & J Music Pavilion, San Antonio, Texas; Moses "Mo" Jeloudrzadeh, of Mo's Place, Katy, Texas; Jerry Hufford, Buck Owens Crystal Palace, Bakersfield, California; Teresa (daughter) and husband, Karl Parker, Last Chance Dance Hall, Austin, Texas; Rodney Collins, of the Troubadour and Music City Bar and Grill, Nashville, Tennessee.

Another time, the lights went out at a show, and everyone was praying for them to go back on. My band and I did not know what to think. We wondered for a second if the owner of the club had something to do with it...you never know stranger things had happened. The owner wanted to cancel the show, but I kept singing with the emergency and it was hot in the building to boot. Come to find out, there was an accident not far away that blew out a transformer, but I told the fans I would still sing in the dark until the cows came home. The bad thing was there was no air conditioning working for the audience and my band. Fortunately, the lights came back on, and we were able to play the rest of the show, and we got paid.

Collaboration in Songwriting

Collaboration in songwriting has always been something I advocated and found inspiring. It kept my creative juices in a win-win situation where the magic rule of three words playing at any one time in a song can give you income on a song, the gift that keeps giving when it is a good song. Residual income is the name of the game in the entertainment world. There is nothing like having royalty checks in your mailbox. Not to mention, songwriting can keep things interesting and your music and name in the public eye.

It was about that time I started to write songs. I did not know how to write a song or "craft" a song as I would come to learn the technology of songwriting. It is not easy, let me tell you. Some songwriters can write naturally, and some do not. In country music, all the greatest songs ever written usually come from someone's heartaches, hardships, and tribulations.

I know every song I have ever written came from where I grew up and how I grew up. If you listen to a Merle Haggard's song or a song by Hank Sr. or Lefty Frizzell or George Jones and you study their words and how those words mesh with their chord progressions, you will see it came from something that happened to them, especially Merle who wrote of jailhouse hardship because he lived it.

While Johnny Cash was running trains, I wrote about thumbing a ride and my time in Mexico. My friend and former Boss, Tom T. Hall explained to me that every good writer of songs or books will tell you to write about something you know. It was as simple as that. For me, that was a good place to start and so it began. Willie told me to make it rhyme and sound real. I always respected and remembered their words on how to write a great song.

Many of my songs would come from events in my life. I tried to write about things to make the listener think about their own lives and what direction they might be going. Songs relatable or where you were the underdog, sometimes from your own making, and then songs of how you were wronged by your job or your girl or society. What I learned was the best songs ever written had elements of lack, delay, and longing for things better despite how bad things had gotten and how you tried to handle it the best you could. One thing I know for sure. It takes courage to write a song because you feel naked, exposed, and vulnerable putting your feelings out there. Worth it? Yes.

Wine, women, and songs were always in the back of my mind when I started to write songs. It is what I grew up listening to and grew accustomed to understanding the power of emotions. Having a drink while all hell was breaking up all round you became the grease to the wheels of one's life, dodging the potholes in front of you while you beg for relief.

I guess all my life I have been looking for happiness and peace. It came from a young age (13) when I took to drinking to forget things I had no control over. God says to never do anything in excess, but when you are young, and your guidance has passed you by, you will take in anything the old Devil offers you. The lines of self-control, boundaries, and excess become blurred to a point where you sometimes lose your way in life.

I recently recorded a song that is personal and raw to me that will be released in 2023. The song is "Don't Expect to Love Me All The Time." It was co-written by my friend Tony Ramey, and the album is called "Building Bridges: A Beyond the Interview Box Set."

I'd like to mention how great it was to sing and write with the talented Randy Van Warmer, Dickie Betts, Bobby Whitlock, James Burton, Jerry Kennedy, Steve Cropper, Hargus (pig) Robbins, Bob Moore, Buddy Emmons, Pete Drake, Johnny Christopher.

My Best Memories

When I lived in Nashville, about every three months, 15 other songwriters and I would go to Magic Springs. We would go and do relaxing things like fish, sing, drink, and eat for about 3 days or so. We all had our own tents, too. Our creative juices would flow where like-minded friends could create music and let our hair down.

Those were some of the best days of my life. I enjoyed being myself and being at peace with good friends. Those were the days. My friends, Chuck and Melanie owned that place. Melanie was my Hairdresser. Great people, I often think about.

Parents: Andres Rodriguez and Isabel Davis-Rodriguez (Family Collection).

Johnny (7) playing a guitar gifted by his eldest brother, Andres Jr., 1959 (Family Collection).

Playing half-back for the varsity football team for Sabinal High School, Uvalde County (1967 Yearbook).

Garner State Park with longtime friends Bob "Bullet" Naegelin (front left) and Randy Willis (front touching his shoe), 1967.

Johnny with his beloved mother, Isabel Davis-Rodriguez (Family Collection).

Johnny was introduced to Happy Shahan by Texas Ranger Joaquin Jackson at Alamo Village Amusement Park, Brackettville, Texas, 1969. Publicity shot/Public Domain.

Johnny with BMI Executive, Frances Prescott, along with singer, Tom T. Hall and Rep in Nashville, Tennessee, 1972. (Publicity shot/BMI).

Johnny with Tom T. Hall and The Story Tellers, Gus Barba, Alan Pace, Rick "LD" Wayne-Money, and Glen McGurt. Nashville, Tennessee, 1974 (Publicity shot/Courtesy of Mercury Records).

Johnny and the Music City Band: Rick Durrett, Johnny Cobb, Rip Willis, David "Rojo" Burns; late, and Merle Counts. (Publicity shot/Photo Courtesy of Mercury Records)

Johnny with Merle Haggard, "the Poet of the Common Man," 1974. (Photo Courtesy of Gus Barba)

With Dottie West, at the Ben-Darrell-Willie Tournament, Houston Woodlands Golf Course, Houston, Texas, June 1983. © Rick Henson.

Johnny with George Strait at the Erwin Center, Austin, Texas, April 19, 1986. © Rick Henson.

Johnny & Tammy Wynette. (Public Domain).

Allen Sowersby, George Jones and JR, 2009
© Chas E. Wilkins "Codak Charlie"
Photography

Johnny and Garth Brooks,1985 (Public Domain).

Johnny Rodriguez Enrichment Center: Charity, Johnny, Willie Nelson, Dolly Parton, Tom T. Hall Corpus Christi, Texas, 1974 (Publicity shot/Public domain).

Johnny recording in the Epic studio with Producer, Billy Sherrill, 1979 (Publicity shot/Public Domain).

Johnny ("Most Promising Male Vocalist") poses with Loretta Lynn, Freddie Hart, and Tanya Tucker, at ACM Awards. 1972 (Publicity shot/ACM).

Johnny and Paul Lynch, Freddie Fender
(Public Domain).

Loretta Lynn, Conway Twitty, and Johnny at CMA Awards
1973. (Photo Courtesy of CMA).

Johnny Rodriguez aka the "Latin King of Country Music" was recognized as an international artist becoming the First Mexican Country Music Star, at age 21. Publicity shot/Public Domain.

Johnny with Rick Durrett and Colonel Tom Parker, Las Vegas (Public domain).

Johnny with Charley Pride at Johnny Rodriguez Enrichment Center (Charity) 1977 (Publicity Shot/Public Domain).

Grand Ole Opry 1974 (WSM/Public Domain).

Johnny with Business Mogul, Buck Owens at Buck Owens Crystal Palace, Bakersfield, California. 2000. (Photo Courtesy of Johnny Mack Williams).

Johnny and Johnny Bush recording in San Antonio studio, 2009. © Chas E. Wilkins "Codak Charlie" Photography.

Johnny with actor, singer, Roy Rogers, and Randy Doyle, Palomino Club Hollywood, California. 1974.
(Photo Courtesy of Randy Doyle).

Johnny and Larry Mahan on his Texas ranch, April 2019.
(Photo Courtesy of Rick Reno Stevens).

Randy Willis, Johnny, James A. Michener, and Coach Darrell Royal.

Johnny, Earl Campbell (Heisman Trophy winner), and Juan Conde (UT equipment manager), at Houston Woodlands Golf Course, Ben-Darrell-Willie Tournament, June 1983. © Rick Henson.

Johnny earned his Black Belt in Martial Arts, World Tae Kwon Do, Seoul, Korea, 1976 (Public Domain).

My first wedding was to bride Linda Diann Patterson Rodriguez-Adams in Henderson, Tennessee, on February 17, 1976 (Photo Courtesy of Linda Rodriguez-Adams).

With daughter Aubry Rodriguez and her mother, Debbie McNeely at Grove High School Graduation, Missouri, 2016 (Photo Courtesy of Debbie McNeely).

With daughter Aubry signing autographs at Andy Williams Moon Theatre, Branson, Missouri, 2015 © Patrice Ash.

Bill Medley, Aubry, Johnny Rodriguez, Branson, Missouri, 2014 (Photo Courtesy of Debbie McNeely).

Johnny with daughter Teresa Ann Parker, after receiving CMA of Texas "Living Legend" Award, Lubbock, Texas, 2020. © Cranston Reid Photography.

Willie Nelson and sister Bobbie Lee Nelson with Johnny and Lana at their wedding in Spicewood, Texas, January 10, 1995. © Rick Henson.

Johnny poses for a publicity shot (Public Domain/Photo Courtesy of Capitol Records).

Me and Merle Haggard, the Hag. Known as "the Poet of the Common Man." I felt honored to be invited to be with him in the same studio. (Photo courtesy by Gus Barba)

Johnny Rodriguez Band: Bruce Carter (Road Manager/drums), David Reynolds (keyboard), Billy McCoy (guitar), Don Sowersby (steel guitar), Mike Hammock (guitar), Kenny Penny (fiddle) 2021 (Photo courtesy of Pauline A. Vega).

Me and my band, John David Aultman (guitar) Bruce Carter (drums), and Gary Goss (keyboard) Buck Owens Crystal Palace, 2016 (Photo Courtesy of Pauline A. Vega).

Pauline Vega, executive producer; Dennis Quaid, actor, singer-songwriter; Tanya Tucker, two-time Grammy Winner, CMHOF inductee; me, Rick Reno Stevens, producer 2019 (Photo courtesy by Albert Castillo).

* * * * *

Chapter 10 Politics of the Music World

"Trust but verify."
– Russian proverb

With every industry and every job, there are rules to live by. Playing music of any kind was no different, but there were different rules for playing and promoting country music. It has been said that country music was closer to God than any other kind of music other than straight gospel.

Country music was always at the heart of the song, revealed in the lives of hard-working people. The rules were that you were not supposed to live out the words of your songs but every star since Hank Sr. did just that. I would come to know that kind of lifestyle myself when I grew up in the spotlight. And believe me, it is a never-ending walk in the darkness of stardom. If you do not have an anchor a family core, you will not live a fruitful and decent life in country music. The words of the country songs I would sing would not allow it as you begin to live out those words of drunkenness and loneliness.

Do not get me wrong; I have been blessed with some incredible gifts. But losing my father and my brother at such a young age sent me on a course where I would use my stardom (to keep from feeling hurt) for my own sanity. My celebrity status is deemed a necessary evil in my life. If a man does that, he is living on shaky ground.

Because I was young when stardom hit me, I did not know the politics of the business, nor did I understand the importance of it all. And believe me, ignorance is not bliss. I did not know the ins and outs of contracts, nor did I know who to trust and who not to trust. On the other hand, I was in a better position than many artists because I had mentors who were telling me about others who got ripped off and suffered consequently. The stories are out there from John Fogerty of Creedence Clearwater Revival to Mark Farner of Grand Funk Railroad to even the Beatles who wound up fighting themselves when they put it all in their Apple Corps LTD and almost lost it all due to bad management. Everyone knows of the decency of many country music stars and the pitfalls the rest of us fell into. I was so young in 1974 by the time my next album was released. When you are hot, the promoters will put you on the same bill as other hot or semi-hot stars. Some promoters would put you on the same bill as the greats whose stars were beginning to burn out to bolster their fan base to piggyback off your rising stardom.

I did concert dates with Dolly Parton at a time when her star was fading after her years with the Porter Waggoner Show on television. Dolly is a super talent and smart to boot. And as for her songwriting, well, do not even try to match Dolly Parton. She has had songwriting down perfectly. Then when Dolly became a movie star, and her songs were beginning to hit the charts with other singers, winning Grammys and Oscars along the way; it was well-deserved.

I will always love Dolly Parton as an exceptional artist. What you see is what you get with that girl. She was always kind to me. I admire Dolly is ability to take life in stride and turn it around to her advantage. Nothing upsets or frazzles her, especially on a talk show or being interviewed by the press. She is clever and professional. I found at the beginning in my own career, the press sometimes was not always on your side, but I needed to be able to roll with the punches like Dolly and others who prepared themselves for fame and all that came with it. In life, it is good to listen and learn from the professionals and stars like Dolly who set the bar high for the rest of us to follow. Never take life seriously... It is a fact, failure happens, and it is newsworthy because, bottom line, negativity and sensationalism sells more papers and magazines. It cannot always be taken personally, but it is always business.

Since I had done shows with Dolly and Waylon and Lefty Frizzell, I began to learn of the politics of the music business. One of those "rules" of the road was to keep your nose clean. For the first years of my time at the top, I tried hard to do just that. But I began to hang around some tough hombres like Billy Joe Shaver and Lefty Frizzell who knew the bottom of a whiskey bottle better than any bartender. I was in the thick of it as well. With no direction on the road and when you are a kid with a pocket full of money and no one to check your behavior, well, you act like a kid!

Let me say a few words about guys like Billy Joe Shaver, who died today as I write these words at age 81 of a massive stroke. Billy Joe was a carefree dude who had songwriting success in Nashville but did not care about extraordinary titles. That is not to diminish his talents at all. So many guys like Billy Joe and Freddie Powers were great at songwriting and were comfortable in their own skin doing what they did best... cranking out their songs. But while writing this book, Billy Joe, Johnny Bush, and my old bandmate, Rick Durrett, passed on all in one month. Sure, makes a guy start to think about his own mortality. Billy Joe lived a hard-drinking life but sure left his mark on the music world through his written songs. Rest in peace, brother. You were a star.

Right after I learned of Billy Joe's death, someone told me that songwriter Jerry Jeff Walker had died the week before. He was 78. That is four country music legends in one month as I write this book. It forced me to self-reflect on my own life. Fortunately, I was always in surprisingly good shape, but death makes you wonder at times like these. Now, there are only about five or six of us old pickers left on this Earth from the old guard. After we go, you know, us old country music pickers, our time will be sealed up and there will be no more links to the past of country music left to play on any stage. So, I will just keep on picking until I cannot pick anymore and not worry about what may come my way.

I remember one night when I was with Lefty and, Willie and Waylon, among other outlaws of the liquid world of courage, we were passing around a bottle of "water" and killing time in a Nashville hotel room. We got drunk and traded stories of this and that with no rhyme or reason to it all. Drinking with those guys reminded me of my carousing days with high school buddies, "Bullit" and Corky Parker. We did not care; we were bulletproof. I was a kid sitting with some of the greatest songwriters who ever lived and to keep my place, I felt I had to compete or so I thought. Billy Joe and, Lefty and even Willie were all Texas boys like me, and we were the outsiders of

Nashville because we really were living out the words of our songs. Nashville could be conservative and clannish at times; you are either in the loop or out of it. And if you are a difficult person, you are most definitely out of the loop. If you are living a life like we were, born of Hank Williams Sr. himself, then you were out of that loop. You were only tolerated because you were selling records and packing concerts. I was heading that way, and I did not even know it. Back then, I didn't really give a hoot. I was on top, and I was riding that mule with all the stallions around me, and it seemed like a good place to be in.

By this time, I believe Billy Joe was living back in Waco, Texas, and Willie had moved to Austin where he and Waylon would usher in the "outlaw" movement in country music. It is not Nashville and thank God it was not. I do remember that Lefty was in bad shape around that time. He had been in the hospital for his heart among other ailments. When you die at 47, you know you have lived a hard life in those years. Lefty did leave a great songwriting legacy, one that I only dreamed I would leave behind. I am fortunate to have known him and for him to have written a song that not only I had a hit with, but one that Merle would have a hit with it when he cut "That's the Way Love Goes." I also had the privilege of sharing a billing with his brother, David Frizzell, later in my career. In the country music world, drinking and divorce were two very real disruptions and if you did enough of both, you would find yourself out of the Nashville loop socially but in the loop as a songwriter because you sure had enough material to choose from. You were writing and singing about the steelworker or the farm hand or the oil field hand who was living the same life as you were through his drinking and divorcing.

I remember when my agent and a promoter were lining me up for some television appearances on shows like the old "Hee Haw" comedy television variety show (1969–1971) with Buck Owens and Roy Clark. They were also talking about me being on shows as diverse as Adam 12. Johnny Cash's summer show and even the Dating Game! It all seemed a little over the top for me. I was not an actor, at least I did not think I was an actor. They kept saying how good I looked on camera, but I wasn't ready for that kind of stardom. My chosen field was singing on stage country music.

Country music seemed to be going Hollywood in those early days of my career. What was really going on was country music was expanding from its hokey beginnings into a mainstream form of worldwide entertainment. To this day, country music has even turned into theme parks like Six Flags and Disneyworld when Dolly opened Dollywood, and the late Conway Twitty opened Twitty City to the public.

It was getting politically correct for country music to be accepted even by Presidents of The United States when booking their inaugural balls. I know I had the honor to play for three distinguished Presidents in my heyday. But I never smoked pot on the roof of the White House like another country music star had done. That may have been true, or it may not have been true, but it sure was a legendary tale in country music history.

So, there I was, drinking with the best of them. Since Lefty died relatively young, I did not want to die that young, but I did not listen to myself. I was somewhat star-struck myself as I sat and drank with these legends. Again, looking at hindsight, if I could tell my younger self anything of value, it would simply be... "straighten up." At the time, however, Willie and Waylon had not hit their outlaw strides yet. A young kid like me had to take the lives of these great stars with a grain of salt and not take them too seriously. It was so hard to do as they were some of the greatest songwriters in country music history, and their songs are still being played today. They were part of those country music musicians I had idolized as a kid living in that four-room house long ago.

Undoubtedly, any musician who wants to remain relevant in this business must learn the business. And if you learn the business, you must understand the politics of that business. By the time my second album came out, Elvis's career had been relegated to grade-B movies and Las Vegas play dates. Parker asked me if I would like to come into his stable of stars and because of his success with Elvis's career, I thought long and hard about it. The promoters went so far as to start a crazy campaign calling me "The Mexican Elvis." When I heard that, I backed up to the fence line to know hitching my horse to a guy like Colonel Tom Parker could be great, but then again, it might not be in my best interest. I declined his offer and even today, I am happy I did. It just felt out of my league, but we did become friends, though. I enjoyed seeing the newly released Elvis movie, and I thought it was done in good taste, with the acting second to none. I admired the King of Rock' n' Roll to death.

Then came other promoters like Jerry Weintraub. Weintraub had guided the careers of stars like Farrah Fawcett and Lee Majors when he was not doing cameos in movies like "The Firm" with Tom Cruise before he passed on a few years back.

In learning the politics of the music business, I made some mistakes along the way. After I left The Storytellers and Tom T. Hall, I did not have the help I had enjoyed during those first years I was in Nashville. Since I had done some old songs as remakes on that first album with Mercury that became hits, Jerry Kennedy and Roy Dea, my Mercury producers did not want to lose that fire for my second album entitled, "All I Ever Meant to Do Was Sing."

"That's The Way Love Goes," written by my friend Lefty Frizzell, would also become a hit off that album. Now I have two hit albums in a year and a half, and my career was beginning to solidify. I had become a bonafide country music star. It happened so fast; I did not know how it felt. Even today, my memory of that success seems like a dream that happened and faded away.

I was either in the studio or on the road at that time doing the star-making machine for me and whoever else was hanging on and getting paid for my success. I guess if I ever had a signature song, it would be "Riding My Thumb To Mexico," which I wrote with Tom T. Hall. Since I had literally done a lot of hitch-hiking in my youth, it was a song that came from my growing up in Texas. As I wrote it, I never would have believed it would probably be one of the most well-crafted songs I have ever written. It remains one of my fan's and my daughter

Aubry's favorite, and I enjoy playing guitar and singing it even today.

Then, in late 1974, I kept cranking out the albums and hitting the road to promote them. Little did I know that I did not have time for myself. I had no personal life to call my own. I was young and a working fool, having little time to enjoy the fruits of my labor. It was one-night stand after one-night stand with no love in between. I had to keep this music machine going not only for myself but for my promoters, my agent, and my band. People do not know that you work for yourself and then you work for others who depend on you even though they are your employees. Tom T. tried to explain it all to me when I was 22 but it had not stuck with me as it should have. I was listening, but I was not learning. When you are a star, you can be blinded by the light of your stardom. If you do not watch out, you can burn out and fade away in the blink of an eye. Then you become a falling star. I worked my rear off for the money in those early days to avoid being burned out.

By this time, it was nearly 1975, and I had arrived. I was known as a Bonafide country music star. I made television appearances on shows like "Hee Haw" and Ralph Emery's "Pop Goes The Country," among many others. I was at a point where they would point me in the right direction and I went, just like a robot. Mercury was asking for a third album, so it was back in the studio, gathering songs to keep it going. Everyone around me knew best... too bad I didn't know I was entitled to have a private life, as well. What I needed most was balance in my life and a purpose.

On that third album, we stayed the course, but we did something wild when we all settled on me singing the Beatles song "Something," written by George Harrison. "Dance With Me (Just One More Time)" was to be the lead-off song with "Something" stuck in there to show my versatility. Little did I know that the country music audience would love it. Jerry and Roy did not think "Something" would come off as a single, but it did. I was shocked that Apple Records LTD., which was owned by the four members of the Beatles who had just broken up a few years before, allowed us to use it. I found out later that all of the Beatles loved country music with George Harrison, especially.

I'm a fan of Chet Adkins, and, you can sure hear it from his guitar licks on almost all those early Beatles recordings. Looks like I got famous off the Beatles after all so the old Spock's band of my school days finally made it, too! Thank God I never had to wear my "Star Trek" ears on stage.

That third album was called "My Third Album." By then, I'd run out of names for my albums, so I'd be like Led Zeppelin and name my albums after the recorded sequence. At least for a while or until someone came up with something better. By this time, I would start listening to anyone with something constructive to say. Promoters, agents, producers, and anyone else who spoke up with an idea. It was at this time that I began to live the life of a country music star, and I started to act like one. I was never a prima don because I grew up poor. But the money and the fame were starting to affect me in a negative way. When you give a 23-year-old young man anything he wants, he is either going to act responsibly or he's going to act the fool. I started acting like a fool. My drinking did not help me either. By the time 1976 came around, cocaine was becoming the chic drug of choice. I hate to say, it became my choice more than it should have, but not at first.

I have had a lot of up-and-coming country music singers who asked me about the music business, and I tell them to beware of it. I tell them to learn the politics of the business so that they will not get ripped off and they will not lose their way. Now, they might listen to me, and maybe they will not. To be honest, I wish I had a family like Tanya's who helped guide her career and kept a close watch out for the vultures flying around the stages of the world when she performed.

You would do well to always remember and heed this... people will lie to you with a straight face. It never hurts to get a second opinion also. But that did not happen, so I had to wing it on my own. The powers that be just threw money at me to pacify and appease me to keep the music going long enough to allow everyone to make money. That is the true politics of the entertainment world, ask anyone who has ever become a star with money. It is a lonely place to be at the top when you are alone and so young. God help the next guy or girl who "makes" it in the business who thinks they can make it solo. My advice is to know who your (tribe) true friends are and get an attorney to create or review your business contracts. You're going to need it written in your best interest so don't let the legality of it intimidate you and don't be the lone ranger. That only makes you appear gullible and an easy target.

Now I am not saying it was all gloom and doom. No way. I bought the material goods...new cars, clothes, and jewelry that money and privileges afford as same as the other stars. The one thing that gave me the most pleasure was purchasing my mother a car and other major purchases for her I in Sabinal, Texas, my hometown. I felt it was the right thing to do to pay her back for all her hard work for raising all of us Rodriguez kids. She deserved it and more to make her life easier.

Whcn you hit the top, your fans do not know what is going on behind the scenes. They think living the life of a country music star is all lights, glamour, love, and a life worth living. It is not. Sure, all musicians want to be on top, to be able to work their craft to please their fans, but the business of life in the world of music is not what you see on the surface. I would learn that from the first time I entered a recording studio for the first time. I was smart enough to see what was going on, but like so many, I got caught up in its superficiality. To be honest, I was too busy working and getting my career to the point of fame and fortune to slow down and take note what was really going on around me. Never take for granted business is always being tended to because you will be surprised it isn't.

Now I just want you to know the simple truth. Being a "star" is the hard part. That is why so many true musicians would rather work in the studio, make records, and write songs rather than live their lives on the road promoting their work. For a while, I loved doing it all. I was young and living the dream, as they say. But after a while, it got to be a burden, the pressure of keeping it all going for my band, my record label, and ultimately for myself and my family. A lot was expected of a 22-year-old kid. And that is a lot of undue pressure for this 22-year-old. I just could not handle it and after a while, it began to show emotionally, mentally, and physically speaking. A few years after my first album, I could see the paint began to peel a little.

To say politics exists in every industry is an understatement. The country music world, especially in Nashville, is no different, especially regarding certain accolades. Last month, Charley Pride was awarded the Country Music Association's Willie Nelson Lifetime Achievement Award for 2020. Many, like me, feel that was long overdue for Charley, a superstar who broke cultural barriers galore, but it never stopped him from making a difference.

No one is more deserving of any award, much less this one than Charley Pride. The way he was treated when some hotels would not allow him to even stay in one of their rooms sure should have made Charley go back to playing baseball, something he was drafted by the big leagues to do in the 1950s as the great player he was coming out of Mississippi. Charley stayed the course and took his fame in stride until he died a few weeks ago as I write this book in 2020.

Finally, I want to tell you up-and-coming pickers that "any success is good success" from anywhere it may come. There is no blueprint to stardom and there sure is no manual for the politics of being a country music star. It is like learning to ride a horse. You jump on and learn from how many times you fall on your head. After a while, when you get angry enough, you either become a first-rate rider or just go home. I never wanted to go home to failure in the record business. If I had never made it to Nashville, I would have just stayed in Nashville, washing dishes or mopping floors until I did. If there is one thing I have always had, it's determination.

I also happen to know I am a driver social style personality because I'm decisive. Knock me down, I am getting back up again. I had that same drive as a young skinny kid playing football in high school, and I have it to this day. I am moving a little slower nowadays. There is no shame in failure, but there is in not trying. Failure is a stepping stone. But let me tell you, I have seen pickers and singers—some of whom were a hell of a lot better than I was—who never made it to the top. At least they can tell their grandkids they tried their best. I know that I will be able to do the very same thing.

After the Grand Ole Opry left the old Ryman Auditorium in downtown Nashville to move outside to Opryland, USA where they had built a modern studio and a theme park for the Baby Boomers, the powers that be decided that they needed to build up Fan Fair meet and greet with the stars into something thousands would come for just that: Fan Fair. Thousands of fans would come hoping to meet their favorite country music stars on one, usually at a table with all your CDs later, posters, caps and t-shirts for sale. In most of the old contracts of the day, it was mandatory for you to attend Fanfare to promote your latest album or 45 RPM.

I have done my share of those Fanfare events and I really liked to do them because I like to meet my fans one on one. Even today, I signed autographs at a memorabilia store in New Braunfels to be in touch and keep my name out there. After 45 years in this business, it is still in my blood to come out and meet and greet my fans who take the time to come see me. I know what I must do to get to a show and can only imagine what my fans must go through and sacrifice, sometimes even travel far to see me. I never want to disappoint them, and that is why I have always selected the best band members to support me while performing on stage, as any country music singer can.

Right before my star began to fade, I did some shows with Jeannie C. Riley. Sweet Jeannie was and always will be the top-notch star she became when she rose to fame with Tom T. Hall's "Harper Valley P.T.A." in the late '60s. Jeannie had a few other hits after that monumental song. It does my heart good when I see her at one of my shows and she takes the time to share a kind word with me about Jesus. She's still beautiful and a fine Christian woman.

* * * * *

Chapter 11 Racism in the Recording Industry

"Cruelty is all out of ignorance. If you knew what was in store for you, you wouldn't hurt anybody because whatever you do comes back much more forceful than you send out."
– Willie Nelson

In life, we all have had to face barriers and learn to overcome them. We make choices in life to deal with our choices when confronted face to face and then move on. What's the point of living in the past? That will lead you to an early death. In other words, I've learned to forgive others and forgive myself by moving on.

We all know people or someone who experienced some form of prejudice and discrimination and led a successful life. Sammy Davis Jr. Charley Pride, you name them... the rich, the poor, the employed, and the unemployed. Luckily, Sammy had Frank Sinatra stand by, defend, and rescue him many times (even financially) like when Sammy was in an automobile accident and Mr. Sinatra paid his hospital bills.

Growing up, my elders had warned me of the signs that were posted in public places like, "No dogs or Mexicans allowed." That is why minorities work hard to feel a sense of worth that we are contributing Americans deserving our place at the table.

When I first started out, I heard the rude and crude comments to my face and behind my back, but I focused and wanted success more than I wanted hate and revenge in my heart. That kind of negativity and toxicity will poison your blood, kill your cells, and major organs as well. Some clubs paid me handsomely and yet had to escort me to my bus due to racism after I performed the gig. The adoration of fans would come later. All in a day's work, I suppose. As strong minded as military soldiers are trained to endure hardships, I trained my emotions to not respond in kind, but to win the battlefield in my mind. It served me well in doing so. Besides, it has more to do with them than it does with you. I vowed long ago to stay true to my fans and to myself by being me and not stooping to anyone's level.

Wide World of Entertainment Tejano Festival was held at HemisFair Plaza. I performed with other performing artists, including Jose Feliciano, Vikki Carr, and El Chicano rock group. Music mogul Don Kirshner was the producer, and it was televised on national TV on ABC Network, San Antonio, Texas.

For whatever rhyme or reason, celebrities change their names all the time. Usually, management in the music or movie industry feels they know best. It happens to the best of us, and it is not necessarily targeted at a minority. It's a common occurrence that has more to do with brand and image than anything else. The following celebrities share their identity and ethnicity who changed or hide their real names to appeal to the masses.

Raquel Welch Jo *Raquel Tejada* to declare Latina the most beautiful and famous California girl of all time, now boasts about their heritage like Mireya Navarro.

Marilyn Monroe's success in Hollywood would depend on hiding her Mexican family origin…the secret was kept well-hidden that her mother, Gladys Pearl, was born in Piedras Negras, Coahuila, Mexico, in 1902. She grew up speaking English and Spanish and assimilated into the Mexican Norteño life along the border. Marilyn would play along with the studio executives' requests because her livelihood depended on it. Despite demands from the bosses and publicists, she discreetly embraced her Mexican heritage later in life. She was fluent conversing in Spanish where towards the end of life she openly embraced her Mexican heritage traveling to Mexico, Baja California, and border city of Ciudad Juarez. She was intentional reclaiming her Mexican heritage even speaking the Spanish tongue in front of others in Mexico.

Marilyn's name was invented to make her a movie star. It was done all the time. Glamor and sex sells. Her birth certificate was never to be read on the theater marquee under any circumstances. Norma Jeanne Mortenson was branded an American image for life, out of fear public California life would not accept her thereby money spent on her would have been in vain and sabotaged her career. Marilyn... Latina? Powerful

Hollywood would have none of it. In her time, a white-majority nation was not ready to give up the image, the brand, the money, and the truth.

Interestingly, actress Rita Hayward Margarita, spoke Spanish even though she had Alzheimer's disease. She was another hidden Hispanic treasure.

People are convinced to change names to sound pleasing to the ear and to the American public. Other ethnicities as well, but not limited to minorities. You would or may not be surprised to know whose name was changed... that is how common these things happened, even today. Let us not spoil the fantasy. Here's a funny one. George Strait was advised to change his name early on to Cain Cooper. Good thing he did not.

Breaking Barriers of Racism and Sexism

"I believe we could paint a better world if we learned to see it from as many perspectives as possible. Because diversity is strength. Difference is a teacher. Fear difference, you learn nothing."
– Pablo Picasso

In the beginning, I was warned by some of my managers that some Promoters stated they would never hire me or welcome me to their honky club due to my skin color and being Mexican. "There's no snowball chance in hell I would hire a Mexican to play in my club." Ouch! Words were much more derogatory and harsher than I mentioned.

And they were not this nice about it. I won't name any names, but these owners of venues know who they are. I never let it bother me too much because I try hard not to sweat the small stuff. I just figured I'd win them over with my talent, personality, and charismatic stage presence once they got to know me. Why focus on the negative and their low vibe? It had more to do with them than it did me. I was confident because I had been mentored by the best legends who took the time to know me.

Time would be on my side, and I was right. Once I got paid well for a show from an organization I will not mention, only to be humiliated and booed on stage, and thrown things at.

Did I keep on playing? You bet. I'm a professional and a man, aren't I? Once my hits started rolling in... these individuals saw the money to be made and jumped on the bandwagon. The choice was obvious, and nobody wanted to be left out in the dust. I'm happy they did, and I smiled a lot playing more honky Tonks.

We felt some racism playing at a few honky tonk venues... how could we not? To see a Texan Mexican cowboy and novelty drummer like my friend, Gus indoctrinated Broadway up and down left an impression. I was a young man who was down to earth and wanted no trouble with anyone. I was like the rest of the artists looking for an opportunity with no money or contacts but had brain radar connecting with other musicians, pickers, and publishers. I was open to advice on traveling the road with my band on the road. We liked Elvis' tailored look and started wearing scarves around our necks and were being chased by women. Finally, my hard work paid off and, before I knew it, I became popular overnight.

In the 1960s, racism and sexism were a common practice, and I always felt bad for my friends and colleagues who had it tougher than me. You were being discriminated against for nothing... your looks, hair, voice, clothes, ethnicity, or worse gender. Federal and mandated harassment laws were not in place as they are today. I do believe some had it harder than others, and some knew how to make it work for them, taking a double standard mindset with a grain of salt. In other words, they learned to grin and bear it and not make any waves. That's because they loved singing and writing music more than the barriers placed upon them. Many rolled up their sleeves and manifested their own success silently behind the scenes using their business sense. The minorities that did this... tolerated the insults and jokes and worked just as hard as their counterparts for less pay. Hardly fair at all. In the end, they survived. Some surpassed their oppressor. Dolly Parton is a good example of a woman who achieved fame and success, becoming a student of the business and taking action.

Action and Brawls

Sometimes, some men in the entertainment business would call me out on something or start something for nothing out of the blue. After all, I did work in honky-tonk bars where a lot of booze flowed and was served in the night. I'd usually just let it go, but I'd react like anyone else would, depending on my mood. This happened to my friend, Merle Haggard, a lot; the man did not play and took no scuff from anyone. First, he'd warn you with his fighting words, then you knew he meant business. Respect.

For example, I was with Tom T. Hall when his brother Harland got on my nerves with his rude mouth. No sooner did I respond than we got into an altercation since he was asking for it. A man must do what he must do or forever be harassed. I didn't have the statute he had, but it was his mistake because I had the strength and youth on my side, which meant I was quick and could move. I knocked him down like a rabbit, and Tom T. stopped the fight. I've been told I can see like a hawk. I've got good peripheral vision, even in the dark. Luckily, in addition to perfecting my guitar skills, I also practice the gift of forgiveness.

Race was an issue in the 1950s through the 1980s, and as big and famous as Elvis Presley was, he felt the prejudice and racial tension others were subjected to. He was told to go back to driving trucks because his music was "N" music. Can you believe that? Do we live in the United States of America and a person is judged and discriminated against for the way you dress and sing? Rhythm & blues played a big part during that time, and Elvis was very much involved with his mother's church in Mississippi. People were slow to change, and music was one thing the older generation didn't want to accept. Some music to them was devil music or inappropriate music to their ears and parents believed it would corrupt their children. My, how times have changed... thank God. Or has it?

* * * * *

Chapter 12 Rodeo Way of Life

"Life can only be understood backwards; but it must be lived forwards."
– Soren Kierkegaard

In case you didn't know . . . you know now. My middle name growing up was "Charro" among my Mexican cowboy family and friends. I've always had a fascination and respect for the elder cowboys, who we called *vaqueros*. They are the real deal. History tells us these old cowboys earned their keep and endured tough times and could handle animals like no other. I believe vaqueros are athletes in their own arena and in life and should be revered.

I love watching all the classic Western movies like my father's father and his sons after him. Yes, John Wayne is on the top of my list, but so was the American-themed Western *High Chapparral* television series (1967–1971) for obvious reasons. Remember, Manolito Montoya? (Henry Darrow). He was the cool one of the bunches and we can't forget beautiful Victoria Montoya Cannon (Linda Cristal). I enjoyed the *Undefeated McClintock*, but *The Wild Bunch* is the greatest, too. Some of the best lines I like are "Aww hell; you ain't got the sense of a jack rabbit," or "They, who the hell is they? They're blowin' this town all to hell." Today, I give special mention to Kevin Costner's all-popular *Yellowstone* TV series.

Vaqueros persevere and preserve a way of life to put food on the table and make ends meet for themselves and their families. According to historian-genealogist John Albitre, in 1769, vaqueros were the first of their kind with the occupation of the Spaniard roots (1519 Iberian Peninsula Iberian) influenced the Indigenous and Mexican men in Mexico, specifically in the Americas where Californios and Texans were born. Many landowners and ranchers turned to the Mexican cowboys for their knowledge of the dominance of horse skills.

The arrival of the Spanish conquistadors bringing cattle into Mexico in 1521 resulted in descendants of Longhorn cattle becoming a central part of the beef and ranching culture in Texas

History. There were no horses before the arrival of the Spanish Conquistadors. The Spanish taught the vaqueros superb horsemanship among the Indigenous and Mexican cultures, where highly skilled workers made a living. Because the vaqueros had been around longer than the cowboy, Texan ranchers were traveling to Mexico to recruit vaqueros to oversee their cattle.

It was in the nineteenth century when the cowboy way of lifestyle took over, running alongside Texas. Later, the Texas tradition of roping came about, and it became known as the All-American rodeo. Non-Spanish speakers struggled to pronounce vaquero, so they settled on buckaroo.

1769, California Missionaries were formed, and the European traditions were handed down to the Indigenous and Mexican vaqueros who inspired the American cowboy in North and South America. Their traditions and superb horsemanship developed in Spain and were perfected on Mexico land from 1500 to the present day.

The Spaniard tales were handed down for generations where the North American cowboy is born. The vaquero could herd, round up, ride, and rope buffalo, horses, and cattle better than anyone. Their livelihood depended on it for survival, and they took to wisdom like a sponge because they could not live long on trial and error. Young vaqueros learned fast and knew their rank to heed the advice of the old-time vaqueros. They would teach them a lesson lassoing you off a horse when you made a mistake a second time—a telltale story told about vaquero and Foreman of R.L. Stockton Ranch, Don Remick Obispo Albite, who taught such lessons to young buckeroos a time or two.

The Spaniard was deeply tied to his horse, and it was more evident when he would ride his horse around the corner rather than walk from here to there. This meant he took take pride in caring for his horse. Who cannot deny the Western's craftmanship with a ¼ plain horsehair rope that was no more evident when a vaquero or Native American could rope and stop a buffalo's head or feet on a dime. Responsible for thousands of cattle, a vaquero's day began at 4 am, and his diet mostly consisted of beef jerky, pot beans, a cup of cowboy coffee, and mush, and a tortilla. The character spoken by the old-timers was one of resilience, patience, and strength to endure the cowboy way of life.

The Spanish word *vaca* (cow) and *caballo* (horse) were imported from Spain to South and North America where Mexico's native cowboys' vaqueros labor and work the ranches and farmlands. From South Texas to open prairies in the panhandle, and in Arizona, there are cowboys hard at work.

These are my heroes and legends that I revere close to my heart. Today, Bandera, Texas is known as the Cowboy Capitol of the world. All in all, it really is a small world where our Spanish influence, Texas and Mexican roots run deep. Sadly, the cowboy way of life as we know it, is going with the wind.

Honorable mention to all Vaqueros and to Tejas Vaqueros—Trail Riders of the elite, Budweiser, Parker Johnson, Kelly Joy, Lance Welch, and Neil Yolderman. These men and 800 others are "real" cowboys and my friends till the end.

Cowboy Favorite

My cowboy favorite was "Billy the Kid" known as Henry McCarty, aka William Bonney, from New York City, New York. A gunslinger/cattle rustler/rancher and Western outlaw, he lived in Arizona and New Mexico. He was a tough hombre who had lots of Mexican friends and hung out with Emiliano Zapata, a peasant hero of the Mexican Revolution (1910–1920) who fought for the people and land reform.

In my humble opinion, those were real cowboys riding, roping, and rebelling while living off the land, drinking and sleeping outdoors many nights under the twinkling stars. He remains one of the most notorious figures from the era whose life and likeness have been dramatized in Western culture, being featured in more than 50 movies and television series. Billie died by age 21 at the hands of Sheriff Pat Garrett.

Cowboy Friends

I first met Alex Fox in 1989 through a trusted and long-time friend named Joey Rodriguez.

Joey is a Promoter for Tejano musician; David Lee Garza Y Los Musicales and he provides sound system for many artists in San Antonio and Corpus Christi area. Joey gave me a ride to the Cold River stables and introduced me to him, "Alex, this is Johnny Rodriguez, Johnny, this is Alex Fox." One thing I will say is by the looks of him (after I looked him over) I could tell Alex was a *real* cowboy because it takes one to know one. From that day on, I decided he was alright in my book.

My next question to Alex would be one that would determine our fate in a lasting friendship, so I didn't hesitate to ask. Alex, "Can you do me a favor and teach me how to team rope for competition in an upcoming rodeo event? It's important . . . I want to learn to heel fast and well." He replied, "Yes, I'll teach you. Be here tomorrow and every day between 1 and 2 p.m. at the Cold River Cattle company." The Cold River Cattle company was owned by Ralph Mitchel and the home of "Texas-style drinking and dancing" in Babcock and Eckerd San Antonio, Texas.'

I asked him, "How much? Cuanto cuesta?" And he made his request known. "Teach me how to play the guitar." I replied, "Deal!" Like the title of my book, *Desperado*, I'm part gypsy-like and nomadic that way and I knew how to barter. That was in the summer of 1996, when my *Mexico Rain* and *You Can Say That Again* album was released and the beginning of a long-term relationship.

I further explained to Alex the real reason for my visit. That's because when I trust someone, I trust them. It may take me a while to size a person up, but I can get a good instinct faster with some than I can with most people. I explained to him that I'd like to enter the celebrity team roping competition with George Strait, and if he would teach me how to heal, then maybe we'd stand a chance to win. Again, it doesn't take me long to examine a horseshoe.

Team Roping is George Strait's passion. He and his son, Bubba, are members of The Professional Rodeo Cowboys Association (PRCA). George and his brother, Buddy, started the George Strait Annual Team Roping Classic Competition in Kingsville. The prizes included a Chevy ¾ ton truck trailer, saddle, and briefcase full of money.

I explained to Alex the event was held annually in San Antonio and that I'd like to enter the Celebrity team roping in conjunction with the San Antonio stock show and rodeo. Moneywise and contestant Kingsville to move to San Antonio stock show and rodeo. Celebrity team roping. Joe Freeman Coliseum. San Antonio Stock Show & Rodeo High Celebrity Team Roping.

Alex agreed to train me for 60 days, and I promised to be an eager student. The event was held every year in San Antonio, Texas. Alex and George are damn good cowboys, and both ropes exceptionally well, so I knew I had my work cut out for me. Alex and I had two months to practice and perfect to heel. It wasn't much time, but we'd work hard at it. The day came when wc had our competition, and George and I placed.

Did I mention Alex is a good conversationalist, too, which makes for good company? I imagine working with animals on the ranch all day is reason enough to welcome company and some of my storytelling whenever I show up. Sometimes, I like to get away and visit the hill country and give him a hand on the ranch to keep my hands busy. I find being on the ranch is therapeutic to my mind. When you meet Alex or see a rough-looking cowboy here and there (Texas has many of them), tip your hat to a guy or gal keeping American ranchers afloat.

I performed with my guitar at a private birthday party and sang "Strawberry Roan." It happened to be my dad's favorite song, and according to Alex, his dad's as well. After the show, I told Alex, "Here is your first lesson," and I handed him my guitar. He knew just what to do with it, too. He instinctively put my guitar away in a safe place. I was impressed. Alex never asked me again for any guitar lessons and I never pushed him to learn. Another thing…since meeting Alex, he has been helpful to me attending some of my shows and sticking close behind me while helping with crowd control and security. He is big enough to intervene on my behalf when things get out of control, yet always behaves like a gentleman around my lady fans and others. Corky Parker is another good friend who does the same. These guys have eagle eyes and can size up a place front to back without anyone knowing they're even there looking out for me.

It sure has made a difference for me to be exposed to the public while performing knowing these guys have my back. It allows me to do my job and better focus on my singing.

My friend, Alex is a real horseman and in his own horse business, he breaks colts for the public to ride or for competitive rodeo. All his life he's trained cut horses. He also makes a living shoeing horse.

Early sunrise to sundown. It's just the cowboy way of life and you either love it or you don't do it.

Well, someone's got to do it and we're happy cowboys like Alex can and do. It's a different way of life that requires many long hours starting at "canto" to "can't.". Another Texan cowboy and friend, singer George Strait, was raised and lives on a ranch in the hill country. Is it any wonder he can sing a great country song?

Now mindful, I mentioned when I first met Alex, he looked to be the real McCoy, no drug store-looking cowboy. Kinda what you see is what you get. If you're into judging a book by its cover, you would be dead wrong about my friend. Yes, he looks rugged and rough around the edges like me, when I'm not on stage, but he is also the most soft-spoken, kindest, well-mannered, and loyal person you could meet on the face of the earth. I do believe that Alex's qualities are a reflection of his parents, ML, and wife, Amelia.

His horse's name is "Pinta." She's the one I wore my Mariachi outfit in at various shooting locations for album cover release at the Guadalupe River and local restaurant.

I moved to a ranch with Alex for the pure wildlife beauty, non-native species, and isolation of it. I've always liked the quiet and the hill country. He taught me how to rope in the 4 to 5 years spent with him. During that time, I walked the area a lot collecting rocks. I'm a bit of a Rockhound and have a decent collection to prove it.

He has also been in some movies with the likes of country singer James Hand, such as a film called *Thank You A Lot* in 2014. He played a fitting cowboy role.

As you can guess, Alex and I are more like brothers than anything else. It goes for his brother, Eric as well. I always felt welcome around the two.

His late father, ML Fox (Mairon Lee) was another good cowboy and was like a dad to me. He treated me like one of his own. I would stay at his place because I felt right at home with his family. Mr. Fox gave me the best life advice I ever took to heart. He looked me straight in the eye and said, "Always be a straight shooter and be honest." To this day, I don't mince my words. His wife, Amelia, was also good to me . . . they both knew and accepted me the way I am. I never doubted they cared about me.

Alex lost his beloved father on March 17, 2019. I respected him immensely and still miss and think of him today.

In the past, I rode horses with Larry Mahan and all those great cowboys and guys in the rodeo circuit. We always had a great time and have memories to savor.

Texas Rodeo

One year, a good friend named Jerry Brandt, President of the Texas Rodeo Association, hired me to play the Huntsville Prison Rodeo. On this day, some cowboys thought they'd be funny with me and pull a prank, but at my expense and safety. Well, unbeknownst to me, these cowboys gave me a spooked horse who was a roping horse; green and not broken and not used to crowds. I always entered at a trot, circling the roping arena, waiving to everybody as I rode in

At the time, I knew nothing about the deceit to take place. They wanted to see if I'd stay on the ropin' horse—all you had to do was barely touch him, and he'd stop on a dime.

I was barely hanging onto the horse's neck, but I was determined not to hit the ground flat on my face, and I didn't. Luckily, there were some steps where I could land on my feet, so I stopped him in front of 30,000 people. I didn't mind the applause—the poor audience wasn't in on the prank. Those cowboys got a big laugh out of me at that one, and I was all the wiser after that. It's also why I still love rodeos today and never borrow anyone's horse I didn't know, but I do trust my friend Alex's horse, "Play Money."

Spotlight in the Arena Spooked

In late 1974, I performed at the Mid-south Coliseum in Memphis, Tennessee. Dressed in beaded denim and wearing turquoise for good luck, I took the lead and rode into the roping rodeo arena on a horse before taking the stage to sing. Galloping smoothly, I circled the arena and rode to stand still in the center. Easy-peasy. The rodeo announcer said, "Ladies and gentlemen, here's what you've been waiting to hear perform tonight. Let's give a round of applause for extraordinaire entertainer and singer Johnny Rodriguez." Suddenly, two spotlights flashed on my face, and the one on the horse cued the high school band to play loudly.

This spooked my horse big time, and he started bucking me crazy. What else could I do? I rode that big horse like my life depended on it (no prize in mind) and had the wildest ride of the night in my rodeo life. I jumped off just in time right up to the flat surface stage to sing "Louisiana Man." Everyone told me I should have gotten a buckle or trophy for the baddest and longest Bronc ride anyone had ever seen. This cowboy earned his pay on that day . . . I could have been killed by that horse. You had to be there to believe it.

Rodeo Competition

In 2006, I competed at a rodeo in Durant, Oklahoma, with rodeo contestant/musician Kevin Bacon. He and I were steer roping, and when I looked up at the flagman/rodeo judge who stops time, I noticed one of them was actor Wilford Brimley. I was happy with our performance, and we placed that night. Sadly, I didn't pick up my buckle win…I was preoccupied with a slot machine, my vice…the devil itself!

Bushwacker

I have a special place in my heart for animals, including horses, cows, and athletic animals. I own two longhorns now and love watching them graze the open space freely. There are also exotic animals on the Texas ranch where I live, so why would I ever want to move when it has everything I love and need? Nature and the wildlife surround and soothe me. This kind of life is not for the faint at heart, but it fits me to a tee. If you didn't know me, you'd think I've become a recluse in my old age. Ahhh, but I am as young as I feel and still have a lot of life in me. I prefer peace and quiet while I'm relaxing at home, away from the hustle and bustle of being on the road. I have always admired the big and baddest bull in rodeo, known as the Bushwacker. He is (PBR) World Champion bull, winning the title in 2011, 2013, 2014, born on June 1, 2006, and is a retired bucking bull at 1,750 lbs. He was inducted into the Class of 2020 in the Bull Riding Hall of Fame in Austin, Texas. Bushwacker is owned by Julio Moreno, a stock contractor for Julio Moreno Bucking Bulls. ESPN Magazine called Bushwacker "The greatest bull of all time." He bucked off 64 of his 66 riders. JB Mauney won.

Friends: Like Family

My relationship with my friend, Charles Koch, and his brother, Ray, goes way back. We also hung out with Teresa's uncle, Danny Snyder, even though he lived in the next town over in D'Hanis. Charles, Ray, and I went to the same Sabinal schools. Still, the four of us hung out quite a bit. It was a small world back then where everyone knew everyone and treated each other like family. I was on a first-name basis with Becky, my daughter Teresa's mom, and her grandma Ruby McReynolds, Charles' mom. I used to assist with whatever she needed help with, along with her four sons. I felt a part of the Koch family. One of them was Charles, who stepped up to be a dad to my daughter, Teresa. He didn't have to but chose to.

In the 1960s, when we were young kids in high school, I would visit, shoot the breeze, and pitch in as needed like family. It didn't matter doing what either, whether it was farming, ranging, or whatever. Once, I pitched in like the rest of the family to dig a cesspool behind Ruby's house. My daughter, Teresa, told me she has the video to prove it. If you could see me now wearing those tall black rain boots three sizes too big shoveling with the rest of them. You wouldn't believe it was me—I was swimming in them. I enjoyed spending time with the family and have great memories of them all. Teresa's grandma would feed me and everyone else working on the place. I think I had a special spot in her heart because she and her family had one in mine.

I revere and hold the highest respect for Charles as well as the entire Koch family. My friend was an honorary family member to them, not by blood, but by heart. I imagine he fell in love with my daughter the first time their eyes met. I know I did. We used to go out with Teresa's uncle Ray, cruising for chicks together. Isn't that what everyone did? Ray had a badass Mustang back in the day, so we knew we were cool. If I can recall, CK used to ride Bronc and rodeo quite a bit, which is something I admired and loved. Terresa's stepdad raised her on ranches most of her life and I am sure that's where my daughter learned the cowboy way. It's where she got her work ethic and learned to persevere. I hope to reunite with my childhood buddies, Charles, and Danny Snyder. Teresa's uncle.

Nigerian Scam

The time I was staying with Alex Fox . . . I was mindlessly gambling online and sending money foolishly to the Nigerians. Yes, we all are fully aware of the scammers and predators who are out there committing identity theft today, but back in the day when some of us weren't as astute when it came to fraud and criminal tendencies. And a few of us were gullible and wishful thinking, trusting strangers not knowing they were up to no good. I'm talking about the day's internet popped in and there were no cell phones to know what we needed to know about the scammers lurking. I'm embarrassed to confess just how much money I squandered believing in a hoax. It started with a stupid email coming from Nigeria congratulating me on an inheritance. Well, I went against my better judgment, believing in a stranger living in a foreign country, no less promising riches I felt entitled to. If it sounds too good, it's a lie.

* * * * *

Chapter 13 Mexican Elvis

'You cannot uneducate the person who has learned to read. You cannot humiliate the person who feels pride. You cannot oppress the people who are not afraid anymore."

– Caesar Chavez

I always felt embarrassed when my record label producers compared me to "the King of Rock and Roll," Elvis Presley, who called me the "Latin King of Country Music." It put much pressure on me to do what they wanted me to because it made me feel like an imposter. I was minus the suggestive "Elvis-the-Pelvis" dance moves, but they didn't care. They reminded me that my popularity made me feel like I needed security wherever I went. The girls were going wild at my shows and came out of nowhere.

I was Johnny Rodriguez, and they wanted me to behave like some Johnny Rodgers figment of imagination. They insisted on having an image wearing flashy clothes, rhinestone-studded jumpsuits, kissing the girls on stage, you name it... the whole nine yards. They were pushing me to imitate Elvis's every move. For a while, I convinced myself I had the ego and green eyes to go with the charade.

Similarities were unmistakable, where girls of all ages hustled and swooned in front of the stage to get a peek just the same. I was told that it was all about my distinctive and sexy singing "voice," exemplifying masculinity and "Machismo" at its best, the "alpha male," if you will, and what red-blooded American woman is not attracted to that! I was told both Elvis and I were natural-born singers because we had the stardom, sex appeal, showmanship, talented voice, boyish charm, winning smile, and old-fashioned manners that attract.

These essential characteristics are spelled sell, sell, sell, and stardom. My head was bombarded with exaggerated comparisons to Elvis. Still, I always appreciate the power of the total package. It's best not to believe everything they tell you.

That is the image press agents and publicists love to convey, and it's an image that's hard to live up to. Understand

I was not trying to compare myself to Elvis, but my handlers felt those elements were essential to stardom. I'd been in the business long enough to know what the promoters and the public wanted. Elvis undeniably had it, so did Michael Jackson, and my managers were now convincing me that I had it, too. It was getting too much, and we all knew who would win—will the real Elvis please stand?

Elvis and I were both into Martial Arts and self-defense. He studied Karate; I earned my Black Belt in TaeKwonDo. World Certified by Kukiwon in S. Korea. That was our way to blow off steam from all the adulation that you shouldn't take too seriously. He liked wearing his karate uniform, which he fashioned to be red on stage. Yeah, he was an original, all right.

Elvis and I were cultural icons in our own way, too. He fought hard for equal treatment for his non-white friends and musicians that others weren't aware. It's because like me he knew talent and wanted the best and got the best, regardless of color. Here was a white musician that suffered prejudice due to his Rock & Roll singing style. They even wanted to put him in jail because they feared his singing style was bucking the system and threatening America's moral fiber. An older generation hated his Black music and provocative dancing moves onstage. I believe it had more to do with the influence of their daughters than anything else.

One racist encounter Elvis had was before he was to perform live at the Astrodome and Houston Livestock Show and Rodeo; his people told him he could leave his black girls (background singers) at home. He refused and told them in no uncertain terms that would not happen, "I'm not going to do that so deal with it or I'm not going to be there!" In Elvis' true fashion, he politely demanded his girls be given the star treatment and made sure his girls looked like royalty, proudly riding with him in the open red convertible. It was a blonde girl who drove them circling the roping arena.

I'm happy to say he and I both performed at the Astrodome and Houston Livestock Show and Rodeo in 1974, sharing the same Marquis billing, and I still have the promotional flyer to remind me. It was one of the proudest days in my career,

I was feeling like one of the luckiest guys in the world to be performing among the greats.

My popularity in country music was visibly seen at numerous concerts with loyal fans. Honestly, I felt like the luckiest man alive when luck had nothing to do with it..

The advantages that I had that Elvis did not have, was I got to travel abroad and that was an experience I will never forget. It was a disadvantage that disappointed Elvis due to the Colonel not making it happen. Unbeknownst to Elvis, the Colonel, a Dutch (Andreas Cornelis Van Kuijk) was not a U.S. citizen, and he could not get a passport.

Another advantage I'm most proud of was my bilingual singing skills; I could sing and speak in Español, another universal language. And that was a considerable asset—women are attracted to Latin singers. My popularity was heightened in this area alone, and the fact that I was the "New Kid" in town and a fresh face made me in demand. Yes, it was nothing short of being labeled "The Latin King of Country Music" and nick-named "Charro" (as a small boy) for the simple reason I was always a cowboy first. Funny, some women fans would later call me the "Marlboro man." And what girl is not attracted to a cowboy! I won't lie, it sure makes a man's head swell up.

On the other side of the coin, Elvis had something I did not: Colonel Tom Parker for the duration of his budding career. The Colonel was fierce in guarding and protecting Elvis' empire; yes, to a fault, and nevertheless, the advantages far outweighed the disadvantages, depending on how you look at it. Only Elvis knew for sure, and the jury is still out on that argument.

One big regret I have is that I missed the opportunity to meet Elvis. I met the Colonel at the famous Peabody Hotel in Memphis, Tennessee, where I had dinner, and you could see in full view the hotel ducks waddling through the lobby following their mama into the hotel . . . it's quite a site to watch the Peabody March and nature doing what it does best. The hotel is the legendary 13-story hotel for its fine dining and resident flock of ducks waddling through the lobby every afternoon to the water fountain. It was here where the Colonel extended an invitation for me to visit Elvis at Graceland.

Unfortunately, it wasn't good timing for me. Who would have predicted Elvis' early demise? I didn't.

The Colonel also propositioned me with the idea of managing me in show business like Elvis. My popularity and career were at their prime during that time, and he knew it. I was fresh meat. It was clear he was on the hunt for newer and fresher proteges.

At the beginning of my career, I was managed by a good and trusted friend, Happy Shahan. Then, down the road, the label companies were more than happy to manage me. But who really manages me? I know the music industry better than most, but wiser is the man who has trust in those who know more.

Hispanic Heritage…My Inspirations

Unsurprisingly, I was drawn to country music because I could relate more to what they were singing about. It was like the music of our people *La Raza.* I was a young kid listening to it with some Mariachi music in my home. It is in line with the Mexican music I sing and relate to. I love both. In Mexican music, it's called Rancheras; you tell stories in a song.

Mexican music and country music both sing stories that are almost the same, just in different languages. You are singing about feelings of love, fear, loss, delay, or unrequited love. I enjoy listening to and singing in both English and Spanish. Country music allows you the courage to express emotions you are too fearful of otherwise. With country music, you are never alone and can always find a song you can sing from your heart.

I have always been proud to represent my Hispanic heritage and Texas roots. It has given me an expanded audience over my counterparts and a competitive edge. One thing I am keenly aware of is that Latinos are the largest minority group, and they are one of my biggest supporters. This is because I speak and sing in Spanish, and I'm so grateful that I do. I feel blessed that my fans appreciate my bilingualism and music.

Latinos are very loyal people, and I am conscious of their pride in my musical accomplishments and the expectations they have of me. Most still hold on to their traditions, especially their Catholic religious upbringing. My people have high standards and can be brutally honest, seemingly crucifying you if you show any form of disrespect or take them for granted. I understand the culture completely. Do them right; they will treat you like family whether you speak Spanish or not.

Latinos love you when you speak to them with the universal language of respect and compassion. It is deeply ingrained in us as a child and never leaves. This is a best-kept secret in Communication 101 as in any ethnicity or minority group, Mexican, Native American, Middle Eastern, Japanese, Asian, Black, and others. Not to say that Anglos don't, but most appear to be self-autonomous rather than embrace the family values of extended family or have restraint in voicing opinions not in the best interest of all concerned. It seems to be more of an individual preference.

While filming Rosie's Cantina El Campo with Kelly Kenning, I used a guitar named "Tex." It is an electric guitar painted with the Texas flag. I also had an electric guitar painted with the Mexican flag, called "Mex." The video was shot at 10 a.m., and we had a free party with food to celebrate. I had to restring it to play with five strings. It was an acoustic guitar. The album and video are called *Coming Home, Cantina*, and it's a great and fun album in the Tex-Mex genre.

I greatly respect the trailblazers before me and those other Country Music, Rock and Roll, Mariachi, and Tejano artists who flourished and made it possible for fellow Latinos to follow. Artists such as Cuco Sanchez, Miguel Aceves Mejia, Antonio Aguilar, Ritchie Valens, Vicki Carr, Linda Ronstadt, Little Joe Y La Familia, Ana Gabriel, Emilio Navaira, and Raulito Navaira, and Los Lobos, Rick Trevino, Felix Truvere, Gabe Garcia, Ruben Ramos, Louie Cruz Beltran, Victor Sanz, and Kadin Hernandez, and Nashville's rising country duo greats with a Latin twist, Kat and Alex.

Finding success in both Tejano and Country Music genres made it easier for me to build bridges with my colleagues and friends. Friends like Freddie Fender (Baldemar Huerta), who

I invited to tour with me in California. Freddie played in the Texas Tornados and Los Super Seven, along with Flaco Jimenez, Doug Sahm, and Shawn Sahm. We always followed our Hispanic heritage, traditions, and Texas roots. Also, my friend, accordion player, Flaco Jimenez who, is a national treasure. I have so much respect for him and always enjoy hearing him perform. I especially love it when we collaborate and perform on stage. I'm a huge fan of his.

Still popular and trending 25 years later is trailblazer Rick Trevino, Austin's Texas native who sang a duet of the popular Ritchie Valens hit song La Bamba on stage. Not only do I appreciate his bilingual musical talents, but I understand he has decent cooking skills as well, so we both have that in common. Rick makes a delicious *caldo soup* and I make my infamous Carne Guisada tacos. I was televised on Country Kitchen Nashville Network TV with actress /singer Florence Henderson on *Who's Cooking With Florence Henderson*, from the Nashville Network. She was formerly known as Carol Brady on the *Brady Bunch.* Evelyn, my former Fan Administrator, put out a cookbook for fans to enjoy.

"Deportee Song" by The Highwaymen

"Deportee" is a profound song with a powerful message written by Woody Guthrie and recorded on Highwaymen's album featuring Outlaw music with Willie Nelson, Johnny Cash, Kris Kristofferson, and Waylon Jennings. I sang a duet bilingual part with Johnny Cash. It is a protest song of sorts. I was awakened in the middle of the night to meet them at the studio to record with the four of them. Now? I'm in bed sleeping. Johnny replied, "Get to the studio, now Rodriguez, we're recording Deportee." I hauled ass over there, sleepy-eyed and all. I'm glad I did because it is a profound and personal song. I can relate and sympathize with the lyrics.

In its lyrics, it brings attention to the unfair recognition of migrant field workers who crashed in California in 1948. Martin Hoffman's music describes the mistreatment and dishonor before and after the tragic accident that only listed the passengers as alleged deportees.

The victims had not been named as if their existence was deemed worthless because of their immigration status—28 migrant farmworkers who were being deported from the U.S. were called back to Mexico after laboring in the hot fields. Guthrie was inspired to write the song for what he considered the racist mistreatment of the passengers before and after the accident.

Four named Americans passed as well, including the pilot. It took 70 years to recognize the crash victims by name with a memorial reading on August 26, 2013. Thanks to the efforts of author Tim Z. Hernandez for spearheading the recognition and research of the crash victims with a Memorial reading all names on August 26, 2013.

The United Farm Workers (UFW) President, Arturo Rodriguez, attended the dedication and unveiling of a gravestone that listed the 28 deportees' names at Holy Cross Memorial on Labor Day, September 2, 2013, in Fresno, California. R.I.P.

The UFW also brought awareness to the public regarding the unjust conditions farm laborers were experiencing regarding basic human needs of dignity and care such as maintaining outdoor bathrooms and access to clean drinking water to other necessities.

As the National Farm Workers Association merged with agricultural workers and formed an organizing committee known as the United Farm Workers Union (UFW), Cesar Chavez and Dolores Huerta became co-founders.

Dolores Huerta went further to fight for women in the labor movement. She challenged sexism and racism in the feminist movement of the 1970s and was instrumental and effective in helping organize thousands of laborers across the nation for better living wages and just working conditions. She was awarded the Presidential Medal of Freedom by former President Barack Obama for her humanity and for using her slogan "si se puede!" in 2012.

English is the universal language, it's true. But Spanish and English are both the most spoken languages in the world. It comes down to economics and tourism; it's productive and profitable to speak both, but being bilingual can earn you a 5 20% salary increase.

There are 470 million Spanish speakers around the world to be exact, and the second most spoken language in the world there are 335 million English speakers. Impressive…facts do not lie.

For economic and geographical purposes, some countries speak more than one language. It's good for communication with tourists; in Europe, 2/3 of the population knows at least one foreign language. Some scientific studies state that bilingual skills are beneficial for the brain and can reduce the effects of aging. In any case, bilingual can increase conversation skills and add to the workforce's value. Speaking Spanish is in more demand for translators and can advance in life.

They say leaders are readers, and readers are leaders. I encourage any of my readers to expand their horizons by thinking outside the box. Do what others won't do so you can have what others do not. Read about your own culture and others. Why not learn about our neighbors who live among us or south of the border. You will be delightfully surprised at how much closer your efforts will bring you to another human being. It may perhaps even expand your business. Do the Indian and Arab businesses here in the U.S. (who most speak Spanish) know something we don't about cultural interrelations?

Learn another language and visit a new restaurant because Spanish is a big part of American history. Our land was owned by Mexico; therefore, many Americans never left and still speak their native tongue, Spanish. Is it possible we can try to understand the descendants of the Americas and the universal language of Spanish in the Americas (South America) that is interwoven into the fabric of our very own culture and history? I did. I dared to be distinctive to sing and share with my audience who I am.

Raising Awareness and Consciousness

It gives me great pride to sing mariachi songs and wear the mariachi traje de charro. My own traje was made of great quality by owner Jorge Tello, known as "El Maestro." He is better known as the "Charro" three-piece suitmaker of Mariachi

L Casa Del Mariachi in Los Angeles, California. He is known for his craftsmanship and designs. He is the creator and designer of Disney's movie, "Tres Amigo" with Chevy Chase, Steve Martin, and Martin Short; and other musical greats such as Carlos Santana, and Placido Domingo. Mr. Tello is the designer of my black and white Mariachi suits with matching boots and an assortment of bow ties. I surely walk taller with dignity when I wear my mariachi suit. It best expresses my personal pride for my Mexican culture. Dressed in pride with my wide brimmed sombrero gifted to me by my daughter, Teresa, I feel most in tune with my heritage where my Texas roots run deep.

Most Hispanics honor their historic roots by living up to their responsibility. We work hard to represent a work ethic and honor to struggle and achieve the American Dream. It is the reason we are used to demanding work. We work with diligence to earn something as basic as putting food on the table to feed our families or saving for college and improving upcoming generations. We are proud people, and anyone we meet, we are more than happy to greet and offer respect. It is when respect is not reciprocated that it becomes a problem. It's called pride "machismo," and it isn't always pretty. It looks like a fight-or-flight, which involves mostly ego, yet many Hispanics relate. We may not tell you you're disrespectful, but if we're offended by you, we will walk away from you.

In every culture there is a hidden boundary of showing respect. For instance, the Japanese have high regard for their elders as do Hispanics, Native Americans, and the Middle East culture. There is much to be said about the wisdom they possess. And there is much to be said about the younger generation, too, who will inherit the earth. But they are inexperienced when it comes to living a full and mature life and fully appreciating culture and respect thereof. As they mature, they, too, start to embrace wisdom and the importance of respect for their elders.

Hispanic Facts

Not all my Hispanic friends speak Spanish, but almost all of them wish they did. I think the smartest thing you could do is turn your car into a university and listen to CDs or cassette tapes while driving. In other words, expand your horizons, your skillset, and your audience. The demographics and number of Hispanics in the U.S. speaks for itself. The Americas really is larger than the United States of America…think of the other country sights you could experience. Spanish is a universal language and an asset. It can open doors for you and has served me well, to this day. English was not my first language spoken... it was Spanish. When I sing in Spanish, it is a feeling and experience, I share.

Data released in 2016 CMA Association highlights a 25% increase in country music's Hispanic listeners since 2010. Also note that 7 in 10 non-white adults polled listened to country music once per week or more. The love of country music is expanding across cultures, especially among the Latin population. It is no wonder that the music is expanding with such Hispanic greats.

Reverend Vincente Fernandez, "Chente" and El Rey, 81-year-old Mariachi singer, who famously sang Ranchera songs, was a hero of both mine and George Strait where George sang *El Rey* at a concert, in tribute. I rerecorded one of Vicente's songs, "La Diferencia" in my upcoming CD, performing a duet with Bakersfield's, Mariachi singer, Daisy Sanchez. We loved this Mariachi singer who romanticized Mexico symbolizing horses, Tequila, honor, women, love, heartbreak, survival, soccer, cockfights, and sports. Chente died 2021. Mis respectos.

The Story of Cesar Chavez

Mr. Chavez was the champion for us field workers who fought hard for fair conditions (bathroom) and pay. To this day, Cesar's sacrifices and recognition for labor workers means something to me as I lived it from the ground up!

Bakersfield's best…My good friends, Merle Haggard and Dave Kirby wrote a song called *The Immigrant* that he gave to me to sing that talks about the unfair practices and hardships the Mexican migrants were experiencing in the 1970s. My hero and compadre dared to care and was unafraid to write and record such a tale-telling song. "The Immigrant" tells the story of migrant workers' plight that only Cesar brought to light. An awareness of social consciousness that makes you think about where our food comes from and who is responsible in America.

"The Immigrant" song is a powerful and personal song to me about the plights of farm workers in the early '70s, when the Bracero Program allowed guest workers to enter the United States to work the Agricultural fields, putting food on American tables until the end of crop harvest. History tells us unbroken promises were made and agreements regarding living arrangements and working conditions were not practiced. Sometimes when it came time to bus these hard-working men and women back to their native country, some weren't paid. It was a time when much social consciousness was divided and raised, where many experienced abuses at the hands of some growers at the expense of the workers earning an honest day's pay. Unions fought hard for better wages and working conditions, such as bathroom facilities, freshwater accommodation, and new laws for pesticides and chemicals. Who would come to the migrant worker's defense? Who would fight against the unfair practices of some ranchers and big companies who happily accepted these workers but weren't honest in their business dealings? Once returning home, if that were not enough, then the Mexicans would face corruption at the hands of the Mexican banks, which held percentages of the worker's earnings. Laborers could not collect what was rightfully theirs. This occurred in the 20th century when the civil rights of brown people were further being exploited. Think color does not matter... think again!

In his lyrics, Haggard mentions how America grew on the back-breaking work of the Mexican immigrants showing up in the agriculture fields. He wrote it, sang it, and gave it to me to sing. It is a song about awareness and being thankful to the worker who puts in an honest day's work to earn an honest day's pay to help America grow. The song was released on *Just For You,* an album released in 1977. I felt honored to sing Merle's song about the migrant worker's plight everywhere.

I challenge anyone who wants quick money but note that I'm not saying it's easy money. If you're willing to convince a contractor for labor work in the fields to hire you, go for it! You will learn a good lesson about what thousands of migrant workers do for an honest day's work. You will have earned your pay. But I guarantee you will have a greater appreciation for what agricultural workers do for a living, be it Mexican American, Filipino, Anglo, "Okies," Blacks, Chinese, Japanese, or Arabs. Not everyone can withstand the brutal sun and hard labor it takes to put food on the table. Nor can many appreciate the labor that field workers do to 'til the land to get dinner on our tables. My family and I appreciate the sacrifices farm laborers make to help feed America.

Throughout my career, I have received many awards and recognitions, but the one that sticks out for me is the one received by the United Farm Workers, former President Arturo Rodriguez, a native Texan (Representing the late Cesar Chavez) of Keene, California compound, coming to my show on CSUB campus.

It was on May 10, 2001, in Bakersfield, California, where I performed two shows for Cal State University, Bakersfield for migrant students who were being bussed in from outlying areas into the University campus to educate them about the opportunity to attend a college, enjoy a presentation, lunch and concert. I know what that is all about from first-hand experience because I picked cotton. I pitched hay. I picked all kinds of crops for a buck, so I knew the plight of the workers in the agricultural industry. It is extremely backbreaking to work hard in the hot sun.

Former President of United Farmworkers, UFW, Arturo Rodriguez, presented me with tokens of a cap and handkerchief (black Aztec eagle insignia symbolized in colors of red and black) of UFW's cause and plight. The Kern County Hispanic Chamber of Commerce assisted with the Meet and Greet for VIP's. Kern County Board of Supervisor, Pete Parra presented me with a Kern County Proclamation Plague and former Mayor, Harvey Hall presented me with the key to Bakersfield. I felt both honored and welcome singing for the county of Kern's youth.

Musician Rick Reno Stevens would help coordinate the entire band, some of my musicians, and some of the local Bakersfield Sound studio musicians. He did a good job too convincing and proving to me his musicians could seriously play. Come to find out, they knew how to play my songs fine... that's for sure.

Some of my favorite Mariachi singers are the late Vicente Fernandez, Juan Gabriel, and Antonio Aguilar; Pepe Aguilar, Cuco Sanchez, Miguel Aceves Mejia, Selina Quintanilla, Ana Gabriel, Daisy Sanchez, and Angela and brother Leonardo Aguilar. Most of these singers grew up on ranchos and embraced their Mexican culture. No one makes love to a romantic song more than these great performers.

Albondigas Soup for Music Lovers: Good for the Soul

Some of the greatest love stories ever told are written in every song. It is the *albondigas* soup for music lovers because it soothes the soul, modifying, relating, and identifying an ocean of emotions to the soul. Speaking of our inner being rather than the injustices felt within having the capacity to choose love or fear. Soul to soul.

Music is to medicine what food is to the soul. Music is and has always been a positive and powerful influence... globally and locally. It is a universal language all its own. Instrumentally or lyrically, it can speak to the mind and heart like no other.

To create it takes passion, purpose, and preparation to be appreciated. To listen to it... one does not need to understand the lyrics because it's an assortment of orchestration of vibrations and its magical when it touches and speaks to the soul. It can match our own vibrations, particularly a low to high, which makes us feel better, lighter, and hopefully, happier.

Playing music is a job I take seriously because it gives me meaning and purpose. It is my rocket of desire to make a difference to others through my music to get my audience through whatever it is they need to get through. I understand the power of the mind and how the spoken words and lyrics in songs can heal. I believe it is human nature to want to connect. Music gives us that and more and only a digital touch away; plus, it's free.

It is my belief that music evens the playing field because it's a universal language that all ears can enjoy. The heart can sing and be nurtured through song. The sound can be compassionate and nurturing. That is the message I love my audience to feel. Giving a great performance was always my goal more than anything else when I stood on stage.

Communication: Spanish Language & Music

Ever since I can remember I wanted to do a bilingual country and mariachi album. The Spanish radio stations would get requests to play my bilingual songs and would in turn play them. I don't think my Anglo friends are aware of this fact since they didn't listen to Spanish radio stations or watch Spanish TV. My brand has always been quintessential Texas and country music, but with my Latin roots and love of Mariachi music that I grew up with, my heart loves to share them both. To put in simple words, Spanish is also my brand. Make no mistake, it is the Spanish language that made Mercury Record Executive Producers sit up and take notice of my musical talent.

In their own words, my former producers had never heard of such a thing in country music, and they wanted to hear me sing it again and then quickly sign me up on the spot. They never told me that wasn't country, or it would never work. I had the voice and the something extra; they could see the dollar signs down the road. They understood they could market me to an expanded market. I was what the doctor ordered for country music's dwindling popularity, sparking a resurgence and time for a new era. I never changed who I was, but some people's perception of me only saw the cowboy side of me not the cowboy *vaquero*. I was always both. All my fans accepted me, eventually, not just the Anglo cowboys, but the Mexican, Native American, and Black cowboys did, too. I will always be proud of the fact that I brought something to a country music genre that was unique during a time when change didn't happen fast enough.

Buck Owens knew this in owning a number one radio station, KUZZ radio and renting space, temporarily to Spanish Univision TV. Recording artist-songwriter Kristofferson knows the importance of being bilingual as he frequently visited Spanish radio stations in the 70s and 80s because he had friends who owned and worked them. He's also fluent in the Spanish language, but few people know this. He is a very intelligent man, obviously. I know a lot of Spanish-speaking people who love country music but until now they couldn't hear this type of music in their own language. Few know that my passion was always to secretly record an entire album combined with country and mariachi music. It has always been my life-long dream to sing the songs of my beloved mother / *canciones de mi madre* (in the same gesture that Linda Ronstadt did for her father, *Canciones De Mi Padre).* My wish came true.

* * * * *

Chapter 14 When a Man Loves a Lot of Women

"The goal isn't to live forever, but to create something that will."
– Selena Quintanilla

Let me first begin by saying that I am a gentleman, a *Caballero.* I am not the kind of guy who kisses and tells or a guy who puts out the names of any woman I have ever loved. I do not care if it is for a long-term relationship or a one-night stand, and I am not going to give out any details. The only names of any girl I have gone to bed with will end with my wives, not any others I might have had that pleasure.

I know they would not appreciate this being a kiss-and-tell kind of book. Personally, I do not pay any mind to those celebrity gossip-type magazines concerning stars. I respect women, although I admit I have not always been good to some. Here again, way too many times I was not in my right mind when something went south in any relationship I engaged. For that, I feel remorse for not behaving as any woman deserves to be treated, and I ask forgiveness as I have forgiven myself and others.

My own mother, my first love, was a wonderful woman with a great sense of humor. I miss her every day of my life that she has been gone. No mommy issues, here that's for darn sure. I am a decent cook because of her. Throughout my career, it has been mostly women who come to my shows, and I love that they do not hold back their love and support of my music. It is safe to say I have had the pleasure of knowing or being with some fine ladies, some famous and some not so famous. Telling you the names of either one will not do me any good. I will let the reader use his or her imagination.

You know a guy uses excuses for how they treat a woman. Some say they were too drunk and were out of their minds and the next day they spent that day apologizing for what they did the night before. You have read about them, the fights between George and Tammy, Johnny Cash and his first wife, Vivian. I do not see any advantage in broadcasting your personal problems in a book or a movie. I think if we have a beef with some women, we need to just maybe put it in the words of a song and make it generic. It at least sounds more romantic and sincere to me. Then again, there are some songs of mine that I do not like to sing because it reminds me of a certain love interest and things that have gone wrong. It is safe to say I have had many rendezvous and love interests along the way and with some famous women to boot. These women were gracious enough to not only allow me to love them, but to even take the time to put up with me in the first place.

When you are a young man in the music business, you are targeted by women. When you are a star and making money and you look half-decent, well, some will claw the paint off the wall to be with you, even if it is for just one night. Such obsessiveness has gone to the extent of some girls behaving uncharacteristically when things did not go their way. I have been told that venue parking lots had their patrons' cars scratched, as shown on video footage.

Was this a way to get my attention from a girl by behaving so aggressively? No. I always liked the girls and women who kept their composure, you know, the kind of woman who would not just fall all over you when they met you. A strong woman who loves and respects herself is ideal, one who does not need me or appears desperate or invasive. My heart always knows which ones I want. These are attributes like kindness, smarts, pretty, sense of humor, and down to earth come to mind and not too possessive.

I guess that is why I fell in love for the first time with Linda Patterson, you know, that young girl I first met at Alamo Village where we shared our dreams of success in what we wanted to do in this life. Every woman I married; I fell in love with her for a reason. I saw qualities in her that made me feel I wanted to grow old and spend the rest of my life with her. I saw a future for us. And, as good as it was at the beginning, one thing is sure... life happens. As mentioned earlier in my memoir, this is a cautionary tale about my vices and that is no easy feat for me to share.

Linda wanted to be a flight attendant and she did just that. Then, some four years after the day we had met at Alamo Village, I was flying to one of my concerts and she was one of the flight attendants on that flight. I mean, what are the chances of that happening? Talk about fate! By the time she was flying for Southern Airways, Linda had turned into this beautiful young lady. She was a Georgia peach, from Conyers, Georgia with a smile that would knock you off your feet. And I fell for her pretty hard.

I was looking for that stability I was seeing in my friend Johnny Cash and his wife, June Carter Cash. June was always trying to get me to church to find a "good girl" and settle down. And Linda gave me a lot of what I needed at the time. At the time she came along, I had been heading down that country road of fast living. I was living out the words of those old Country songs where the guy was not worth much of anything. Who knew?

Linda and I were a good fit for each other at the time. She had realized her dream of flying the friendly skies and I had done the same, only my dream was a little more grounded. I think that although she was surprised that I had become a country music singer, she didn't steer clear of me. Linda was comfortable in her own being and really did not need any man. But she wanted a man, a husband, and a family, eventually.

I gave her my number and told her to look me up should she ever have a layover in Nashville or any city she might hear of me playing a concert. She did follow up (fortune is in the follow-up), and I sure was glad she did. After a few months of long-distance dating, I asked her to marry me! When we both had some free time, we spent a wad of money to have a lavish wedding complete with tuxedos and limos and fancy suites in the best hotels for our honeymoon.

Linda looked so beautiful in her dress and honestly it was one of the happiest days of my life. But for some reason, happiness always seemed to pass me by. Some of it was my fault, some of it was due to circumstances. Who knows? Looking back now, I see a lot of it was on me because of my restlessness. I had always felt I was on the run from something when in fact my happiness was right there in front of me all along. To this day, I am still searching for my place at the table. Maybe it came from my growing up poor and wandering around the countryside looking for where I was supposed to be. I honestly do not know.

As I write these words, I can only wonder, so I will just keep on singing and searching. It is my lot in life, I guess. Tiring to say the least.

All good things must end. Married life is good for those who can live it. I could not live it. I was not the marrying kind, at least not at that age. I had come to find out that I was not much of a husband to my bride. Now I could blame it on the music business, the women I kept meeting and then the booze and the drugs and back again, but that is not really it. Like a man commits to his job, you must want to commit to a marriage. I just could not do that as I found out I wanted to play my music and live my life on my terms. It does not work that way, not in a real marriage anyway. When you are married, it is on our terms. They say you got to walk beside a woman as she walks beside you. Well, I was always trying to lead on the dance floor and that is when you tend to step on someone else's toes. Marriage is a different and special kind of dance where it takes two to tangle in sync. Communicate and compromise are key words.

Linda was too good a girl to let me run around like I was doing soon after our marriage. We lived in my home in Hendersonville, and we would party with some of the biggest stars ever to hit a stage, but the cracks in my character began to show with everyone around me. Linda saw it and that is why I think she did not want to have a child with me until I had the courage to change. I never did and she was gone. My attitude "my way or the highway," was just not going to work for someone as special as Linda. Back when I got married, the divorce rate was around 35 percent. Today, it is 55 percent.

Seems like getting married is a losing proposition from the get-go. Some people can do it, and some cannot. My parents were married their whole lives with a lot more troubles than I ever had, and they made it work until my father passed away. I do not know how those old couples did it. They were poor and struggling and still managed to keep it all together. My guess is they learned to cling on to each other and get through life, caring and sharing with a "I Got You Babe" attitude.

That is what you call a sacred bond and vow. "To have and to hold form this day forward, for better, for worst, for richer, for poorer, in sickness, and in health, to love and to cherish, from this day forward, until death do us part." I guess my generation is the beginning of the end of what is called a successful union. Still, I will not ever give up on love and the sacrament of marriage. A lasting commitment and lifetime partnership with a special someone. Call me a romanticist, but I still wish upon a star and my heart remains hopeful.

If a man ever needed fuel to write songs by, I found it in my first marriage to Linda Patterson Rodriguez. By the time we married, my star was fading a bit, and I was still trying to hang on to my stardom. I took a lot out on her, blaming her for this and that and treating her like a scapegoat as I tried to keep my place on the stages of America. Misplaced anger for sure. It is easy to lash out at those closest to you, and that is what happened. I wanted my cake and I wanted to eat it, too. No woman wants to ever compete with another woman. I was too immature to know that fact.

I had grown up in a small town with small-town values, but I needed guidance from someone on how it all worked or was supposed to work. It was my fault for sure. I really was playing "A Game That I Can't Win," as the song goes in my upcoming CD, *Building Bridges*. It was the first time in my life with regard to a woman where I was deeply sad at how it all turned out. I felt like a failure, realizing that I just was not marriage material. Still, I would try marriage three times more, and engagement a few times more, too. I just never seemed to get it right.

After that marriage went into the sky on the wings of a dove, I was out looking again, but not for a wife, just an array of lovers. I poured my mind into staying on top of the country music world. My next album was aptly titled *Songs About Ladies and Love*, which had a huge hit on it entitled "We're Over." Now you could say this was about my first marriage to Linda or maybe a girlfriend I had found to replace her, I cannot remember. There was another song on that album called "I Just Can't Get Her Out of My Mind" that could be about my failed marriage or another song off that album called "Just Get Up and Close the Door," which was a huge hit for me, too. That song was a longing of sorts where I was looking for a woman who would stay with me instead of just hooking up and her leaving after the loving was over. It was also about a guy who was messing around with his wife and found himself begging this girl to close the door and come back to bed so that there might be a future to their infidelity. Either way, my songs were beginning to mirror my life at the same time.

In time, every man looks for that one "Queen." Ladies, (beware!) when you follow a singer backstage unless invited, it usually means one thing. For a musician like me, the only thing on my mind during those days was a good time. Please don't fool yourself because you're not fooling my band or men. This is the fatherly advice I would give my daughters. If you're looking for love, you won't find it backstage or behind a singer's bus. You will find heartbreak because hurt people hurt, and people aren't always in a good place. Keeping it PG is usually not what's on our minds.

The truth that I learned later is that some of those women got pregnant. Maybe more, I don't know. If you lived during those days, sex was easy, and the girls were held responsible for taking the pill, so things stayed on course. But when you have a lapse of judgment and one-night stands, it was a spur of the moment, and the girl may not have remembered to take the pill, and the guy did not think about protection. We all know it is not right to blame the girl just because guys can be lazy.

In those days it was careless to not be as responsible as men and women should have been. When abortion became legal in 1973 it was another option for women but there were still many young women who still could not see themselves using this contraceptive method. I pray that I did not cause any girl to resort to that alternative.

But later, in my life, I would learn it wasn't so that just because you don't know about pregnancy doesn't mean it isn't so. I will get into that later in this book. Safe to say when you are young, rich, and dumb about responsibility, you make some stupid choices as you really are blinded by fame. I am not making excuses; I am just being honest with you. I have always tried to be honest with you in my songs, so I want to be honest with you in this book.

By this time, I was doing TV shows to broaden my exposure outside of country music. Those shows I mentioned earlier, well I managed to suck it up and do them despite not really wanting to do them. I'd heard that Elvis was getting tired of all those films he'd made in the 1960s and wanted to get back to the music and he did so in 1968 when he did that TV special in an intimate setting with his fans and his songs. The words of one of my songs, "You Always Come Back to Hurting Me" shows that to be true because we all try to get back to the days when we were the happiest in our lives.

Some of us are gluttons for punishment, so we go back to a long-lost love who hurt us because we found out it was better then than it is now. If that makes any sense, you are as lost as I was back then! Ha! I am no philosopher, but I know the core of my mistakes with women. I will not say my marriages were mistakes because they really were not. I married a woman I admired and loved deeply at the time. Unfortunately, during my life, I did not have my act together long enough to make the marriage work. I was more co-dependent than anything and didn't know it. Today, I can earnestly say that I learned from each long-term relationship, engagement, and marriage.

I was going the opposite way as my managers kept pushing me to TV and even a movie! The more my name was out there, well it meant more money for them. It was all for the gain and game of fleeting fame. They even wanted me to do a movie when I had never really taken the time to study the art of being an actor! What, me a movie star? No way. I did not want to be an actor or any good at it. I remember the great Roy Orbison felt the same way, but to appease his handlers, he did a horrible Western movie called "The Fastest Guitar In The West" in which his guitar was also a gun!

I can't believe Roy's manager even allowed him to be in a movie like that. I did not want to be laughed at as I know Roy's fans laughed at that sorry excuse for screen time. I heard later that Elvis was embarrassed of some of his movies because the scripts were basically the same thing. I did not want to leave any kind of film legacy, so I quietly declined the movie business even though I did a movie, called "Nashville Girl" that I am still embarrassed to admit.

One thing about family and friends, they will tell you the truth, if you ask. I had a blast and was proud to be cast in the movie called, "Down with the Barrio" that some of my friends starred in as well. My good friend and Tex-Mex singer, Little Joe Hernandez, recommended me to the Director, Cesar Alejandro who featured me in the movie, along with Tony Plana, and friend, Tejano singer, Ruben Ramos, in 1996.

No, I decided to stick to what brought me the fame I was enjoying. A few TV shows were fine with me, especially "Hee Haw" as I performed in nine episodes. I enjoyed doing "Hee Haw" because I was around some great country music talent. Some of them were real cutups or jokesters and the show really was all about stupid fun with corny jokes and skits. The stars of the show, Buck Owens and Roy Clark, were still at the top of their careers and getting to pull off jokes and puns with them was a hell of a lot of fun.

I will let a secret out about "Hee-Haw." Some of those players were off-color about it off-camera. For the most part, though, they kept it pretty clean as Minnie Pearl and Grandpa Jones were Christians. I especially liked doing those cornfield skits to the tune of "Oh Where, Oh Where Are You Tonight?" I did one in Spanish that brought the stagehands to their feet. We had to do a lot of takes to get it exactly right, especially with comedian Archie Campbell. "Pfft! You were gone."I did a lot of those shows to keep my mind off my loneliness. I was thinking if I just kept busy, I could forget things that were going on in my life at the time. As fast as I rose to the top of the country music world with women all around me, I was still lonely sometimes. The women and the booze kept me company but like everything else in life, it is a shallow replacement for what is real happiness and contentment. To love and be loved unconditionally. I think of world-renowned comedian Robin Williams, who was the most beloved actor but still could not escape the need to commit suicide.

Mental disorders such as Depression is a deep and serious conditions when you're trying to self-medicate. I guess that's why June Carter Cash and Loretta Lynn were always trying to keep me on the straight and narrow. God bless these fine ladies. They thought of me as a little brother and only if they could get me into that church house, I would straighten up and settle down. They were sincere women who knew all about lonely guys filling their void with alcohol drugs, and the groupies while I was on the road 250 days out of the year.

And that is another thing: I was running with the biggest country music stars of the day and some from yesteryear. I could say I had the best of two worlds. I was living in high vibrations in the country music arena and at the same time, living in low vibrations as well. Who knew? I met talented and sweet women like Jean Shepard and another one named Connie Smith.

In those days, Johnny Cash, Roy Orbison, and Jean Shepard all lived down the road from each other in Hendersonville, Tennessee. The beautiful and talented Connie Smith and I met when we did shows together. What an angelic and distinctive traditional country music voice she has. She also sings Gospel and Christian. The crazy thing is Connie would meet a future country music star Marty Stuart when he was 11 years old, and Marty vowed to marry her when he got older. They married in 1997! I told you Nashville was one crazy place to be back in those early days. It is a place where you can make it or break it. The choice is up to you. If you are strong and courageous enough to see your dream come true and still believe in yourself then having faith in God to hold onto will see you through.

I bring up these women because female country music stars were loyal to their husbands and boyfriends, more so than us men. They did not want to be known as tramps because Nashville has long attached itself to a godly lifestyle contrary to the word of our songs, the women who made it big stayed the course when it came to loyalty.

I guess when Kitty Wells sang "It Wasn't God Who Made Honky Tonk Women," that song became the rule of thumb for all the female singing stars back then. The country music female stars of today try to keep it that way too with some stars boasting of their long marriages. George Strait and his wife, Norma have been married 50 years! That is both commendable and a testament that with commitment, work, and unconditional love, true love prevails.

It is safe to say I have loved a lot of women in my time and the best way to describe it all is my music paved the way. Oh, I was decent looking back then, but I didn't view me as any kind of Earth-shaker. I was also Hispanic, which was a new breed in Nashville. I was something of a novelty, I guess. Girls looked at me as a singer and my coal-black hair as something different. There were always 20 or 30 girls that Christopher Cross sang about at the old stage door when he'd come off the stage after a show. It happens to me as well... many women looking for more than an autograph, if you get my meaning. It sure was a recipe to break up a marriage. Being a star of any kind will always have that element of temptation and blueprint for marital failure if you let it.

The song that describes my sentiment, though, is the one sung by friends Willie and Julio Iglesias, "To All the Girls I Loved Before." I think my friend Julio would agree that I could sing that one well. Simply because I did love them all in my way and am appreciative of any time they gave me. Right or wrong, they got me through some hard times and nights, and we enjoyed some fun times. In closing, I forgive those who broke my heart and ask forgiveness from those hearts I broke unintentionally—no hard feelings on my part.

I dated and went out with a lot of women, but I messed up anything and everything by me, myself and I. If I still have them as a friend, I thank God for it. I've learned Life's lessons *consejos* that a woman doesn't want to compete with another woman, a job, or with addictions of any kind, ever. It appears I fall in love easily, but it's the stick and staying in love that's not so easy to find. I also like settling down with the right person when the time is right. God knows I've been engaged enough times to vouch for this. Beautiful and talented actresses like Robyn Bernard and Lisa Thornhill come to mind. The first one was that I was happily married by a District Judge, but sadly, not for long; the other was the *one that got away*.

Once, I was at my friend Randy Willis's beautiful 8,000 sq ft home, where he hung photos galore of celebrities mounted on the wall. For obvious reasons, he and I knew tons of people in the entertainment industry and in life. Well, one night, we both had dates coming over to the house. I asked him politely to remove the photos of the girls on his wall. He said, "Why, Rodriguez?" I replied, well, I want the girls to feel comfortable and not intimidated by all your celebrity photos of any gorgeous drop-dead women.

He looked at me for a second and said, "Oh! okay." All the photos came down in a New York minute. My rationale is I'd rather people act naturally around me and get to know and like me for me and vice versa. It was the same home Randy hosted his annual Darrell Royal Pickin' Party over many years at his Austin home. Coach Royal never missed one. I didn't either.

Later, at Randy Willis's 5,000-acre ranch in the Texas Hill Country, I noticed he only had photos of family and cowboys on the wall. When I mentioned that fact, Randy said, "Yeah, I had the ranch house decorated in "Early John Wayne." By then, Randy did not drink any alcohol and hated drugs with a passion. He said I should do the same. He was sold out to Jesus and founded Operation Warm Heart, which fed and clothed the needy. He had seen the results of alcohol and drugs daily helping the needy, not to mention me.

Finally, I would go on to have three more marriages in my life... so far. I will tell you about them later. I will say that being a country music celebrity in the early to late '70s wasn't any different from what it is today. I remember girls writing messages to me in lipstick on the window of my tour bus and hanging panties and bras on the mirrors with their phone numbers scribbled on them. When George Strait hit it big in 1982 with his first hit, "Unwound," he, too, was getting the same panty party left on his bus. The only difference was that George had Erv Woolsey in his corner, and he was manageable. As my fans and I matured, I was getting granny panties instead of bikinis.

The love of country music between male and female fans will never die. I am sure many hardworking men had been dragged to the concert halls and county fairs I played at by their wives who were my long-time fans. Luckily, I have a lot of male fans, too. It is just they do not always come out of their shells and approach me as the female fans do. A simple Texas gesture as a tip of the hat offers me their appreciation for my music.

I have to say that the women in my life have always been special to me. My mother, my sisters, female fans, and my lovers. All of them. I am a big supporter of women and even though I have never been a perfect brother, son, husband, or lover, I have always regarded myself as a man (sober!) who respects women because of my beautiful mother. It is just the times when my respect had holes in it for my failure to control my substance abuse and alcohol consumption that made many a woman run the other way.

Did I blame them? Never. Oh well, I chalk it up to being who I am, and I can always blame it on my time in the spotlight right down to the times I was wasted. Lessons in life have taught me I should have been a better man about it all. God bless all women. I'd like to think I'm a better man now.

Women... My Type

I've always loved women... it's no secret. I find them attractive and mysterious at the same time.

Women are beautiful to me, period, and the more personality, the better! Just like any other red-blooded man, I'm looking for that diamond; the "one." I love a non-judgmental girl, who can laugh and have fun. Someone comfortable in her own skin to hang out; and is confident. In my youth, the kind of girl I enjoyed being with hasn't changed much today. I've sowed my wild oats, but I'm not looking to settle down anytime soon, but should I get the desire, you can bet she'll be a keeper. The good Lord willing.

* * * * *

Chapter 15 Losing My Family One by One

"Death leaves a heartache no one can heal... Loves leaves a memory no one can steal."
– An Irish Headstone

There comes a time in a man's life where he will reevaluate what is important in his life and that conclusion will come down to God and family, including your children. Surely, you want nothing more than to shield the ones you love. You consider your child's health to be just as important as your own. You also know that taking care of family requires protection more than anything to safeguard them against harm. In other words, what pains them pains a parent.

For the love of family…I lost family members through the years that still fills an empty hole in my heart. There isn't a day that goes by that I don't miss and think of them. My dad, Andres Rodriguez, Sr. (January 1972); my mother, Isabell Davis Rodriguez (1999); baby infant brother, Raul Martin Rodriguez (January 1950); my eldest brother, Andres Rodriguez Jr. (April 1972); my eldest sister, Ofelia Rodriguez-Gomez (March 2013); Reynaldo Rodriguez (March 2010); Manuel Jesus "Jesse" Rodriguez (October 2008); and Valeriano "Vale" Rodriguez (September 2005).

As I mentioned early on, I lost my dad and my eldest brother, Andres Jr., my biggest influences, and heroes in my life, when I was young. Their unexpected death turned my world upside down and devastated me to no end.

There was a lot of love between the entire Rodriguez family, and I believe my siblings saw something in me that set me apart from all my brothers and sisters. This is no way in any shape or form to say my other brothers and sisters did not have talents because they did. It is just that I was to reach a higher success and notoriety in terms of money and fame than they did, which doesn't make me better or them not equal.

Looking back, they were the winners of my family because they lived their lives in peace with families of their own back in Sabinal. My older brother, Reynaldo, became the mayor of our hometown…talk about taking on a job that takes guts playing referee with people you grew up with while they are riled when the city raises sewer and utility rates. Keeping peace and community awareness requires diplomacy.

I have known pain and suffering from losing loved ones; I carry scars that remind me of cherished memories that live forever in my heart of family long gone.

I have survived thanks to the prayers and support of my family and friends. It is my faith and my music that has carried and gotten me through in life when I didn't think I could sing any longer on stage from my heart. Still today, I continue to perfect my craft, singing and writing songs that keep my eyes to the sky.

My mother, Isabel, was a saint, and I envied my family who stayed back home to remain close and care for her. Me, I was always on the road making a living. When I made it in the music business, like Elvis when he bought his mother that pink Cadillac, I bought my mother a car. I helped my mom with whatever she and my brother Ricky needed while in her home in Sabinal where I grew up. Mom deserved much more and instinctively knew how to make a house a home. Everything she did, my mother did with love, prayer, and God's blessings. To this day, that yellow house in Sabinal is still standing.

My mother would even get on a plane and attend Nashville's Fanfare every summer. She enjoyed meeting, greeting, and sharing stories with my fans at my booth. I could tell she had a great time, and my fans loved and enjoyed mingling with her. It was not uncommon for her to invite some new and familiar fans to her home.

After my mother died, my younger brother Ricky moved into my mother's house. He and my sisters, Antonia and Eloisa took loving care of my mom in my absence. Whenever I would tire of the road life, I'd want to get back to my Hispanic roots and go home. I'd stay in one of the bedrooms and hang out around town with old friends and spend time with what was left of my family. The same thing happened when fame hit me; I knew where to go. When the word was out, I was back in town, many of my old friends and a lot of new fans would come over for autographs and pictures. It made my fans happy, and it made me happy, too.

My star was beginning to fade a bit where just the old loyal fans would show up, and we would pick guitar and drink beer, among other libations. We would have guitar "pulls" of our own way into the night when the local police would ask us to keep it down. Small-town America will always have a curfew with little time for crazy musicians playing into the night.

After living the high and good life you come to terms with the man in the mirror and you ask hard questions of yourself. To wear or not to wear a mask. I am talking pre-COVID. You come to terms with yourself and realize that being your authentic self is worth more than fame. Once you understand your value of self, it gives you more freedom than you've ever known. You understand it, you appreciate it, and you ease into it. Now, when I wear a mask, it's for my own safety and choosing due to the COVID-19 virus and not because I'm afraid to show the real and vulnerable me.

My faithful friends and family know and accept me for who I am. I'm comfortable with and trust my tribe and I know how special they are to me. They know who they are, and, in their presence, I lay my burdens down and be still and, in that moment, we are ourselves happy and in peace where I too, can be the real me. It's not a feeling I get with my fans when I'm performing on stage. My fans are on a different level and give me a sense of accomplishment for my work which is different from my personal friendships.

To my lifetime friends who are more like family from the beginning to the end; here's to the good times and more to come. See you on the Sunnyside... Corky Parker, Charles Gammill, Thomas "Twig" Phillips, Donald Sweat, Bob "Bullit" Naegelin and Randy Willis. Thanks for the memories.

In those early days of my life and times in show business, I felt the need to get away. It would feel overwhelming, and I would go home to bring me down to Earth. My other intention to be home was to finally eat some real Mexican food. Now, contrary to what many think, Taco Bell is not Mexican food. Authentic Mexican food can only be found in Texas; in Mexico and Arizona, Mexican food has a different flavor, and in

California. Reminds me of that old Roger Miller song "You Can't Go Skating In A Buffalo Herd." Therefore, you cannot find real Mexican food in New York City or Billings, Montana. It was one hell of a friend of mine who had more talent in his little finger than most of those who thought they had talent at all.

The truth be told, Mexican food can be found anywhere. I have found that out in all my traveling on the road. Yes, even in Chicago if it comes from old family recipes handed down and cooked with *amor* and *sabor*, which are two primary ingredients. A lot of fans have gifted me with their expressions of love and support, in one way or another. I'm happy to say there have been many girls who wanted to impress me with their cooking attempts, especially Mexican food. I must admit they did a decent job putting their heart into it trying, and that's what counts.

So, many times I would find my way back home, sometimes with my tail between my legs from some drunken stunt I had pulled in a place I should not have been. It was a place where my family knew me well and would not put up with the star-making machine that was trying to change me. They treated me like they always treated me. I had spread some of that money around when it was flowing in like a river of green, but my family would always take me in stride and never try to placate or appease me.

Besides, my siblings were never shy about telling me the truth or what they heard about me in Nashville. Ouch! That one hurt big time, especially hearing it from my mother. If a friend wanted to hurt me, stooping that low to tell my mother was a surefire way to go. Still, I could not point the finger at anyone... the blame and shame were mine. I accepted responsibility for my immaturity and vowed to do better each time.

There was no denying my time in the spotlight was dimming, and the huge concert halls I had been playing in were drying up; I was losing and grieving for my family, one by one. I had cousins and nieces and nephews who were dying and grandparents who were passing on, too. It happens to us all. There is nothing we can do a thing about it. Just because you have a few extra bucks and a face of fame, it does not mean you can do something about your family passing away.

We are all going to die; that is a fact. No one will ever get out of this life alive.

Benjamin Franklin said, "Nothing is certain but death and taxes." Having a nice bundle of money makes no difference when you lose loved ones. Somehow, you think it will, but it does not, believe me. No amount of money or fame can change what God has written under your name in the Book of Life. So, you'd better have your house in order because you never know when the Master will come knocking!

It does not matter if you are a God-fearing person or not, we all wonder where we are going after we die. Some people do not care because they do not know the Bible. Those who do need to just live out their lives until God calls them home. We will all have to answer that call one day. It will not matter if you believe or if you do not, that phone is going to ring for you one day.

One thing is for sure, I do not do funerals well. When Rick Durrett and Johnny Bush both died as I was writing this book, I sent flowers as a show of respect and acknowledgment of my time with them on the stages of America. I'm sorry, but I try to avoid sadness if I can, God knows I have had it all my life. There were times when one of my family members or good friends died while I was on the road, all I could do is send flowers to offer my condolences and let them know my heart and prayers were with them.

I do not profess to be a devout Catholic as in my youth, but when the chips are down, and you are losing your family, your home base of family, you tend to call on God for relief. Since I have been in jail a time or two and survived COVID-19 and illness, I have a lot of time to think about life itself. I have seen guys who were facing some real time in prison suddenly find Jesus on the jailhouse floor but that is not how it should be.

I know many who have found themselves in the same position I have been in, and they would grab hold of Jesus when they found themselves in times of trouble. They say the item found most frequently in the trash cans outside the jailhouses of this country is the Bible. It is too bad they use Jesus while they are locked up and then throw Him in a trash can when they are free only to find themselves back in jail searching for Him once again. I am just as guilty of that as anyone else. Jail is a lonely, cold place and praying to Jesus is more comforting and hopeful than feeling alone. You feel safer and at peace. I find myself praying for contentment these days more than anything.

Since I was raised in the Catholic church with my family and directed by my mother, I never put Jesus first in my life because I took it all for granted. My rationale was being a man and a country music singer will not allow it. There is just too much sin to pass around that you will grab on to because you are out in the world playing star-making machinery with the popular song.

You are 25 years old, and you are far away from home and family, so you tend to forget your spiritual roots. You go with the flow. When I started to get in trouble as an adult, I still did not allow Jesus to take charge of my business as I should have. My mother worried so much about me out on the road playing music that I had to try and convince her I was doing fine. She worried about the drugs and the drinking and lived a part of her life waiting to get that phone call or read in the next day's newspaper or maybe hear on the television news that her country music star (son) had finally burned out.

I simply was not getting the message, but I was making a mess out of my life. I know she and a lot of my fans and friends prayed for me which is why I believe I am still here to write this book. It saddens me to see many of my friends and favorite singers of country music have passed on like Tom T, Merle Haggard, Johnny Cash, Johnny Bush, Jerry Lee Lewis, and Loretta Lynn. All gone now, but never forgotten.

Kris Kristofferson, Willie Nelson, Barbara Mandrell, and I are some of the only ones left from the '60s and early '70s in country music. So many have passed on and in just the past 10 years. So many of my own family have passed on, too. It affects me both deeply and sadly more than anyone can know. And I have tried to take it all in without feeling down too low. It is easy to get depressed when people you know are passing on. You cannot do a thing about it so you might as well thank God for their lives here on this earth and move on down the road.

I missed so many funerals of my cousins and other dear family members passing on while I was performing on the road, or in the studio working. Keep in mind there were no cell phones back then and only three television stations. You had to wait for the bad news from your family when they found you playing somewhere, God knows where. When I was at my peak, I was playing all over the world! Some of my family would pass on while I was in Poland or England or even way down-under in Australia whereby the time I learned of their deaths; they were already in the ground.

What else could I have done but buy some flowers, show my respect, and grieve in silence. So, throughout my life that is what I have learned to do. It was my way of acknowledging their lives and how their lives were a part of my life. Why I am still here outliving others is a mystery of life itself. But the Bible says God has a plan for our lives and it really is in His hands. You just got to live your life the best you can. My good friend Kelly Kenning wrote a fine song called, "God's Got This," and that song is on point and says it all.

I used to go back to see my family and friends in Sabinal, Texas up until the year 1997 when things changed in my life and that told me it is better to stay away. It is my way of living well enough alone, for all concerned. I only have a few siblings left and I miss them terribly... more than they know. I am 70 now and still making a living today, doing my shows and playing my music. As for my family, so many have passed away.

That does not mean I do not miss my family. It just means certain circumstances in my life prevent me from visiting them more often. Besides, the last time I was in Sabinal, there were so many new people who had moved in while the others moved away. I guess that happens in those small towns as every generation passes on or moves away. The population of Sabinal has not changed much and has stayed at about 1,700.

Not a lot of my family members come to my shows even today. Because I am mostly isolated at the ranch down in South Texas. But when they do, they sure light up my life and I'm happy to see them. I know it is hard for them to keep track of me and my concert schedule. Someday, soon, I would like to have one of those great big family reunions that so many Mexican families have every year as a tradition of respect, but since so many have passed on, there's not a lot of us Rodriguez's left. We all know that the name Rodriguez is as common as Smith or

Jones is to the Anglos, but as far as my familia is concerned, there's not many of us left in my hometown.

Like my veteran friends, Gus, Bullit, and Tommy, I know my days are numbered on this old Earth, but I am in surprisingly good shape for my age. And I am still hitting the stages whenever I am booked. Playing music is what keeps me going and nourishes my mind, heart, and body. It is *albondigas* (meatball) soup for my soul. As for my family, well, they kept me going when I was a young star through their unwavering love and support. Safe to say I was blessed to have a solid base back in Sabinal, even though I did not go home often. I have much love and respect for my Hispanic heritage and traditions.

Losing my family over these past 50 years has hurt me as does everyone who loves family. I guess if I did not have my music I would be in bad shape. For everyone and thing God takes away, He gives you something to keep you going. Country music has always been my escape (on and off stage) from the sorrows of life. I have lived it and I have sung about it. I guess I always will until the day God calls me home.

Finally, I have seen how the love and support of a family unit has kept a singing star's life in check. I have seen how some of my musical friends have had their families close to them, proximity-wise to keep them feeling safe and secure. And it has made a huge difference in their life. I never really had that, but I am not bitter about it. It has been my own doings and choices in life I have made. I have learned to survive through it all without any regrets for the past and have no worries about the future. I try my hardest to live in the present. When I was young starting out, time was on my side. Now at 71, every day is a good day, and I am grateful to be standing above ground and not in the ground.

The Center of God's Will

What I have found out in my life through lessons consejos *and* wishes desejos of course, is when you are not trying to be the engine that makes it happen... God happens. I learned I was my own worst enemy not knowing who the demons and enemy really were. And, sometimes, it was me! Fear cripples' people if you let it and I found out it came in many shapes and sizes in the disguise of jealousy, insecurity, anger, anxiety, lack of sleep and illness. But I discovered in my journey in life that Jesus Christ is the greatest physician, not drugs or alcohol.

You can beat your mind up by having a mindset of lack and limitation that stunts your growth from moving forward, experiencing too many tribulations to count. I believe it becomes a self-fulfilling prophecy if you don't change. One day you wake up and realize something has got to change and it might as well be you. I understand the power of thoughts and words and I intend to use them to my advantage and to praise God. In the name of the Father, the Son, and the Holy Spirit.

In Remembrance

I would like to pay homage to my deceased family who are no longer with us. My beloved parents, Andres Sr. and Isabel Rodriguez; brother Andres Jr., who died in an automobile accident; Reynaldo, who died of heart disease; my beloved brother, Jesse who died from cancer; my brother Vale, who died from a complication from a fall; my sweet beloved sister, Ofelia; and nephew, Vincent, who was a proud veteran of the United States Air Force (Former Aircraft Armament Systems Specialist), who died of cancer.

In my culture, it is called *Dia de los Muertos*, and keeping a loved one's memory alive is celebrated in traditional music, dance, altars, food, candles, and prayers.

When my brother, Jesse, died from stomach cancer, I went to visit him before he passed. He was always good to me and good-natured to be around, always smiling. Sure, like brothers, we fought, we'd make up, and we'd laugh and cry. He even hired me to work for his concrete construction company where I could save enough money to follow my dream in Nashville. Lying in the hospital bed, my brother told me he liked my handmade knife, so I gave it to him. He also complimented me that he liked my hat and boots, so I removed and laid them before him, too. He was my brother . . .no other words could describe my raw emotions more than the heartfelt words. "He ain't heavy, he's, my brother." Perhaps because Jesse and I were more alike and relatable, I felt closer to him, and I loved him very much. No sooner than leaving my brother's side in D'Hanis, memories would flood my mind at the thought and the grieving would begin. How in the world was I to endure being without my brother for the rest of my life?

After saying my goodbye to Jesse, I would receive a call from Kandy Walker less than twenty minutes later, that my beloved brother and friend had passed. R.I.P.

My brother, Vale, had an accident that took place at a dance hall in Uvalde, Texas, where his son, Vale, was scheduled to perform. My brother's injury took its toll as he had fallen off a ladder. He had backed up his truck bed behind the stage to remove a tree limb that was in the way. That was the kind of man my brother was—helpful. When I heard the news, I was worried sick about his recovery and suffering, resorting to saying many prayers for my brother and his family.

It was another huge loss losing my beloved brother, Vale. He was a good family man who loved his children and family very much.

My brother, the late Reynaldo Rodriguez, served in the U.S. Air Force and that made him a hero to me. Next in line, he became the first Mexican American Mayor of Sabinal and served two terms. We were proud of him as we were of my other two veteran brothers, Vale and Jesse, who also served in the military. So was Jesse's late son, my nephew, Vincent Rodriguez.

My youngest brother, Ricky, served on the city council of Sabinal as a Board member. He worked many years for the Uvalde CISD as a Special Education Teacher. I always thought he was the smartest of us all. Each of my brothers contributed to my persona and being in ways that will always be a part of me. We shared the same blood, traditions, and values growing up as kids getting by and well into adulthood.

One of my brothers gave me some simple and important advice that I've ever used—he advised me just before leaving for Nashville, "mind your own business and don't meddle." He was right. It keeps me out of trouble. Today, I continue to practice staying in my own lane. The other is to be honest. Being honest and true to me is what got me where I am today. I've learned to follow my hunches and listen to my intuition.

COVID-19 Too Close for Comfort

My own family members had a close call with COVID-19, my beloved sister, Antonia, and dear cousin, Mary Esther. To be honest, I was praying and sweating bullets at the same time. I'm thankful to God they pulled through. Not everyone does. Prayers were answered during a difficult time for my family, but my faith in Him comforted me. I come from a family who mourns and reveres a celebration of life in private to be left with our memories and deep, heartfelt sorrow, but I am compelled to pray for each of my siblings, deceased or alive.

I'm also sending my prayers to the many friends and family we've lost over the years and to the people suffering in the world. I thank my heavenly father in the name of the holy spirit, Amen.

The good news... is that God's grace and mercy is yours for the asking. On the road to humility, it is the road less traveled but will get you where you want to go the fastest. It took me a lifetime to learn this gem. Only a few friends are aware I've been witnessed to about Jesus as my Savior, but many do not know that I am at peace to witness about Jesus sharing a platform in my book.

Walk by faith and not by sight. Show up and never give up because you are never alone with Jesus Christ living in your heart. Bless you and keep you with favor and mercy giving you, His peace. If you haven't guessed by now, I am not a religious man, but I am a spiritual one. Who knew?

I've been transformed and transitioned to a new way of being and living. I've learned not to be bitter, resentful, and prideful, but instead I'll be defined by me and my Holy Father. If my hardened heart and stubborn mind could be broken, so can yours if you receive in Jesus' name.

* * * * *

Chapter 16 Changing Labels, I Married Willie's Daughter

"Every new beginning comes from some other beginning's end."
– Seneca

By the time 1979 rolled around, I had a pleasant and successful run with Mercury Records. I had hits, I had been a country music singer, and I had made myself, Mercury, and other people a lot of money. But I could feel it was time to move on. I didn't leave Mercury for Epic without having a few of my best-known hits with another cover, "Reflecting," that I still sing at my shows today.

I had done an album called "Reflecting" and then another called "If Practice Makes Perfect," where I charted some hits like "We Believe In Happy Endings" and "I Couldn't Be Me Without You." However, I could see a downfall in my work as I charted songs, and the hits were few and far between at that time. I was getting used to having hit records played on America's country music radio stations and then all the way to England, Canada, Germany, and even Japan! I was always shocked at how much the Japanese people love country music.

The business mogul also built a restaurant and museum called "Buck Owens Crystal Palace." It's where tourists from Japan and worldwide come to savor Buck's tasty chicken fried steak and dance at his beautiful and famous museum and stage. And the Aussies love it, too. I did not know much about those countries and their cultures, but because country music tells a story of people's lives, we all have that common denominator of love, loss, heartache, romance, and wanting a better life for ourselves. The words of country music seem to be relatable and universal to us all.

Right before I changed labels, I cut a song called "Desperado," a hit by the Eagles. The song was written by Glenn Frey and Don Henley, who played in Linda Ronstadt's band. The song spoke to me in more ways than one. First, as a drifter and all the despair I experienced in my life due to death, drugs, and divorces. I agreed to record on the condition that they would not single the song. I did not do many covers of pop or rock songs, but this song really spoke to me, and I loved the Eagles music anyway. Just as I had done with George Harrison's "Something" when he was with the Beatles, "Desperado" became a huge hit for me on the country music charts. The song was a perfect fit for me in many ways, which made it feel natural for me to sing.

Because I did not do a whole lot of what us country music musicians used to call "Belt Buckle Rubbing" songs—also known as slow-dancing songs—I thought I had done a fairly good job on that song. "Desperado" climbed up the charts to Number 5 and then fell back. I wanted my fans to see that I could do more than just honky tonk country music, and Roy Dea and Jerry Kennedy, my producers, really went all out on those arrangements and instrumentations in the studio, complete with strings and background singers. Both songs were done very well. And occasionally, I'll be driving down the road and one of them would come on the radio to bring back memories of a time I was at my prime.

Right before I left Mercury, I cut a song that I still use in my act today that really is a crowd pleaser. Sung in English and Spanish, "Love Me With All of Your Heart (Cuando Caliente El Sol)" is a love song that tugs at the heart. The chord progression and the words match perfectly and it's the kind of song that gives the audience and listener food for thought in what might be going on in their lives or defining a long-lost love that was won and lost and maybe won again.

There is not an artist of any musical genre who does not like to hear his or her song on the radio. It is a super cool feeling. We know that if our songs have touched your hearts for a time when something good was going on in your life, you can bet it makes us feel we have accomplished something when we hear one of our songs on the radio, especially if it is years later after you recorded it.

So, I'd run to the end of the road with Mercury Records and my time with Roy Dea and Jerry Kennedy was over. I learned so much during my time with them, lessons that would help me in new contracts I would sign with other labels later. I was the most blessed fresh-faced kid when those two guys and that record label took a chance on me when I hit Nashville. Here I was a young man with a great career despite country music taking another turn in the road to newer singers all wearing cowboy hats. Music comes in circles and sometimes changes altogether. The stars that see it coming are the ones who stay on top. For me to stay on top, I needed a change. That change would come in the form of Epic Records with a man named Billy Sherrill where the grass seemed greener on the other side with a bonus to boot.

Billy Sherrill was one of the greatest producers Nashville has ever seen. One day a young girl with three kids and a mountain of blonde hair from Alabama just walked into his office and demanded he make her a star. By the time Billy accepted her challenge, his new protégé had so many hits they were always meeting at the bank. That big blond-haired person was Tammy Wynette. Besides being a great producer for Epic, Billy was a fantastic songwriter.

He and Tammy wrote what is widely known as the greatest country music song. When they got together, they wrote "Stand By Your Man." They would go on to write and hit the charts many times after that. There was hardly any room for the rest of us. Billy was the kind of guy who could give my career a new direction and he did.

I had a respectable number of hits with Billy. My first one on Epic was "Down On The Rio Grande." The song was written by my friend, Bill Bolinger. I asked Bill how he would spend his royalty check, and he proudly replied he would buy himself a bass boat. Unfortunately, it never happened. My friend and roommate was killed in an automobile accident just 18 months after my hit song.

Billy then advised me to get back to my roots because songs with a Texas cowboy flavor never go out of style. He had a unique way of producing hits. When the song demanded it, he had put in the strings and full chorus background vocals. Billy had done it too, with Charlie Rich and given Charlie two of his biggest hits in 1973 with "Behind Closed Doors" and "The Most Beautiful Girl In The World." Billy was a songwriting fool and when he put his songs with the right artists and the right production, Grammys would start flying and the money would begin to flow.

My albums with Epic and Billy were "Rodriguez Was Here" and just plain "Rodriguez." I know Billy was trying to keep things simple for me. He knew I was a different kind of country artist, like Charley Pride. We both had the ability to bring in a whole new audience to country music. Because I had the ability and the novelty to sing in Spanish, he made sure that would be my signature and brand of my music going into the '80s. He utilized my Spanish language to the fullest when the song called for it. I felt understood and blessed to have his support as an artist.

"North Of The Border" came out and climbed the charts but the novelty of my singing style was fading by this time. Now that is not to say I was going to just die off musically. No way! I had the pleasure of recording up until the late 90s before life changed for me in a very real way and that caused me to search for a new place in country music. As did Johnny Cash, George Jones and Merle Haggard began to level off career wise in the 1990s, their styles were also tapering off, too. I know they sure were verbal about it all. They began campaigns against corporate radio airplay who would stop playing their records, even the new ones they would cut.

Yep, the times were a-changing in country music and the old guard did not like it. Sadly, there was not a thing any of us could do about it. George Jones even sang about it in his song "Murder On Music City Row." He was upset that the radio stations stopped playing our music, that they had "murdered" our music and replaced it with the new "Hat Acts" such as George Strait, Alan Jackson, Garth Brooks, and Clint Black. Do not get me wrong; those guys deserve to be where they are in the scheme of things. I just wasn't ready for the fast change.

They had the talent, that is for sure. But us old guys saw the handwriting on the wall and there was not enough room for all of us to play two different kinds of country music: old country and new country. The lines were blurred between the two, but it was the youngsters who would prevail and us old guys would have to live as living legends. Our music venues began to get smaller, too. But the one thing that never got lost in the shuffle was our fans. They never let us down and would always show up to see us live. When cassettes gave way to CDs, our fans followed suit by buying our old albums in a new sales format. During my musical life, my music has evolved from LP (Long Playing records) to 8-track to cassettes and now CDs. I guess the next thing will be implants where they will just put a blazing chip in you and the music will play in your head all day long! I guess that will happen in the year 2525. There is no telling what is going to happen to music in the future and we sure will not know what format it will be in.

So, Billy Sherill and I kept trying to sell my music in what was to become a new music store: videos. I shot a few of them, but for some reason, it just was not catching on. Same thing happened to all the old stars I had come up with. We were the old cats still trying to hang on to what we got. Billy saw that in me, and he tried to sell me with the songs we had put together. When MTV rolled out, Rock 'n Roll began to gather audiences it never had before.

Country music fought MTV type promotion which is why country music fell behind in sales in the past 20 years. It cost musicians a lot of money in the process. By the time country music television came online, music videos were fading out. Johnny-come-lately promotions always came too late. I was lucky Nashville took a chance on me back in the day with my original and innovative use of the Spanish language (Bilingual Country).

My last two great songs to hit the charts were "Foolin" in 1982 and "How Could I Love Her So Much" in 1983. After that, I charted more times, but being on the top was fading fast for me and my career. Johnny Cash and Merle Haggard found themselves playing the smaller venues, you know, rodeos, county fairs, and large dance halls instead of Carnegie Hall or Madison Square Garden or even the old Astrodome where we had all played at one time. The same thing happened to me. What is amazing is all of us got to play Carnegie Hall and The Grand Ole Opry plenty of times before we faded out. Not a lot of country music stars of today can lay claim to playing in one or both of those majestic venues.

My time at Epic was just about over with going into the 1980s. Country music was changing once again. It was the "Hat" crew's time to run the charts. You know country music was changing when guys like Merle, Johnny and George could not get airplay. I could not either. We had had our time in the sunshine of fame and fortune. Some of us old guys could take it, and some could not. A few of those old stars decided to check out on their own, if you get my meaning. Sure, was a sad day when you would hear one of them who decided to kill themselves. Not me. I am going to die with my boots on when I get the call from up above. That or die trying, singing, loving, and living.

Before my time was done center stage, I was looking for love again after my divorce from Linda. I knew I was not the easiest guy to live with and it would take a special woman to put up with my drinking, partying, and drugging. When I was on top of the country music world, I drank in celebration, and I basked in my success. When I was on the downside of my career, I drank in despair trying to play catch-up and stay relevant on the charts and in recording new material.

I always had a reason to drink and run around and most of the women I was with during that time knew there was no way to tame me. I was a ramblin', stumblin' man, living life one day at a time and it was probably killing me softly. When I was in my 40s, there was not a woman who could put a halter on me, much less saddle me up!

I was still doing shows of my own and with other stars, most notably with Willie Nelson. Old Willie and I were two peas in a wilted pod—drinking, smoking pot, and partying hearty, all in good fun. We were not nearly as bad as the Rockstars who were way out there, but we sure knew where the parties were and never hurt anyone hangin' out.

I performed at Willie's "Farm Aid" one summer with Roy Orbison and a slew of stars who were there to help the struggling farmers of mid-America. I met Cher and her husband, Gregg Allman. Now, I'd only met the Mystery Man with the huge black shades one time when I passed him one day in a studio, we were both recording at, and I could see there was something special about him. He was a soft-spoken man with a wagonload of talent. He was a legend and after I shook his hand, I knew I had met one of the greatest singing stars of all time. Even Elvis said that Roy Orbison was the greatest singer who ever lived. A fact not a lot of people in business would argue.

Roy was on the 'Farm Aid" stage and after his set, Willie and I went on stage. I had met Willie's wife at the time, and I had met his sister, late Bobbie who played piano for him most of his musical life, but then when I met his daughter, Lana, from his first wife, Martha, I saw more than one pretty girl there. I thought, "Wow," she is nice, but young. And, of course, she would be nice, she is Willie's daughter, right!

Willie is not only the best Musician in Texas but also a great human being. Lana Nelson was not a musician, but she is intelligent, pretty, and talented. Again, she was only 16 when I first met her, so nothing came of that except a talk and walk on the beach. Later, her forte was in costume design. She had worked on Willie's album "Red Headed Stranger" and a few other projects Willie was part of. They were then and are now a tight-knit family who work hard on stage and play hard together off stage.

Married To Lana Nelson

In 1994, I was staying at Randy Willis's Austin home in Austin. Bob Cole called and asked Randy if I would be willing to do an interview with him and Sammy Allred on KVET radio. I agreed and asked two friends and Longhorn football legends, James Street and Doug English, to join us. At the end of the interview the KVET private hotline rang, and Bob Cole answered. "Let me speak to Rodriguez," the voice on the line said. "This is Darrell Royal." After the short phone call, we agreed to all meet at the *Broken Spoke.* Randy called the owner, James White, to make sure they were open, and that set off a series of events that got me married to Lana Nelson.

At lunch, I mentioned Randy's birthday was that week. Sammy Allred chimed in and said that he and his band The Geezinslaw Brothers, were playing that weekend at the Broken Spoke. Sammy added, "Why don't y'all come out, and we will celebrate Randy's birthday too?" We both said sure. What Sammy did not say was he and Bob Cole would be plugging the birthday celebration on Austin's highest Arbitron-rated country music show, The Sammy, and Bob Show on KVET. Now, we didn't care, the more the merrier. It was good publicity.

Sammy was huge friends with Willie Nelson and his daughter Lana Nelson. The entire Nelson Family seemed to be there when Randy and I arrived. Lana introduced us both to her fiancée and Willie's attorney, Joe Turner. Little did I know that I would be married to Lana Nelson three weeks later.

The show was a big success. So much so James White suggested we celebrate my birthday at the Broken Spoke the following week. I explained my birthday was a week before Randy's. James responded, "No one will care about that little detail." Once again Sammy and Bob promoted the hell out of the event. And once again the Nelson Family was there. But this time I was surprised to see Lana was not with Joe Turner. She explained they had broken up. That night started a whirlwind romance that was at a supersonic pace.

When I was dating Lana…we were inseparable. Every night, Randy drove me to meet Lana. We ate at every restaurant in town. On Christmas Eve, 1994, Lana called me and invited Randy and me to Willie's home for Christmas Eve. She'd asked me the day before what Randy and I were doing for Christmas. I said just watching old movies.

During that time, Craig Dillingham and Karen Brooks stayed at Randy's Austin home until they decided to rent a condo near Willie Nelson's Pedernales Recording studio. The condo was just up the road from Willie's home, golf course, and recording studio in Briarcliff. It was called Whitecliff Condos. It would be there on January 7, 1995, that I asked Lana Nelson to marry me. Three days later, we were married in Willie's movie set in Luck, Texas. The night before the wedding, Randy and I bought a 6-pack, sat on the 9th green of Willie's golf course, and discussed the last three weeks. Soon, Willie's security drove up on a golf cart and said, "Oh, it's you. I'm pickin' at your wedding." It was Bucky Meadows. He joined us for a beer.

The courtship was so fast that we had not time to plan our honeymoon. After the wedding, Willie, my bride, Randy, and I hung out for 30 minutes at Lana's home until Willie and Randy politely excused themselves.

We continued after the wedding to visit a lot of restaurants and clubs in the Austin area. One night, we had dinner at a restaurant called the Top of the Marc in Austin. We were with Lana's sister, Susie Nelson, and my friend, Randy. After dinner, we tried to decide what to do next, so we checked out the Karaoke bar called the Common Interest on Burnet Road. It was dark inside, so I thought I'd try karaoke. My choice of song was *Ridin My Thumb to Mexic*o. I was acting on the spur of the moment, having fun. When I was done, I could hear someone in the audience comment, "Gosh! He sings just as good as Johnny Rodriguez."

When I was married to Lana, there was this one time I got in a lot of trouble when I took off to a 4th of July gig where it rained that night. Soon, it dawned on me that I had clumsily left my bride behind on the bus and when I got back home, I got yelled at like nobody's business. Deservingly, she chewed me up and down and spit me out because I forgot about her and left her behind at the ranch. I mean, she cussed me good and blamed everyone around, too. How was a guy to make up for that one? Lana is as red-blooded American as anyone can be. She's got strong native American genes to prove it, too, which means she can stand on her own.

During the marriage, Randy negotiated a free car for me for a year with insurance from Roger Beasley's auto dealership. While I was out of town doing a show, Lana called Randy and asked, "Can you get me a car too?" Randy called Roger and asked him. Roger said yes if he could play one round of golf with Willie. Lana called Willie, and he agreed. When I got home, Lana showed me her new car. When she explained how she got it, I told her Randy Willis could not have cut that deal without using my name. "What do you think Daddy's name is, chop liver?" she said.

When you marry someone's daughter who thinks enough about herself and her daddy, she will always come to his defense. Well, if that doesn't remind a guy who stands taller in her eyes, I don't know what does. You don't ever want to come between a daughter and her father.

I was drinking and trying to clean up and drinking again. Around this time, I checked into rehab at Starlite Recovery center near Center Point, Texas, but I did not take it seriously. I was only going through the motions and did not want to change yet. I tried to because I was in love with Lana Nelson, and she was worth me trying. She was a combination of both her father and her mother, plus she was a great cook taught by her full-blooded Cherokee mother, Martha. You name it, boy could she cook—her enchiladas were to die for. We managed to stay married for 7 months, knowing the end was near before we started. I was hopeful Lana would be the one to change me for the better, like Linda, apparently, there was not enough soap to clean me up.

I do not know what the hell Lana was thinking by letting me put a ring on her finger, but she let me, and I wanted to. We were old enough to know each other better, so we tied the knot like we both wanted to. Willie said it was alright with him if we hitched up, so with his blessing, we danced down the aisle to the altar.

People Magazine did a short story about our wedding; many said it would not last. Well, seven months later, Lana was gone. It seems she could not change me either, so she got out while getting out was good. I do not blame her. I must have been a fool to think that guy in the mirror would ever change. And Lana must have been blind to think I'd change when she saw I was back to my same old self right after the wedding.

I was not a bad guy. I was just set in my ways and too stubborn to be any different. There are just some guys who needed a type of woman to handle them. That was me. Johnny Cash was like that and the only woman who could tame him as much as he could be tamed was June. Lana and I finally called it quits after a second try, and then we got a divorce.

After Lana and I divorced, I was on the prowl once again. I tried to make it work with her, you know, cutting back on drinking and partying. In the end, I just was not the marrying kind back then but like a lot of things I have done in my life, I never listened to myself. I had already been married, and I did not have anything to show for it that counted very much, but I do now. Like in a sad Country song, those rings I put on my wives'fingers and mine were, in the words of one of Charley's Pride's songs, "were just way, way too tight."

I tried to stay in touch with Lana from time to time, but she moved on with her life. So did I, but not before more looking for love in the craziest of places I could find. I heard that she worked as a costume designer on "The King Of Luck" and "The King of The Roadies" movies. I believe she is in the family business consulting and producing (videos) in the music arena with her dad.

I thought this might put me in a bad light with Willie; after all, blood is thicker than water, and it is his daughter he loves most. Luckily for me, Willie Nelson is the most easygoing guy you will ever meet. He is a soulful man, a spiritual man who does not let life get to him if he can help it. I believe he takes the path of least resistance and lives life with as much ease and peace as he gives to others. Is it any wonder he is the most beloved person in all of Texas and perhaps, in the world? Granted, he loves his daughter more than I do; I still count my blessings. I was in Willie's world, if not for a brief time.

I could probably complain about a lot of things and justify in my mind all the things that went wrong in my marriage to Lana. But as you have probably guessed by now, I messed up another good one because Lana is a good woman, and I was just being me. Lana is very much her mother's daughter and her father's pride and joy, where the apple doesn't fall far from the tree.

So, I had married Linda Patterson, Robyn Bernard, and Lana Nelson but that would not be the end of my episode in matrimony. I also became engaged in between because I really was the marrying kind and fell in love with each woman I proposed to. Why didn't it pan out? Well, your guess is as good as mine, but I'm sure it had more to do with my addictions than it did with my love interests. I was engaged to drop-dead gorgeous model-actress Lisa Thornhill and songstress Lorrie Morgan, daughter of George Morgan.

My next and last marriage would gift me something no amount of fame or fortune could ever buy. Seriously, it would be the greatest thing I would ever do in my life. They say the greatest things in life are free. Well, when God gives you something so precious, there is never a price tag to it. What I would get out of my fourth marriage would come to be the finest jewel and possession I could ever hope to be blessed with. Despite what others may say, in my book the mother of my child, Debbie, will always have a sacred place in my heart because my daughter's heart belongs to hers. And there's no way, I'm going to break it because I would be breaking my own. It doesn't take a rocket scientist to comprehend this, and if a person doesn't, then he needs to be hit on the head with a boulder.

Marriage to Debbie McNeely

In 1998, a good friend, Tom Foote, revealed that he had a friend who liked my music, so he gave me her number, and I talked with her on the phone. Tom was George Strait's long-time tour manager. We arranged a meeting of the minds at my next George Strait concert, where I was opening. Unbeknownst to my friend, I would meet *the one,* my fourth wife.

Well, we hit it off. I liked her from the start. She was petite, good-looking, intelligent, and blonde with sky-blue eyes. She lived in San Marcos, Texas, and owned a Salon. Her name was Debbie McNeely, and I saw something special in her. I wanted to ask her out since there was no ring on her finger. Our first lunch date was at the famous and touristy Mi Tierra Café Y Panadería, owned by La Familia Cortez for eighty years in San Antonio, Texas. In Spanish, *Mi Tierra* means my land and *Panadería* means bakery.

Debbie would come to be a savior of sorts to me, like Nancy had been for George Jones. My burdens did not seem heavy when I was near her. She was this all-American girl and she worked for herself styling hair. I found her to be strong-willed, intelligent, fancy-free, a horse lover, and she had style. In a way, I saw I had met my match, and I saw myself living again. Whenever we went out together, we had fun.

I knew I would have to slack off the drugs and the drinking if I wanted to keep a gem like her in my life. So, I did just that. Debbie saw I could fit into her life, too, and we started talking about marriage and maybe a family, you know, kids and such. Me with kids? The happy go lucky singer, confirmed bachelor, settling down with children and giving up my life of bachelorhood and all? No way, but yes, there was a way. All I had to do is set aside my wants and desires long enough to allow time for others needs and desires. Debbie McNeely would be that person. At least, I was hopeful she was the right woman for me.

So, I got married... again. Only this time I was in it for the long haul. I learned quantum lessons from the past and I was determined to do better with my newfound blessing. Debbie knew all about my time in rehab and my binges of drinking and drugging. I vowed to clean up my act and concentrate on our lives together as well as trying to revitalize my sagging career. It was a daunting task as my free-wheeling lifestyle of fame and fortune was a hard habit to break, even when it was all going downhill from the time it peaked in the early 1980s.

Married life was bliss. My bride and I went on a honeymoon to Europe, where I did a couple of shows. We had a wonderful time, too.

Then, with the news of a child coming into the world, I was ecstatic and nervous at the same time. What a responsibility having a child would be for a free agent like me and before I knew it, we would name our precious daughter Aubry Rae. Because of her, I had a new purpose in life and felt determined to change for the better and become a family man. A child will do that giving you a new lease on life, along with hope for the future and the chance to take care of God's creation is bigger than anything in life.

The innocence of it all. I wanted to only protect her and Debbie to the best of my ability and look forward to the future. I had hope and knew I was blessed with new love and life. From the moment I laid eyes on her and held her in my arms, I knew she would have me wrapped around her delicate pinky finger for life. She was all mine…no doubt about it.

I had come from a large family but having one of my own was different. And it was a different time, too. I was more committed and understood the love of a child more than I ever did... talk about feeling overly protective. When I was a kid, all my brothers and sisters would leave home during the day doing whatever they did and come home at night and my parents did not worry.

When Aubry was born, I felt I had to worry about everything and everyone. I worried someone would harm or kidnap my little girl because of my celebrity status and old lifestyle. Whichever the reason was, the anxiety was overwhelming, and it put a lot of paranoia in my mind. I felt restless and uneasy. I did not understand it until now.

In time, issues came to surface no matter how hard I tried to make a marriage work. In my own way, I really tried to be a good husband and a doting father to my little girl who was the light of my life. Debbie saw my struggle, too. She married a celebrity who was used to getting his way, used to the adulation, and used to the wayward lifestyle.

The disappointments and pressures were taking shape. Debbie started talking rehab again for me to straighten out. She really cared for me and wanted me to help and save myself. But my touring on the road and trying to chase the dream of being back on top kept that talk to a bare minimum. Again, I did not have any of it. How could I? My machismo pride would not let me stop to heal. I was the head of the household and felt I was doing the best I could (considering the circumstances) for my family.

Goat Reunion Visit

In 1998, I was invited to revisit the Bob Davis Ranch, where the descendants of the goat owners resided. I took Debbie, pregnant with Aubry, to my hometown of Sabinal, and we returned to our roots at Garner State Park. It was a big deal in conjunction with the Texas Parks and Wildlife's 75th Anniversary (1923–1998). Along with my friend, Randy Willis, we went back to visit the Davis Ranch, where it all began with the goat, but this time, we visited its descendants for promotional purposes. The people on the ranch were friendly.

Debbie had told me getting back to my roots could be a way of waking me up to what was important in my life. She was always grounded and good at supporting my musical career. In rehab, they always tell you faith, forgiveness, and family are the best medicines to get right with your life. So, I agreed. I did not just for Debbie but for Aubry, who would be coming along soon. I believed and felt my future never looked brighter.

I feared they would not take kindly to me and be upset. Before meeting these lovely people, my main concern was that they did not hold a grudge. Randy Willis reminded me that their goat (mohair) business would have gained notoriety and sold many goats after the incident. I told him I hadn't thought of it that way.

Angora mohair is used beautifully in upholstery, furniture, and rugs, and it dyes beautifully. I should have visited them much sooner. I enjoyed my visit, and I even caught a goat and took loads of photos with the many goats on hand. There is a YouTube video about Garner State Park and Davis Ranch visit. It is the one in which Randy Willis keeps yelling to the goats, "Run! he killed your grandma."

Garner State Park Reunion – 75th Anniversary

Randy Willis produced the 75th Anniversary of Texas Parks and Wildlife at Garner State Park. Larry Holden of Country Music Magazine featured the celebration. I performed at the Homecoming concert at the park's outdoor stage near the park's entrance. Governor George W. Bush attended the Pickin' Party the night before, sponsored by Southwest Airlines, Ozarka Water, and others. We met at the private pavilion on the other side of the Frio River for the Pickin' Party.

Memories flooded in as I thought of special friends Janet Blalock, Ma Barker, Denise Barker, and countless other friends we all hung around with. I think of my old friends and wonder how they are doing today.

I often wonder what my life would look like today if it had not been for stealing goats. I've asked that a lot! Knowing then what I know now, I can honestly say I probably would have ended up selling tacos or playing music at the side of the road. I say this because I am a survivor and entrepreneur who would have worked with my hands and lived off the land. A local news program came out and did a live feed on us, and it felt good again.

I was away from home often during those early days of my marriage to Debbie and the earlier years of Aubry's life. In hindsight, I regret losing this important bonding time between my wife and daughter. I do not know why I was the way I was. Perhaps it was the desire to succeed and overwhelming power to protect and prove something or fear of the unknown... who knows? I do know we are ultimately the decision maker with who and how we spend our time. A song that comes to mind for me is Rodney Crowell's song "It Ain't Over Yet." I think that would be a good song for Tanya and me to record. I do believe, too, that I am a driver (social style) with an addictive personality and too much of my energy went into my work. Consequently, my marriage suffered. Something always does when done in excess with little or no balance.

The bulk of my career was between the years of 1972 through 1982, ten great years of stardom. By the time I married Debbie and became a father to Aubry, my star was struggling to shine on a slippery slope. The hits were not at the top. I did make a record change by signing with Capitol in 1988 and I had charted my last hit record with "I Didn't (Every Chance I Had)." Man was that song prophetic! I had not done much on the charts or from 1988 to 1998 and being with Debbie and settling down I thought just might put me back at the top. Maybe that drastic change from star to daddy would be strong enough to spark new interest in a new career.

At least for a while, I thought Debbie was "the one." After all, I was in love, at peace, and happy at home with my family. I would learn more about effective patterns of communication and compromising skills in a marriage with her than with anyone before. Due to extenuating circumstances and refusal to make changes to make our marriage work, we divorced.

My daughter Aubry is her father's daughter where the apple does not fall far from the tree, and she's a beauty like her mom. I hope she pursues her interest in music a little bit. She likes to sing and write songs and I have all the confidence in her to be whatever she sets her mind to achieve. My daughter is not only beautiful and talented, but she is smart too.

On Divorce

The pain of it all. It is never easy, and no one plans it. All I can do is forgive myself and push through the guilt and regret of it. God knows I punished myself long enough. What I would like my exes to know today is that I have grown and moved forward in my life and wish the same blessings for them. I have learned the hard way that there is no rational purpose for guilt and dwelling of pain about the past. It only delays our growth to evolve and push forward to better and improved relationships where communication and compromise are at work. If I learned anything, I learned, *we* is a much better word than *me.* Sadly, you can never buy back time.

A Blessing In Disguise

One evening, while I was dating the lovely and gracious Kandy Walker, she was sophisticated-looking as we all got out. Her sister, Elizabeth, happened to accompany us when we went out corralling at the Stockyards. It's my favorite place to be in Fort Worth, Texas, and I often went there. There's plenty to do there, and it's just my kind of place with the rodeos, dance halls, and night clubs, and shopping going on there. Well, we hit the spot at this one club to have some drinks and this pretty waitress there kept serving us drinks and naturally, I kept tipping her.

We all were having a great time, and our waitress was always smiling giving us great customer service. Towards the end of the night, I paid for our drinks again and tipped her one last time. The following day, we headed to breakfast at Lil' Red's Saloon and when I reached in my pocket, I only had a $100.00 bill. Let me remind you that I started out with $1,800.00 cash in my pocket. Somebody was happy and feeling like they won the lottery, the next day, but it sure wasn't me. I guess if she was having a bad day that night…someone was about to make up for it and make her day. Hopefully, the waitress will pay it forward in some way. The moral to the story is to charge it!

Not All Mushrooms Are the Same

Another blessing that happened to me, again, was while I was at my ex-girlfriend Kandy's ranch near Laredo, I was looking to get high, maybe have a hallucination trip and a healthy snack at the same time. Unfortunately, I accidentally ate a poisonous mushroom unbeknownst to me. Thank goodness Kandy's sweet daughter, Hailey (5), was there to witness everything. She looked up at me and innocently said, "Mommy said, don't eat those mushrooms, ever!" No sooner than hearing her words, it was the last thing I remember her saying. She was my angel in disguise at the right place and time.

All I know is I was feeling sick, and I was in excruciating abdominal pain. Kandy immediately called the Poison Control Center, and they walked her through medical assistance adding, "He could have died." I do believe the mushroom had attacked my liver and kidneys that were starting to shut down. My stomach had swollen, and I was sick for a good week. That was a narrow escape.

That's what poisonous mushrooms do within hours they attack your liver and kidneys causing death. Poisonous mushrooms grow in the back yard and are not edible.

Mushrooms are superfoods and can aid medicinal purposes, and improve health, but it is wise to keep in mind that there are myths and facts that exist. Even scientists in labs make mistakes. A good mushroom has a nutty flavor and has lots of protein. Never eat mushrooms raw but cook them instead.

* * * * *

Chapter 17 Touring to Survive

"People may not remember what you said, but they will remember how you made them feel."
– Maya Angelou

Many fans have asked me in the past few years what the hell have I been doing in between playing county fairs, small theater venues and rodeos. Well, I am still here! And if I have a voice and a guitar, I will be on stage somewhere. It has been rumored that I had died! I am not the first country music singer who has been mistaken for being dead, that is for sure. We all have our valley between hits and appearances where the fans have lost track of us. From 2005 until 2015, I was still working on the stages of America at the same time my bookings were not as well known to the fans of country music.

My fan base, however, has never let me down. They continue to follow me to the ends of the Earth. Sure, it was bikini panties and short shorts in the beginning of my career, but now it is granny panties and old tie-dyed t-shirts. I do not mind. I still love 'em with all my heart. I guess we are all sagging a little bit and getting those gray strays in our hair, here and there. I practice aging gracefully and embrace it. I do not hide or fight it. Everyone will always have an unsolicited opinion of how you should or shouldn't look. Why argue? What is the point! The main thing is I love seeing happy faces when fans come to see me sing. It makes my day and puts a big smile on my face, too.

To this day, I still hit the road, touring. Since my keyboard player, Gary Goss, has retired, I have added a couple of new pickers for my concert dates. I hired a rhythm guitar picker named Billy McCoy and brought in David Reynolds to take Gary's place at the keyboards. I have kept my steel guitar man, Don Sowersby, my lead guitar/fiddle man, Kenny Penny, and the foundation of my live band, Bruce Carter on drums and Mike Hammock on bass. They make up a great live group that can really fill up a concert venue with solid country music. It costs me more money, but it is worth it. Every band brings a unique culture to the group. The qualities I mostly look for and demand in any band relationship who plays for me are competence, professionalism, respect, and team spirit.

Of course, having these attributes along with the ability to communicate makes up for excellence and the assurance of continuing the "Rodriguez Sound." It's what the fans expect, no less will do. I do not want to beat a dead horse to death, but today's country music just is not Country enough for me. I suppose it depends on the radio station you listen to. Willie's Roadhouse Classic Country still plays traditional music, and it is just what I love.

When you leave out pedal steel or a fiddle, well, you have left the country out of country music. Some may disagree with me and that is okay. But the closer you are to Hank or Jones or Haggard, the closer you are to what country music is all about. It is not to say, I do not listen to new artists and new music or enjoy other genres time to time, I prefer playing what I love most. Of course, I still enjoy some variety at times and will listen to soft rock 'n roll and other music for a change.

Others would be surprised to learn just how versatile I am as far as other artists and to know I am a fan of others, too. I have been having some real problems with my strumming hand that's causing numbness and stiffness of my fingers and hands. The strife and struggle are a battle for me to the point where I'm not able to sign autographs like I used to. It could be carpal tunnel or rheumatoid arthritis setting in. Throughout my career, I was never at ease just standing out front with a mic in my hand.

I made a lot of television appearances standing out front with just a microphone in my hand. I had agents who thought it would be better that way, you know, the visual aspect of showing all of me for my fans. When I was young, that was fine with me because I had such a large female following who apparently thought I was some sex symbol. Since those days are pretty much over with, I need a guitar to help me keep pace with the songs I sing. I am more comfortable with a guitar in my hand than not. At my age now, I accept the fact that my body is not what it used to be. Strumming a guitar for 50-plus years has taken a toll on me. I am not going to lie. It is hard on this old man! But my love for playing will follow me to my grave no matter how much I hurt. I am just bull-headed enough to die with a guitar and a song in my heart.

I remember when Johnny Cash was in a wheelchair and in the studio in 2001, still doing what he has been doing all his life. His career had slowed down, but he was always relevant to his fans and all who knew him. A young whipper-snapper producer convinced old Johnny to record one more time. Rick Rubin put together what was to be Johnny Cash's last album, and it was a huge success. It even brought in a new and younger generation that appealed to Johnny's music. I was thinking the same thing, that maybe I had one last CD in me, too.

I will not quit. You cannot keep a good man or woman down who will not quit. I need to play. I need my fans, not so much for the adulation but for the inspiration they give me on stage. I have always had the most loyal fans any artist could ever want. They keep showing up to wherever I am singing on stage. It is what keeps me going and if I ever lose that, if I ever hit a stage and there is no one out there in the audience, then that will be the day I stop this madness I call my passion and career. Until then, as a dedicated and hard-working performer, I will continue to always show up.

Just as Johnny Cash found himself a young and talented producer who believed his days were not over just yet, so did I.

Missed Opportunities

When I look back to the fantastic opportunities I have been afforded, I would be amiss if I didn't share the regrets and wasted time, I put myself through the missed and near miss opportunities. There were too many to count due to my addictions and poor choices. I have learned not to dwell and leave myself in a mess. What has changed? First, understanding that experiencing a near miss is okay. In other words, you can be more conscious and prepared for the next opportunity that is coming around the corner — having a mindset of staying on track and moving forward *adelante.*

They did not call me an "outlaw" for nothing, nor did I associate, record, and hang out with the outlaw mentors and friends for nothing. Johnny Cash, Kris Kristofferson, Waylon Jennings, Willie Nelson, better known as "The Highwaymen." We were men to be reckoned with and were ahead of our times for sure, mainly because we were open to the people and places with some degree of conscious awareness. We were excited about getting out our messages so that we could all have a voice to be heard. It was our way of story telling what we knew and what we wanted to share with the public. We didn't want to live in fear or boundaries.

If not for showing up late or not at all, whichever the reason, I would have been on the album cover with the Outlaw gang as the fifth band member. It turns out I missed my opportunity by choice and not in my best interest in the end. We all can relate, I suppose, at some point in our lives. You know the sayings, "Wish I could've, would've, and should've." I try not to live in the past but try to learn from my lessons. On the album, I am singing a bilingual duet called, "Deportee" with Johnny Cash. It's one of my favorite songs and means something special to me.

The Eagles

Then, I attended the Eagles concert at the Dome, featuring Glenn Frey, a favorite singer/songwriter of mine, along with Linda Ronstadt. I was told I was one of Linda's favorite country music artists and I appreciated her telling her band members that and recommending me to record Desperado.

Of anyone's rendition of *Desperado*, I believe Linda knocks that song out of the park better than anyone.

At this Dallas Cowboys stadium concert, I stepped away to take a cigarette break when others told me later that *The Eagles* invited me to come on stage to sing a duet with the band. I had no idea the band would make this gesture, so the timing was not in my favor. It does no good to cry over spilled milk because this undoubtedly was one of those missed opportunities that I sure would have loved to have taken place. It could have been a sweet memory, no doubt.

I probably regret the most in my life is not meeting the King, Elvis Presley. It is not like I spent my entire adult time "wishing and hoping" because that's not the case. Elvis, the Manager, the Colonel, approached me and told me Elvis wanted to invite me to meet him. At the time, I was very flattered, but the timing was off. I had an engagement with a date that I did not want to miss, so I declined the offer. Again, it was a regret I thought about a whole lot, especially after Elvis's passing. The Colonel extended his interest in managing me as well, and I declined that one too. That one I did not regret.

At the time, my career was soaring, and as anyone can attest, I am unmanageable. Of course, I have evolved since my younger and carefree days due to competition and age that I do not have the energy or time to do it all today. If you are smart, an artist will evaluate the pros and cons and take in good counsel, providing you with an attorney review and drawing up a contract that is in the artist's best interest as much as the Managers. I have learned the importance of having counsel for significant decisions in my life.

In the music industry, it's a must when it comes to business. Having an attorney review any agreement is something many artists, including myself, have learned the hard way. The entertainment business can be a double sword and necessary evil due to the nature of the beast. It pays to look after your interest and have people who you trust and care about have your back. Paying an attorney makes that happen because you're paying for the service in your interest.

Funny story—I was away from my Tennessee home for a while, and when I returned home, I came home to a surprise: a hot mess. I had forgotten to lock the animal door and discovered a party going on in my kitchen floor without me. There were snakes and tom cats raiding my snacks. Then something creepy rubbed my leg, and it gave me heebie-jeebies, so I jumped away. It was a damn raccoon.

Going Home, Leaving Nashville

In 1994, I left Nashville and headed home to Sabinal, Texas, to my mom's yellow house on North Pickford Street. I find it interesting how a man when he is alone will find himself in body, mind, and soul wanting to go home.

When you're young, it's funny how you can't wait to find your way and move away from home fast enough. Ironically, when I headed to Nashville, I felt compelled to leave Texas to make something out of myself and to help my mother who had recently lost my dad and my brother in one year's time. It was unbelievably painful trying to get over the loss. I just felt that I had to leave my childish ways behind and make it or break it. Fortunately, a lucky star was following this wandering star.

In any case, the same reason I left Texas would be a big part that was calling my soul back to home. Anyone that knows or would meet my mother knows she compared second to none. She was the most loving, humorous, and kindest person you could ever meet. In every way, I was my mother's son and proud of it. I would have done anything for her. She loved everyone and she enjoyed meeting and talking to my fans and friends, often welcoming them into her home for conversation, no doubt about me.

The funny thing about show business and fame is that people think they know you, but they don't most of the time. Usually, it's only an illusion in their mind unless they are my true friends and can say they know the real me. The truth is I have many sides to me, and I am not one way or the other, especially when it comes to my Hispanic culture. I've been accused of only liking and dating a certain type of woman and ladies I'm here to tell you, it isn't so. I enjoy a woman for who she is and the heart she shares and words she expresses from within. I know boys who would disagree, but I don't know a man who wouldn't agree.

* * * * *

Chapter 18 Sex, Drugs, Rehab and Back Again

"Insanity is doing the same thing over and over again expecting different results."
– Albert Einstein

It all started with a bad car accident that injured my chest. Then I got addicted to pain pills and had to go to the Treatment Center to get off them. It was a challenging time for me, but I kicked the hamster wheel to live.

In AL-Anon classes they say that 1 in 20 drug users possess a membrane that causes them to become addicted to alcohol and drugs. It can stem from hereditary, psychological, or physical craving to inherit this disease that is hard to kick. What are the chances that I'd be roped in this category?

Suffice it to say, I lived a lot of my life, during the drug period on auto pilot which means I was just going through the motions. I was not the best person to be around and should have known and done better. There really is no excuse except to say I was in a stupor and couldn't and didn't want to get out. My addictions took total control of my life. What you saw on the outside was not always what was inside of me. Little did I know that I was running from me. If only I knew then what I know now. You know what they say about hindsight. It's 20-20. Do what I say and not what I do. Yes, I can see clearer now and can talk about the deepest despair that I lived through. It was pure living hell and a nightmare and one I never want to revisit.

Drugs

According to the 2020 National Survey on Drug and Health, 5.2 million people in U.S. households use cocaine, ages 12 and older. Those are staggering numbers, for sure where Drug Awareness is key for American families to cope and seek help.

People thought cocaine was safe to use and not addictive in small amounts. At least that is what we were told. Yeah, not true. It is a powerful addictive stimulant made from coca leaves/Cola Kola nut. In 2020, approximately 19,447 people overdosed.

In 1979, I experienced cocaine for the very first time. It did nothing for me, and I couldn't figure out what was the big deal. I only took it because a big celebrity friend of mine who I looked up to turned me on to it. The only difference is he quit the habit but when I tried it again, I got addicted in the worst way…hook, line, and sinker. At that time, everyone was deceived into believing it was safe to use; that's why the drug was so popular and the thing to do. We were misled to believe the addictive stimulant made from coca leaves/Cola Kola nut wasn't addicting. Surprise!

At the time, I was smoking three packs of cigarettes a day, no exercise, and had a terrible diet. The year was 1979. I was freshly divorced. I was pretty much in a bad way, and I was hurting unbeknownst to anyone. It was my way of numbing myself to escape the insufferable pain I was feeling. Drugs only compounded my problems and as a sad country song goes, I was headed for a train wreck with the wrong antidote to cure me. It's kind of like old Buck's song, "Hello Trouble," says. I was an easy target for anyone to influence and introduce me to drugs.

Once, even an acquaintance (doctor) convinced me and turned me on to LSD. Imagine paraprofessionals even getting fooled, it's no wonder us laborers got scammed. I figured I would be okay since I was in the company of a professional and licensed physician. All I can say about that is I may have been in good hands, but it still was a wild trip. One, I won't be choosing to ride again.

Luckily for me, the experience didn't turn out badly. The funny thing about being a celebrity is you meet other people in respectable careers who are mesmerized with fame that they, too, can have a lapse of judgment and experiment with drugs, sex, and vices they never thought they would.

Earlier in my career, I was heavily into drugs and spent and lost a lot of money. I had justified $250,000 spent that I could afford so, why not? That attitude did not serve me well in both my personal and professional life. I've got divorces to and financial setbacks to prove it.

Alcohol and drugs were my coping mechanism and vices: resorting to amphetamines to go sedating to sleep, pain pills, and morphine to numb the pain or whatever else was given to me or I could get my hands on. What I learned is cocaine causes heart attacks, strokes, seizures that can result in sudden death, especially is mixed with alcohol. Not to mention it alters brain structure and function, used repeatedly. I say this to help, warn, and save a life.

A vicious downward spiral of addictions to alcohol, drugs, gambling, sex, and work. I'm work in progress trying to balance my life. It's something I work at every day... to relax.

I'm content in my life today, because I know that my life is just as relevant today as it was throughout the decades and back then during my success.

The most responsible thing I did was surrender my Class C driver's license. I figured I wasn't ready to give up alcohol cold turkey, so I couldn't see myself risking the life of someone else or myself. The MADD, the nonprofit organization against drunk driving, brought social awareness to communities seeking to stop drunk driving. I paid attention and didn't want to be a statistic or in the news, so I made a conscious effort to do the right thing for me and others, giving up control and being reckless while under the influence of drugs or alcohol.

The best thing that happened to me was going to my first Alcoholics Anonymous (AA) meeting. Of course, there was Cocaine Anonymous (CC) meetings, but AA is the one that really helped me. A way to get an honest answer when you want to know the truth about what a person looks like, or their life is all about, go to an AA or AL-Anon meeting which will help family and friends to better assist problem drinkers to identify principles and affirmations to get through the process. I highly recommend the meeting for healing.

I still drink and smoke marijuana, but the program and staff teach a person how to live. It really did. It taught me how to live a better life and that helped me grow a lot. Somewhere along the line, possibly due to drugs, my mindset was stuck and my emotional growth impaired. Some of the staff, I call my friends.

Rehab can be very expensive... effective, but expensive. It can cost approximately $1,500 a day for six months. I was in and out of them between the years 1991 and 1998, for a total of seven times, sometimes due to intervention of family and friends or sometimes because of business to give me an opportunity to clean up and save myself.

I had turned into good-time Charlie, who felt like a failure. I was still doing drugs and drinking and playing the field... again. I was approaching 40 years old, and I was still acting like a kid. When you make it big, you act big? When you lose it, do you try to stay the big shot? What is so strange is you never know you are spiraling back down until it happens. Something happens that tells you it has happened. The smaller crowds, the things you must handle and put up with that you never had to put up with before. You do not have the handlers anymore. You do not have the hotel suites nor the perks that come with it anymore.

More importantly, though, you do not get the respect you once had. And finally, you do not have the respect for yourself as the star you once were. It is a real downer and eye opener. Then the darkness starts to set in, and alcohol and drugs numb the pain and begin to fill the void every day. Then the bottom hits you when you use sex just for the sake of having sex (because it's available) and getting drunk to forget about your sorrows. (It sounds like a bad Country song in there somewhere).

It is hard to accept change sometimes. I am not going to gloom and doom my career currently, but the reality of the shift from being a Country star to where my career was going at the time sure did not help my ego much. The girls at the back door of the stage were getting older, too. My fan base was getting smaller, and so were the venues. It was all irrelevant, but I had a case of mistaken identity, evidently, and I needed to grow up. I did not recognize the man in the mirror any longer.

I also had to get my own band if I wanted to tour but I could not afford a full-time band on a payroll. Stars like Barry White and Chuck Berry used local musicians whenever they went out on the road as their careers dwindled, which seemed like a good idea to me, but I did not like hitting the stage not knowing how good or bad those musicians might be. Once I was comfortable with a band, I wanted to stay with that band, and I didn't mind paying them their worth.

So, I put together some guys I had known that had day jobs flexible enough to be called on a moment's notice. These guys are the salt of the earth, and they will stay with me for the next 30 years. They are loyal, competent, and very professional. They could also be counted on leaving their day jobs and hitting the road with me, then returning to those jobs the next week. And they stayed with me up until recently when one of them died like Randy Reinhard and Gary Goss, my musical director and keyboard player retired. For 34 years, I could count on these guys to be there for me, and they were.

I got it in my mind that no matter who hit the stage with me, if they were professional, then I would not worry as much about them being musicians. I knew I had to have the best. It has always been an asset for me to follow my intuition, selecting the best... qualified musicians and a great song. This COVID-19 virus has thrown a wrench into my touring with my band. I also heard that many bands just disbanded because of this years-long virus.

Many great music venues just closed shops, putting thousands of good people out of work. This pandemic has been a disaster to every one of us, especially in the music business because we rely on that mad money everyone has for their play time. I was only glad my band had day jobs where they, at least, still had a paycheck coming in.

There were times my band was rightfully annoyed at me as I was not at the top of my game. I was doing drugs to keep my mind off the downturn of my career, and I was missing gigs and missing the words of songs I had been singing all my life. When you miss a gig or cancel a gig, you not only upset your band, but you also disconnect from your life blood: Your Fans.

Once you start violating that rule, you begin to become your own worst enemy. George Jones comes to mind. George was a great friend to me and was one of my favorite singers of all time. He went through tough times and was in the same downward spiral I was going through. He was missing concert dates and upsetting his fans and his management team. He was drinking so badly that he had health scares that had his family and friends lighting candles and praying for his recovery.

Then he met someone special like Nancy who saved George from himself. I did not have a Nancy to save me, and I was not going to marry just to find one. I decided to go with the flow and keep things real. If I had ten fingers and a voice to go with them, I would have had a chance at staying in the game and on stage. Like I had done since I hit Nashville in 1971, I told myself I could still rely on myself. The problem was that I had a strong work ethic and worked too much, but I also played too hard.

The TV appearances were regulated to occasional spot-on shows like Ralph Emery's "Pop Goes the Country" or a spot on "RFD Country Cafe," with the great Jimmy Day leading a small but talented band of studio musicians who just wanted to play together for fun. I had been on Buck Owens "Hee-Haw" during its time as a hit show and I had been on Johnny Cash's summer replacement show as well as other TV shows. I liked TV appearances but being shy by nature, I just did not fit in. My agent at the time kept telling me exposure is the name of the game, so I did as I was told even though it did not really help my career that much. When you are in the music business for 20-plus years, you are basically relegated to being a nostalgic act.

Every star that has ever been there can tell you when he or she was at the top of their game. They can tell you their "star" years, too. No matter what the decade is or ever will be, the buying and radio-listening public who buy CDs are between the ages of 14 and 35. Girls buy (85% of the lion's share of CDs more and differently than boys do. Women tend to buy from the song and the singer's looks while men buy from what they like to hear while working or drinking or whatever they are doing at the time. Speaking of timelines, my time was '72 to '82. I think back at other friends in the music business as to when their time was. Buck Owens's time was between '63 and '75. Merle's time was between '67 to '80 while Johnny Cash's time was between '58 to '75.

As for Dolly, well, there is no time limit with that lady! She is timeless! But we all had our time. She has sold over 100 million albums, and they don't call her "Dolly Lama" for nothing. The thing is it is hard to give up your time to a young and rising star as you once were. Maybe it is an ego thing, I do not know. But it is real and to survive you accept that your time is basically up. However, to thrive you keep on keepin' on and not worry about competition or what others are doing. "Ego is not your amigo." That is a phrase I have coined to remind me to be humble, grateful, and mindful that a relationship is more important than who is right or wrong or any material gain. It fits and will keep a person on the right track, in business and on a personal level.

As I toured and Debbie stayed home with our little girl, I began playing at state fairs, rodeos, and small concert halls. One day I was booked in Poteet, Texas which is just down the road from my hometown. This is the town where George Strait was born, and they are famous for their Strawberry Festival. With Debbie not looking over my shoulder, I slipped back into the drugs and drinking. I figured I could slide a little and convinced myself everything would be okay.

I ran into an old bull-riding friend from long ago, Casey Tibbs, who challenged me to ride this 5,000-pound monster, so I obliged. I did not care, I thought I was still 25! I got laughed out of the arena. Big time singing star flopped on his behind. What was I thinking? Not! I need to remember the basics... Safety first. Here's a thought: if you care about your friends who are under the influence, do not dare them because they will most likely try something they usually would not if they were in their right mind. We all know of people doing crazy acts due to peer pressure, let alone acting under the influence of a substance, only to regret it. Top that with cell phones are everywhere to record your ill-attempt efforts. As much as I love rodeo life and I have lived it since I was a kid, so they can have it! It does not pay enough because the bull always wins!

At times, my Bushwacker mentality (referring to the infamous PBR Champion Rodeo bull) can get me into trouble that makes me act like a fool. The only way I will ever have anything to do with a bull ever again is on a plate with steak sauce! Maybe on a mechanical bull ride for the fun of it at Billy Bob's Fort Worth, Texas. I can do that one and come up with a picture or two as proof.

Then, while on that Texas tour, I rode on a trail ride in Kingsville, Texas, on a mule. I guess I was the laughingstock because I would do just about anything to break into a song for a laugh or a reason. Again, I was acting like a single young buck which had been long gone by then. I was doing things to have fun. Far be it for me not to be the adventurist type, feeling like a kid at heart. I was trying to keep a smile on my face at the same time I worried I was losing my place in the only world I had known since I was young. Again, I filled up the jug and passed it around for good times that just were not there. For 4 ½ years, I rode in the San Antonio Rodeo 13th Annual Trail Ride Master on a mule named "Popeye the Swarme." We had fun on that trip, too.

In Corpus Christi, Texas I was really flying higher than a Georgia pine—and I do not mean in an airplane. I saw a spirit and it came to me, talking to me, telling me things. It showed me parts of my life from the time I once broke my arm and still played a CMA Music Fest with Tom T. Hall, T.G. Sheppard, and Jeannie Sealy, to those crazy trips to Mexico with my buddies getting laid out on jobs working cattle and pitching hay. That spirit guide would not go away that night. It followed me on that four-mile walk I had made as a kid walking home, poor and without a car. Then it flipped and showed me the first new car I bought with cash, then to the house I had built for my mother when the money was flowing like lava out of my money-making volcano. It showed me my mother cooking over a hot stove for all of us kids. Beans again with tortillas with some homemade pan dulce (sweet cake) for supper. And yes, I still love a fresh pot of beans today... unlike others who ate beans every day like me but will not eat them again. The spirit guide showed me, too, how hard I worked to learn to play chords on a guitar. In short, it flashed and showed me part of my life.

I thought that only happened when you were just about to die. Maybe at that time, I was just about to die, I do not know. I understand now that I was on a trip from some drug I had taken. Goes to show you the risk you take not knowing what is in a substance that can lead you where you might not want to go. What a slow, strange trip it turned out to be... a mystery that haunts and deters me today.

Then the spirit guide showed me when I was young and frustrated and went down to the Marines recruiting office to sign up instead of being drafted into service to head out to Vietnam as some of my closet buddies had done. It showed me the pet crocodile I once had and when I once worked as a hunting guide, chasing white-tail deer in the South Texas brush country. I am lucky I did not get bitten by a poisonous snake. This spirit did not pull any punches. It showed me when I was at the top of my musical life as I sang the national anthem at Cowboys stadium in Dallas, Texas.

There I ran into a buddy, Randy Owens of a popular Alabama band that day. About that time, I had a hit record that was climbing the charts only to stall and fade away. The song was "Just Get Up and Close The Door." There was a similar song by Keith Whitley at the time called "Don't Close Your Eyes." Both of those songs had the same unrequited theme of a woman in love with someone else while still giving herself but making believe. Poor old Keith. He had a woman who loved the hell out of him in Lorrie Morgan, but he loved the bottle a little bit more and drank himself to death. I was on the same path with those mystical spirits creeping about my head. I did not want to wind up like Keith. I did not want to lose Debbie and my time with Aubry while she was a little girl. I had some real choices to make and as I look back at my life now, I wished I had made some different choices.

So, it was back to rehab to get things right or I was going to lose my amazing, beautiful wife and my precious little daughter. I had to at least try for their sake and put aside my self-sabotaging ways. When that spirit cleared, I went back to Starlight in Kerrville, Texas, where I had been before to dry out. Starlight was an excellent place to rehab because they cared about you getting straightened out. But again, you must want to get cleaned up. They will help you, but in the end, it is all up to you. It is the old 'man in the mirror' routine. You can either tell him the truth, or you can lie to him once again. I kept lying to him and myself, wasting everyone's time.

In my life, I would try to clean up several times. Starlite Recovery Center near Center Point, Texas, helped me. Randy Willis had gotten me into Starlite twice and La Hacienda north of Center Point near Kerrville once. He never told me what it cost him, and I never asked, but he began to hate drugs with a passion after that. The treatments worked for a while. But it was always me screwing up and winning and losing at the same time. You would have thought interventions among family and friends would have convinced me, but I was always in denial. I remember a counselor at Starlite told me once they were not going to put up with me the next time. I have been there two times already over the past 15 years. I was like a boomerang, back and forth. Then, like a yoyo, up and down. But I had to try, I needed to try! They never told me I was a lost cause, but they knew I could be. I just would not stop what I was doing addiction-wise.

While I was trying, and that was the operative word, trying, I was seeing my country music friends doing the same. George Jones started showing up late to his gigs. Merle Haggard was giving his PR man fits but managed to stay out of the newspapers and always still hit his dates. These greats loved performing for the crowds their way and could do it with their eyes closed. Johnny Paycheck was picking up George's baton and missing dates due to being only plain too drunk to stand up. He really did tell them to take their job and shove it! You must remember these were my heroes who became friends who I idolized at a time in country music when I was a kid. These men showed me acceptance and friendship when I was alone and needed it most.

I was clean and sober when I did that Farm Aid for Willie Nelson in 1985. I was trying to control my intake of booze and laying off the drugs, except pot. To me, the pot was a way to mellow out and can be used for medicinal purposes, you know.

Willie was the mellow-out king! And he never cared about what anyone thought. During those times, I watched as great stars like Willie and Roy Orbison, who also did Farm Aid with us, were respected. These great men were legends in the music business. And guys like Ray Price. The funny thing is when Ray Price died, there were empty seats at his funeral. Can you believe that? Ray Price, the direct link to the king of country music, Hank Williams Sr., had empty seats in the church. I was stunned... no COVID-19 then to worry about social distancing of sort. I am just old school and did not understand how Mr. Price did not get the respect in death he was supposed to get. It shocked me. Did that mean his star had faded as mine was fading? Has country music become such a cold business that it has lost its soul? If Ray Price could not be respected in death, where would any respect come from for the rest of us in life?

From the years of the nineties on into the new millennium, the country music world was big on doing tributes to stars who had died. John Denver, Johnny Cash, Tammy Wynette, and others. Other country stars were asked to be a part of those tributes in song or for a promo about what the star meant to other artists. Country music musicians have always been a close family and instrumental in coming to one another's aid in times of need. God only knows I would jump at the opportunity to express my appreciation and respect for needy entertainers.

Rehab and Intervention

Rehab can be expensive — effective, but expensive. It can cost $1,500 a day plus for six months. I was in and out of them between 1980, 1981, 1985, 1991, 1993, 1995, 1998, and recently. I was given an opportunity to clean up and save myself and my career voluntarily through the intervention of family and friends.

There comes a time when you can be detached from your body and mind, and sometimes your friends and family will care enough to challenge you. That's what my good friends did to me. My former boss and friends Tom T. and Alan Brown tricked me into rehab intervention by staging a party under false pretenses. Yes, that got me there in a New York minute. I even brought my own BYOB (bring your own bottle), as did they. I was pretty upset to be deceived like that and was sore for a while, but I knew it was for my own good and appreciated my friend's caring to step in. I agreed and surrendered to commit to treatment.

How could I not? These were friends and family who I loved, looked up to, and had the utmost respect for. I could not have been with a better or more competent team and winners like Coach Darrell Royal and Earl Campbell. They cared enough to share their concerns for my mental and physical health and overall well-being. At the time, I didn't appreciate it... today, I do.

My support came from friends who courageously addressed the elephant in the room. I learned that steps to recovery from alcohol and drugs affect the entire family and circle of friends. Structured conversations between loved ones who struggled with my substance use and disorder, felt free to express their feelings of hurt and pain constructively, and often supervised. It was staged, necessary, and well-received.

My drug use had taken its toll on everyone I knew or who knew me. Friendships and meaningful relationships were either destroyed or harmed because of my addictions. My true friends saved my life from the addictions of cocaine, heroin, meth, amphetamines, and overuse of marijuana and saved me from myself. They paid for my treatments. No man needs more than good men in their circle who give him tough love and support. How can I repay such friends? I am sharing my personal experience in this book to make a difference, even if it's a dent.

I had been in rehab for many reasons. Sometimes, to commit and show a judge, I would clean up my act if he would give me a break on a misdemeanor and minor charge I might have committed for drinking or drugging. One time, I had been busted out of Oklahoma for carrying some drugs. I made bail, and between my lawyer at the time and myself, I admitted I needed help and was sent to rehab. I had been in rehab in Texas at Starlight twice, and they told me not to come back! Talk about a low blow to my ego. Ouch.

Then, I went to La Hacienda near Kerrville to get the treatment. It was a revolving door I kept walking through. So many of us country music players did such madness. That is no excuse, but it is the truth. Sometimes, it made national news, the local five o'clock news or the paper, and now the internet, but after a while, when you are known for it as much as your music, it gets old, and they just do not print it or announce it anymore. It is old news.

I overheard Johnny Cash tell someone when he had gotten out of rehab or a church dunking to cleanse his soul from drugs and drinking: "What is a man if he doesn't have spirit?"

And what is a man's spirit if he can't connect that spirit with the master of life?" I took that to heart when I heard that. I was always looking for something to keep me alive and kicking when I found out the drugs and drinking had abandoned me. My only difference was I did not seek it from God (my higher calling) as I should have. I do not know why; I just never did, and to this day, I still seek that peace I have seen in others who have lived a life like mine. I figured if they could be happy, so could I. I also discovered it's a step-by-step process and not overnight.

Unbeknownst to my fans and readers, I have always been shy. It is my shell. I have used it to my advantage to observe and become a student of the business and a name. It has served me when trouble came my way. Addictions that come with Touring, especially drinking and women. That is just part of this Earth for us, not just me. I was brought up in the church before God, but I never came back when I needed to. Being shy to a fault has always been a defensive mechanism for me. I do not always like it, but that is who I am. I cannot change it, so I live it.

Besides, it is humbling for me to stand back and observe others. I find people refreshing and most interesting to know.

I do not want to get to "rehab in a circle when we all tell each other our problems," but I will tell you we all have traits that define us; some of them are God-given to help us cope with life. I know my strengths, and I know my weaknesses. Both make me unique. I can and have gotten up in front of thousands and thousands of people to sing and play, but when the lights come down, and I am behind the curtain once again, I lean on the things of the Earth to cope with my place in life. It could be the fame or the adulation of the screams, standing ovations, and the bright lights, I do not know. I do know it breathes life into me. When I was performing and connecting with the crowd, there was no greater feeling at that moment.

Merle Haggard once had a rare interview with Dan Rather (1991) in which Rather asked Merle, "You have all the money you need and you don't have to perform, why do you still do it?"

I will never forget his answer when Merle replied, "Because, if I do not, I will die. I need them (the audience) as much as they need me." I can relate to what Merle and others who share this same sentiment. Here is what I do know is when the show is all over with every night, I am alone with me, and I must deal with that. And I do not always deal with it in the right way. Silence can be deafening. Usually, I will turn up the television or radio and drown out the sounds in my mind to escape. It does not matter to me what movie, sports (fishing) comedy, or news. It is all the same to me and serves the same purpose that I need to amuse and distract me.

* * * * *

Chapter 19 My Daughters

"For where your treasure is, there will your heart be also."
– Matthew 6:21

In my dilemma to right myself long enough to be the father to Aubry, my wife Debbie insisted I be…I did a lot of soul searching. Then, it felt like a ton of bricks hit me when I learned I had fathered another child! More children? What! My good friend in high school, Corky Parker, got hit with the news, too! We both learned we had daughters from girls we had dated in high school. It's no laughing matter when you learn many years after the fact that you have another daughter, well, you man up in whatever way you can. In the past I always used humor in a tough spot because it is the easiest way to deal with shocking news, but this came out of the blue.

I discovered I have another daughter. Her name is Teresa Parker, and she met me at one of my concerts when she was in her late 40s. She is married to a good man, Karl Parker, who's also a musician. She has children (now in their 20s and 30s) who had children, which were now my grandchildren and great-grandchildren. This was too heavy for me, but I took it all in because my daughter matters. In short, I acknowledged the truth. I only wish she would have found me, though before she was 40. Corky had a daughter about the same age, Monique, who became fast friends with my daughter, Teresa.

This newfound daughter of mine was conceived unbeknownst to me, while I was still in high school dreaming of being a singer. My wish had come true for my two daughters to meet and know that each is available to accept and support one another as sisters. We all want our kids to have someone to lean on when we go, right? So that connection is out there for them to enjoy if they want to.

I have known a few country music stars in the same position who discovered they had fathered a child they did not know. Some may say we are irresponsible for having children out of wedlock, reckless love; well, maybe that is true. I just know that I am not alone facing an unknown predicament as this and welcoming the addition in my life. Teresa may have been a secret but I'm just thankful her mother made her reveal.

We all make mistakes, especially when we are young. But I can say that Teresa was never a mistake by any stretch of the imagination. She is a blessing to me as every child should be.

When you are a kid in high school and you have sex with girls you like, life happens. With my case, the girl who I was responsible for getting pregnant, Becky, never said a word. For reasons known only to her, she quietly went off and had a baby without telling me. Perhaps, my life might have been a lot different had I known. I do not know. Did she choose not to tell me out of fear of being ostracized getting pregnant in a small town with all the gossip and prejudice she would have endured—being pregnant, and from a Mexican to boot—at a time when both were looked down on unfavorably. The truth is I was in the dark about it all until Teresa and I finally met.

The first time Teresa and I came face to face was in 2016 at one of my concerts in Pleasanton, Texas. My first impression was, "Boy! She sure looks like my mom," and I could not stop staring as I noticed the resemblance of my mother's features. Teresa was 45 years old. With the assistance of friends, it became a reunion of sort, and we have the happy pictures to prove it and we would meet up again with my beautiful granddaughters at future concerts. I can candidly say I do not regret it one bit now. It is part of my life, and it is out there for us all to deal with. How we deal with any challenge is key to having a successful today.

Anyone that knows me knows I am protective when it comes to my family. I do not like living in the past or the future, but I do practice living in the present with as much harmony, happiness, peace, and family privacy as I can. My daughters know that I'll do what I can to help them in any way.

One of the most comforting things about finding out about Teresa is that she grew up in a good home, that her mother, Becky, and stepfather, Charlie, a pal of mine, treated her good and gave her a stable home. Charlie and I hung out in high school, and he has always been a great guy and friend. It gives me peace knowing my flesh and blood was provided for and loved. Also, knowing, the time I spent with Becky, her mother (along with her secret pregnancy) when we were just kids in a small town had not been a mark against her. I went off in search of a career to find myself while Becky lived a normal life; a life that could have ended differently had she tagged along with me.

In the late '60s and early '70s, having a baby out of wedlock was a scandal in a small town. Tongues would wag and fingers would point in a way the girl might run to the abortion clinic. God works mysteriously, and I feel blessed Teresa's mother, Becky, did not do that. After I found out and we met, Teresa and I bonded not only as father-daughter, but also, we have a personal connection where we can now lean on each other. For that, I am grateful. I am also grateful that her adoptive father, was good to both Teresa and her mom. It is clear he helped shape her into the fine young woman she is today. Teresa is an ambitious woman who recently retired as chief of operations, having worked in the construction industry for over 33 years. I respect my daughter immensely ad am proud of her own achievements she has accomplished as a woman and an entrepreneur. She is one of those people you wished you could go back in time and do it all over again, but we are enjoying getting to know each other now. She's beautiful, intelligent, and knowledgeable in the construction industry.

Now along with Teresa, I have my daughter, Aubry. Debbie has raised our daughter into one of the most grounded and stable young ladies you would ever want to meet. Man, I am one lucky man *hombre* because this young lady is something else. She is beautiful—and smart, too. That is not just me talking! And she is pursuing a music degree minoring in business law in college. At her age, I got the same singing bug that she inherited from me. Aubry's voice is sweet, pure, and original; and when she sings melody, she sings from her heart (she gets that from me!) with a beautiful smile that captivates the audience. Call me biased, whatever, but to me she sings like an angel, and I enjoy singing with my daughter on stage, every chance I get. It gives me pride to do so; especially when I hear her sing in Spanish. Besides, she sure makes me look good! Keep in mind that I in no way wanted her to go down the path I went down, my chosen profession, even though it could be a good path given a little more caution than I had. Debbie never pushed her that way either. Debbie is a good mother. She is protective, but not a stage-type mother. I remember my own mother telling me I was good but that I needed to understand the odds against me in the music business: A Mexican boy trying to sing country music? Heck, I might as well set my sights on being President of the United States! But my mother never discouraged me either. She told me the truth about her concerns for me being away from family, but she also gave me her blessing. Besides, she was so busy with all of us kids . . . who even knew one of them would ever break out to become a country music singer or anyone prominent in the community, but we all did in our own right. My mother, Isabel, was proud of all her children. One thing is for sure, we are law-abiding citizens and good people at heart and private, to boot.

Now that Aubry is singing and has set her sights on country music, I am not going to discourage her either. It is her life to live. But, as my fatherly duty, I have warned her about the pitfalls in show business and what she would be up against. The tricksters, men, players, sabotagers, and suffering that goes with surviving before thriving. I always want her to know I care about protecting her heart and best interest in the arena of business.

I am only glad there are not the same old prejudices today as there were back when I started. Again, the late Charley Pride and I had to fight off racist demons for a shot at singing country music. My friend, Charley, was yelled at on stage, *go back to picking cotton,* and there were one too many promoters who yelled, *No Mexican will ever sing in my club*. I am happy to say that once I made it and was in demand, the club owner was more than happy to have me sing in his club and paid me good money to do it. Demand and supply will work every time—so musicians, practice your craft. I am so glad America has grown up enough to set aside some of that menacing mindset so that my Aubry can have a chance should she want to continue her journey into country music.

I have had Aubry come up on stage with me to show her how much I love and support her and sing duets. The song

"We Believe in Happy Endings" is one of our favorites and we do it well since she was about 17 or 18. Although she was like me, shy at first, she has pushed herself to get over her reticence and now commands stage presence with her guitar to sing the songs she loves to sing. There is no father in the world who is prouder. It is a hard business, but if a young talent has some guidance, she can make her mark. There would have been no Tanya Tucker without the protection and guidance of her father, Beau Tucker. He was like a father to me as well. Tanya toured and opened for me at my shows, and we would sing duets on stage where there was always a watchful father's eye. Selena Quintanilla had the same father's eye protection as Abraham.

Dottie West had Shelly. Loretta Lynn had twin daughters and her sister, Crystal Gayle, while Dolly had her sister, Stella. There is nothing wrong with siblings and children following in the footsteps of their kin who have become celebrities. Aubry can sing and she can write songs, too. So, I thought if Aubry wanted to really pursue a career in country music, I was not going to be the one to try to stop her. I told her I would give her every contact I could but that only she could make it on her own. I told her the music business does not care who she is the daughter of as it did when I was starting out. The music business only understands talent and money. I have confidence in my daughter, and she is two steps ahead of the game. In today's music world, competition is stiff, and it feels colder than an igloo in Alaska. That is just the way it is, and I am not going to say anything different. You deal with it with the knowledge you have and make smart decisions in your own best interest. With that in mind, you have a slight edge over the others who do not know better. It is a warning of sorts for any young kid wanting to get into the business. Be ready to stand on your own two feet with integrity and your head held high using your God-given talent. Do not fall into the traps of the music business, that being fighting off the addictions with drugs, alcohol, gambling, sex or fighting off the demons, including friends in disguise. Aubry is my daughter and she needed to hear the truth from me. I am a firm believer that blood is thicker than water and I aim to protect my daughter at all costs to let her know and others that she is loved.

However, I will advise my readers on what to do to have a competitive edge in the music business. First and foremost, show up, have faith, believe in yourself, perfect your craft, and know your real friends and mentors. Lastly, it's good to keep in mind that the devil is in the details. Get your hands on "This Business of Music: Definitive Guide to The Music Industry" 10th Edition by M. William Krasilovsky and Sidney Shemel with contributions by John M. Gross and Jonathan Feinstein. It is the Bible in music and is available on Amazon. Run, don't walk, and use an attorney to draft and review contracts in your best interest. In a nutshell, work hard and take care of you. Do not assume for a second others have your best interest at heart, unless they've proven it to you. Heed the lessons and do not learn the hard way as many artists do.

So, yes, I made my personal family most unconventionally. Having Aubry at 46 and then learning about Teresa in my sixties is no way to start a man's family. But it had become my way. I thought about having Aubry hit the leg of a tour with me while on college break. I was still hitting television shows from time to time, and I thought it might be fun if she tagged along. I did the TNN show "Stone Country" in 2013 where a collection of us seasoned guys sat around and talk shop and sing our old hits to each other. On this one show, I sang "Pass Me By" and then "That's the Way Love Goes." The late Jim Ed Brown was the show's host and artists such as Crystal Gayle, Lynn Anderson, and Little Jimmy Dickens sat listening. My fatherly instinct told me timing was not right as I do not think Aubry was ready. You have got to be prepared and strike when given the opportunity. Aubry has the right idea playing it cool and easing into her spot in country music. I respect that. She has the looks and the talent to make it on her own without any help from me. Any decision she makes will be her call, but I am sure Debbie and I want her to complete her degree to fall back on should things change . . . and they always do! An important fact about a college degree is no one can ever take that away. It's something you earn through hard work and sacrifice.

I remember that taping on "Stone Cold Country." Besides those three stars I have named, T.G. Sheppard and Larry Gatlin were also sitting around. A little story about T.G. I've toured with him, Mickey Gilley, and Johnny Lee, and I still do to this day when the gig is proper. T.G. is a nice-looking dude and he tries hard to keep it that way. He has this thing about his hair. It reminds me of that old song, Werewolves of London, *with the line.* His hair was perfect, that's T.G. Shepard. He keeps that hair of his always looking perfect. You have to give your fans what they expect, not just what they want. I wish mine could always look good, but it has a mind. To this day, I still love performing shows with these old friends and seeing that they also want to be on top of their game for their fans. So, do I. One thing is for sure, your friends, like your kids, can always be real and honest with you.

My relationship with my daughters means everything to me now more than ever for obvious reasons. You just cannot stall time. Communication and compromise really are key both in a personal and professional business. I have learned to listen more than speak . . . the hard way. COVID-19 has impacted our lives profoundly and has made it necessary for us to behave and do business outside the box to be effective.

I have taught Aubry that being an opening act is a solid stepping stone to letting the public know who you are as a country music singer, not just as Johnny Rodriguez's singing daughter. She has the talent and personality to bring to the table. The audience will fall in love with her. When I used to tour with veteran stars like Hank Thompson and the Brazos Valley Boys, I would use Hank's band for my set, and then they would bring on the other acts, usually 30 to 40 minutes per act. It would be a fantastic way for Aubry to get noticed. I remember the pay was good because what one star's fan base has come to see them, gets to see me and my fan base. Those package shows are a great way to network, collaborate, and bring in the crowds. Venues love it! They sure sell a lot of beer and whiskey. Stars, two for the price of one! Take copious notes—if you are not networking with others; you are not working. No pay.

I also warned Aubry of the pitfalls of living the country music life. It is hard and harsh as it gets, at the same time. I told her I often drank too much applejack liquor to manage it. I just do not want her to get overpowered by the same struggle. In hindsight, I had it good. Fortunately, it had not taken me long to have hit records. They say you must pay your dues and Aubry knows that is the way it is done. My rise was unique, an almost novelty way of success by singing bilingual songs. Aubry could do the same now that it is 45 years later, and it just might work. I strongly believe so. I can see it now, her singing the "Songs of My Father (Canciones de Mi Padre)," like Linda Ronstadt affectionately dedicated to her own dad.

Right before I married Debbie and had Aubry, I accepted whatever gig came along. In 2009, I did a duet with the late, great Johnny Bush. We cut a song called "The Rio Grande Runs Red" and followed it up with "Old Worn-Out Cowboys." Well, that is what he and I were, a couple of old worn-out cowboys from Texas, born, bred, and raised. I think that is what I was doing in Austin, Texas when I met and was smitten with Debbie. I remember her and I dating in and around Austin. I also remembered doing Austin City Limits with my band led by the late Rick Durrett. We did ACL two or three times, and I sang a new song I was hoping to be a hit called "Back on Her Mind Again." It got some airplay, but by that time, the new "Hat Act" (George Strait, Clint Black, Garth Brooks, Dwight Yoakum) had taken over the country music scene.

I can remember a time when these newcomers were at mine and George's show, admiring our music and wanting to meet the two of us. Before long I was tapping my toes to the beat of the drum and sound of their voice and songs. What can? I say? A musician knows good music when he hears it, and I'm a fan too.

Now I know country music loves to pay homage to its seasoned stars. I played "Country Road TV" hosted by Whispering Bill Anderson. That show would give us old cats some airtime, you know, me and guys like David Ball and Moe Bandy. They even let newcomers like Mo Pitney, who has a mountain of talent to play some songs. I thought of those reputable venues should Aubry desire to play them to open her careerI told Aubry to take whatever show or gig you can get to advance your career as long as you get to keep your clothes on!

After all, I am a man, and a dad and blood is thicker than water. I will always speak my truth with my daughter to guide and protect her. One thing I can honestly say about my daughter is she is smart, and she listens.

Aubry does not take my celebrity status for granted, and she does not hesitate to ask her dad for advice on music matters, being the songwriter she is. Reaching out to her fans and mine, she has a kind, giving, and polite heart. Did I mention how smart and hardworking both my daughters are? In my opinion, that will always give them a competitive edge. To show Aubry how much I love and support her as an artist, I have her come up on stage and sing with me. The song "We Believe in Happy Endings" is one of our favorites; we do it well together. There is not a father in the world who is prouder.

I just want readers to know how proud I am of my daughters, Aubry Rodriguez and Teresa Parker. God willing, Aubry will achieve success as a country singer in her own right (if that is her heart's desire), and my daughter, Teresa will welcome, support, and cheer her younger sister in the manner she has welcomed me her dad on and off stage. Continuing the "Rodriguez Sound" legacy perpetuates our love for each other, country music, and the fans who come to see us. Now that would be a real kick in the pants and make me happy. As Aubry decides to travel this road as a country music singer, I hope you will give her the support you have given me throughout the past 50 years. For me, that would be a great family tradition. We all know the fans make it all happen for all musicians.

I read somewhere and can vouch first-hand that there is no greater feeling than "The most precious jewels you'll ever have around your neck are the arms of your daughters," wrote the poet Altaf Qadri.

* * * * *

Chapter 20 Riding High in April, Shot Down in May

"We must all suffer one of two things. The pain of discipline or the pain of regret."
– Jim Rohn

In 1998, I found myself living in limbo while going through a rough patch in my life, not knowing what half of Texas would think of me.

In a split second, tragedy can strike anyone. I always felt haunted that the worst thing that could happen to me was to hit another person while driving my car and be responsible for their death. For the longest time, the thought sent shivers down my spine... I haven't driven for years and carry a Texas identification card to prove it. In my teens, I used to ride my thumb... today, I let Uber drive me to get where I am going... just not Mexico-bound.

For me, it happened in the early hours (in my own mother's home) after a long day. One shot took the life of another man in an unfortunate accident.

There were threats and rumors spreading and calls ringing left and right; hoaxes or not, one never knows. All I know is that threats were something I did not take lightly, and I feared not so much for me but for my family. If that was not bad enough, my wife, Debbie, at the time, feared for her safety and left me with my baby girl to live in another state. It broke my heart. Out of fear for their safety and well-being, I isolated myself from those I cared about most. No doubt, my own children would wonder about my whereabouts, but it felt like the right thing to do in my heart.

After the assassination attempt of President Ronald Reagan by John Hinckley Jr. in 1981, where bullets ricocheted off his limousine and struck him down, I was not going to be the next statistic. Athletes and Entertainers of all genres must be extra careful nowadays, whether in their homes or at a public venue. Self-preservation and safety come first; I'm wiser now about remembering this. It is easy for a celebrity to let down their guard from all the adulation from fans, but it's not prudent.

The Lowest Point in My Life

After being acquitted by jury for the shooting incident, about one year later, I was shopping in the vegetable section at a HEB store in San Antonio. Always looking over my shoulder for obvious reasons of threats targeted at my life, I am observant of my surroundings. In passing that day, I spotted a lady with two little boys. They appeared to be twelve and ten years old. Five minutes later, one of the boys tugged on my shirt. I said, "Yes, son!" He boldly asked, "Mr., are you a real criminal?"

I was speechless, feeling blindsided that this child questioned me this way and could think that I was a bad man. I can't tell you how appalled I was to be confronted in public any less. God knows what was said to him about an incident they knew nothing about except what was in the news.

I felt I was being judged and on trial a second time for something I was acquitted of in the court of Texas law. I felt sickening, pitted at the bottom of my stomach. To be seen guilty in the eyes of a child was the worst punishment I could have been handed in a local grocery store. It is hard for me to recall this memory because it still bothers me if I dwell on it.

Still, I would like to thank all the individuals who expressed a willingness to help me during a difficult and emotional time. You know who you are. Your kindness, hospitality, protection, and generosity were much appreciated.

On a serious note, I kept a low profile after the shooting, and I feel bad about that. I didn't want anyone retaliating against my children, friends, or any family members. I made a choice out of a sense of duty to sacrifice their safety to live a normal life without me and the scandal. They say time heals all. I pray it so.

Hangin' With The Guys

In 1999, after an unfortunate incident, I moved in with a friend, who happened to belong to the Bandidos Motorcycle Club. I stayed with president and chief, Mando Martinez, in Corpus Christi, Texas for three years. His invitation came at a time that was perfect timing for me. I really had no place to go, nor did I want to intrude on anyone. I just wanted space and privacy to lay low and let time pass.

One day Mando's sons, Eric and Shane (age 18 or 20 years old) and I were standing outside the main Biker bar, in Corpus Christi just piddling around. These two strapping young men had just caught a 7-foot King rattlesnake. I quickly grabbed the King rattlesnake by the back of its neck and flung it in the air where it landed on a table where 10 badass Bandidos (biker members) were sitting. Well, you've never seen a bunch of bad asses jump up and take off running so fast as when that happened. Yeah, it was funny at the time, but I ended up having to run away because one of the Bandidos was hot on my trail.

The truth is I could not hold on to that rascal any longer because its snake hide was incredibly strong. The boys will vouch for me on that because they could see for themselves how I was struggling to hold on.

The boys and I were running like hell as fast as we could, too, but one of the Bandidos was firing off his pistol running behind us. I could still hear him yelling "I'm going to kill you... you little S.O.B." His name was Bob Dumas, and it took me some three months later to get the nerve to apologize to him. He's a great old guy that I love, but I'm glad I did the right thing manning up and approaching him out of respect. We laughed when I said I would have run, too, and tripped all over myself, if it were me.

The thing about a rattlesnake king is if bitten and the bite is left untreated, a person's organs and bodily functions break down, resulting in death within 2 days.

The boys are grown, healthy and still doing well, today, and so is Mando, their dad, who lives in Corpus Christi, Texas.

In Another World

There's another side of life that my eyes have seen that I never talk about for obvious reasons. I tend to be that way when certain memories are too painful for me to talk about. Most men are... it's how we were conditioned as boys to toughen up and man up, showing no emotions. I'm not saying it's a good thing, I'm just saying it's why men become attracted to women who aren't afraid to be vulnerable to show emotions and be themselves. It allows us to do the same.

If you want to see me shut down and make me, feel uncomfortable, then get personal or overstep your boundary with me. In doing so, I will learn more about you than you will ever learn about me. Let me best express myself in my own time or in a song…it's the cowboy way and who I am.

Everybody has a story; a matter that comes to mind is one of family and honor "first" and learning to have boundaries. However, many people feel closer to their friends than they do with their own family, but not everybody does either way. This really hits close to home for me because I have a relative, Chacho short for muchacho *boy* who served time in prison for killing another guy. The provoked young man was defending his elderly uncle who had gotten beat up by a thug. Chacho sought revenge and shot the guy down with a machine gun that cut the man in half. Sounds gory, I know. My cousin took the matter into his own hands... vigilante-style. He paid dearly for it and lives to regret it. I'm not justifying his actions by any means, but at the time, he was addicted to heroin.

It stands to reason just how many people are in prison today sitting in their lonely and isolated cells wishing they would have walked away in the heat of passion. We see on social media the Karens or senseless incidents of honor killings, road rage, anger, and hate crimes at their worst.

My acquaintance with friends like Danny Berlanga of San Antonio was not widely known. They even wrote a book about him, *The Heroin Merchant*. I go way back with these guys when we all flocked together. Those days are behind me now and I'm at peace with where I am today. To describe me best back then would be "street wise." I always did accept people and places and found both intriguing to know. It's the desperado- lifestyle in me. Texas will always be my favorite place to live.

May we never forget the sweet and bitter memories of loved ones who lost their lives in one way or another.

The fact is people from all walks of life like music and I am always happy to meet anyone without judging who and what they do for a living if they love my singing. It went without saying for me to extend the same non-judgmental attitude to family and friends who made a mistake in their life.

My friend and singer, George Strait, had just given me an expensive black felt cowboy hat; with a personal note written to me that same year. Knowing my cousin Chacho is a huge George Strait fan (who isn't?), without thinking much of it, I intentionally gifted him my hat that I valued more than anything. It was my way of saying take care of yourself while incarcerated—paying your debt to society and not giving up.

I pray that he has kept and worn my Strait hat and it has helped him stay on the *strait* and narrow to move forward in life. If not, then I regret having given him my hat that meant a lot to me. I've gifted and thrown a lot of memorabilia of mine to the fans in the audience like buckles, shirts, clothes, and cowboy hats, but they've all been replaceable to me. I'm happier being a giver than a receiver, but a hat like Strait's is special to me and has emotional attachment to it. You can't put a price on it.

The truth is... I intended to give hope to a young man who made a poor decision acting on his anger. I have never taken back a gift in my life, but I sure would love to have that hat back if he's willing to give it up. George is my buddy. Chacho, if you are messing up in life, gimme back my hat—if not, then keep it.

The Bandidos have come a long way and have changed their public image considerably for the better. Most members are respectable and quit brawling in public and cleaned up their acts finding jobs and commit no more than minor offenses. I appreciated Mando being kind enough to let me hang my hat at his place, along with his hospitality.

I wasn't afraid of staying with the Banditos because 99% of these club members are law-abiding and hang together for the enjoyment of riding their Harleys for adventure. Whereas 1%were considered "outlaws," but we all got along alright. Members come from all walks of life, and their camaraderie is something else. They are a tight-knit bunch of guys, and they have a lot of fun riding together. "Ride or Die."

Sometimes, some of its members would even visit my shows in Texas. After all, I was dubbed "Outlaw Country" genre with my pals, Waylon (the pioneer of the "Outlaw" movement), along with Willie, Kris, and Johnny. We enjoyed seeing these motorcycle club members at our shows. Their presence revitalized our careers and synergized us when Nashville Ameripolitan halted our progress and slowed us down.

Other women joined the notable "Outlaw Country" genre, including Loretta Lynn, Tanya Tucker, Jessi Colter, Sammi Smith, Miranda Lambert, Gretchen Wilson, Rachel Brook, Gina Jones, and Bri Bagwell. These courageous and strong women sing their hearts out with their own songs.

I always felt protected around the Banditos (have you seen their stature and muscles?) I just tried staying out of the way. These guys are amazing and strong men with an unbelievable amount of self-confidence and loyalty to one another. They know a lot of people and have a wide sphere of influence, mostly the ones who like to ride their Harley's with them. There is no freer feeling than going on a good ride.

The Bandido family's act of involvement for charity work in San Antonio is an impressive record for their dedication to the community proving they are worthy of recognition and praise. Still there is room for improvement in crime to stop some of the fighting and bickering that occurs. I stayed with the Banditos for three years and have friends who are motorcycle members and love to ride.

Their appearance might look a little gruff, probably to give the impression they are the meanest group of guys to attract new members, but they are changing their public image all the time and getting involved in lots of community events, especially when it comes to kids. Still, there is room for improvement in crime to stop some of the fighting and bickering that occurs in any organization, civil government, and family.

The club continues to make strides and changes over the years for a different and more positive image. There are approximately 10,000 Bandito members and most share their passion for riding their Harley Davidsons.

Hide-out to Open Range

From Mando's, I moved in with my musician friend, Kelly Kenning, and his dad, Ray, and brothers. These two men are the most upstanding Christian men you could meet. Their ranch is in South Texas, where the incredible wildlife roams free. I'm talking Bison. It's paradise to me because it's remote and I get to view and take in the deer and exotic animals living there. No place gives me greater peace.

My buddies and I have shared a lot of good times together cooking, kicking it, and playing and writing music. We have loads in common, and music is our number one interest. I've been blessed to have great friends throughout my life who remain friends with me today. I can honestly say I am most happy about this fact.

* * * * *

Chapter 21 Living Out the Songs of My Life

"Don't wish it was easier, wish you were better. Don't wish for less problems, wish for more skills. Don't wish for less challenge, wish for more wisdom."
– Jim Rohn

Now we are back to 2005 and then onto to 2010. My hits are all gone now, but their memory is not gone. Memories are here forever. I am still picking and singing to crowds, sometimes smaller, but no less important to me. I still give it my all, even though the smoking and the drinking has battered my voice where I have my good days and my not-so-good days behind the microphone. For the past 30 years, I have had a top-notch band headed by a great guy named Gary Goss to back me up on the road. He played keyboard and did my backup singing and as I write these words, has recently retired. He has had a teaching job for as long as I can remember. We had some wild and fun times on the road even though we started together in our late 40s and into our 50s. Age plays no part when you love to play and have the Rodriguez Sound band to back you. They are a class act.

Along the way of my musical life, I have shared the stage with the best and most famous country music recording studio musicians (50-piece orchestra). Still, I can safely say my touring band are some of the best and most dedicated I have ever had that pleasure to share a stage with. After Gary, I had, ironically, a policeman named Bruce Carter from Conroe, Texas, who had drummed for me for 20 years. Bruce is my Road Manager, the backbone of the entire team. I am hoping he will hang around till the cows come home. After all, he is still a young man. I try not to wear him out with my occasional shenanigans I display to break the monotony.

Then I have Mike Hammock from Waxahachie, Texas as my bass player for 25 years on the road with me. His day job has been working in the electrical energy industry and driving a truck. He stands back on stage and uses that bass of his to support the foundation of my songs. What a great guy and professional he has been for me and the band.

I have had a few pedal steel guitar players in my time, like the great late Randy Reinhard, who I miss till this day. Then we have the phenomenal Don Sowersby. He is old school country, a pedal steel player who knows when to fill in and knows when to shine. He is just as comfortable in a recording studio as he is on stage. We all feel the onset of aches and pains of age, (due to lack of sleep) but old Don will probably die with his hands on the old double neck. He is still able to load up and hit the streets so I can perform on stage when called upon. None of these guys ever complained about a thing.

Finally, I get to tell you all about Kenny Penny who has played off and on for me on lead guitar and fiddle. If there is a picture of a musician who is a journeyman, it is Kenny. He has played with almost everyone and has played in too many studios and stages, to name a few. He has made an impressive living with strings of all kinds for many kinds of artists. Guitar. Lead guitar. Fiddle. If it has strings on it, Kenny can play it. There is no one finer or more hardworking. He plays his instruments with love behind each song and just has what it takes to deliver to the audience! Kenny is a musician's musician. He is like that running back that will get you 4 yards every time it is 4th and 4.

No musician worth his salt can tour without a solid band on stage behind him. Hands down. I have been one of the most fortunate singers who has a band that will follow me through my ups and downs and carry me when my downs are too many. I have been blessed in that department from former band Manager Rick Durrett to Gary Goss. I am not the easiest guy to get along with on the road, especially since we were doing some 60 dates a year before the pandemic of 2020. When that Twilight Zone thing hit the music world, it was hard to accept not being able to play venues because of the social distancing restrictions of the crowds. I suppose we were luckier than most states, because Texas businesses stayed open the longest during this trying time. I miss playing when I want to play. I have never allowed anyone to tell me when and where I can play my music, even in jail. Most musicians are like that. It is our rite of passage just as it is our first amendment right to speak our minds. This virus that has plagued our nation and our world in 2020 as I write this book that is the mother of all confusion, we have no control over. I have never really been controlled, as you know. But this pandemic is the real deal and we have had to deal with it out of necessity than despair. What is so sad about not coming together to enjoy a common music bond has hurt people who need country music to live. Club owners, waitresses, cooks, busboys, and everyone who works in music, the service industry, etc. That is the real letdown for this whole scenario. They are the 80% of workers who really run this nation! I feel bad for us musicians but for the rest of the working community, too. Still, I am confident we Americans will get through it together with fervent prayer and God's help.

So, for the first years of the 2000 century, I have been living out the songs of my life, the songs I have written that have become hits that still pay me residual income to live off. My life has been that mailbox money and money earned from gigs off the road. There was a time when I was rich, and money did not mean much to me. I was young and thought that since I had made it in country music, I would be rich forever and that money would never dry up. That is a lesson I had to learn the hard way to wake up to. I have seen with my own eyes some great singers die penniless and poor. We have all heard of those dire circumstances and stories. They are sad and heartbreaking. I do not need to name any names; you know who they are. But it is safe to say they made their mark on this profession which we musicians have chosen and hopefully that they have gained life's real reward in Heaven. I can only pray when my time comes, I can say the same: regardless of how much money I have when I die it meant little to me. I did it for the love and joy it gave me and my fans and music lovers everywhere. I've seen many Musicians play longer than they probably should have. I sometimes wonder why they did, only to pass on when they could have stopped. I'd like to say I will not do that, and I will know when to stop before my health fails me, but I guess we love the music business and people too much to quit.

As the new millennium moved on, I kept on the road for many reasons. I kept redeeming myself from mistakes I had made in the past and to atone for the ones yet to come. I had missed some gigs. I would forget to stay and autograph for the fans. Some nights the sound was bad, or the gig was sluggish, so I became indifferent to everyone. In my mind, I was justified in expecting perfection not only from myself, but from others. It was not on purpose; I was just a man being moody and temperamental sometimes and ungrateful. Most of the time, chalk it up to lack of rest. I felt I had been trapped into being just another musician making a living instead of being the star I used to be. Stardom can be a curse in that when it moves on, you are left with only one memory. It can spoil you, making you want more of it and on the other hand, it can make you resentful reliving the past over and over. I would not change a thing with the career I have had. It still has been a blessing. Today, I am work in progress and making lemonade out of lemons thanks to COVID-19, I am reflective on my life, being still, and feeling grateful every single day. Circumstances can literally awaken you and bring you to your knees.

Sometimes the road was weary for me, so much so that I had to cut back on dates. If I had done that, I would have hurt my band, which wanted to play and needed the money. They had families to support, too. When you are a "star," you cannot think of yourself alone. You must think of the others who have worked to help you keep on keeping on. They never quit on me. Moe Bandy had a song out while I was on top, and it said something to me. It was called "Hank Williams You Wrote My Life." I recall that song from time to time when I think of drinking with guys like Lefty Frizzell and Billy Joe Shaver. They lived out the words of Hank's songs as I still do. It is the nature of the beast in country music, I guess.

There were times I was a little too messed up to play, and that was wrong. It was me trying to cope with life that had changed so much I had been through. Little did I know that feeling the need to mask and hide my pain off stage, was showing in my performance on stage. Way too many country music stars find themselves in the same boat. When you are at the top, it is all good, the money, the fans, the women, the songs. When the star begins to fade out, you are on stage working your behind off, trying to prove to the fans you have still got it. It is so exhausting, and it takes the wind, sometimes, the fun out of it. Funny thing is not your fans, nor your friends want to tell you how bad it looks. Guess they are trying to spare my feelings. It is like that scene in the movie "The Blues Brothers" where the fans are as drunk as you are and throwing bottles at the chicken wire in front of the stage! Life on the road is a rowdy one—and a lonely one, too. You have no family to come home to, just a dusty old hotel room with a lumpy bed and boring cable shows that should have been taken off years ago. I kept fighting things, believing I was too good to be through.

I was playing a show in Ft. Worth in 2018 for promoter Joe Belinsky when I got a surprise call from the producer, Jerry Kennedy of Mercury Records. He worked on my first album at Mercury and said he would love to be on stage with me to receive my award one last time, but he did not fly. Jerry was the musician who had played that nice dobro riff in Jeannie C. Riley's hit "Harper Valley P.T.A.," written by my old friend, Tom T. Hall. He is a great studio musician, songwriter, and producer. He is one of those guys who could wear many hats in the music world and do it all with class. God bless him. He sure was good to me, and he taught me so much about the workings of writing songs and how making music behind the control board was a job well worth taking your time to produce a fine album the fans will want to buy and you can be proud of. The business of making music is half of the job. The other half is promotion and marketing and that's another job.

I recall that, in 1985, I was asked by many other country music stars to fill in on road shows. Now you do not want to get me and Willie and Waylon and guys like David Allen Coe or Johnny Paycheck on the same bill or you had run out of beer before the first set was played. But someone was crazy enough to do just that when I agreed to a gig in Austin, Texas at a new outdoor venue called Southpark Meadows. Kris Kristofferson, Leon Russell, and Johnny Bush were all there, too. When Faron Young showed up, nothing good could come out of that for sure. Faron, who they called "The Singing Sheriff," could work a bottle better than anyone since Lefty. Acting up was just part of his show. A lot of us veteran acts were acting like kids on stage.... behind the stage, too. Some of us never grow up. We were always and forever youthful. Still am.

California Country

I used to perform a lot of dates in California, mainly in Los Angeles, San Francisco, the central coastal area, and in Bakersfield—home to business mogul late Buck Owens, and country music icon Merle Haggard. Buck owned the number one KUZZ radio station and the beautiful Buck Owens's Crystal Palace (museum). He also owned some radio stations in Arizona where his son, Buddy, managed them for him. One day, the mayor of Bakersfield, Harvey Hall, presented me with a Proclamation and the Keys to the city. I told Buck I was going to be participating in the Bakersfield's Veteran's Day Parade, but I did not even have a damn horse to ride on and old Buck said, "that's all-right Johnny! You see that classic Pontiac Grandville of mine stored in the museum, well, you are going to ride in that car." He instructed DJ, Dan Robertson, and Joe Stormont to drive me in the parade. Promotion Manager, Jerry Hufford retrieved the car for me where he had this beautiful white Pontiac Grandville stored so I could ride in it following the Our Lady of Guadalupe Catholic School float. I was performing a Benefit for the Nuns and the children. I also was honored to be Grand Marshall in Bakersfield's Veteran's Day parade. There must have been 40,000 people in attendance. Bakersfield knows how to honor its Veterans with patriotic pride. It is where Congressman Kevin McCarthy lives.

Now this old white 1971 Pontiac Grandville beauty (looks like a Cadillac.) has a massive set of Texas long horns on the front hood, deer horns on the hood, and pistols for door handles. It was gaudy looking like hell, but I was proud to ride in it and wave to the adoring and smiling fans.

An interesting tidbit about this one-of-a-kind show car is Elvis bought the car for his mama, Gladys, but she was disappointed it wasn't pink and didn't want it. Well, Buck did, and the rest is history. Buck bought the fancy car from Nudie Cohn, the tailer who made rhinestone-studded jackets and pants for Buck and his band.

The Manager told me later that Buck never lets anyone drive that car but him. I do believe though I saw a photo with singer, Dwight Yokum in it with Buck when they recorded,

"Streets of Bakersfield." In a way, Buck was my brother from another mother. He and Roy Clark were so hospitable to me when I would do their show, *Hee Haw* ("Pfft You Were Gone"). Since I had done it 8 or 9 times, I knew my being a Mexican gave the writers some new fodder for jokes, but it was light and all in fun. I really did not mind because they were all tasteful jokes, as the show was a family show bent on being funny instead of offensive. I would not have done it if I thought otherwise. I try not to cross the line in situations that could compromise my integrity. Besides, my family keeps me in check and would be the first to tell me so. Remember "The Beverly Hillbillies?" That show cracked me up with Granny and her potions and lotions. Who did not love watching that stereotype show or "Mama's Family?" You were always sure to get good laughs family dynamics in action. How America lost its sense of humor, comedy-wise is a mystery to me. Nothing is more dangerous than losing the ability to laugh and then laugh at yourself. Nothing wrong in wanting things to get back to the way some things were when times were simple and innocent.

When I was bouncing around Los Angeles playing clubs like the Palomino, I would get invited to some great parties along the way. One day, a friend, Michael Trutills, took me to the Playboy mansion (Chicago was the original clubhouse) where I met Barbie Benton, who was Hugh Hefner's squeeze at the time. She was this beautiful and fine playmate who just happened to be a smart girl, very driven to become a star out of Hefner's shadow. If there ever was a party 24/7, it was at Hugh's mansion where you had run into movie stars, sports stars, and guys like me who added a unique perspective to the conversations that ran all night long. I knew if I stayed too long at that place, I would have trouble getting back out on the road. Let me just say it was a wild ride for this country boy.

What can I say about my idol and friend, Merle Haggard? I still choke up knowing he is gone. Merle was a man's man . . . the real deal, and everyone loved him. He impacted my life more than he ever knew. One thing is for sure, I could always show him in my own way, my respect and gratitude as an artist and as my friend. Merle had a harder life than I did. Jail. Prison, but we both lived in poverty as kids and were given our first guitar by an elder brother—Merle had his brother, Lowell, and I had my brother, Andres. In his childhood he lived in a (refrigerator) railroad boxcar that his daddy converted into a house and his mama, Flossie made into a home in Oildale, California.

In 2016, Theresa Spanke co-wrote with Tony Brown a special song for Merle, "The Boxcar Song," that he liked very much, enough to invite Teresa to open and sing her song at the Fox Theater. What an honor.

In 2019, after recording in Bakersfield and on my way to the airport, I requested to visit Merle's newly relocated childhood boxcar home at the Kern County Museum. A thousand memories flooded my mind as I visited his past. It was a sobering feeling moving from room to room where my friend grew up. I missed him looking at his past while reminiscing. We both lost our fathers at an early age. Mine from cancer and his from an aneurysm and a stroke resulting from a prior car accident. Another common bond we shared was family. We both had siblings we could lean on in good and tough times. My family was much larger than his, and Merle had his sister and protector, Lillian, who was also his confidant. Merle would call his sister in the wee hours of the morning to have her listen to the newest song he had just written. The last one is "Kern River Blues." Merle had plenty of reasons to be bitter all his life. But he had turned his life around when he got out of prison and he and I became good friends. Country music was in his blood; I can tell he knew it was mine, too. You could not fool Merle about country music . . . he knew it inside out and he lived it. We may have lived in another state from one another, but we shared our jokes, songs, and smiles across the miles.

We often recorded the same songs because our deliveries (vocally) were similar. We both had hits with "That's The Way Love Goes," which happens to be my second favorite song (written by Lefty Frizzell) and we had done many a-shows together throughout the years. As a kid, I tried to sing like Merle, that smooth voice over a gruff interior always got to me when I was listening to him in the late '60s while working in South Texas at some job I'd been getting paid for. Little did I ever believe I would ever share a stage with the Legend and become friends. But it happened. I cannot tell you how many nights I set up singing Merle's "Sing Me Back Home," trying to match his style. I am still working on it to this day! There are some you cannot imitate, and Merle's style is one of them. Merle set the bar high when it came to country music. And that is a good thing! It gives the younger generation a place to go when looking for inspiration to be better than they are. In time, I developed my own signature style, but not without reminding myself who I was influenced by some of the greatest country music singers in time, including Merle Haggard, Buck Owens, and George Jones.

I remembered Merle telling me the story of seeing Johnny Cash when Johnny did a show at Folsom Prison in 1968. He was in for robbery. Johnny took Merle under his wing when he got out and helped him get some doors opened. Never in my wildest dreams did I ever think I would be a part of a string of country music singers who had lived the jailhouse Blues like Johnny Cash, Merle Haggard, and myself as we had done in our lives. It was a unique fraternity of sorts, but it was what it was, amazing. I also remember Johnny Cash sharing with me that doing that gig at Folsom was biblical, that in the Bible God tells us to feed the hungry, clothe the naked and visit those who are in prison and in need. Cash had done all three and, in my lifetime, I have tried to do the same, give back. Playing benefits for me goes way back to playing the Jerry Lewis Telethon for Muscular Dystrophy and other dates where someone was in need.

In Recent Years

In the past couple of years, I would go back to Nashville for Fanfare, and I would play studio gigs such as Country Road TV, or I would play with those great studio musicians in a "guitar pull" of many of us seasoned stars like Jim Ed Brown, Lynn Anderson, Connie Smith, and Larry Gatlin. But when your time had passed, fanfare was really set up for the new talent. It is where the up-and-coming stars would work the crowds at their booths and sign autographs. I would do it, too, when they wanted me to, but when your time had come and gone, there was not much space left for you and any new talent when you had not had a hit in years. Keep in mind that I am not bitter at all. I had my time in the sun, and it was one hell of a ride. It is kind of amusing and fun to see how the new kids on the block handle that wind of stardom that hits 'em. Some take it to the top and others fall by the wayside after a few hits. It is all about how you manage it. If you cannot, then it handles you.

In the past few years, I have resigned myself to being who I am, a veteran country music singer who feels blessed to still be around. Older stars like Shelly West, Barbara Mandrel, David Frizzell, Jeannie Sealy, and the great Jimmy Capps backing us up with his band all gathered from time to time to show the "youngsters" that our voices are still relevant despite being out of the limelight that had made us stars in the '60s and '70s and onto the '80s and '90s. I was fortunate to be able to still sing during those shows (coliseums and wonderful venues; big and small) and I made it a point to keep off the sauce and put away the smokes long enough to give my voice a rest when I knew I needed to sing my best.

Whenever I got frustrated with life, I would want to go out and do something, anything that was positive. It made me feel like I was paying forward and doing something for the greater good and not for me. I stepped in to help build a new church in 1978 as I recorded a song in half Spanish/half English called "Love Me with All of Your Heart." It is a beautiful love song, one of my favorites and a real crowd pleaser. When I can hit the notes exactly right, it still brings 'em out of their seats!

It took me back to my days when I hit Nashville, and the novelty of my English/Spanish songs were introduced and became a hit.

One last thing before I move on. I was playing Austin City Limits in Austin, Texas during the first years of my fame. Now keep in mind I was becoming a "star", and it was too much for me. I was getting booked on the biggest stages and venues in America and Austin City Limits in 1978 and '79 was fast becoming the must-stop when playing a gig in Austin. I was on stage and the crowd was really getting into my set while the band was spot on when I called up the old Hank Williams classic

"Jambalaya." As we started the song, I got the first verse down, and then, lo and behold, Willie Nelson showed up out of nowhere, grabbed a nearby Stratocaster, and joined in with me. It floored me! I knew and liked Willie, but this was too shocking for me. By this time, he was a real star, doing movies and having duets with musicians in all walks of life, changing Country and Western music into the outlaw movement with Waylon and Kris and Haggard. It was a total surprise to me that he would take the time to come on stage with me. But that was Willie, and it still is to this day. He only cares about music, not fame. A gentleman and a humanitarian to boot. You must respect Willie for that, I do. And that is what makes him the true definition of being a star.

I have heard lately that Willie's slowing down some (like the rest of us). He is 89 as I write this book, and his health keeps him safe at home in Austin, Texas, where he records with his sons in his personal studio. The other day, I heard his son, Lukas, sing and play in the studio and if you close your eyes, Lukas sounds exactly like his father when Willie was young. And I mean exactly! Merle Haggard's sons, Marty, Ben, and Noel also sound just like their late father. Man, I love it when the kids of the old stars get up there and do the very same thing their fathers taught them and had done during their careers. And if my daughter, Aubry wants to continue my torch, well then, so be it. I will be just as proud as Willie and Merle are of their own kids. All I can do is support her all the way and guide her from all the trappings of the country music life of which I know all too well! She is smart enough to know the pitfalls (beauty and fame can be fleeting) of working in the music business. I am sure of that. It is up to me to teach her the rest that no one ever tells you about.

Even though my career has slowed down, quite a bit of my friends in this business have seen in their careers, I still have the same heart desires and drive I have had all along. Your body tells you one thing, but your mind tells you another. You still have the ability but let us be honest, 50 years singing for your supper takes a toll on your vocal cords. Still, my red beating heart ticks and tells me to keep on singing. Recently, I have had trouble with my strumming hand. I have had to see a doctor to look at the ligaments in my hand as the pain from years of playing has finally taken its toll. But like everything else in my life, I am going to fix the problem and keep on strumming if I can. I guess I will live out the songs of my life until I die. I really would not have it any other way. It is who I have been since I was a kid. From the time I picked up that guitar at the age of 8, I have been chasing an elusive dream . . . it was all I could think about was to achieve a seemingly unattainable dream, heart desire, and goal. Why not me? I never dreamed I would live the life I have lived in country music. I really did hit the "big time." All I need now is to remind myself I can keep on singing for my beloved fans as long as they never give up on me. Better yet, I keep on keepin' on, so I never give up on me. Lord knows I pray for contentment in my life. It is a good feeling staying in your own lane doing what is right and helping others when you can. It sure makes me feel good giving while I am living.

In the Name of Charity

"Everyone shall give as he is able, according to the blessing of the Lord your God which He has given you."
– Deuteronomy 16:17

The Johnny Rodriguez Life Enrichment Center was established in the 70s, benefitting the handicapped and impoverished youth in Corpus Christi at the Memorial Coliseum on South Shoreline. I was approached by the director, Ed Lowe, to help the children, and I didn't hesitate to do so because I've always had a soft spot in my heart for kids. I felt even prouder that my celebrity and Renegade's friends jumped on the band wagon with me to perform. They didn't waste any time rolling up their sleeves, committing to show up for the kids. You can't imagine how that makes a man feel knowing we would be getting involved in something bigger than ourselves to serve others in need.

Lives were enriched and changed through all participant's collective and heartfelt efforts. Word got around that there was one hardship a young girl named Maria was having because she did not have a bed. My good friend, Willie, heard of her hardship and anonymously bought a bed for this innocent child. That is the caliber of person Willie is all about. He has a heart of gold like the others who showed up for the kids, not asking anything in return. The Telethon was covered by news reporter Nancy Jo Purdue of Channel 6 TV at the Memorial Coliseum on South Shoreline.

Celebrity guests included Tom T. Hall, Willie Nelson, Dolly Parton, Waylon Jennings, and Charley Pride, who performed on stage. These people have good souls and would do anything for children and their fans. I had lots of fun playing games and interacting with the kids and families for this charity.

Community support and a legion of fans in Corpus Christi were tremendous and could not have been more successful of an event for the children.

Its annual event was held for three years in a row and a lot of money was raised. However, one day, it was sadly brought to my attention that all Texas finest was all in vain because misappropriate of funds was discovered.

Unfortunately, the people who got hurt in the charity were the children. I had no choice but to walk away. What I can say in all honesty, is I had a lot of fun being a part of the Johnny Rodriguez Enrichment Center, because of the kids, fans, community, and artists that came together for a worthy cause. For that, I have no hard feelings or regret, but I do have good memories bridging the participants and community together.

The news scandal eventually died down and had more to do about the organization's director than it did with the volunteers and celebrities who worked hard for the benefit of the children and did not deserve the backlash.

Later, I would participate and sing in the End Hunger Network, Veterans, Law Enforcement, and other benefits for deserving citizens in need and of merit.

Another Benefit that especially hit a soft spot for me was singing for the Nuns and children at Our Lady of Guadalupe Catholic School in Bakersfield, California, in 2000. Those children performed my song, "Ridin' My Thumb to Mexico," for me, and it blew me away.

In 2017, I would do a Benefit for the Montalvo House (a Texas Historic landmark) in Brackettville, Texas which brought back great memories for me. I performed at the Buck Owens Crystal Palace in Bakersfield, California, hosted by Dr. Homer Montalvo, a descendant of the Montalvo family whose non-profit organization is dedicated to the restoration, preservation, and maintenance of the Montalvo house.

Another charity event close to my heart was the Astroworld Festival in Houston, Texas. I have a weakness when it comes to kids and enjoy giving back when I can to support a worthy cause.

I played at the 150th Anniversary of the Wounded Knee uprising. I have always had a special place in my heart for Native Americans and sympathize with them over the atrocities and injustices of ethnic cleansing and forced displacement that were inflicted on them at the hands of fellow Americans.

I am an advocate of Native Americans who were subjected to ethnic cleansing and forced displacement. And who can ever forget the atrocities of the Cherokee nation, The Trail of Tears, and others nationwide? History says it so. I do not like to get political, but sometimes there is an appropriate time to use the platform you are given when it concerns humanity for the greater good.

In the late 1970s or early '80s, I was doing a show in Anchorage, Alaska, for missing children of America. I drove the lead dog sled of mushers at IDITAROD, an annual Trail Sled Dog Race done in early March . . . I thought the slogan would make a cool Koozie.

* * * * *

Chapter 22 T is for Texas, and B is for Bakersfield

"There is no limit to the amount of good you can do if you don't care who gets the credit." – Ronald Reagan

In 2017, I began to think about one last-ditch effort to record another album. I was looking for someone who still believed in my talent and felt I had something left to offer. It had to be someone who thought I still had the desire, passion, and deliberate intention to create music before deciding to move on down the line.

When I put out feelers for such a producer, Rick "Reno" Stevens (ANR Records) came along. Rick is and has been a producer, reputable singer-songwriter, and guitarist in Bakersfield, California, since his early teens. His production credits include working with Lorrie Morgan when he lived in Nashville. When I explained that I wanted to do something new and fresh, Rick was on board. He produced with Bakersfield studio musicians who pride themselves on the Bakersfield Sound. Executive Producer, Pauline Vega mentioned the idea of adding traditional mariachi music in the mix making it a bilingual album; it would be a novelty of sorts making me come full circle providing opportunity to return to my humble beginnings where I rose like a phoenix singing in Spanish. I have always wanted to get back to my Hispanic roots, the music of my people, and sing some down-home mariachi music completely, with dueling violins, stand-up bass guitar, and some Mexican horns thrown in for effect.

I told Rick that it was time to bring in some extra fire power in the studio, something to get the new CD and a little something extra for my fan base. At this time, I had spoken to some old friends who were keen about coming to Triple Seven Recording studio to lay down tracks to make the CD something the public would want to buy after some 20 years of me not being in the studio. It sure had been a while and I wanted this CD to reflect the signature work I had done in my past, along with the new. When I shared my idea with Rick he was thrilled and wanted the same thing as me. We calibrated and collaborated effortlessly and that is an essential ingredient to achieve any kind of success.

I performed a lot in the Bakersfield area for many years and I liked playing there from time to time. Buck Owens had invited me (before and after) the times I had been there hanging around with Merle Haggard, pickin' and grinning.' In many ways, Bakersfield looks a lot like South Texas where I come from and since it has a large Hispanic population and culture, it felt like home in many ways, not to mention it is widely known for its country music. Guess, you can call it the "last, little, small town." I do.

Anyway, it was arranged. An old friend and I were to sing a duet. I remember feeling nostalgic and moved at the same time seeing my friend, Tanya Tucker. She looked beautiful as ever wearing her pink hair for a great cause (cancer for a friend). She walked into Triple Seven Studio with all the confidence and a flair that I remembered her having. We were to sing a duet called "A Game That I Can't Win," written by actor Dennis Quaid. The album would be called, *Building Bridges: A Beyond the Interview Box Set.* Now this was 2019 when Tanya's career was hitting some high marks. In 2020, she won a double Grammy Award after many years out of the limelight, and her star was beginning to shine once again. "A Game That I Can't Win" is a traditional country song about unrequited love complete with the same rhyme, chord progression and meter as many of my old hits. I had not done a duet since my time with Charley McClain when we did a song called, "I Hate the Way I Love It." I remember hoping that duet would match the duets of the old country that Loretta and Conway and George and Tammy had done. When Tanya sang and we blended our voices together in that Bakersfield studio, I knew we had something special; I could feel it in my entire body and could not have been any prouder. She was on top of her game, like the professional she is. It was old school country and I believed given an ounce of airplay, it just might be a hit. Tanya deserves it, and Dennis and I would love it.

Now this was important for me! Having my "sister" from another mother, Tanya Tucker, in the studio with me for the first time made my day, it was something we had wanted to do all our musical lives since we were literally kids in the early '70s. Actor and musician Dennis Quaid came into the studio to boot. Now Dennis is also a Texas boy. Tanya is from Seminole, I am from Sabinal and Dennis is from Houston, so Texas was well represented on this CD, and it does not get any better than that. There definitely was a theme going on there. "T" is for Texas Red Dirt and "B" is for the *Bakersfield Sound* and Twang.

Dennis is not just a great actor, he is also an exceptionally great guy and musician who plays guitar, and piano. He has his own band, Dennis Quaid, and the Sharks, and writes songs as easy as anyone can. Who knew? He contributed two songs to my CD that he and I sung as a duet together. Dennis told me he got the idea for "Montana Hills" from a movie set his brother, Randy, was in called *Missouri Breaks* starring Marlon Brando and Jack Nicholson. Ironically it was about horse rustlers.

I wrote a couple of songs for the album, one with my friend Tony Ramey, "Don't Expect To Love Me All The Time," which is personal to me. He and I got together and talked about women and relationships. The song is also about unrequited love. We both agreed that as creatives we both can be moody, cantankerous, and plain ornery. A warning to those who still want to go down that road with us, and what to expect if they do. It is a testimony to the strength of women who have loved and cared for artists and stuck by them. Tony has a CD *Under the Gun* and Soul Survivor coming. He has written for well-known artists including Willie Nelson, *The Bible, the Bottle, and the Gun*; George Strait, and Trisha Yearwood.

And to top it all off, I proudly brought in my talented daughter, Aubry, into the studio to lay down a track we do together all the time, "We Believe in Happy Endings." I was excited about collaborating with my daughter and always enjoyed singing with her on stage or in the studio every chance we got. Aubry also lent her vocals on Quaid's two songs he wrote, "Montana Hills," and "A Game That I Can't Win," and one I co-wrote with Tony Ramey, *Don't Expect To Love Me*.

As the session progressed, I knew I had something special working with Rick Stevens as Producer, Pauline Vega as

Executive Producer and Pariecee McGriff as our Engineer. Like a song in perfect harmony, the Rodriguez A-team fit perfectly and was as good as any Nashville studio production. I had not realized how much I missed being back in the studio creating music. I felt like a man without water in the desert, thirsty for more. It was magical . . . a one-for-all and all-for-one attitude. Sometimes, you do not get that in a big corporate-sponsored studio. It was a dream come true and the CD is set for mid-November 2023 release date. Of course, setbacks can happen with circumstances behind the scenes, as they usually do.

I was in pure bliss with these two heavyweights in the studio with me. Thank you, God, everything in your glory. I just kept shaking my head, trying to keep my cool at the thought of this CD becoming my life's latest, most diverse, and unique recording. The studio band was top-notch, too. We had Skip Edwards, keyboard; Jay Dee Maness, steel guitar; Vern Monnett, electric/gut string guitar; Neil Morales, drums; David Wulfekuehler, drums; Mario Carboni, piano; Kyle Appleton, acoustic guitar; Chad Watson; Ernie Lewis, fiddle; and David Varnado, violin. Even Rick Stevens got in on the action by playing acoustic guitar and adding some background vocals, along with Tanya Tucker and Aubry Rodriguez.

Things were falling in place, and momentum was taking shape. I felt good knowing the angels were on our side. The musical arrangement could not have come at a better time or gotten any better than this.

My heart skipped a beat when Pauline and Rick brought in Bakersfield's best mariachi singer, Daisy Sanchez, who had formerly opened for El Rey de la música ranchera, the late singer Vicente Fernández, *Chente.*

Accompanying Daisy was the infamous Mariachi San Marcos, a full backup band that filled the studio with the sounds I had heard on the radio in that four-room house I grew up in as a kid in South Texas. The players were what you want—professionals to perfection. I knew it when they came in and set up and we began to practice. Not to mention the group went beyond the call of duty helping with translation and music arrangement: Manager Mauro Laris, guitar; the late Luis F. Laris Sr., bass guitar; David Pena, trumpet; and Carmen Dias, violin. The musician's push was magical and accommodating. There is nothing like the feel of a real mariachi band in all its force. And they do not need any microphones to fill a room. I felt like I had died and finally went to musical heaven as Bakersfield did not disappoint me with its professionalism, hospitality, and newfound friendship.

My latest album is a lifelong dream of mine that Rick Reno Stevens produced, starring Dennis Quaid and Tanya Tucker, who made it come alive. I sure hope my fans love it as much as I do. Country and mariachi music are my two loves, my two passions in reverence to my Hispanic heritage and traditional roots. That is why my album is dedicated to my beloved late mother, Isabel, songs of my mother, *Canciones de mi Madre*. Mariachi genre is mexican dance music played by trumpets, guitars, violins, and vocals with *Gritos*.

My new country and mariachi CD is my gift to my fans for your continued support all these years. From your warm greetings and generous and thoughtful gifts, showing up to my shows, driving and flying to my shows, listening, and dancing to my songs, promoting me through kind words and buying merchandise. My sincere gratitude comes by way of Texas from my heart to yours.

I had a lot of firsts happen for me when I was guest producer for recording artist, Amber Digby, on her upcoming album, *Heroes, Mentors & Friends*, on Heart of Texas Records. Tommy Detamore produced that album, and I was asked to lend my vocals on it which brought back many memories of my days with Jerry Kennedy and Roy Dea at Mercury Records on my very first album. Singing "You Go Around" and playing on an album is one thing; co-producing it is another. That is why so many artists will not try to do both at the same time. It is a lot of challenging work!

So, I keep on keeping on. I was in the studio in 2019 beginning a new CD and then it was back on the road again. As I write these words, there is a vaccine out right now to contain or eradicate it so that us musicians can get back on stage. In the words of my friend, Dolly Parton, "I don't do politics." I make it a rule to not discuss politics or religion either, for business reasons, alone. Offending one fan, is one fan too many.

Relationships are more important to me than anything else. That is my own opinion and business stance.

2020 Setback

2020 has been one of total chaos for the music world, especially the live music scene. On the bright side, it has also been a time of reflection for me. I have been able to stand still long enough to explore hidden and repressed feelings inside of me that I wasn't able to feel or process while I was moving all the time on the road. Yes, the light bulb has gone off . . . Country singer Tim McGraw's "Live Like You Were Dying" sings it best. Give it a listen as does Tanya Tucker's newest release, *Bring My Flowers Now (While I'm Living)*. Two powerful message songs featuring Brandi Carlile who she collaborated with in 2019 and a single, "Ready As I'll Never Be." While I am mentioning great songs, Dennis Quaid has a good one, too, "On My Way to Heaven," which Dennis wrote and dedicated to his late mother, Juanita. If you are letting circumstances get you down right now—and we all do—I ask you to get some quiet time and listen to those three songs. You will gain perspective and be glad that you did. As you have helped me over the years, I am taking the liberty to help you get through this isolation period. Some of us are handling it differently (better or worse) than others but take it from someone who knows about regret struggling and trying every day to forget. Remember, if you believe, any situation can only get better and I am confident in saying, "This, too, shall pass." I am thankful a great song comes along now and then and reminds us to choose love and life during challenges as these, because God is Love.

From the time I was playing at Garner State Park for my friends as a kid to just recently singing as a veteran, I have never had anything stop me from booking and playing for my fans. This COVID-19 pandemic has hurt me and all other musicians who love to play and sing out in public. It has almost killed us, musically. I know it has killed hundreds of musical venues that rely on us traveling musicians to make money. I have managed to do a few shows in 2020 but keeping myself well and alive as is first and foremost the safety of my fans is more important to all of us. I have encouraged everyone during those shows to take all precautions to stay healthy and continue to listen to country music wherever they see and hear it. We are America and we will get through it. I have faith in God to assure me of this. Not to undermine, the seriousness of a pandemic and death, but I have been through and seen worse, that is for sure.

I have been trying to cut back on my smoking. I still roll up my own cigarettes with Buglar tobacco and I still take a nip or two from the various libations that show up, but I have been trying to take better care of my health as I approach 70 years old. Having this new album CD coming out along with his 2021 along with this book, well, it looks like my future has never looked brighter for me to live it. I sure hope to see you at one of the shows I am lining up for the new year. When this pandemic is over and at least under control and we can hit the road again, be looking for me! My booking agent at Third Coast Talent Agency, Carrie-Debbie Moore, can line up dates for where and when I can come to see you near your hometown. I am not through with performing for my fans and friends yet. You will be the first to know when that curtain comes down.

Now, when I was coming up in this musical world, music videos were becoming the thing to do in the '70s. I had done some videos for my hits such as "Run for the Border" and a few of my songs such as "You Can Say that Again." I do not know when we will do a video for this new CD, but Dennis Quaid and I have kicked around the idea of videotaping his "Montana Hills" song he wrote, that we both sang a duet. It is incredible. When that happens, you can bet I will do it. First and foremost, I just want to get the music out there for my fans to have a listen to what I still have to say. Now that I am one of the last of the old country music singers of yesterday, I want the young market to know that they can still listen to what true country music is really like. And, if anyone of the rising musicians are incline to perform a duet with me, I am more than happy to oblige. I believe the duet I have done with Tanya will bear that out. "A Game That I Can't Win" is true-blue country music. I sure hope you will take a listen. And if we are lucky, maybe Tanya and I might take the stage together in a few of the concerts planned in

2023. Miracles and wonders happen when you least expect them. Wouldn't it be a hoot to perform with Texas's best superstars?

I am learning from today's youth and what talent they bring to the country music industry, regardless of whether it is the same music as mine or not. I feel a sense of pride and responsibility when my young daughter asks me for musical advice or wants to learn and sing my bilingual songs. Guess, I am showing my age because I have learned to just appreciate music of all genres, period. Just as I have learned and been taught and inspired by country music greats, including Tanya and most recently Dennis, who have taught many something of value listening to their music. You would be a fool not to observe, listen, and learn. Still, let us be mindful that we are all placed on earth to teach and help each other, be it through our songs, lyrics or spoken word.

Home Is Where I Lay My Head

So many fans have asked where do I live? Well, I live wherever I hang my hat, remember! You do know I sing a song called "Desperado," written by the Eagles? No really, I have an apartment in San Antonio near my long-time friend Rick Gipprich's place and it is perfect for picking and singing and having get-togethers with old friends. We even let some gringos in for added color. When my other old friend Ray Koenning, who owns a Texas ranch, offered me a place to get away, I took him up on it and I keep a nice place there. There is no way you will ever get as close to complete solitude as you do when you are on a South Texas ranch, out on the edge of nowhere where the coyotes and bobcats sing at night while your BBQ fire cooks a meal. You can find a setting right out of a John Wayne movie. It does not get any better than that with exotic animals roaming the open space where privacy is at its best. Trust me, I like it that way. It really is and reminds me of God's country and I love spending time there. I am in Texas.

While on the ranch, I play, write, and sing to amuse myself and pass time. I used to ride horses but at my age, they tend to ride me. It is so beautiful on the ranch that I will shoot some arrows (archery), or photograph different sunsets and scenery of nature's beauty, life in the West. I'm thinking about putting together a calendar of sorts displaying my photos I've captured while on this exotic ranch and in the wilderness. Too, there is nothing prettier than staring at a clear blue or star-lit Texas sky at night. It is my way of sharing natural surroundings, shooting the west as my eye sees it. It is what I live, day-to-day. I live a laid-back life when I am down here with no one around, just me, myself, and I. Every now and then I hang out with the ranch hands, who slaughter a pig, deer, or game meat. I also practice my Karate moves by the moonlight, and during the day I throw my knives and hatchets at these huge tree stumps I have set up. I do not need any video games to keep me company to pass the time. Long ago, I decided to live a simple life. I have been living a simple life for all my 70 years on this Earth. That just might be a recipe for happiness, peace and harmony living in God's country. I only know it works for me and keeps me grounded and balanced from being on the road and touring.

I believe in happy endings. It's true . . . I keep my life the way of a drifter and nomad of sorts, a "Desperado," if you will. And I describe me living in the past as a Desperado, not as a desperate person, but one who lived much of his life in despair. Today, I wake up with a smile on my face almost every morning providing there is not a new ache or pain in this old body. I sit outside taking in nature's vitamin D and I look forward to the day with enthusiasm and thankfulness. I am not trying to be poetic or anything, but I really do prefer living and making a wish under the Texas twinkling stars. My humble opinion, they are the brightest and the best anywhere around. I have never had a problem getting a place to sleep from my days as a kid camping at state parks, to living on a friend's couch during my first days in Nashville, to the peaceful places I live in today. Look up a picture of a "Fortunate Son" in the dictionary and you will see a picture of me, Johnny Rodriguez, the last of the country music drifters that old Hank sang about way back when.

America has been good to people like me. Sure, I have had my ups and downs, that's life, but America is the only place to be. There is a song by Brooks and Dunn called "Only in America." That song is my life. No matter our skin color or where we come from, America gives us the chance . . . it does not matter what profession we choose; we all get a chance. It really is about talent, attitude, and character over skin color. I often say, what God gives you is your gift, what you make out of yourself, is your gift to God. Sure, seems like it is someone else who is making a big deal out of it just to make a buck. I think we need to do a little more work and worry less. How 'bout you? I have a philosophy that keeps me in my own lane, "Don't sweat the small stuff. Life is what you make of it. Do not be anxious. Just go out and make your own dream come true. If you think you can, you can. In the words of labor leaders Cesar Chavez and Delores Huerta, "Yes, We Can! Si Se Puede!"

I have had so many ask me what is it like being a country music star? Well, it is fun, seriously. But it is not everything and it should not be. I have watched my once super charged career come down over the years to what it is today, and I have learned it has happened to be the best there ever was in this business. Johnny Cash, Merle Haggard, George Jones, and I saw our careers come to a point of no radio play of our songs as the new and upcoming talent took over. In time, the same thing will happen to the great artists of today—George Strait, Garth Brooks, and Taylor Swift when the following string of talent comes along to take their place in the music world. It is the cycle of life, and you get to decide how you respond. Me, I stay detached from situations that I have no control of. I am smart enough to know that I can only control my own self. I accept it. Take the path of least resistance, and live out my life staying true to me, myself, and my music. I've reached a point in my life to go with the flow as I have neither the energy nor the desire to swim upstream anymore. You will not find this man on a set with an open shirt, a fancy hair style and an electric guitar trying to be something I am not. That is not me. Like Charley Pride sang years ago, "I'm Just Me." Well, that is what I am, just a small-town boy who made it to fame and fortune and managed to keep his head on his shoulders through it all and stay alive so far. God is not through with me yet, so I will keep singing with a song in my heart. I may have fallen hard off a horse, a time or two, but we are not over yet. My motto: We are passing through.

* * * * *

Chapter 23 We Believe in Happy Endings

"Life is not measured by the number of breaths we take, but by the moments that take our breath away."
– Maya Angelou

Over the past two or three years, I have been getting recognition in the country music industry. Country Music Association of Texas Directors, Mary Minter, and the late Troy Bates have worked hard and supported my musical endeavors to be the recipient of the 2020/2021 CMA of Texas "Living Legend" and "Top of Texas" Award in Lubbock, Texas (2019, 2020). Now, this honor means a lot to me for two reasons. One because of its founder, the late James White who I hold in high esteem and owner (along with his wife, Annetta), of Austin's famous honky tonk, *Broken Spoke*.

They both were good people dedicated to preserving Texas dance halls and country music, a traditional and special way of life. In prior years, the two always greeted me warmly and made me feel at home in their Western hospitality. I believe my photo, with many other singers, still hangs on the wall.

The other reason the CMA of Texas award means so much to me is that I am standing in the company by my fellow Texans such as Willie Nelson, Lefty Frizzell, Jim Reeves, Roger Miller, Marty Robbins, Tex Ritter, Kenny Rogers, Gene Watson, Paula Nelson, and Ray Price.

Lastly, I just want to add that I respect what the organization stands for promoting and preserving country music's legacy while representing musicians in the business. Too, there is no greater feeling for a musician than winning the esteem and recognition of your peers.

Carrie Moore of Third Coast Talent Booking Agency out of Nashville, Tennessee (Carrie and Debbie) is still with me, booking me in the venues which I am sure will revive after the mandated closing through 2021.

As I write this book, it is hard for me to fathom that I have been doing this music scene for all these years, a span of five decades. I have seen a lot of things; some I should not have seen and some I had no control over. And the stars I have met along that same path are the "who's who" of country music of all time. I have shared the stages of the Americas with great country music stars I only dreamed about. Never in my wildest dreams did I believe I would share any stage with my heroes. Meeting and playing with Merle Haggard and George Jones had to be the most surreal experiences of my life.

As a young Mexican boy growing up loving country music in South Texas, I would listen to these two men sing and try to learn their phrasing and deliveries. It was pure country that will not soon be matched by anyone that I see coming up the ranks of today's country music stars. There are some out there, but to be real country, they are going to have to write the songs of love, lack, yearning, deceiving, drinking, and fooling around, and happy love songs where the boy meets and gets the girl. They are going to have to have the bare-knuckles instrumentation that Hank Sr. had on stage, forever supporting the songs without playing over the song. When you get away from all of that, you are not country. Keep it simple and sing your story... you'll keep 'em coming back for more!

We all face addictions and vices and fight off demons in our lives. Some eat too much, some gossip too much, some gamble too much, and some have sex too much. Some abuse and do others wrong all the time. Such is life. I'm not saying it's all good or bad, but we are on a life journey until we can meet in the middle. For me, it was about fighting addictions and the demons that sounded like me all the way around and not feeling good enough.

I co-wrote a song about this battle in *Don't Expect To Love Me All The Time*, with my friend and songwriter, Tony Ramey. Good enough to and compared to who? None of it matters. I am here to tell you... you are enough. It does not matter what other people say or think about you. It matters what you think of yourself. I have spent a lifetime punishing myself and figuring that one out when I was good enough, all along. Just be yourself and be humble and stay kind. It's key. Tim McGraw sings this amazing song best, *Humble and Kind.* I like hearing him sing it in Spanish, too. Proud of him for that and now others are copying the right cat. Being born out of poverty or of color is not a curse, but it is if you rehearse it in your mind over and over.

Another song that gets me is Alan Jackson's, "The Older I Get." What matters is what you think of yourself. Tell yourself, tell your children who they really are in your eyes, because you cannot expect anyone else to tell you or them the truth. Breaking barriers of poverty, skin color, and demons is not any excuse. For me, using the God-given talent I was fortunate to have in my life—and then getting rich and famous while just a kid became too much for me. That shot to stardom became my demon. The music industry afforded me a lifestyle; one that came with pros and cons, but mostly privileges of materialism, friendships, and opportunities. It is true to an extent, "there is no business-like show business."

They say you must pay your dues in this music business before you taste stardom and the riches that come with it. I paid my dues all in two years of reaching Nashville. I have read stories about so many who came to Nashville, bounced around the city and its clubs for 10 to 20 years and never scratched the surface of fame and fortune. I guess the saddest part of that is they were probably just as talented as me and others like Johnny Cash and George Jones.

That can only prove it takes a lot more than talent to make it in the world of country music. You have got to have a little bit of luck and a whole lot of being in the right place at the right time. I say these things about my success not to brag, but to let you know how thankful I am for the life I have led. Have faith in you and in God. Be grateful, as am I and will be for the rest of my life.

Regrets? Of course! I could write a book on those alone. I often wonder why I am still here, and others are not. I guess God will call me when the time is right. For now, I am just going to do what He has called me to do: play guitar and sing until my last breath. I believe that God blessed me with talent to use the instruments of my voice and guitar to connect with others. For all my faults, I cannot see anything wrong with doing just that! God sees the good in me to serve him the best way I can give him praise and glory through singing my country songs, in His name. To some, I might be called the Latin King of Country, but there is only one king. Jesus Christ, my savior.

From the beginning to now . . .We believe in happy endings of any kind and anything that has ever come my way. When I count my blessings, I am most thankful to God for these... My ex-wives. My kids. My family. My friends. My fans. And now you, my readers. All these gifts bestowed on me give me happiness still today. And if you ever meet me at one of my shows wherever that might be, know the greatest happiness I have ever known on this Earth was playing music and singing for you.

While you were sitting in the audience, I was feeling your heart and that is why it was easy for me to sing with all my heart *gusto* to yours. Just know that my appreciation of your love, applause, kind words, and support over the years has sustained me. I not only survived but thrived because of you. And if God has a choir up there in Heaven, I sure hope He has a spot for your amigo (without an ego) so that when it is my time to go, I will be happy for the rest of eternity.

New Chapter in My Life

Back on the ranch where I live, my amigos, Alex Fox and cowboy Craig of Bandera, will be helping me to train my longhorn steers, a black one, and a white one... Sol y Sombra means sun and shade. Alex and Craig both live in Bandera, Texas (the hill country). When they're done, my longhorns will be more approachable to others.

The greatest part of this story is there are no public appearances, just me living in the middle of a pasture of cows, longhorns, and other exotic animals roaming and running wild. I have seen more Bald and Golden Eagles on the ranch than most in the wild. I love the sight of it all. It gives me peace living a simple life. I've lived the so-called good life and met people from every place imaginable. Do I miss it? Yes and no. There's something to be said about being a recluse, voluntarily or not. Buck Owens, as did actor Marlon Brando, became one later in his life. I've had my taste of "The glamour life," and I can testify that it does not equate to happiness. Fame is attractive and intoxicating, and with all that comes with it, like money, it is lonely without someone special to share their riches and rewards.

There are no gigs, no fans, no applause. Just a cell phone, TV, and me. I have a lot of time to get to know me where my thoughts are mine and mine alone. There's the good news. I'm tuned in to my radio frequency in my head, where the law of attraction begins with me. Tuning in to me for the first time, turns me on. I'm a new me. It's my journey home to be the best I can be with me. I realize now I was never in control. Once the dust settles and you learn from your mistakes, the best thing to do is keep moving forward.

Reflecting on my life experiences has led me back home on the road to finding myself and what gives me peace and happiness. My goal and inspiration for the longest time has always been to give a great show to make my fans happy. And now that I am semi-retired, I am at peace and happy now. And I wouldn't trade it for the world.

Writing in my book makes me recollect the difficult and hard times and the celebrations of 70 years of my life. Still, they were the best times if I am to be honest with my soul searching that has brought me to this place. If I had known then what I know now, I would have written this book a long time ago. I have no idea if my book will give hope and encouragement to a handful of readers or not, I will be thankful if it helps one. I never once cared for the star treatment, but I always wanted to sing my best to my fans. Today, I much rather be a light in my reader's eyes if my book shines a light or means anything to others than from the stage.

Today, I am practicing and learning how to play the harmonica on my own, and I'm enjoying it a lot. It's always good to learn something new…stimulation is good for the brain and all-around mental health. My friend Brian Black (Clint's brother) said he would teach me anytime I was ready, and you know he's an excellent harmonica player. He and his brother, Clint, are talented musicians who I've performed with on stage.

What are my plans... well, I can't see me slowing down any being I'm blessed to still be healthy? Music is always in me to do something creative, still, so I'm still open. Besides, I'm always pitched to work on some project or another, so you never know. I may take on a venture in the future.

In June 2022, I returned to Nashville to support my daughter, Aubry Rodriguez, who was performing in the Sons and Daughters of the Legends sponsored by Third Coast Talent Agency, Carrie, and Debbie Moore, who are popular entertainers themselves. I always enjoy singing on stage with Aubry when we can. Our favorite duet is “We Believe in Happy Endings.” Everything went great and it felt good to see everyone’s faces. I’m very proud of my daughter and all she has achieved in her life.

My friend, Rodney Collins and wife, Jennifer successfully own the bars, The Troubador and the Music City Bar and Grill in downtown Nashville. I am very appreciative of Rodney and his brothers, Ron and Richard Collins, Steve Smith of Tootsies, and Al Ross, for their help and friendship during my stay in Nashville, 2022–2023. It was supposed to be a short visit and here I am still enjoying my stay in Nashville. The two men are masterminds when it comes to building businesses. I’m impressed with their creativity, integrity, and other endeavors they’ve got going on in the future…in my book that makes them Nashville’s best movers and shakers to come along.

* * * * *

Chapter 24 A Hand on My Shoulder

"For God so loved the world that He gave His only begotten Son, that whoever believes in Him should not perish but have everlasting life."
– John 3:16

Spiritual Reveal

Christmas Eve, December 24, 1995 – I would spend this holiday evening in a solemn mood, watching a Christmas movie gift, *Addams Family Values*, from Lana Nelson, with Randy Willis at his Austin home.

Within an hour of finishing the movie, Lana Nelson called and invited me and Randy to Willie's home for Christmas Eve.

It was a cold and calm Christmas Eve. When I shared Lana's invitation with Randy, he said, "Sure, but first, I must ask you a question that's been on my mind for a long time. Christmas is a good time to ask it."

"Johnny, are you born again?" This is a question I've been asked for most of my musical life. My reply probably took my friend back and led to a spiritual marathon on Christmas Day that lasted for hours.

Surprisingly, I shared about myself as a young boy, raised a Catholic, and served as an altar boy. Randy replied, "You have religion, but do you have Jesus." He explained many people have just enough religion to inoculate them from knowing Jesus.

As an adult, I told the story of a shopping experience I experienced with a good buddy, Donald Sweat, who worked at a swank men's retail store, Alamo of Nashville, on Lower Broadway.

This business sold flashy clothes and I'd buy lots of stylish shirts in different colors if I liked one style, spending a fortune on stage clothes. Donald was my teen-age friend since our Garner Park days, and he was always a good friend to me. I liked seeing him knowing he would witness Jesus to me every single time we'd meet face-to-face. He was patient too; lending me his ear when I needed one. He was not judgmental, but always attentive and kind. I had money in my pocket, so I wanted to splurge and buy new clothes. Texas Ranger Joaquin Jackson was accompanying me, and I had money in my pocket to burn.

I had missed Donald's friendship and asked him if he'd like to go on the road with me, but he declined saying his life was headed in another direction and explained he had just accepted Jesus as his personal Savior. He began witnessing to me about accepting Jesus as my Lord and Savior.

At the time, I obliged but merely was going through the motions. I confessed with my mouth to appease my friend, but my heart was not in it. I often reminisce about all the kids that I worked and performed with and played around with at Alamo Village and in my youth. Those were great times for me, and I will always think of them all as my college Alumni because of the bond and personal growth that took place between us.

I admitted to Randy that later in life, I accepted Jesus Christ, and I meant it. I noticed whenever I accepted Jesus in my heart; my life would drift back on the right path, and I would feel good about me. I would get a feeling of peace and contentment that brought me closer to Him. I used to think I was lucky in life…now I know better. Anyone that really knows me knows I am not a religious man but make no mistake I believe in God and know Jesus as my Savior. I knew it then as I know it now.

It is an unknown fact that I have a Prayer Warrior, known as "Dee Dee" (Carmen Cordova of Ignacio, Colorado) who tells anyone who will ask, "I pray daily for all my prayer children, and Johnny is a special soul because he believes in the power of prayer and what it could do for his loved ones. I canvas my prayers for Johnny and his entire loved ones for good health, happiness, and peace, in Jesus' name."

I will be the first to say I practice meditation to quiet my mind, to be positive, and to live by my mantra—to live in the moment. Living in the past serves no one and is a complete waste of time. Trust me, I know! Besides, I enjoy my quiet time in the morning, soaking in some sun and letting in that good old fashion vitamin D. It is in my solitude where I gain my greatest strength and come to know me and God best. I have no problem going to church but find for the most part I enjoy talking to God one-on-one, best these days. I never pray for myself because it makes me happy to put other's needs above my own. I'm able to give back the lion's share to those in need.

It would be another three years later that another marathon-spirited session would take place. This time, it was the death of my mother, Isabel who died in May 1998. It is a wound that still hurts deeply, so I think of the happy times most.

My faith is simple... have a leap of faith and keep on keeping on and choose love and life. My passion and purpose in life are to stay alive and well and have a level of gratitude. Living in the flow and bliss line. Follow the yellow brick road. I am not a superstitious nor a religious man, but I am spiritual because I believe in God and accept Jesus as my savior.

That's What Friends Are For

"Be still and know that I am God."
– Proverbs 46:10

In 1979, I came across another good friend, Billy Ray McNair, who was working at the Alamo Restaurant in Arkansas where we got to visit and reminisce some. My band was having a bite to eat, and I was on my tour bus when my friend joined me. I shared with my friend that I was going through a rough patch in my life getting a divorce and doing drugs that were taking a toll on me. My buddy listened then witnessed the word to me about accepting Jesus as my Lord and Savior. At the time, there was no pretending. I did accept Jesus Christ into my life and meant it... every word. R.I.P. buddy.

Honorable Mention

There are two ladies who I met in the country music industry that I admire and think about today. They are singers Jeannie C. Riley and Connie Smith, wife of Marty Stuart. Jeannie was well-known for her Harper Valley PTA hit song and Connie for both her country and gospel hit songs. We became friends as both are devout Christians who aren't afraid to witness to me face-to-face. They have no way of knowing how much they moved me with their words of faith and wisdom whenever I'd see them. They may have thought their words were falling on deaf ears, but I can attest they were not.

Many times, Jeannie would show up to a show of mine and after she would witness to me. We'd get to talking about matters of the heart that I enjoyed listening to very much. I found her to be spiritual and with the presence of Jesus in her heart. Jeannie, thank you for your soothing and inspiring words and all you do in Jesus' name. I was listening to you the whole time.

I respect Connie, too, for following her heart when her family, spirit, and religious beliefs were calling—she chose all three. Lucky for us because she recorded gospel albums, including spiritual showstoppers, "How Great Thou Art" and "Peace in the Valley." I appreciate and thank these two God-fearing and loving ladies not only for their music, but for caring enough to share the word or song of Jesus when I needed to hear it most. They didn't have to, but they did. God bless these ladies.

Deep Dive for Our Lady

In Acapulco Bay, Mexico, near the island of La Roqueta, the statue, Virgin of Guadalupe (Virgen de los Mares Acapulco), is submerged approximately 90 feet down in the ocean. She is also considered the Empress of the Americas from Chile to Canada and can be seen some days when the water is not stirred up.

I anxiously scuba dived deep into the ocean water and kissed the statue, and then came back up to surface. That was a personal experience for me being the statue is more than a religious icon to Catholics everywhere. It has to do with my Mexican identity and faith that not everyone gets... she symbolizes everything from motherhood to feminism to social justice. Honestly, she has more to do with the way I was raised and trained in the church than anything else. In my youth, I had to go to catechism to learn about our Catholic teachings to receive sacraments. I was being trained to be a soldier of God in Baptism, First Holy Communion, Eucharist, confirmation, reconciliation, anointing of the sick, and Marriage.

My religious training has always been in the back of my mind and has gotten me through a lot of hard times when all I had was my faith. Later in the evening, I went over to a bar and sang with the Mariachis. That was a fitting thing for me to do … singing mariachi music is something I always like doing when I get the chance. I was in celebration mode feeling uplifted by our Lady's promise of love, mercy, protection, and deliverance. Our Lady of Guadalupe is credited with bringing many blessings and miracles to everyone worldwide.

I stayed at the Acapulco Princess Hotel, a resort hotel where I spent my honeymoon with my first wife, Linda. Here's where all the rich and famous people visit and participate in the ambiance and food. Howard Hughes lived on the top floor while we were there.

I remember they had the best breakfast and quality Tequila at the resort. Randy Willis later owned a home on the ocean near the Princess Hotel. He sold it years later when kidnappings became a treat.

A Turn In The Sun Movie

In 1979, I recorded and released a country gospel that I wrote, "A Hand On My Shoulder." It is also a song that my good friend, Kelly Kenning, recommended to me to a television producer, David Von Roehm, for a movie, *A Turn In The Sun*, a Kerry Wallum Production and Luck Tales Production.

I'm proud to say that my friend, Kelly wrote eight songs for the movie and received in 2017 the TCMA for "Christian Country Songwriter of the Year," In 2019, he received CMA "Cowboy Western Music Song of the Year" and "Album of the Year" for *A Turn In The Sun* from CMA of Texas. In 2020, he received the award "Songwriter of the Year" from CMA of Texas, and Christian Country Single of the Year for "Bible on My Dash" from the TCMA.

The movie is a pilot, but it will be a good movie to see when it comes out. The movie shares a faith-based message that everyone will enjoy. The following year, I received the CMA of Texas Awards: "Living Legend" 2020 and "Top of Texas."

My Love, My Passion... My Trusty Guitar

Long story short, good-bye to my trusty friend, if you will... my guitar. It has been music to my ears and has always provided me comfort for the pure joy of strumming it. To be honest, it's been good too, for my mental and emotional well-being. It attracted, bonded, and opened doors for me more than anything or anyone could. It built bridges of friendship and was always a great confidence builder for me. I can't tell you how many hours of practice I would put into it to perfect my skill... way more than 10,000 hours, I am sure. I paid my dues and made the sacrifice to master playing sometimes with bleeding hands and callouses but playing still gave me an elated feeling.

I have been blessed by God to play my guitar for most of my life. Unfortunately, Rheumatoid Arthritis has locked-in my fingers where I can't strum my guitar anymore. I fought hard to keep playing, but my hands will not allow that, and it breaks my heart to admit it. All I know to do is to give it a rest, but I have taken up learning the harmonica on my own. Known as a French harp, the brass instrument is used worldwide. It's a great face exercise too using your using your face muscles which is good for wrinkles. Its origin comes from Germany, and it takes approximately a good 3-12 months to learn simple major scales and chords. Plus, it is easy to transport. I pray daily for contentment in my decision and my future. I have returned my beloved blessing to the giver, and I'm left to admire listening to other guitar master's when I can.

My Lasting Advice

The greatest weakness lies in giving up. The most certain way to succeed is always to try one more time.
– Thomas Edison

My advice is simply to take a leap of faith... keep on keeping on choosing love and life. My passion and purpose in life are to stay alive and well with a level of gratitude. I am not a superstitious nor a religious person, but I am spiritual because I do believe in God and accept Jesus as my savior. As my good friend, Corky Parker says, *See you on the sunny side.*

My philosophy today is making the dash (live your life between birth and death) It's what you do and who and how you live your life in between. It is about relationships.

Living in the flow and bliss line. Follow the yellow brick road and reach for the stars. Today, my happiness is a reflection in my faith because no matter what hard times I may be going through... my faith gives me hope. From cradle to grave, I will have a song in my heart and love for my savior 'til the day that I die.

Like my late mother who was surrounded with reminders of her faith to sustain her, I wear my Catholic scapular; worn on my shoulders that symbolizes "a gentle yoke of Christ. It is more than my lucky stage shirt, lucky charm or a rabbit's foot, but my reminder to know I am with Him and He is in me. I go with God, and it is his music puts a song in my heart.

My Journey Home

The greatest part of my story now is I'm enjoying life. I've lived the so-called good life and met people from every place imaginable. Do I miss it? Yes and no. Not so much the appearances and hectic schedules rushing here and there, but I do miss my fans a lot. What I'm mostly resigned to do for now is keep living in the middle of a pasture of cows, Texas long horns, and other exotic animals roaming and running wild that I get to view anytime I want. I love the sight of it all. It gives me peace living the simple cowboy life. It is who I am. My residence is remote, and I like it that way. I'm alone... just me, myself, and I probably for the first time in my life.

I have just a television and cellphone to keep me company and the animals and critters surrounding me. I think you can appreciate the quiet when your entire life you've performed on the stages of America where it's fast-paced and there is no time to be still. Imagine finally taking the time to enjoy the sounds of the ocean waves or spending time with loved ones in the hill country where peace speaks to your heart and soul. And you listen to the sounds of silence. Nothing is more freeing in the mind.

The good news is I'm trying to regain the luster of living in my father's house where my heart makes its journey home. It's been quite a spiritual journey for me writing this book. Home is also where I found comfort and peace in my mother's protection of prayers. All my reflections from the past, both good and some not so good, have been sweet and welcoming memories.

Music has been with me through the highs and lows in my life from my childhood up to my professional career. From the good and celebratory times to the despairs, disappointments, and deaths. And, I say with all sincerity that it's all been an amazing opportunity that has led me to my spiritual journey home that I am excited about life, today.

I'm done trying to figure everything out on my own and trying to put all the puzzle pieces together. My soul is right where it belongs... it is right with Jesus. It took me a long time to get there because I stubbornly did it my way. Once I stopped running and got still, I figured it out. I embraced and listened to the silence and learned fast that the best practice is to surrender and let Jesus take the wheel. I'm at peace in my life and happier about it. There's no going back. I choose love and life.

I don't strum my guitar these days due to rheumatoid arthritis, but I have taken up learning the harmonica on my own. Known as a French harp, the brass instrument is used worldwide. It could be seen as a great face exercise too using your muscles in your face which is good for wrinkles. Its origin comes from Germany, and it takes approximately a good 3–12 months to learn simple major scales and chords. Plus, it is easy to transport.

Self-Reflections

This book project is the best thing that I have ever taken on and for obvious reasons being what I have come to reflect and talk about has triggered many memories and thoughts. Some good; some bad. But, if I'm alive, it's all good.

There was a time in my life where temptation; addictions of drugs, alcohol, and sex took over my life where through life lessons I learned to feel the pain; confront the lion in the room; and move forward to heal and to love and forgive others, but more importantly, forgive myself.

My God is bigger than I am, and I've learned that my past addictions do not define me, neither are they the sum of my life as a person. All I need to do from this moment on is to be still and listen. I finally get life and know what my real passion and purpose is about. To be thankful for all I have and am and will be in His glory.

So how do I pass my time these days? Occasionally, I work out (pre-COVID) at a local health club in San Antonio and walk when I have time. I'm more transparent today since my spiritual journey focuses on healing my body, mind, heart, and soul. I no longer play my guitar, but I do take the time to heal my hands of time in between learning the harmonica.

Lastly, if my book inspires or helps one person; this will have been worth it. I personally, never really cared about coming in first or last in any race that I didn't ask to be or compete in. I just wanted to play and stay in the game until the end of the race. That's the story of my life. In the end, I was able to level out the playing field which opened doors not only for me, but for others to follow. And that is the best feeling in the world. In my book, that's a win-win situation.

The truth and nothing but the truth. This book means a lot to me in more ways than one. Not only is it a big piece of my legacy, but it also stands for my journey in life and what I've been through to arrive here from the beginning to the end. I've been very fortunate in life, and I know it. Despite the despair, hardships, and pain that I put myself through, today I feel lucky in my life, again. I have hope for the future. It's important that my book tells my truth, including the good, the bad, and the ugly. Because when it comes down to it, drugs may have destroyed my career to a large degree, along with broken relationships, marriages, and my voice, (slowly, but surely), but it did not kill my soul. I fought the good fight until the end, until I surrendered to Jesus; Thank God.

I Take A Lot of Pride In Who I Am

For the love of Texas... nothing gives me more pride and a sense of accomplishment than being called a Texan *Tejano.* It's where a lot of my hero friends are from... some not well-known nor come from money but are who I call unsung heroes and friends. These are men and women who have heart and character to be true to themselves and to their Jesus and never judge me. Many have sustained me through their prayers, assistance, and faith in me; sometimes believing in me when I didn't believe in myself.

There are also many well-known celebrities and figures in my life who I look up to who are my heroes too, and have inspired me through their actions, songs, poems, and words; and they have no idea just how much. I am a fan of such individuals.

Some of them don't even know me nor do I know them, but to the ones I do... I feel blessed to know them.

As mentioned in my book, I've been privileged to meet and visit influential and high-ranking people from all over the world. And I love sharing with others such acquaintances because I want others to know just how amazing and intriguing, they are off stage and in person as they are on stage. It's just who I am... I enjoy sharing not to boast but to share an experience.

This is what I hope I accomplished in my memoir—baring my soul and sharing my life singing country music, rock and roll, pop, and folk songs not only to the masses, but I'm also grateful to the stories of musicians who sing their songs. These entertainers have enriched my life and influenced me through their music, in melody and harmony.

In his book, *Decision Points*, George W. Bush admits that drinking and smoking had become bad habits to him and further explains that he had a habitual personality where he couldn't stop smoking for eight years. Yet, once he made up his mind, through his faith and God's grace, he was able to overcome and stop. I can't tell you what reading that meant to me for Mr. Bush to be vulnerable and share in his own words his burdens for all to see got me to thinking that anything is possible. You can be proud of our former President for a thousand reasons, but his reveal and perspective changed my life to always keep singing with a song in my heart. Imperfections and all. Today, I have discernment and wisdom to know that life is worth it and it's okay to share my heart and be vulnerable without judgment.

Moving forward *Adelante* in life is key...especially if it happens to be living on a spacious ranch with nothing more than surrounded by nature, animals, and the coyotes howling. Give me a view with a Texas starry sky, lit up and twinkling high in the night and that is where I'll be. My soul is healed and finds comfort in its peace and gentle breeze that frees me. It's a dream come true to be calm and to be still.

A little friendly advice. Dare to care to be your own man or woman. Let others do what they will, you are responsible in the first instance to yourself. Hold on to your own principles and values and believe in God, always.

HE will never steer you wrong. COVID changed a lot of people's lives. It halted work for me and my band for a good while, but I decided to muster all the strength and faith in me to get right with myself with the Lord's help. For some reason, he listened and gave me peace. His gospel music was sweeter as were his written words. Like in a music studio, in life... raise your vibes and eyes to the sky. Be the voice for the better to make our world a better, brighter, and lighter world. You can do it no better than in music with words, melody, in a song.

In the end, what worked for me was to be still and listen to Him. I am awake *despierta*. My life is a living testament today to know that *There, but for the grace of God go I.* I consider each day a gift and blessing to have favor with God and vocals to sing and speak in His Glory. Don't believe it? Believe it. I will not deny it.

I have to say, I miss playing my guitar and melody today. I live a simple life, like my father before me; nothing gives me more peace. I am enjoying just planning what I am going to eat next. No stress there because I like to cook and eat.

On the other hand, it may sound surprising to you, but sometime, I get so high reading His words that I am not hungry for food. It's because my soul is being fed, instead.

One last thing I'm proud to say I'm happy my parents gave me the gift of language, speaking Spanish fluently as a child. When I arrived in Nashville at age 20, the environment made me feel uneasy only because it felt different. I didn't know how the locals would receive me, but in time, I let them in, and I decided to just be myself. It was then I appreciated the locals and all of who I was, including my ethnicity and foundation of who I am. Today, I sometimes wonder what would have happened in my life if I didn't have the foundation I was born, bred, and raised with that my parents invested in. And if I didn't have the asset to speak Spanish. I can say I'm thankful to God for it all.

Challenging Times

"I used to be afraid of the dark until I learned that I am light, and the dark is afraid of me."
– D.R. Silva

I feel that we Americans will be stronger and more successful for living through these challenging times. We are better conditioned to cherish and relish relationships with family and friends more now than ever before. For me, I've had to make lemonade out of lemons and make the effort to reach out to family and friends I love. Staying connected is the best way to let your loved ones know you care.

They say a person has 50,000 to 70,000 thoughts per day. I'm disciplining my mind to be more positive, creative, and productive with the down time and social distancing time I'm dealing with. It has more to do with mind control believing in the power of positive thinking and God. And anything the opposite is fear and darkness. The depth of the human mind and soul is limitless and when you set your mind to deliberately creating what you want... anything is possible.

The heart wants what it wants, and human connection is vital and makes life more meaningful to thrive rather than survive. What matters most is that we are free from the chains of doubt, worry, and not feeling enough. A lot of us choose to be authentic, kind, and helpful. Releasing ourselves from emotional bondage or judgement of others and ourselves. It is a much better place to be. COVID-19 showed us what hard work and unconditional love and deep faith looks like. Choosing love and life over despair and doom. Love and faith can see us through having the resilience of the human spirit.

The COVID-19 pandemic came out of left field—no one saw it coming. For me, it is serious. I'm all for using precautions to reduce the spread of the virus. Like it or not, I'm a senior, up in age, even though I am a kid at heart and act like one at times. It keeps me feeling young doing things out in the community and meeting people. It's what I love best about singing on stage. I get to meet all kinds of people from all parts of the world, and it intrigues me, but most of all it gives me pleasure seeing people having fun and dancing on the floor.

Through my music, and all the latest technology that it provides, I hope to expand more and take advantage utilizing social media to reach new and existing fans. I'll be the first to say that I have the greatest fans in the world, and I am most grateful for their continued support. I pray that they are well and staying safe, and I have faith that we will be celebrating soon with music and within time.

I believe that our mission and purpose in life is tied to finding our "why" Adjusting and living in a pandemic could feel like being in hell and back. Only the survivors of the fittest will get through. Some will not only help their own families during a crisis, but some will extend their efforts to help others.

I've lost longtime friends who passed on these past two years. It's hard to find the words to express my loss but you should know... aside from the small tokens of my deep regard to affection, these giants John Prine, Charley Pride and Tom T. Hall, Mickey Gilley, Johnny Bush, Naomi Judd, Loretta Lynn, and Jerry Lee Lewis. They will always be on my mind and in my heart. Truth be told they were all a major part of my memories and musical career.

Remembering Those Who Have Passed

You know, I have read about other singers over the past 60 years who made it big, and they just could not handle it. Why? Because along with the fame it brings... along comes the stress and struggles of it all. Let me tell you that becoming famous is not as easy or glamorous as it looks. There is no bragging in me because that is not who I am. I'm proud to have been in the presence of some fine people and all, but you won't find me being braggadocious about it.

What happened to me in the world of country music has been told many times before. The only difference is I am still here, and some are not. Why? I cannot answer that. I would only reply what I always say, *by the grace of God go I* is my only guess. Everyone keeps telling me I am not a cat and I really do not have nine lives to keep landing on my feet. There is nothing else to contribute it to... it appears God really does have a hand on my shoulder, as the song says.

On December 10, 2021, I turned 70 years old. I have been playing country music for a living since I was 20 years old, that's almost 50 years of my ups and downs on the stages of the world. I do not know how long God wants me to be here on this Earth, but with your help I will be remembered for my songs and not some crazy prized goat story that put me in jail a long, long time ago! I will tell you this, every day is a blessing for me to live another day and it's something I don't take for granted.

As I write this book, my old drinking buddy Billy Joe Shaver died of a heart attack at age 81. Talk about a guy living out the words of his Country songs, Billy Joe was that man. He was one great songwriter who loved to sing and play like no tomorrow but was known for his words and his hell raising more than his singing and stage presence. He could be as cankerous as another and then he'd sober up and give you the wad of $100s he always carried in his pocket to make up for it, especially to his bandmates who he'd fire and rehire time and time again. All I have to say about my friend, Billy Joe Shaver, is rest in peace, old buddy. You finally found the heaven you sought here on Earth all your life.

The time I spent writing this book prior to and during COVID-19 forced me to notice a few of my old friends and fellow musicians pass on. We are all getting old, that is for sure. They say the older you get, the more apt you are to see more and more people your age die. It kind of makes you feel alone and think about your own mortality or demise. I suppose the best way to look at it is when your friends all die off it is part of God's plan. I will say it is hard to accept for you know your time cannot be far in the future. When Johnny Bush died, I thought of the time he and I did some studio work together and how we both were just excited to be working together and doing what we still love to do... sing.

Then I got to thinking, "Why worry about what you did or what fame you had or how much money you made singing for your supper." You must be thankful you even had your time in the spotlight where there are a million who hit Nashville and never even made a dent in the fame and fortune you were lucky to have had. What I have come to understand is that materialism means nothing without having the ones you love and who love you close by to share your life with. And half of those who did not make it were probably more talented than you were!

I guess the beauty of it all and what really matters most is to recognize that God gave you a talent and you tried your best to give it back to others. I know Bobby Bare, Billy Joe Shaver, and Johnny Bush had talent—that is for sure. And I know they left their mark on the world of country music. I just hope when it is my time, I will be thought of in the same way as all the talented musicians I have ever come to know or had the pleasure of sharing a stage with. That is a sweet memory to have.

Loss of Brotherly Love

"There is no love like the love for a brother. There is no love like the love from a brother."
– Astrid Aluda

It is with a heavy heart that I share my deepest and most recent loss of my beloved and younger brother, Ricky. After losing the last of my brothers I've never felt so lonely and hurt, yet at the same time I feel more responsible to live each day with thankfulness and purpose. It wasn't supposed to be this way. Me outliving my younger brother. Thank God I have my two sisters, Antonia and Eloisa and all my siblings' children, still living.

My Legacy

In closing, I would like to turn once again to my daughters, Aubry and Teresa, whose unconditional love and spirit have taught me more about life, forgiveness, and accepting others than anyone else ever could. Words cannot describe the happiness they give me. I have admired and observed them both from a distance and am impressed at the maturity, kindness, and emotional intelligence they show others. My daughters are my pride and joy, and I couldn't be prouder of the aspiring and accomplished women they have become. Naturally, I am thankful and credit their mothers for raising them to be all they can be. It is my promise and prayer to be the best dad they need me to be. You both are my world and God's blessing.

My advice to you is to walk by faith and not by sight. Never give up and listen to your spirit guide. You will never be as beautiful as you are today and remember to always wear your mother's and grandmother's smile. Love, dad

* * * * *

Chapter 25 Legends and Friends

"Don't get so busy making a living that you forget to make a life."
– Dolly Parton

How do we know when a person is wearing a mask or is being their authentic self? Some people on and off stage feel the need to be what others expect them to be. Learning to have the courage to break the belief and chains to feel free to be yourself and not have what Oprah Winfrey refers to "the disease to please everyone else." It's not easy because we become like chameleons to fit in wherever we go, forgetting that the only thing expected from us is to be and please ourselves. Eventually, we learn, it's okay to just be yourself... you are enough, you are loved, and you are worthy. It's that "aha" moment that sets you free when you understand our only responsibility is to love ourselves, first. I finally learned to separate the Human being from the Human doing. It made all the difference in the world.

Fame and fortune are not all that it's cracked up to be. Sure, there's the A-list actresses, actors' athletes, and slinky-type models, but as they say, "beauty is fleeting." Take it from me, it is true! Actor James Garner once told me, "Never ever seek fame. It's not what it seems." My friend Coach Darrell Royal always said the same thing. You are constantly wondering if people love and like you for you or because of your celebrity status. I found myself constantly testing seemingly friends to find the truth.

Believe me, I had my ways of doing this too and it worked like a charm. I would divulge a little about myself and before I knew it, rumors were spread to kingdom come. There's something to be said about the worth of a person who has integrity and values friendship and would never stoop to entertain rumors or gossip about you. It is said "The only way to have a friend is to be one." Ralph Waldo Emerson.

Mardi Gras and Dolly Parton

On March 2, 1974, Dolly Parton and I performed on stage in Baton Rouge, Louisiana, at LSU. It was a package deal where we drew in a good-sized audience, which also featured country Rockabilly singer Billy "Crash" Craddock.

Dolly's first number-one hit, "Joshua," was in February 1971, followed by "Coat of Many Colors" later that year.

On the day of our show at LSU, Dolly's song, "Jolene," peaked at number one! Four months before, my song "Ridin' My Thumb to Mexico" reached number one. It was my second number-one single.

I called my friend, Randy Willis, who had rented a home near LSU to work on his master's degree, to see if he would join me at soundcheck. He agreed. By the time Dolly's bus arrived, Randy had rolled in, too. Dolly and her best friend and personal assistant, Judy Ogle, dropped by my bus and mentioned she wanted to get something to eat after the show. I told her I knew a place where we could make that happen. Randy agreed we knew just the place to go. The four of us hung out until my road manager, Phil Jones, said, "It's showtime." I went on stage first, and Dolly closed.

Between sets, I asked Dolly and Judy if they would like to go with Randy and me to New Orleans for Mardi Gras. It would also be a great way to celebrate your number one hit 'Jolene!" Dolly and Judy loved the idea.

After the show, we set out to begin our trip. First, we stopped at 7-Eleven for a bottle of wine for some celebration and hung out at Randy's place just long enough for me to change clothes. Then we all loaded up and headed to New Orleans for Marti Gras, about 90 miles away. We were excited to eat at the French Quarters and then head to Pat O'Brien's Bar and Restaurant on St. Peter Street. It was the first time both Dolly and I had visited New Orleans.

On the way there, Randy played a demo entitled *Louisiana* 1927 by Randy Newman. I said that gives me an idea for a song. Newman's song was sad but powerful about the devastating 1927 Mississippi River flood. So, I decided then to write a "light-hearted song."

Next, Dolly asked if I'd like to ride on her bus the next day to Alexandria, Louisiana so that we could write songs together. She added that she had agreed to visit a children's hospital there and perhaps I might like to go, too. So of course, I said, "sure!" In Nashville, "it all begins with a song." Besides that, who could say no to the children or to Dolly?

Randy seemed to know his history about New Orleans and shared some facts. He and his cousin, my former Producer, Jerry Kennedy, were born in Louisiana.

We arrived in New Orleans around midnight, and Randy pointed to a couple of famous sites. The one I remember was *A Streetcar Named Desire*. It was the inspiration for Tennessee Williams' masterpiece. He added that the route ran down Royal Street, through the French Quarter, Desire Street, and back to Canal Street. We made our destination and parked near Canal Street.

Dolly and I were like tourists taking in all the sights and aromas as we drove by the above-ground tombs and mausoleums. "Does Marie Laveau's ghost hang out there?" I asked. I recalled my friend Bobby Bare saying he was releasing a song about the Louisiana practitioner of Voodoo shortly.

After parking on a side street off Canal Street, we headed straight to Pat O'Brien's in the Vieux Carre (French Quarter). Pat O'Brien's is famous for its hurricane cocktail, which they invented, and there are twin "dueling" pianos, too, where local entertainers take song requests. Their dueling piano bar was the first of its kind.

Our drinks were served in hurricane glasses shaped like a hurricane lamp. After a drink, Randy approached and tipped one of the entertainers playing the dual-Baby Grand piano. At the beginning of the next song, the player nodded at Dolly and said this one is for you, compliments of the gentleman. As he played *Tennessee Waltz,* Dolly got teary-eyed. She then arose and tipped the pianist. He nodded at Randy and said this is from the lady. Next, he played "The Yellow Rose of Texas" and a few bars of "The Eyes of Texas Are Upon You." My friend, Randy Willis, was beyond himself. The four of us were like kids in a

Candy store... having the time of our life, taking in all the ambiance and gaiety.

We next headed down Bourbon Street to check out the other clubs. One of us said this looks interesting. The sign read, "These famous people have walked through these doors." When the waitress at "The Famous Door" approached us, she asked Dolly, "Can I ask you a question? You look just like Dolly Parton?" Dolly sweetly replied, "No, but I'm always asked that."

Then, the waitress turned to me and said, "Are you Johnny Rodriguez?" I said no, but I wish I had his money. The Famous Door is called "the heart" of Bourbon Street.

It was about 2 a.m., so we figured we had better head back to Baton Rouge to make it to the children's hospital and our gig in Alexandria the next day, not looking half-dead. That's when I was approached by a homeless guy on a side street near Canal Street asking for money. "Mister, I'm hungry. Can I have a dollar?" I said, "Sure," and pulled out my wad of cash. When I did, the guy shamelessly grabbed my money right out of my hand. Dolly was standing next to me. The guy took off running, and I instinctively sprinted after him in hot pursuit, as I did in my high school track days. The distance was about ½ the size of a football field.

I left Randy and the girls behind me, hearing Dolly yell, "Randy, don't leave us." He stopped and ran back to Dolly and Judy to ensure their safety.

Unfortunately, my cowboy boots were not designed for me to run as fast. The culprit was wearing tennis shoes, which gave him a slight edge. But I did catch up and tackled him. I scolded him, "Look, man, don't do this anymore... somebody's going to hurt you one of these days for doing this kind of crap. I would have given you the money." I took back my money and gave him a $20.00 bill. Before walking away, I told him, "I would have tipped you more."

We dropped Dolly and Judy off at their hotel in Baton Rouge, and I couldn't help but notice the sun rising over the Mississippi River. Then, Randy and I crashed at his house, catching up on much-needed sleep. Still, when we got on the bus the next day, none of us were feeling spry.

We headed for our trip to Alexandria. That's when Dolly said she wanted to sing some songs for us. She had two buses, her bus and the band bus, and she said, "why don't you'll ride up with me on my bus? I replied that sounds fine, knowing good and well, I'm getting drunker.

Dolly gave us a tour of her bus, decorated with butterfly wallpaper. Dolly loved butterflies. She even wrote a song about them called "Love is Like a Butterfly." In her autobiography, Dolly says she was fascinated with anything that flew as a child. Butterflies were her favorite. Even today, they are her go-to design on stage.

We go down the road in single file 1, 2, 3 buses. Inside the bus, Dolly and I are sharing stories, kicking around ideas about music, and talking small talk, mostly me. We sat across from each other at a booth and started playing guitar.

I picked up my guitar and said, "Here's one I'm going to release later this year," but I did not write, "We're Over." After that one, I said, "Here's one I just thought of last night. It goes like this... There's a place next to my home state called Louisiana.

Next, Dolly said here are two new songs I'm working on, as she began to pick and sing the first song. Randy and I looked at each other with amazement as she sang, "I Will Always Love You." We both knew it would be a hit the first time we heard it. She said, "I've got one I haven't finished." She sang, "Love is Like a Butterfly." Both songs were released that year.

Dolly's butterfly wallpaper began spinning in my head about that time. Unfortunately, I had too much to drink the night before. Randy was our designated driver, so he only had a few drinks and was bright-eyed and bushy-tailed. He never was much of a drinker anyway. Suddenly, it hit me. I was feeling dizzy from drowning those Hurricanes down at the French Quarter. I wanted nothing more than to lie down. As the bus swayed in the road, I felt sicker. I was paying for my overindulgence, drinking too many Hurricanes with too little sleep.

In the middle of her singing, I ran to the bathroom but didn't make it past the hallway. I threw up in Dolly's hallway. Man, I got sick, but I'll never forget what she said... "I guess you didn't like the song." That's classy, Dolly... non-judgmental. Oh, Lord! I looked around and said this isn't my bus, remembering, "Oh shoot, I'm with Dolly!" I passed out. I looked up and told the driver, "Hey man, pull over, I don't know what I'm doing... I was here singing with Dolly, and I guess I got sick." He replied, "Yeah, you did." He didn't complain, but I guess he cleaned up my Hurricane mess.

I called my bus driver, Curtis Webb, via Dolly's CB radio. "Breaker 1-9," I mumbled to follow us to Dolly's Hotel. We made a pitstop that night, and all ate gumbo and jambalaya. We wondered what Hank Williams was experiencing when he wrote "Jambalaya (On the Bayou)."

I was asked to judge a beauty pageant in Alexandria. I did not want to have 50 females mad at me, so I decided to go fishing instead. I think that was the next best thing to do.

The next day, Randy and I rented a car and headed to the small town of Longleaf, which was near where he was born. As we walked the banks of Barber Creek next to his family's old homestead, I thought of the Frio River, where I learned to swim. We debated over which one was the coldest to swim. We agreed that both were too cold to swim that day.

After stopping by a tackle and bait shop, we decided to fish Cocodrie Lake near Longleaf, where Randy learned to fish as a boy. I discovered a St. Croix telescope fishing machine. I'd never heard of such a thing.

I also finished that lyric, "They got beauty queens and fishing machines. We ate gumbo until my dish was clean. For a Texas boy, it was a bundle of joy Louisiana."

Dolly and I played The Texas Prison Rodeo in Huntsville a few weeks later and laughed about our Louisiana adventure. Then, I asked her if she would play a fund-raising telethon for the Johnny Rodriguez Life Enrichment Center in Corpus Christi, Texas. Private citizens started the enrichment center due to the government's inability to subsidize handicapped youth in southwest Texas. She agreed. So did I.

Willie Nelson, Tom T. Hall, Charley Pride, and Waylon Jennings.

By this time, Dolly had written and released "I Will Always Love You" in 1974, I had written "Dance with Me Just One More Time" (about a girl I knew in Hondo, Texas) and "We're Over," written by Barry Mann and Cynthia Weil. Both of our songs had reached top chart billing, so we were on a roll and had momentum going for us.

Dolly announced she had ended her seven-year business partnership with Porter Wagoner, including switching labels. He was not happy, and she was not pleased; he was not happy. She wished to go her separate way. She starred on the *Porter Wagoner Show* for seven years and felt she more than met her obligation staying on his show for five years. Dolly was ready to evolve and move on in her career solo.

Randy and I felt honored that Dolly sang her amazing songs to us first (on her bus) that the world would come to know in 1974. In appreciation for all that Wagoner did for her, she took her infamous song "I Will Always Love You" and marched into his office to sing it to him, not knowing how he'd react. Porter responded emotionally, "That is the best song you have ever written; if you let me produce it, you can leave your contract."

Dolly left Monument Records, owned by Fred Foster, to go onto RCA Records. Fate proved she did the right thing, launching out on her own. Her song shot to number one on the Billboard Country Music chart. It was just business, and the rest is history!

Dolly was raised in the Smoky Mountains and came from a large family. She was born one of twelve children, and I was born one in ten. We were raised poor but were also reared in a home with a lot of love. We concluded God gifted us with a voice and blessing, and our gift to Him is to use it for the greater good of serving others.

Bob Wills Birthday Bash

In 1973, I played a concert sponsored by Acon Entertainment at the San Antonio Municipal Auditorium in San Antonio, Texas. It was the last time I saw the Western Swing singer Bob Wills perform on stage. It was at his 69th birthday celebration, and I was honored to sing his crowd-favorite and hit song, "Faded Love."

Bob's wife, Betty, tenderly wheeled him onto the stage for him to belt out his famous twang yell, on cue, "Aw-Hahh!" It was priceless... Bob still had it in him, and the crowd and I loved it. He was paralyzed and disabled in his late elderly years, but he was on stage in good form and happy to be there thanking his adoring fans.

Thanks to Leon Rausch, the lead singer for Bob Wills and the Texas Playboys, for arranging the concert for me to play and be a part of Bob's special birthday.

Country music singer the great Mr. Tex Ritter, and cowboy movie stars were also there to perform on stage. Tex was known for his timeless hit songs "Jealous Heart" and "Hillbilly Heaven."

I found it ironic that here I was on stage with two of my favorite country singers, whom I admired to re-record their music early in my career. Their songs made hits for me and for them, reviving them with a new twist. It was surreal and an honor to perform with them on stage. It was a great night of entertainment, and everyone had a grand ole time.

Willie Nelson

"Once you replace negative thoughts with positive ones, you'll start having positive results."
– Willie Nelson

A 12-time Grammy Award winner and over 12 Country Music Association Awards in his outstanding musical career, no one has worked harder and deserves accolades recognized by his colleagues and fans than Willie.

I can't think of another artist and friend who has done more for country music or another Texan than Willie. The man has a heart of gold when it comes to helping others. He leads by example by being a true humanitarian. He gets invited and asked to help at a lot of benefits and charities, but he never asks to get paid a dime. He will at times that his band gets paid or insist that no one gets paid. That means he does it for free and if Willie does a benefit for you, it's because he believes in the cause and trusts both the promoter or organization. For those reasons, you can be sure it will be successful.

Willie is the first to describe himself as a hillbilly from the Hill Country in Texas. He's a good man and I think it's funny because in many ways, I'm a hillbilly too. All kidding aside, you couldn't find a better human being on the face of the earth. There's not a mean bone in his body and his kids all take up after him being good people.

I performed at Willie's first Farm Aid Picnic and at his Fourth of July Picnic. I can tell you there's nothing like it being on stage in front of all of Willie's beloved fans. He is always surrounded by family... one big happy hard-working family. They work hard and they play hard together. The Nelson family band, line-up include Lucas Nelson, guitar; Monica Player; Mickey Rafael; Billy English; and Kevin Smith, bass guitar.

In the beginning, when I had my band, Willie used to sit in my band. Talk about having the best of the best on stage with you. And I played on stage with him and his band, too. There is no greater feeling like it because first, it's *Willie*, and second, because the crowd loves Willie.

Willie is an outlaw icon in country music and one of the four original Highwaymen, including Johnny Cash, Waylon Jennings, and Kris Kristofferson. I always felt enormous pride that I was asked to join the fantastic group and sing a duet in Spanish on the album with Johnny Cash.

One thing you can say about Willie is he's a giver and when he gives, he gives big; and he prefers that it remains anonymous. He wants no credit. You must respect a man like that. It was during Willie's Farm Aid concert where I met Cher and Greg Allman in Champaign, Illinois, and John Fogarty and so many more. I was honored to participate and sing on stage with Willie at his great concert and benefit. The lineup is always superb offering the best of the best but more importantly Willie's mission is the same as the day he started in 1985 which is to raise awareness and monies for America's farmers to stay on their farms.

Brenda Lee

Brenda, a fabulous singer, was a good friend of mine. She sang rockabilly, pop and country music and happened to be my all-time favorite country music female singer along with Loretta Lynn, Tammy Wynette, Tanya Tucker, Dolly Parton, Reba McEntire, and Faith Hill, Crystal Gayle.

Once she was having a million-dollar party at Opryland and I wanted to go, so I thought I'd ask a blackjack dealer and friend of mine (who wore my road jacket) to get us in. By that time, I see and hear this tiny and distinctive voice about 25 to 30 yards away on the carpet yelling at me "Rod is that you, you little bastard! I'm sorry JR—I didn't recognize your million-dollar smile." I'd always let her joke around with me like that.

Buck Owens "Streets of Bakersfield"

Buck was a Pioneer for his signature of the Bakersfield Sound and lead singer/songwriter/guitarist for Buck Owens and the Buckaroos band of Bakersfield, California. Owens had 21 Number 1 hits in a row on the Billboard country music charts: and 42 top 10s. He stopped recording in the 1980s but ventured out to other lucrative ventures like opening Buck Owens Crystal Palace Restaurant.

What is the Bakersfield Sound, well, he explained to me that he favored a telecaster, and the twang sound was more about the people and places as much as it was about the sound? According to Robert Price in his book *The Bakersfield Sound*, it describes hard-working people who lived in or migrated to Bakersfield for a better life to live and work. I like Buck's music a lot—it's real country; distinct and innovative.

Migrant workers were coming from Arkansas, Colorado, Missouri, Oklahoma, Texas, and other places. It's music with fiddle and guitar that's played and sung from the heart and soul and is a language and story of its own through song. It's unique and unlike the Nashville sound. Buck putting Texas, Flaco Jimenez to play accordion in his "Streets of Bakersfield," is alright in my book. I think he was courageous and an Outlaw like Willie, Johnny, Waylon, and Kris. Everyone had a lot of respect for Buck.

Buck always seemed proud that he and I were in a lot of ways like each other because of our backgrounds. He said he related to me being we were both brought up poor adding I was a poor Mexican kid and admitting he was an *okie boy,* himself. He knew how to make you feel welcome. I liked that about Buck. He was also very honest, kind, and funny. Plus, some of Buck's music has a Tex-Mex, Norteño flavor, like his signature song, "The Streets of Bakersfield."

Buck was a good man, and he was always good to me. We both admired the same musicians and friends. Whenever I came to perform in Bakersfield, he would make me feel welcome and insist we sing a duet on stage.

Throughout my visits to Bakersfield, I always felt at home, like I was still in Texas. Much of that came from the good people who know and love their country music and the heroes who sang it.

Buck was co-host, along with Roy Clark on the popular televised Hee Haw variety show for 17 successful years featuring many country music singer guests: Merle Haggard, Loretta Lynn, Roy Rogers, Charley Pride, Johnny Cash, Dolly Parton, Garth Brooks, Conway Twitty, George Jones, George Lindsey, Tammy Wynette. I was a guest on his show as well. It was a boatload of fun. Many of these guests were also his friends who expressed their appreciation of him playing their music, sometimes when other stations would not. He was also a business mogul and more fortunate than most to be surrounded by family in his business empire.

Buck was married to Bonnie Owens and had a sister named Dorothy, who was Vice President and Business Manager of Buck Owens Television-45. She was responsible and the backbone of all of Buck's prosperous endeavors. A very intelligent woman who looked out for her brother's interest and he looked out for his sister's Dorothy. Buck inspired many country music artists nationwide promoting their music on his KUZZ Number one radio station: *Bakersfield's Best Country* and KUZZ's Bakersfield's News Leader.

Today, his family dynasty still owns and operates the Buck Owens Production Company, Inc., and Buck Owens Crystal Palace, a museum and restaurant where I have performed numerous times and invited by Buck to share the stage with him. His son, Mike, managed and operated two radio stations in Phoenix, Arizona, and Buddy, his other son worked there as well. The stations were sold to Jacor Communications, Inc 17 years ago for millions. Buck's son, John, has a band called Johnny Owens and the Bakersfield Sound; they perform onstage at Buck Owens Crystal Palace Restaurant once a weekend per month, and is booked at other events throughout the U.S. Buck's nephew, Mel Owens, is CEO who oversees the Buck Owens Production Company.

Buck was known for his showmanship on stage and successful radio stations he owned in Bakersfield and in Arizona.

He knew good talent when he saw and heard it too such as the likes of Roy Clark, Susan Raye, Bonnie Owens, the Haggard Twins, Brad Paisley, and finally, protégé Dwight Yoakam. He was a perfectionist, straightforward, but likable and a good communicator, paving the way for others... whenever he did record, he did it his way. He inspired and was inspired by some of the great musicians: Merle Haggard, Garth Brooks, and Dwight Yoakam. Admittedly he was a fan of their music, too. If Buck liked you, he would share his thoughts and truth, but most of the time you would be in the presence of his great sense of humor, hearty laugh, talent, and life advice.

Buck sure did help a lot of people and not just in the music industry. He was held in high esteem by the Cal State University of Bakersfield among its athletes as well for his scholarship support. Amongst musicians Buck was beloved by many for him playing their music on the radio, especially when Nashville stations considered some too country, including Merle. If you can believe that.

A lot of us veterans remember those days and know who and why we're grateful to the stations and DJs who wanted to play traditional country music for their listeners. The world was a better place because of Buck. What few people may know about Buck is that he was loyal. If he liked you once he did business with you, you were his customer for life. He just was loyal that way in friendship and in business. Singer Loretta Lynn went on a TV interview thanking him personally for playing her music when Nashville and others wouldn't. Buck was a true trailblazer in the country music industry, and his legacy will live forever in the hearts of many country music fans.

Johnny Cash: On A Need-To-Know Basis

I thought about the world of my friend, Johnny Cash. The two of us shared secrets of sorts, mostly about music, relationships, and how and where we hid our drugs from others. He had his ways and I had mine. The one he shared with me that I got a good laugh with was where he hid them in his closet. His smokes. To me it was an obvious place when you think about it. He would stash his drugs in the inside of his black coat pocket in the closets. And since he had so many, he'd forget what jacket he hid them in because he could afford such an extensive wardrobe.

One day in 1988, I received a call from him out of the blue. He told me he was in the Baptist Hospital in Nashville, Tennessee, which wasn't far from me, so I went to visit him. He told me he was heavily guarded, but he'd let the guards know I was coming to let me through. I was familiar with the place and had been in Rehab and treatment nearby for drugs, but I hadn't told anybody. And I knew the hospital escape route, too. That was when I was at nearby Parkview Hospital.

Once there, I checked in and dummied up. I walked in like I owned the place because I was familiar with the grounds inside and outside. Security was tight at the door. He was happy to see me, and I was happy to see him. He told me, "I'm alright, Johnny, but I want a hamburger bad, please!" I looked at him stunned but I didn't bat an eye.

I received my orders to go to iconic Brown's Diner, a greasy and dingy-looking joint that you could easily get addicted to, but a staple in Nashville, Tennessee. He even instructed me how he wanted it, too. "Make sure it is a double patty and don't tell anyone." I didn't.

I merely obliged a friend's request. Go in and out of the room through the fire escape way," he had insisted.

"Okay, John." I teased him a bit, but never once asked him why he was in the hospital in the first place. Guys are like that sometimes; we don't ask personal questions to appear not to pry. There's a common thing with men—it's called on a need-to-know basis. For me, it's a cultural and generational thing; man code, if you will. I figure if someone wants me to know something... they'll tell me. It has nothing to do with me not caring, it was me not quizzing him out of respect.

I never once asked Johnny why he was in the hospital, and he never told me. He seemed well enough, but he sure wanted me to get that hamburger for him. No big deal, we all have heard family members and friends tell us the same thing. Hospital food was never anyone's favorite. We all want ice cream, a steak, whatever our food fancy might be... seeming harmless enough.

Returning, I found him sitting on a chair strumming his guitar on his lap. I left him in hog heaven and at peace enjoying his burger to die for.

About two weeks later, I ran into his wife, June Carter, at the Opry House, and when she saw me, she did not hold back. She scolded me, "Johnny, did you give my husband a hamburger in the hospital?" I replied, "Yes, ma'am, I did!" She continued to firmly admonish me, saying, "Johnny Rodriguez, you almost killed Johnny."

He had coronary bypass heart surgery the next day that lasted three hours, and he almost didn't make it! Waylon Jennings had triple bypass surgery at the same time. Hindsight, I realize now he may have been under the influence of medication before going into surgery. Unbeknownst to me, Johnny had 90% blockage in the main artery.

I would find out later that both Johnny and Waylon Jennings were hospitalized in a few rooms down the hall, and I had no idea. I discovered Johnny went to visit Waylon, but the doctor noticed Johnny's skin color did not look right and insisted he be tested and wheeled in for surgery. The two would share the same hospital floor after surgery per their insistence—Johnny for coronary bypass heart surgery and Waylon for a triple bypass surgery. Both were life-saving surgeries for the two of them.

I was shocked! Every time I would see June or speak to her on the phone whenever I'd call, she was always caring and witnessing Jesus to me. It's something I remember about her and how she loved her husband deeply.

Like me, my friend John faced the addictions of drugs and alcohol in his early career and fought like hell to beat them. Morphine, prescribed for injuries would be his relief of extreme pain he endured. Johnny was kicked in the chest by one of his tall Ostriches on the farm which broke 5 ribs and caused internal bleeding. Injuries and substance abuse, age, and the loss of his beloved wife, June, took its toll on my friend's frail body, mind, and heart.

Naomi Judd... My Saving Grace

Naomi Judd (Diana Ellen) was a Kentucky-born singer/songwriter who won a Grammy with her daughter, Wynonna, in 1983. She is also the mother of actress Ashley Judd. Naomi Diana Ellen Judd, her Biblical name, symbolized pleasantness. During the time we dated, daughters Wynonna was just 11, and Ashley Judd, seven years old. Her future husband would be Larry Strickland, a long-time backup singer of Elvis Presley, who turned Manager to Naomi.

In the early 1970s, an unfortunate situation happened to me that turned out to be fortunate for me. Someone special saved my life. My friend Naomi Judd came to visit me after a show where I performed at the Great American Music Hall in beautiful and old San Francisco, California. Lucky for me, it was before she was a well-known singer and star, but she happened to be a very qualified and good nurse.

After the performance, I was in my hotel suite when I mentioned to Naomi that I wasn't feeling good. What I didn't tell her is that I could feel my heart racing out of control, and I felt a lot of pain in my heart. She was able to calm me and put a wet towel around my neck. I did not reveal to her that I had taken cocaine earlier, but she recognized I needed immediate medical attention. The next thing I knew, she called the ambulance, and EMTs headed me out of my room. Thank God for First Responders who arrived on time. I remember my band staring at me in dismay lying in a stretcher and rolling down the hallway into the ambulance.

I will forever be grateful to my beautiful friend, Naomi, who saved my life. She was not only at the right time and at the right place, but she did not judge me. She comforted and stayed with me like a true friend when I needed someone the most. Her competence and demeanor were my saving grace. Who knows what could have happened if Naomi would not have been there? The Medical staff administered treatment to me, giving me Narcan (naloxone), a lifesaving injectable medication that reversed the effects of a drug overdose.

I was then sent home in 4 hours, which is a shocking fact, but it happened. I was lucky it wasn't fatal. My body could have suffered irreparable damage, or worse, I could have died. I may have taken a lot for granted back then as if I was a cat with nine lives. But I realize today that friends are precious and few, even though I admit I've been blessed with the best, and only God knows why. For this, I am eternally grateful. Cocaine use is dangerous. I took a lot of risks in my young and adult life, filling my body with toxins for no good reason... "to be higher than a Georgia pine?" Honestly, I'll keep my beer and marijuana, but I'm no longer willing to allow cocaine to destroy my brain, kidneys, liver, and entire life. It is the real killer.

Naomi was deservingly inducted into the Hall of Fame the day after her untimely death in 2022. When I heard the news, I was shocked and deeply saddened by my friend's death. The cause of death ruled mental health disease by suicide. My prayers go out to daughters, Wynonna, Ashley, husband, Larry Strickland, her friends, and entire Judd family.

I find it ironic that the woman who was compassionate and merciful beyond belief with someone like me... careless with my own life that she rescued not thinking twice to save me. Rest in peace, sweet friend. I wish I could have saved you.

John Denver

The late John Denver was a singer/songwriter, actor, pilot, and humanitarian. He was a solo singer and one of the most beloved entertainers of his era, at the age of 53.

He and I used to work together on ending the World and Domestic Hunger Project, along with many other celebrities. He was the co-founder and spokesperson against famine traveling to Rwanda and Africa to promote this worthy cause and I was honored to join him. He used the platform and stage to raise consciousness of the cause and donated his own money proving he not only talked the talk, but he walked the walk. John was brilliant at fund-raising and believed in what he was doing serving others. On stage I sing one of my favorites of his that he recorded, "Some Days are Diamond."

Dottsy Dwyer

Dottsy and I met at the Alamo Village, where she worked for Happy Shahan. She also attended the University of Texas, majoring in Special Education until 1975. Dottsy and I toured together on the road, where she sang at some of my major shows. Both Happy Shahan and I were happy to help her secure a contract with RCA Record label. She went on to record "Storms Never Last," written by Jessi Colter, which became a top 20 US country chart hit, and next recorded the pretty and popular song "I'll Be Your San Antone Rose," on Dottsy's *The Sweetest Thing* album written by Susanna Clark.

Today, she lives in Sequin, Texas, with her husband, attorney Robin Dwyer. I'm always happy to see her in Sequin when I perform at the Theater for promoter Tracy Pitcox's shows. She is a great singer and has always been a good friend. Between 1975 and 1985, Dottsy recorded for RCA Records. Manager Happy Shahan and I were instrumental in securing her the contract deal and happy to do it because she deserved it. She is beautiful, talented, intelligent, caring, and hard-working…the whole package.

Former President Jimmy Carter: Hail to The Chief

How lucky am I to have been chosen to open and perform for U.S. President, Jimmy Carter, along with recording artist, Johnny Paycheck, whom I had performed on stage with before. We both were to sing on stage for 15 minutes for our President, who was running for re-election at Texarkana in 1979.

The event was held at the Texas side on the courthouse steps, which were closed off for this big event. It was a special concert and fundraiser for Carter's re-election campaign that I was happy to lend my support to. It was well-known that both the President and Carter's brother, Billy Carter, were huge country music fans…lucky for me.

Everyone was anticipating the convoy rolling down the road on schedule where a high school band was ready to perform in between bands. As you can imagine, secret service men were postured rampant and dressed incognito, but who can't spot the "men in black" when you see them?

Johnny Paycheck's band started to play and as he walked on stage to sing one of his more popular songs. Then to Paycheck's surprise, the high school band in the stand on cue started playing the Presidential theme song, "Hail To The Chief." Feeling frustrated and slighted, Paycheck turned to his band and told them to play "Take This Job and Shove It." He didn't take kindly to the band interrupting his performance and saluted the audience with the bird (finger) before turning away and walking off stage. Most witnessed a ½ pint of whiskey in his back pocket. Secret Service was behind the stage ready for the President to give his speech.

Unfortunately, there was a breakdown with Johnny Paycheck's performance solely due to circumstances and timing. On the other hand, I know all too well how being under the influence of alcohol or drugs can cloud your judgment and make you overreact to circumstances (real or imagined) that you normally would not if sober.

Sometime later, I would receive an autographed book from our 39th President, Jimmy Carter, who wrote me a handwritten personal note of appreciation in the inside front cover. My former boss, Tom T. Hall, was responsible for President Carter mailing the inscribed book by President Carter to me. That sentimental gesture means a lot to me and remains in safekeeping to this day.

Little Joe & La Familia

Jose Maria De Leon Hernandez, better known as Little Joe Y La Familia is a great buddy of mine, and we go way back since 1978. Around this time Tejano and Tex-Mex music was just getting started to mix with country music genre and we were quite aware this was happening fast. We wanted to jump on the bandwagon. Little Joe was very popular because he offered great music and diversity, singing bilingually, as well. I met him at a show I was performing at the Lone Star Café in New York. We both visited after the performance. We knew of each other, but we didn't know one another personally. It was also his birthday that day. I love him and his wonderful family, especially his son, Ivan.

We've shared the stage together singing duets and have had some good times and laughs together. We mainly appreciate each other because we share the same traditions and values. We even worked on a movie together that he recommended me to play a gangster and I always appreciated him putting in a good name for me to the producer. Ruben Ramos was also in the movie, *Down For The Barrio*. We both got involved in a musical charity event for the End Hunger Network as that is a cause that is very close to my heart and Little Joe has always been involved in great causes such as United Farm Workers, too. He always lends his platform where he can give the people a voice.

Little Joe and La Familia Horns is a great band that I enjoy very much. He and I both love Mariachi music and have shared the stage with one another many times. That's the kind of music I grew up with too. In my household, my sister loved the Supremes; we had a mix of music, all types of music and records around the house. Little Joe and I bonded both inside and outside of the music business and every time we see one another, we catch up and laugh our heads off like old times. My amigo is a massive and mighty *Chingon* badass.

Ed Ames

I remember at the Hilton Hotel; I was told that Ed Ames wanted to meet me. He is an American singer of Pop music/Actor who was born of Russian Jewish immigrants and 1 of 9 children. He was of dark complexion and starred in a popular TV show with Fess Parker, co-host, called *Daniel Boone*. He portrayed an American Indian in the role of Mingo. He was also good at Tomahawk throwing as demonstrated on Late Night Johnny Carson show.

Guy and Susanna Clark

One winter, my friend, Gail Burkhol and I were going down the road to visit a friend at their log cabin home in Hendersonville, Tennessee. The car ended up stalling on the side of the road, but a car stopped for us. It turned out to be Hank Cochran, country music singer and songwriter who had major hits by Patsy Cline, Ray Price, Eddy Arnold, and others. He was kind enough to lend us a hand. I did not even recognize him, but Gail did.

We got back on the road and headed to Guy and Susanna Clark's home and told them our story that Hank gave us a ride. That was the first time I heard the ballad "Pancho and Lefty," that Townes Van Zandt penned and released in 1972. I was first turned off because I thought Townes disrespected Pancho Villa and didn't have the song right about him. It was just my opinion at the time. Townes Van Zandt, a singer/songwriter who played fiddle, replied that it's not about Pancho Villa.

In 1983, outlaw country legends, Willie Nelson and Merle Haggard released the album, *Pancho and Lefty*, and did a phenomenal rendition of the song, which was suggested by Willie's talented daughter, Lana Nelson. She also directed the music video with Willie and Merle featuring Townes in several shots, which were filmed in the Cantina at Alamo Village. I thought that was a nice touch. Guy and Townes often listened to recordings of poet Dylan Thomas for inspiration and Guy in his youth loved Mexican songs and would learn to sing songs in Spanish that were influenced by his father's business friend, Lola Bonner who sang in Spanish. It really is a small world anytime it comes to a person's sphere of influence. You just never know where the universe takes you and synchronicities take hold. The adage: it's not what you know but who you know.

Colonel Tom Parker

I've always known I've had a good memory. I can remember names, places, and songs like nobody's business, but I hear Elvis had an exceptional memory, too. That's always been a huge asset to me in my career. During this time, my popularity was at an all-time high, and Elvis's Manager, Colonel Parker, knew it.

Roy F. Zinser grew up in Monroe, Wisconsin. He changed his name to Parker who served in the U.S. Army and went to work for a traveling circus. The Colonel admitted he knew nothing about music, but he did know plenty about Showmanship, the same way Rodeo Producer/ King of The Cowboys, Cotton Rosser did for Flying U Rodeo providing family entertainment for over six decades. These two legends were masters at getting a favorable reaction from the audience to want to buy more than their ticket to get in the show.

Elvis' manager, "The Colonel," was a shrewd businessman and he knew the importance of publishing, marketing, and the promotion business better than anyone. He also knew the art of Sales selling merchandise, and he especially knew how to spot talent when he saw it. All were key ingredients for success and profitability. Everyone knew who he was working for, the King of Rock & Roll, and his priorities and interests benefited Elvis and no one else. That's because he was invested in Elvis—50%.

When Elvis was alive, he wanted to record Dolly's beautiful song, "I Will Always Love You," which flattered Dolly, but the Colonel demanded half of her publishing rights to her song. At that time, for obvious reasons, that didn't happen.

I read somewhere that Elvis sang the song to his ex-wife, Priscilla. Again, Dolly did not budge. She knew her worth after fighting so hard to get what she worked hard for going out on her own. She eventually ended her contract with Porter, but not without hard feelings. The deal with Elvis did not happen.

Hindsight, as big as Elvis became…who knows how big the deal between Dolly and Elvis would have been in the long term? No one could have predicted his early and unfortunate death. One can only speculate the huge success that business arrangement would have been for Dolly, but again the lady is blessed and has worked hard to accomplish all that she has.

Colonel Parker was insanely protective of Elvis. He didn't believe in overexposing his artist, Elvis, with the media feeling less was best... being a mystique. He advocated following a blueprint not to overplay the market. The Colonel believed the crowd should be leaving the building wanting more. He also insisted that Elvis would only play for a sold-out crowd, so some venues got smart and put less visible chairs out. That's what you call business and creativity at its best, thinking fast on your feet. If I learned anything from businesspeople, it is "the devil is in the detail."

I would run into the Colonel a second time in Las Vegas where I opened for George Strait. The Colonel and George were talking shop about movie possibilities, voila *Pure Country*, released in 1992. This meeting reminded me of the missed opportunity I was offered to meet Elvis in Graceland.

Earl Campbell: NFL Hall of Famer

Earl Campbell, "the Tyler Rose," is an American Pro Football Hall of Famer 1991 and NFL Legend (Most Valuable Player, 1978) running back drafted by the Houston Oilers 1978–84 Woodlands, Houston, and New Orleans Saints, retiring in 1985. He became the first University of Texas Longhorn to win the Heisman trophy after leading his team to an undefeated season in 1977. Campbell came from a large family, the 7th of 11 children raised by Ann Campbell, who he adored. I probably haven't changed my set list in 30 years, but Earl's favorite song of mine is "I Just Can't Get Her Out of My Mind." Once the two

of us sang a duet on stage and I really enjoyed watching Earl sing the heck out of my song with all his heart and soul. Few people are ever invited on stage with me to sing, but a friend, indeed, is always welcome to share the limelight for the joy of it.

A great memory and adventure of mine is when my friend, Earl, invited me to go to a football game. He said, I got an extra ticket, and we can go with another buddy of mine, football running back, Herschel Walker. I said, "Yeah, let's go!" I sat in the middle, Herschel was on the left of me, and Earl sat on the right. It's funny too because as excited as I was to be there with these two gentle giants, I couldn't help but notice how one leg of theirs was one of all of me. I was so excited to be among these two football heroes that I couldn't stop smiling the entire time.

There are only four Official State Heroes of Texas... those favored sons honored are inducted due to popularity and fame include: Stephen F. Austin, Davy Crockett, Sam Houston, and Earl Campbell (1981). As Earl wisely suggests, "Take your hits and keep moving forward." Earl resides in Austin, Texas and enjoys spending time with his grandchildren.

OJ Simpson

June 17, 1994, was the first day of a two-day event for Darrell Royal's annual "Ben Willie Darrell" golf tournament and concert at the Woodlands Country Club north of Houston. Randy Willis and I drove to the club, the day before, to get an early start. We watched the movie *Tombstone* and then parted ways in two awesome bungalows Coach Royal had arranged for us.

After 18 holes of golf with Coach Royal the next day, I napped. I asked Randy to give me an hour's notice before my set. That evening, when he awoke me. I asked, "How is the audience?"

He hesitated a moment and said. "I have good news and bad news. Which do you want first?" I said give me the good news first. He said, "The Houston Rockets are on TV playing the New York Knicks in the NBA Finals." A fourth of the crowd is watching that on one of two giant TV screens in the lobby. That's not too bad, I said. Randy then added, "That's not all. OJ Simpson is on the other TV screen in a white Bronco with a gun to his head." I turned to Randy and asked how many were watching that. "The whole damn planet," He said. Well, then, what's the good news?

"Coach Royal said you only need to sing five songs. Here's my suggested setlist: "Pass Me By," "Desperado," "Ridin' My Thumb To Mexico," "Just Get Up And Close the Door," and "That's The Way Love Goes."

The audience glued their eyes to the two TV screens in the lobby and not on the stage. It showed OJ Simpson, "Juice," former NFL Football Player (running back) and news broadcaster riding in a white Bronco being chased in hot pursuit by LAPD on the Los Angeles 5 freeway. The driver was OJ's former teammate and friend, Al Cowlings, who made the plea on a cell phone that he was taking OJ to his mother's house while OJ held a gun to his head.

The scene was being played out amongst 95 million Americans watching live TV. Ironically, in my audience sat Coach Darrell Royal, who introduced me to OJ years earlier, and Coach Bum Phillips. On the TV screen, "The Juice" was in a 35-mph police chase for an hour. A caravan of at least 20 police cars chasing renowned football star accused of capital double murder. This was big-time news! No one could believe what they were seeing on the big screen.

Coach Royal said as we watched the scene, "OJ is going to kill himself." Bum Phillips added, "I once coached Al Cowlings as an assistant coach."

I was shaken up and asked Randy what we should do now. He said, "Watch another movie. How about *Wyatt Earp*? We can compare it to *Tombstone*."

So we did.

Terry Bradshaw

Terry is a former professional football player who played quarterback for the Pittsburgh Steelers and has been a television sports analyst for Fox NFL. He's also a great actor and singer, releasing country music albums. My friend could sing his ass off, too. After coming to a few of my shows, we'd ride around town just drinking and shooting the breeze.

Once, he left his jacket on the bus where everyone was asking the next day, "whose green jacket is this? I mentioned it belonged to Terry. To this day, he and I are great friends.

I also knew Tommy Kramer, who retired from football and was also a great athlete, golf player and a great guy. He was from San Antonio, Texas, and quarterback for the Minnesota Vikings. Tommy and I liked to have good times.

Coach Darrell K Royal

The Eyes of Texas: Hook 'Em Horns. Coach was an all-American football player. He served as Head Coach at Mississippi State University, the University of Washington, and the University of Texas Longhorns (1957–1976). Coach Darrell Royal was not just a legend and beloved Texas Football Coach but an outstanding human being. He is among the greatest men known in Texas Longhorn history for his achievements, ethics, and legacy. Only his team would relate. He was digging in the trenches with them because he talked the talk and walked the walk alongside his football players.

He was a good man of personal strength and integrity. I can still hear the coach's "royalism" to this day. When he wanted to emphasize the importance of consistency and its value, he emphasized friendship. He would remind us, There's an old saying, "Dance with the one that brung ya.'

Another one I liked was about a true winner. "To be successful as a team, you must bring all the parts together and play as one heartbeat." To say he was one of a kind is an understatement. He had a great sense of humor and didn't mince his words. I sure liked and respected him, as did everyone who knew him.

He would jokingly say, "She turned a cold tail to him," when he wanted to make a point about a breakup. It was funny as hell, and you'd listen, too. He was one of a kind.

The coach made a lot of good raising money for the community in causes close to his heart, like golf tournaments and music for the University of Texas, children's health, Alzheimer's research, and other worthy causes he would lend his name and likeness to. His favorite song of mine was "Jealous Heart."

Being in the presence of this good man and coach was always nice. And a bonus for me is that he would request my presence at some event... golf fundraiser, music event, or Pickin' party. Anybody and everybody wanted to support Coach Royal's athletic and music fundraiser events. There was always the best food, music, and camaraderie in a great location.

At the Ben, Willie, Darrell benefit, I met Bud Lee, a great songwriter who wrote "Friends in Low Places," which Garth Brooks ended up singing. The first time I saw Bud at a party, he looked like a hippie dressed in a t-shirt and jeans. I liked him initially, and he struck me as super friendly, creative, and talented.

Coach Royal was a big man; I don't just mean stature-wise. I'm talking about his character and what he stood for. The man had high standards, and he expected those in his circle to stand up for something, too. Friendship and loyalty meant a lot to Coach. Whenever Coach requested me to be somewhere, I did my best to oblige because I had that much love and respect for him. In my eyes, he was a gentle giant and legend.

I loved that he liked my music and me. My only request would be Randy Willis, who spearheaded an annual Pickin' Party honoring Coach Royal at his massive home in Austin, for my band to be paid, but never me. Randy paid them out of his pocket. He was like a son to Coach Royal.

Anyone who is anyone would feel honored to be on the A-list in the company of some great people performing and attending. Some people would want to volunteer to be amongst the celebrities lined up to appear. Such artists as Willie Nelson, Charley Pride, Mikey Newbury, Kris Kristofferson, Waylon Jennings, Rita Coolidge, and Sonny Throckmorton, to name only a few. A favorite memory of mine is when Coach asked me if I wanted to play golf with Mickey Mantle and him... I still think highly of it. I remember asking Coach Royal if he thought asking for Mickey's autograph would be all right. Coach said, "Sure, go ahead." So, I got out of the golf cart and went to the clubhouse for lunch, where I asked for his autograph. Mickey, sure enough, obliged and signed a basketball cap. Some SOB stole my Mickey

Mantle cap, but don't ask me where it is today. Again, I guess someone needed it more.

Death and pain sting the heart like no other. I know because I've had my share of death and sorrow in my life. And due to COVID-19, we've all seen and heard of more of my friends passing on than I'd like we'd like to think about. My idol, Coach Darrell, has known the same feeling upon the death of his son, David Wade (1972), and separately his daughter, Marian, who also died in a car wreck a decade later in 1982.

Willie Nelson's son, Billy, died on December 24, 1991. Again, the pain cuts deep into the heart and never leaves you when you lose a beloved child or loved one. One thing is certain—their blessed memory is cherished and forever remembered in our hearts.

Darrell was a good husband to his wife, Edith, and a devoted father who loved his daughter, Marian, so very much. His daughter's death was indeed a somber and sorrowful day for the man I admired and looked up to. I felt his deep pain and loss as I, too, was no stranger to grief. At the news of Marian's death, loyal men gathered, embraced, and stood in a triangle in solidarity as nothing more than friends, saying not a single word. No song comes to my mind that could describe the emotions more fitting than the beautiful and heartfelt lyrics of the "Healing Hands of Time" written by Willie Nelson.

I understand that two weeks before Coach Royal's Alzheimer's condition worsened, he requested that the Kyle sisters sing the beautiful lyrics of the "Old Rugged Cross" to be sung at his funeral service and celebration of life from I will cling to the old rugged cross... "til my trophies at last I lay down," to I will cling to the old rugged cross... "til my burdens I, at last, lay down"... And exchange it someday for a crown."

It is a powerful and consistent message that conveys Coach Royal faith and love of God, the Almighty merciful and not that of his career or any earthly award. Knowing this made me feel as if I was at the funeral for my friend, as I was, if only present in spirit. The ceremony closed with the UT Marching Band playing "The Eyes of Texas."

The biggest compliment I heard that Coach Royal said about me was "Johnny took Nashville by storm because he introduced a new culture and language that took off." This acceptance from a man who was bigger than life and someone everyone idolized and respected will always mean the world to me. He saw something in me that only his players will ever know how I feel. Coach genuinely and undeniably loved and cared for his team, family, music, and people.

Ralph Emery

Ralph was a popular country music DJ, radio and television show host who happened to be a close friend of mine and neighbor in Nashville, Tennessee. And every now and then I would host his shows in his absence. He always booked and interviewed the best celebrity and talented guests on his shows. It was a great experience and a lot of fun for me to do.

While a guest on his show, I remember him asking me, "Johnny is there a song you wish you should have sung." I replied, well, before I commit to a song, a question I ask myself is... is it good for me? The song was called, "Day Time Friends Nighttime Lovers," by Kenny Rogers. I prefer ballads with a mid-range tempo or fast dancing, and this one was slow.

Ben Peters, a neighbor of mine, pitched it to me, but I passed. When I discussed it with my then-wife, Linda, she didn't want me to record it because of the cheating reference, so out of respect for her, I declined a hit song. I made a conscious decision because I loved and valued her opinion.

There were other times I'd pass on songs and then find myself driving down the road when someone else would be singing the same song. Sometimes, I had a gut feeling it was a good song but would talk myself out of it. Life is funny that way where a song would be a good hit for someone else.

The best of the best artists has turned down songs for one reason or another. For Patsy Cline it was 'Crazy." She didn't think it was country enough. Imagine that. Luckily, her husband, Charlie Dick and record plugger, Hank Cochran (Publishing Company for Willie) was both persistent in getting Patsy to record Willie's song.

About this time, the music coming out in country was more about relating to the sign of the times. You were understanding the essence and universal language of the heart, in other words feeling an ocean of emotions that were crying to be shouted out.

It's the reason I've always loved and related to country music and artists like Kenny who gave a voice and expression to a situation and sang it in their songs.

Charley Pride

On my first tour as a single artist, I worked with the "one and only" first Black American country music superstar, Mr. Charley Pride. It was an honor to know and open for him. He was one of a kind, and I learned much about him and his fantastic talent. He was a professional through and through, and we became good friends. His presence demanded your respect and admiration; and he was easy to be around. Charley remained one of the biggest names in country music, recording over twenty albums. Today, I still sing his crowd-pleasing songs in his memory, "Is Anybody Going to San Antone" and "Kiss An Angel Good Morning."

Charley was a snazzy dresser, too, and I told him so. Once, he passed me by and said, "Son, it's almost show time; you better get dressed and ready." I replied, "Charley, I'm already ready!" I was dressed casually in a t-shirt and jeans while Charley was dressed for his fans to the nine. I respected the man a lot and how he loved to sing for his fans. His legacy will live on through his sons, Dion and Kraig's music

.

Erv Woolsey

Erv Woolsey is a powerhouse manager and an incredible businessman who believed in and supported me in my musical career in the early 1980s. He has an eye for talent, but he's no nonsense, too. He takes business very seriously and if you follow his blueprint and best practice for maximum success, you will be steered on the right path. You will also become what it takes to be an even greater country music star and in the process of becoming a better man.

Erv is George Strait's Manager, and he knows how to groom an artist turn star with talent and a voice. That's because he knows what it takes to be a Superstar in the making, but more importantly, how to maintain that status. He's also a great and caring human being who I think the world of.

In the beginning, while under Erv's leadership, George opened shows for me when he was getting started. I believe he had about two hit songs by that time, "Fool Hearted Memory" and "Unwound' and he was becoming bigger than life. I was fortunate to work with the two of them. Soon, I began opening shows for George, and life was good. It was a sweet deal. I consider them both friends to this day. They are both men of impeccable integrity and are respectable business and community leaders in country music history.

I performed at the Trap Night Club, at the hands of the master, owned by promoter Erv Woolsey in Nashville, where Erv, along with his son, (guitarist/singer) Clint, produced an album, *Live at the Trap.* They even had a mechanical bull to ride. I was happy to be on stage singing with the best band, Jody Maphis, Rick LD Wayne, Mike Solee, and Gary Goss. Clay Walker and Big and Rich were there. It was a blast singing for the crowd and seeing family and friends. Randy Willis leased a tour bus. We rode it from Austin to Nashville. Randy and Erv were both from Wimberley, Texas and attended Southwest Texas State University in San Marcos, as George Strait did. He and Erv Woolsey were hanging out on the bus when Randy's friend Casey Kelley arrived. The second Randy said, "Erv, meet Casey Kelly," Erv said, "Cowboy Rides Away." Casey had co-written the song with Randy's friend Sonny Throckmorton years before. Erv had never met Casey. Sonny was going through a divorce and was staying at Randy's house, as many people in the music business did when hard times came. It made for some incredible music around his campfire at night. I dedicated a song to Randy on that live CD that night. One of his favorites was "That's the Way Love Goes."

What I remember most are the numerous times my friends Erv and George went out of their way to help promote and support me, not only as a friend but also as a performer. Whichever the case, I appreciated both men for making me feel like a part of the team; I will forever feel indebted to them for their generosity, counsel, and belief in me. Even sometimes going out on a limb. They both gave me the opportunity of a lifetime to be a part of the cowboy music dream.

I may have had the voice and career success for decades, but my two stellar friends had the stick-to-it-ness that it takes to sustain success and get bigger and bigger.

James Michener

For this is the journey that men make, to find themselves. If they fail at this, it doesn't matter much what else they find.
– James Michener

I attended a fundraiser for Darrell Royal in Austin, where over 50 celebrities attended. I was honored to accept an invitation to sing five songs at this event. I remember mainly wanting to sing "Wind Beneath My Wings." Considering the special guest in attendance, I thought it would be a special touch. The singer before me, Gary Morris, had the same thing in mind and started to sing the same song. I turned to my keyboard player, Gary Goss, and said, "Scratch that one," I sang my next best song. It was an honor to sing in Mr. Michener's presence. He is a true master.

James was a prolific author and philanthropist who donated more than 117 million to universities, libraries, and museums. He and his wife, Mari, donated 35 million to the University of Texas in Austin, a Center for Writers where he had his own office. He was raised as a Quaker and in extreme poverty. By the time he graduated from high school, he had visited 45 out of 48 states. He was the assistant visiting professor of History at Harvard University and remained helpful to all. I met this teacher, naval officer, and political advisor who sold over 100 million books. He won the Pulitzer Prize for his first work of fiction, *Tales of the South Pacific*. James wrote over 40 books and is well-respected in the literary field for donating to museums and supporting university students.

Farrah Fawcett

Willie invited me to the Backyard in Bee Cave, Texas. Randy Willis and I drove to the gig in his pickup. Darrell Royal asked if we'd like to sit on stage with him and a couple of other folks. Randy sat by this Texas-feathered blonde beauty on stage. They chatted throughout the three-hour gig. After the show, I asked him what Farrah was like.

He said, "Farrah, who?" Farrah Fawcett, I replied. He smiled and pulled out one of his business cards from his wallet with her name and phone number on the back. I asked if that was for me. He smiled again and said, "Not hardly." She was in town filming a movie at Willie's Luck, Texas movie set.

Farrah Fawcett, actress and fashion model better known as One of *Charlie's Angels*, in the 1970s television series. She was from Corpus Christi (University of Texas, Austin, majored in Microbiology) and turned to Hollywood after a publicist discovered her.

Frank Mull

Frank was a genius at marketing and production, and his expertise greatly impacted my thriving career that I would remember to incorporate for the rest of my life. He was the Manager of Capital Records in the Sales & Marketing Department, and he was quite the mover and shaker. He knew the music business better than anyone and proudly shared his expertise with pal Merle Haggard on how to succeed in the Music industry. He lined up writers and the Magazine Village Voice for about 30 different interviews in New York, Manhattan,

Sydney, and Australia. I consider myself lucky to know Merle and his incredible team by association. Frank would also share nuggets about show business marketing tips with me when Merle was around. He was the kind of guy who was generous with his words and sound business advice.

I'll never forget the time when Frank took me to the Barnum Brother's Circus to make a point with me about presentation, appeal, and money. It was in that ring where I learned the true art of showmanship and how to attract and mesmerize the crowd and get them to want to spend their money. It was a lesson I would never forget without rhyme or reason not to. I am grateful to Frank because it's been a lesson that served me well in my musical career. I know the importance today about selling merchandise, brand, and your most important commodity, yourself. If I can remember, I've worn my favorite colors and matching handkerchiefs and scarves on stage at my shows, since. The traditional cowboy singers did as well. Marty Stuart and Roy Rogers comes to mind. Merle was lucky to have him as both a life-long friend and manager.

Garth Brooks

Life is a funny thing... I remember the first time George Strait and I were doing a show at the Grand Ole Opry in Nashville, Tennessee, in 1982. We were approached in the green room if we would like to meet two rising newcomers named Garth Brook and Clint Black. George looked at me and said, "Well, Johnny what do you think? Shall we let the whippersnappers meet us?" I said, "Yeah, let's do it; tell them to come backstage in the Greenroom dressing room at 7:15 p.m. and we'll all meet." I had this coat hanger that I was spinning around and around... it drove George crazy. As usual, I was having pre-performance jitters and it was my mechanism to calm me, at the time. I liked Garth's enthusiasm and down-to-earth personality. I saw the drive, the stars, and rockets of desire in his eyes, just as I had seen those same stars in the mirror when I was just starting out. Clint Black had the same drive and look.

Garth is an Oklahoma "okie" cowboy with a great big heart who always wore his cowboy hat. I liked that about him and felt kinship with him the first time we met. He is attributed to revolutionizing the Nashville Sound as much as anyone who came before or after him. Garth is 7-time CMA Artist of the Year and Winner of 9 Diamond Awards, selling more than 100 million albums. In my book, that makes him special.

What I admire and respect most about my friend, Garth, aside from his tremendous talent, is his priorities in life. First, he's a family man... they come first. In my book, that makes him unique. After a divorce in 2001, he retired and both he and singer, Trisha Yearwood took time off from music to devote time with his family putting the children's and their mother's needs first, making the transition of divorce smoother. Focusing on co-parenting, worked at its best between the three... Brooks, Yearwood, and ex-wife Sandy Mahl. They even live close to one another. In 2005, Garth returned to music.

Also, what makes him unique is that he's a songwriter in his own right having a great appreciation for songwriters because he likes to choose various songwriters and use their skills that will make his songs unique. That alone distinguishes his own style gaining in popularity and relatability with his fans and colleagues. He doesn't have an ego to just make money for himself, it stretches beyond himself as a collaborator and a team player in the music industry where everyone wins.

In 1998, a memory comes to mind that I will always be grateful to Garth for his kindness and generous gesture. I was going through a rough patch in my life after a shooting accident that I was acquitted for by jury. There were threats on my life and rumors that the Mexico Mafia was going to kill me…It was something I did not take lightly, and I feared not so much for me, but for my family.

The next thing I know is country music great and friend, Garth Brooks sends me his million-dollar, 45' bus from Oklahoma to one of my shows in Utopia, Texas for protection. I will never forget his thoughtfulness. Friendship is one thing I never take for granted. Anyone that knows me knows if I can return the favor or repay in kind, I will.

I remember it like yesterday hearing from a friend that Garth got down on one knee to propose to Trisha Yearwood in front of 7,000 fans at Buck Owens' Crystal Palace, outdoor stage, in Bakersfield, California on May 2005. It was witnessed by Buck Owens standing nearby when the audience went crazy with Garth's romantic gesture when she said "yes!" Trish was one teary-eyed woman and Garth, was one happy man. I was happy to hear the good news from my Bakersfield friends.

He was also in town for the unveiling of the bronze statue made in his likeness, along with other great country music legends such as Merle Haggard, Willie Nelson, George Jones, George Strait, Elvis Presley, Hank Williams Sr., Bob Wills, and Johnny Cash. The ten statues were made by sculptor Bill Rains in their honor and for their vast contributions to country music history. The project took two years to complete. The Hag and Jones were on hand to acknowledge the unveiling of their statues, too, along with other country music artists to perform at the Legends in Bronze concert.

Garth is a competitor in the music industry, but the only difference is... he doesn't try to be. His talent alone outperforms a lot of entertainers just by being the best he can be. You must admire his commitment to want to share the limelight giving other songwriters an opportunity for him to hear their songs. He likes the variety and freshness of other songwriter's work and he's willing to give them credit singing their selected songs. That's a man of integrity.

George Jones and Tammy

I hadn't been to Nashville for very long before I met singer/songwriter the one and only George Jones. I always felt fortunate to have met him early in my career; also, I considered him an international star for all his long list of hits. When I met George, I was living out of the trunk of my car, basically. George and Tammy, both invited me over to have supper with them, so I went over, and it was a big and delicious meal. It had been a long time since I enjoyed a home-cooked meal, and we had a good time. Suddenly, George said, "I want you to come with me I want you to look at something." He opened his jam-packed and extravagant closet door and gave me all kinds of beautiful suits. They were some Nudie suits made by the great tailor Nudie Cohn, who made all the Western clothes for famous stars, actors, and entertainers from all over the world.

I learned George had given me about $80,000 worth of clothes! George mentioned he had gained weight (due to Tammy's good home cooking of beans and cornbread) and he wasn't able to fit in his fine suits; some he never even wore once. He claimed a 29-inch waist that had expanded to 34 inches. He told me I reminded him of his younger self when he was first starting out, and he wanted to help in any way instead of his clothes going to waste hanging in the closet. Well, I just couldn't believe my luck and shared my story of George and his generosity helping a newcomer like me. What was even better that were the kind words he had to say about my talent and my character as a man and how he thought I was going to make it big in country music. Feeling grateful, I carried his custom suits to my trunk and took them home. I couldn't get any better endorsement than that, and from my hero. On top of that, all the members of Tom's band wore the same outfits with ties and boots to match. Tom took care of that, paying for those clothes as they were part of his stage act.

All the members of The Storytellers had to wear the same outfits, complete with ties and boots to go with the suits. And if you left your tie somewhere, he would dock your pay $20 and pull out one from a box he kept on his band bus. Tom was as good a businessman as he was a musician. Later, I would buy extra ties and sell them to band members who had forgotten theirs. It was beer money! I kept those clothes George Jones had given me and wore them early on in my own solo act. Later, I would get to share the stage with George Jones for another dream come true for me—when we would do some package shows along the way.

I mention tidbits here and there of my friends because their successes indirectly helped, motivated, and healed me of my own insecurities of not feeling good enough. I came into the business green and if it weren't for the generosity and kindness of these country music greats, I probably would have given up and moved back home. It wasn't easy being away from home and family at an early age coming to Nashville.

Because of special friends, I felt a sense of kinship with these talented and good-hearted people that moves me even today. He was called the Possum, the Rolls Royce of Country Music, and No-show Jones, but to me, George was a good friend of mine. In that arena, the man knew how to talk the talk, but more importantly, he walked the walk. George also opened up his club in 1976 on Printer's Alley in Nashville called George Jones's Possum Holler Club. Lots of up-and-coming talent played for the club before Jones sold it. Another story I have about my friend George Jones is when we met up with the beautiful and vivacious Playboy Pin-up bunny, Barbi Benton (1969, '70, '72, '73, '75, '85) who sang at the same place in Canada. We all had fun playing that gig and shooting the breeze. We were far from home, and a casino is an attraction and place for chance. And, though exciting with its glitz and glamour, George and I were in a hurry to get home.

Barbi was on Buck Owens' *Hee Haw* show (comedy sketches) and is a very intelligent and talented singer and model who was engaged to Hugh Hefner at that time. She also was the woman behind the iconic Playboy mansion having discovered it on the market and convincing Hugh to buy it. She was only 16 years old when she met Hefner. What a life she has led. I had only visited the Playboy Mansion once.

George Lindsey

On occasion, I use to stay with actor and standup comedian, George Lindsey, in California who is a great guy. He is best known for his role as Goober Pyle on the TV series *The Andy Griffith Show*, *Mayberry RFD*, and on *Hee-Haw*. He was a smart man and the first person to introduce me to French crepes. We call them omelets here in Texas. The two of us would talk about everyday life and normal things. Just two friends killing time before a heavy work schedule. George was not the duffus character that he portrayed on TV in real life. He was an intelligent man and a college graduate, too.

George Strait

I first met my friend and icon George Strait around 1981 at the San Antonio Convention Center. Reba McEntire and I were headlining an event benefiting the Bexar County Sheriff's Department. On this day, it would not be an ordinary day, but a fated one that forged a friendship.

For some time, Randy Willis's CPA's R.C. Reed and Company's receptionist in San Marcos told him her husband was a great singer. Randy always smiled and told her he wished her husband good luck. He had heard stories like that many times and brushed it off, trying to shield me.

Before this show in San Antonio, the receptionist approached Randy backstage. Randy said, "What are you doing here, Norma?" She replied, "My husband is opening for Johnny and Reba tonight." About that time, her husband walked up to Randy and said, "Hi, I'm George Strait, Norma's husband. Is there any way I could meet Johnny?" By this time, Randy had become a fan of George's music, not knowing he was the singer Norma kept mentioning at her office. Randy said, "Sure!" Randy walked onto the bus and yelled, "Are you decent Johnny?" I walked out, buttoning up my shirt.

After the introduction, George said, "I'm a huge fan. When I heard "Pass Me By" on the radio while stationed in the Army at Schofield Barracks in Hawaii, they said you were from Sabinal. It made me homesick. I'm from Pearsall, which is not far from there."

Rodeo life is a big deal for George. He's a real cowboy who always endeared me to him because of his character and lifestyle. You can say I felt a kindred spirit about him. Plus, I'm only six months older.

The cool thing about George Strait and me is that we did it, and that means something different to each of us because we were raised only 60 miles apart, which is why I say this. We both know where we came from, the hard work it took to make it, and how it feels to look back. It's a feeling that never disappears but reminds us of our humble beginnings and sacrifices to get here.

My favorite photo of George and me is posing with actor-singer Gene Autry, "the singing cowboy," taken at a concert where he and I performed at the Erwin Center in Austin. Gene recorded the holiday classic favorite "Rudolph the Red Nose Reindeer," though he was born in Tioga, Texas, he lived in Studio City, California.

George Strait likes the melody first and then the lyrics second in a song. It must sit right with him in that way. His songs almost sound poetic... "I've got some oceanfront property in Arizona, from my front porch you can see the sea. If you'll buy that I'll throw in the Golden Gate for free." Yeah, I'd say he's a master at song selection for sure.

Once, I took a buddy with me to visit George at his ranch in the Texas Hill Country, where he had invited me to visit him. I was looking forward to seeing my friend, but I didn't want to overstay my welcome, so I instructed my driver to pay attention to my body language and secret code because when it's time to go I'm ready to run. Usually, it's a hand gesture in the air. We had a pleasant visit, enjoyed a few drinks, and felt relaxed—always a great time hanging out with George. Before long, he says, "Johnny, let's write a song together." That's when my hand shot up, and I started walking to the door, saying it's good seeing you... "George, you gotta live 'em to write 'em." My driver didn't miss a beat. In a flash, we jumped in the car and were on the road headed home.

Anyone who knows me well . . .knows my secret knock code, too. I will answer the door if I hear it because I know you're a friend of mine standing at the door.

George loves spending time working on his ranch and with family and he's just a likeable guy, aside from his singing and celebrity status.

Erv is George's manager, and I know for a fact, at George's insistence, that I was blessed to be a part of an amazing team. I will forever feel indebted to George and Erv for giving me that opportunity. A lot of water under the bridge transpired, but I consider them both my friends. They are both men of integrity and phenomenal community business leaders in Texas, Nashville, and Las Vegas.

A note to George Strait: Call me. I won't let that "okie" interrupt our conversation. We both love you, George.

Jerry Lee Lewis, "The Killer"

I remember getting on stage with Jerry Lee Lewis at the Republic of Texas Biker Rally concert in Austin, Texas. It was a last-minute decision to go. I was at Randy Willis's home when he said, "Jerry Lee's playing tonight 30 minutes from here. We took off for the gig within an hour.

Jerry Lee invited me to come on stage with him. We sang a duet, "What's Made Milwaukee Famous (Has Made A Fool Out of Jerry Lee and Me)." I'm happy I got to sing and get a photo of him with my friend Jerry Lee Lewis. Randy Willis and Jerry Lee discussed two things after the gig: horror movies, which they both loved, and publishing. Jerry Lee wanted to know if he should be paid for production using his name and likeness in a new play on Broadway entitled *Million Dollar Quartet*. Randy owns two publishing companies. Within a few days, Jerry Lee's manager called Randy, and he gave him an entertainment lawyer's name in Manhattan.

I performed at a show in Denver, Colorado, where the Denver Nuggets NBA Basketball team played next door with the likes of rock and roll icon Jerry Lee Lewis. I felt honored to be introduced on stage to sing with him.

I'm a big sports fan, and we were playing next door at the Mile High Stadium, where the Denver Broncos basketball building was erected. Most of the time, I was in the dressing room and didn't see Jerry's entire show, but my band told me about it after he finished. The venue had rented a baby grand piano for Jerry to play, but that didn't stop him from giving a performance that knocked his audience's socks off when he stood up, kicked the bench out of the way, and then played the piano with his feet. It was during his last song and grand finale. The crowd went into a frenzy and wanted to hear more. Lewis was the greatest piano player who ever lived, and they branded him wild after a brawl... the killer!

Jimmy Velvet

Jimmy Velvet is a great friend of mine, as he was to Elvis Presley, too, for twenty-two years. At one time, he owned the largest Elvis memorabilia collection in the world as President and CEO of the Elvis Presley Museum, across from Graceland. He's known as the "Godfather of Memorabilia," as quoted in *Rolling Stone* Magazine.

In the '60s, he was known for his Number one song, "We Belong Together." It's always cool seeing my friend, Jimmy, at my shows.

Joe Cocker

Joe Cocker and I performed at the Orange Blossom Festival at Daytona Beach, Florida; I opened the show for him in the summer. He was the headliner. It was a super-hot day, and we were burning up. The performer asked me to sing another song, another, another, and another. Finally, I said, No this is enough! I'm out of here. When I walked off stage, the crowd went crazy. When Joe went on, they did the same thing and wouldn't stop. My band and bus were located directly behind the stage.

Joe danced on stage for 2 to 3 minutes to "You Are So Beautiful." And then stepped off stage, taking off. The crowd went crazy again, feeling cheated. It was a huge audience, and they were mad. My band heard a thumping sound on the bus. Disgruntled fans were looking for Joe, who had long fled the scene.

Hot-headed thugs were causing a ruckus rocking my bus and throwing oranges thinking Joe's bus was ours—clearly a case of mistaken identity.

Johnny Bush

Johnny Bush Shinn III was nicknamed the Country Caruso. He was best known for co-writing the song, "Whiskey River," with Paul Stroud on the RCA Victor label in 1972. It's a song he wrote for himself, and it became a signature song for his friend, Willie Nelson. He played guitar, fiddle, and drums.

When I first started off my bus broke down in San Antonio. I didn't know how I'd make it? I was in a bus with six people, but Johnny Bush said, "Don't worry, take my driver." He saved my ass that day. I always knew God blessed me with amazing friends because my friend, Johnny, was one of the good ones. R.I.P. amigo.

Kris Kristofferson

I first met singer/songwriter Legend Kris Kristofferson in early 1976. I met him at the Exit Inn, a club in Nashville. At that time, I had a motor home, toured with my band, and was living a good life. We visited my motor home, smoking weed and hanging out. We rode around in the streets for 2 ½ days oblivious to everything. I have to say time passed fast and before I knew it, it was time to pay the fiddle and go home. That meant facing my bride, Linda Patterson, who I hadn't seen in days. I knew I needed to think of something to return to her good graces. I thought I'd better play it cool, so I asked popular and charming Kris if he'd go home with me to smooth things over. He agreed to play along. I walked into the house, not knowing what to expect. Convincing Kris it will be cool. I yelled, "Hey Linda looks who's here? It's Kris Kristofferson!" The next thing I know is a shoe is flying directly and swiftly at both of us. Suffice it to say, it didn't work. Linda wasn't impressed with either of us. Her stoic expression on her face told us she wasn't having any of it.

Kris is a fine gentleman, scholar and one of the best writers in the business. He also speaks fluent Spanish and is a good friend of mine who sings medleys that I love to sing at my shows. We have something in common, too; Bobby Bare helped Kris get started in the music business like he influenced me. Most probably Jerry Kennedy and singer, Mary John Wilkins, had a heavy hand in it, too. Mary wrote "One Day At A Time." I really admired and loved her and will forever miss her.

Lawrence Welk

I loved The Lawrence Welk Show when I was younger and throughout my career. I thought it was so well televised and perfect! It was the longest running TV show in history from 1951 to 1982. You really got to see the best musicians perform, who were disciplined and high caliber. They really weren't stars or household names, but band leader and show host, Lawrence, groomed them to be. He treated everyone like family calling the crew by their first names.

There were times I'd be so engrossed in his show that you couldn't pry me away to get ready for a show and if you changed the TV channel, I'd insist you turn it back on. Yes, I always gave myself enough time to get to my shows, safely.

Mr. Welk was from North Dakota but of German descent and appeared shy due to his heavy accent. He didn't speak English until he was in his early 20s, but he knew show business and showmanship at its best; it came across loud and clear. His Saturday night show was a tradition to watch, at least it was for me for the longest time.

He was an accordionist, and the music on the show was calming, bubbly, and light... champagne music. Staying true to his show's wholesome image, even their commercials were carefully thought of. You never saw a cigarette or beer commercial, nor did he have comedians on the show in fear of offending anyone.

Here's some tidbit... who knew that the popular hit single, "Tiny Bubbles," was initially written for Welk in 1966, but he turned it down. Instead, it was given to Don Ho who made it his signature song. I could still see him in my mind's eye with his conductor baton in hand, hearing him say, "A one, and a two and a three."

Reba McEntire

Reba is a singer/songwriter, actress, savvy businesswoman, and a beautiful lady and soul. She was born in McAlester, Oklahoma, to parents Clark, a champion calf roper, and her mother, Jackie, a singer who strongly influenced her life. For a reason, she is known as Queen of Country, dominating the industry and selling more than 75 million records worldwide.

I remember the first time I opened for Reba McEntire at a show. The crowd sure loved her stellar performance. Her talent as a country music Superstar speaks for itself. Reba also sings country gospel, not to mention she's a real cowgirl to boot (that endears me to her in my book) who competed in rodeos as a barrel racer, and she was good. Reba could knock your socks off singing the National Anthem better than anyone.

Some of the best times of my life were meeting and opening for country music heroines and heroes.

Red Skeleton

My favorite comedian was Clem Kadiddiehopper, "Red," a very nice man who shared stage tips with me. One of them was to reduce stage fright, he told me, "Look above the top of the audience's head, Johnny... they'll never know you're not looking at them in their eyes." It works. My other favorites were Henry Cho, Phyllis Diller, Lucille Ball, Carol Burnett, Joan Rivers, Don Rickles, George Lindsay, Robin Williams, Eddie Murphy, and Mexican comedians Cantinflas, Paul Rodriguez, Cheech and Chong, and George Lopez.

Roy Rogers

Roy Rogers was an American legend actor and cowboy favorite of mine. He named his horse Trigger, his German Shepherd dog Bullet, and his 1946 Jeep Nellybelle. His wife, actress, and singer, Dale Evans, was from Uvalde, Texas, and her horse's name was Buttercup. Roy was famous for saying, "I never met a man I didn't like," when I met him, I knew exactly what he meant. He was true to his word because he was an absolute magnet, and you couldn't help but admire him.

In 1979, I did a 30-day tour in beautiful sunny California by way of route San Diego to north of San Francisco. I spent a lot of time in the LA hub and got familiar with a lot of the hot spots, like Palomino Club, the Horse, and many other venues.

At one of my shows, we were approached by Roy Rogers, Jr. (son of Roy Rogers, Sr.), a musician, vocalist, and fan of country music. He asked, "Would you like to meet my dad?" We jumped at the opportunity to meet everybody's childhood hero. He told us to meet him at the museum in LA, so my manager, Randy Doyle, and I went to the museum. It was an exciting and cool place to sightsee and tour, too.

In the museum were statues of Roy and Dale, his horse, Trigger, Bullet Nellybelle, and his jeep. Before long, Roy Sr. walks out, apologizing for his dusty cowboy appearance and explaining that he was working in the desert with his bull. He was accompanied by his blue heeler cow dogs, which were used to herd cattle. We felt as if we had known him all our lives. He was a super nice guy.

Roy took us upstairs, where they had a private room and a kitchenette. He said, "Listen, I need to freshen up, but I won't take long. I need to go change my working clothes." He disappeared to a bedroom to change and returned looking like the Hollywood legend in the fancy getup he wore on television shows. It was quite a treat for us. Roy even taught me some roping tricks I got a kick out of.

One of the tricks he showed me was with a gun he showed me how he practices standing on a bed twirling his pistol from his holster. We met with him for 20 to 30 minutes, and he took us outside to show me some neat rope tricks. I felt honored to get special lessons from Roy, which will always be a cool memory.

Roy Jr. would come to see more of my shows in California. Nick De Stefano, who played vocals and percussion, played for my band here and there. He formerly played for the band, Toto, and sometimes filled in for my band.

I was invited to visit Roy at his California ranch thanks to his son and my Road Manager, Randy Doyle. We didn't make the visit, but Roy came to my show at the Palomino Club, pulling up in his jeep like a regular guy. I liked that about him; he appeared good-hearted and down to earth.

Selena Quintanilla

Selena, a cultural icon, was better known as the "Queen of Tejano Music" for her music and fashion in the '90s. She was in Star Mania, always under the eye of her protective father, Abraham Quintanilla, with good reason. I have two daughters, so I understand that one well. Selena was beautiful, talented, and vulnerable, and born before her time. The two of us and a few A friend of hers, the talented Shelly Lares, got to spend time together at shows, talking music in the presence of her father.

It breaks my heart that she died unnecessarily at the hands of an obsessive fan turn Fan President and Boutique Manager in 1995. She loved singing with all her heart, mostly Tejano music, and she loved her fans. She could sing any genre if she wanted to, and she proved it when she crossed over beyond Tejano music. I firmly believe that Selena could have reached the stars by crossing over to any genre because she had unlimited potential and talent. That kind of beauty inside and out is ageless and timeless but not without risks. I wish she would not have gone alone to confront her attacker, the evil Yolanda Saldivar. That woman robbed us of our beloved Selena, who had a pure heart and just wanted to sing.

There's no telling how much bigger she would have gotten. She possessed an incredible presence and spirit that made her the star she was. No one could deny this fact. She was a role model for many Latinas and Latinos, and we hold her in the highest esteem for her achievements and keep her in our hearts,

Stephen Spielberg

At the Southerners Atlantic, Georgia Supper Club concert, I met movie film director, producer, and screenwriter Steven Spielberg. He was introduced to me by a Teamster friend of mine, Jack Boultinghouse. He is one of the most successful movie directors of all times and it was an honor for me to meet him.

Spielberg also came to one of my first shows in San Antonio and re-introduced himself to me. Jurassic Park and Schindler's List were his most famous and well-known movies. Spielberg filmed his first movie, the *Sugarland Express,* produced in Pleasanton, Texas. Goldie Hawn and William Atherton starred, and it was his first hit. He was well on his way to greatness.

A fact about this man is that Stephen refused payment for his work in the Oscar-winning movie *Schindler's List.* I don't know what else will if that doesn't tell you something about his character and integrity.

Tanya Tucker

Tanya was a young girl (13) when she got started in the music business. We were both young and free-spirited individuals and we both worked hard on stage, but we played hard too, laughing all the time. I was (22) with a bullet. My first impression of her was one of innocence and fun loving, natural and having a great sense of humor. We toured together where she opened for me. Sometimes, she would come out of nowhere and join me on stage. I never minded that she did. Why would I? She had come on stage with that big, beautiful smile and spread her contagious energy galore. The crowd would go crazy seeing the two of us. She and I would also look out for each other, too, both on and off the stage. I always felt protective of her and still do to this day. I imagine she on the other hand was glad when we no longer toured, and she didn't do that with me anymore. Tanya matured fast in the business world but managed to stay balanced. You'll never meet a truer friend who will tell her truth to a friend on any level when you need to hear it. There's not another generous and kinder soul than Ms. Tanya Tucker.

In the early 1970s, singer, songwriter, and my friend, Tanya talked me into having some fun and yelled at me to hop on a dirt bike with her. Well, after getting over stunning me that she could even ride that thing, I had to hold on to dear life quickly. She drove that bike like a horse, fiercely without a care in the world. I thought throughout the whole ride she forgot I was riding behind her. I mean she flew over hills, bumps, holes, you name it all for the thrill of it. I really was scared riding with her on that bike. Finally, without warning, it happened: the bike got stuck and stopped. As I stumbled off, I was feeling dizzy and wobbly at the knees for sure. Not Tanya.

I felt like I was riding with little Beau because her father was this tough and fearless man, and she emulated her dad's fierce qualities. I think he raised her independently and was free-spirited to be like him, but in a good way. That man did anything he could for his little girls Tanya, LaCosta, and family. Nothing stopped him. Beau even sometimes gambled calling the shots... for seed money or to have the opportunity of his daughters making it into show biz. It's a tough business to crack, and he knew he had to be in the thick of it if he was going to protect and promote his little girl. That meant making sacrifices for the greater good. I respected him for that. He took courageous steps for the welfare and interest of his entire family with his adoring wife, Juanita, by his side. Tanya was close and loved her mama, too.

Afterward, we enjoyed a nice dinner with her parents and brother Donald in their lovely home. I always felt right at home with Tanya and her welcoming family.

In 1972–1973, Tanya Tucker and I toured together at Del Rio Civic Center with Texas Billy Gray (leader and fiddle player) and the Cow Towners, in Fort Worth, Texas. Pearl Beer was the major sponsor, so much so that it was distributed in every club imaginable. It was a sweet contractual deal. Tanya's sister, La Costa Darryl was part of the opening act at times, too. Both girls were fresh, dynamic, and highly talented.

For one full year we must have played in every Honky Tonk joint in Texas; some were even rough places to be in where chicken wire was placed across the stage to protect the singers from flying bottles from the misbehaving' hell raisers. We played five to six days a week. We all worked very hard, but we loved singing on stage, perfecting our craft and enjoying the cheering crowds.

Set List consisted of: "Louisiana Man" (yodel), "Good Time Charlie's Got The Blues" (Charlie Rich), flip side on record (bilingual) 'I Wonder Where You Are Tonight, Faded Love" (Bob Wills), "Pass Me By (If You're Passing Through)," "Easy Come, Easy Go" (Waylon Jennings), "Jealous Heart" (bilingual, Tex Ritter), "There's Goes My Everything" (Jack Green), "I'm Moving On" (Johnny Cash), "Me and Bobby McGee" (Kris Kristofferson), "For The Good Times" (K.Kristofferson), "Sunday Mornin' Comin' Down" (K. Kristofferson), and "I Rather Be Sorry" (K. Kristofferson).

There's even a yodel and impersonation that I performed of the following: Buck Owens ("Love's Going To Live Here"),

Marty Robbins ("Devil Woman"), Faron Young ("It's 4 In The Morning"), Roger Miller ("Kansas City Star" with a yodel).

Charley Pride ("Is Anybody Goin' to San Antone"), Kris Kristofferson (Webb Pierce) "There Stands A Glass." This entire performance was recorded (reel to reel) by Rip Willis, drummer which he recorded on a CD for both Tanya, La Costa, and I to enjoy.

During this time, I had hit songs, "You Always Come Back To Hurting Me," and "Ridin' My Thumb To Mexico," "Louisiana Man," and the *Introducing Johnny Rodriguez* album. The two that I had written about were fast climbing the charts. Tanya had "Delta Dawn," "The Jamestown Ferry," and "What's Your Mama's Name Child," which were all popular hits with the crowds.

My manager, Happy Shahan, predicted Tanya would be a top-ranking singer and was he ever right about that. He was a promoter at Alamo Village Amusement Park (where I got my start performing in entertainment) thanks to him, so he knew talent when he saw and heard it.

My schedule for a year was a brutal one where I was also including taking time out to head to Nashville, Tennessee then cut a summer replacement for the Dean Martin show, cut a half of my album, *Introducing Johnny Rodriguez* and cut Buck Owens's *Hee Haw* show. How I managed to tour and always be on one project or another; and keep my sanity, I'll never know.

I always wanted to record with Tanya, but we were just kids when we started and were always on a different record label. I'm happy to say that we finally made that happen and recorded a duet together in Bakersfield, California, called, "A Game That I Can't Win" beautifully written by actor, singer-songwriter, Dennis Quaid. It is produced by Rick Reno Stevens of ANR Records and is expected to be released in 2023.

We recorded at Triple Seven Recording Studio, in a quaint and isolated location where the mighty Kern River flows, surrounded by the Kern River oil field and rigs operated by Chevron Corporation. I even got a picture of the site which reminded me a lot of Texas.

Tanya's friendship has always meant something special to me. In many ways, she was like my little sister. She calls me her "buddy." And today, I still see her in that same light and am proud of her accomplishments. I could always trust her personal and professional advice to be in my best interest and vice versa. I appreciate my friend for caring enough to share and keeping me in mind. She's a good woman with a good soul.

It makes me happy to see that my trusted friend of many years has found true love and is happy with her ex-boyfriend and fiancé, singer/songwriter, Craig Dillingham. She deserves all the flowers now and happiness in the world and Craig is the man to give it.

One thing I always loved about Tanya was her personality and ability to sing any song. She knew them all too. If you asked her to sing Midnight Train to Georgia, she could belt it out. Tanya has always been a powerhouse, but she is also an entrepreneur where she proudly has her Cosa Salvaje Tequila on the market. And she continually cranks out new and improved hit songs that are relatable and identifiable with her unique signature style. Ever since I've known her, she's had nothing but a pure heart and raw talent. That is a fact.

Merle Haggard

In my book, two-time Grammy winner, and Hall of Fame singer/songwriter, the late and great Merle Haggard known as "the Hag" and The Poet of the Common Man will always be my hero and the greatest country singer of all-times. I cannot say enough about my friend whose music was timeless and his friendship priceless. He was a man's man popular with every man and woman on Earth. There is not a day I don't think about him and the mentorship he gave me teaching me the ropes in and out of country music.

In 1974, a friend of mine named Audry Winters, who worked for "Music City News Magazine," knew that Merle was my hero and had arranged for me to meet her at a restaurant. That's where I met the beautiful and talented Bonnie Owens who I'm a big fan of as well. Bonnie asked me if I wanted to meet Merle. Yes! I said. I love his music. They invited me to RCA Studio B where Merle would be recording. I was beside myself and ready to head out to the studio in Nashville to meet my hero as a fan.

My impression of Merle was that he was bigger than life. I observed him in the studio as reserved but extremely talented and professional. None of us said a word to one another. I chose to keep quiet, step back in the background and observe the master at work. I could not believe I was there in the first place. The Hag spoke to no one. I opted to give him his space, feeling privileged to be in the same room with him. Little by little I gained his trust and respect.

I liked Merle immediately. I sure did love his music, so he really was a hero to me. I'm always asked what I liked best about him. Well, for me his talent goes without saying, but as a human being he was second to none. I always felt good being around him and liked him most because he liked me.

Surprisingly, I got invited to a second recording session and this time Merle spoke four to five words to me and I was excited about that. Then after, each time I saw the Hag he'd open more with me and eventually he and I would share a song here and there. It meant a lot to me because he did not let others in easily. Merle came across guarded, but you couldn't blame him. I was one of his biggest fans and now he was my friend, and the rest is history.

Merle became the face of Bakersfield, putting it on the map, and I became the Latin King in Country Music. Not bad for two small town country boys who did good. We both loved country music and had vocal talent with a tremendous knowledge of recording and education in the hard knocks of life. We enjoyed our privileges, adventures, advantages, and a truck load of opportunity.

Both coming from small country towns but big in oil and agriculture, where I worked the fields, and Merle being surrounded by oil rigs and fields born in Oildale, California, we had a lot in common. Is it any wonder, he knew I could deliver and sing a controversial song he wrote, called, "The Immigrant." It is a song about the plight of the migrant workers who come to the US to work but are looked down upon and taken advantage of - much like the displaced okies looking for work in

Bakersfield, California. A story behind the song that Merle and Buck could relate to.

In the mid-1970s, when I was in my early 20s, Merle must have heard that I got myself in a jam because he said to his friend and manager, Fuzzy Owens, "Bring me that bag!" To my blessing and surprise, he then handed me a brown paper bag. And here I still am, an old goat reminiscing and choking up at the thought of my friend. Merle was my other big brother from another mother; an "okie" one at that to top it off. He was my hero when I was a child, and he was my hero in my time of need, and still is today. There isn't a thing neither of us wouldn't do for each other. He knew it and I knew it.

He was always a mentor to me, giving me the best personal or professional advice in the music business. I trusted him and he trusted me and because of him, I mentored others in turn and have paid it forward just as my good friend taught me. I also keep his memory alive singing his songs and praises.

In 2014, Merle was playing a concert at the Selena Auditorium in Corpus Christi, Texas. I went to the show with my friend, Kelly Kenning. We had just got on from the ranch and didn't want to wait in line with the crowds, so we had a seat at the Corpus Christi Fish Restaurant instead. We thought we'd take our time and eat a bite of fish. Suddenly we were approached by a man who looked like a police officer. We were approached by one of Merle's people and asked, "are you Johnny Rodriguez?" "I replied, "Yes." "Well, Merle wants to see you in his bus," I said. "Alright, but how does he know I'm here?" The guy replied, "he knows!" When he led us to the bus, I got in to hear Merle say, "Rodriguez, where the hell have you been? I wrote 15 songs for you to sing." I told him I'd been in Texas singing at my shows. Well, true to his words, Merle sang every song to me. And they were all good. He added how he would put three different bands together and produce my next album at his home studio in Shasta, California. We agreed to make that happen. To say I was blown away is an understatement. I enjoyed every minute of it. To this day, when I think about what could have been, I am mostly grateful that Merle wanted to do it in the first place; produce and work with me on a project with the master's hand in it.

Merle introduced me to his son, Ben, and crew member, Alex, on the bus, and I introduced him to my buddy, singer-songwriter, Kelly Kenning. Unfortunately, time and circumstances prevented us from making it a reality. My one big regret and missed opportunity. When I think of what memories could have materialized out of that one getting together to work and spend time with my friend, all I can do is shake my head in regret. I try hard not to think about that missed opportunity.

Merle's mother, Flossie, and sister, Lillian Haggard-Rea, supported his musical career all their life. After his mother's passing, Lillian especially was close to her beloved brother. Merle would call her after a late-night concert to share whatever was on his mind, mostly reminisce about family members who had passed or mention a newly written song.

The last song Lillian ever heard her brother sing to her on the phone that he was most proud of was "Kern River Blues." It was the last country ballad written and recorded by Merle in his home studio about his memories leaving Bakersfield in the '70s.

The two of us had a lot in common, both of us coming from humble beginnings. Merle was raised in a converted box car and lived in a three-room house. Merle went to jail at an early age, and I went to jail early in my youth; he hitchhiked a ride on a freight train, and I thumbed my way to Mexico for the thrill. I had Garner State Park and Merle had the mighty Kern River. Losing our fathers at an early age played a big role in our search to fill a large hole in our hearts. My father died of cancer when I was 16 and Merle lost his father at the tender age of 6. Another commonality we shared was I had received a guitar from my eldest brother, Andres, at age nine. Merle received his first guitar from his brother, Lowell, at 12 years old.

One blessing both my daughter, Aubry, and I are extremely grateful to Merle for, is him allowing my daughter to share the stage with him. My ex-wife, Debbie McNeely, gave Merle a haircut before the show in Nashville and when they were done, he turned to my daughter and said, "well, kid alright are you ready…you're up next."

It was déjà vu and reminded me of the first time I performed on the Grand Ole Opry stage…pure coincidence and luck for me when Don Gibson missed the curtain call, and I was told, "You're up in 3 minutes." For Aubry, it meant so much to me to know that Merle saw that "something special" in my daughter that only a man of his caliber could, and he chose to share and expose her talent with his captive audience. That's something... a moment in time no one can take away from you.

Debbie told me he told Aubry after her performance, "you did great, kid!" As Aubry's father, I can't tell you what that meant to me and my daughter, a young and impressionable girl to have both our hero and friend have that much faith in her singing expressing his affection to my daughter.

Merle knew me, liked me, and he accepted me the way I am. In my eyes, Merle will forever be mine and daughter Aubry's hero. There are no words to express how much I miss my brother but singing his songs keeps his memory alive in my heart.

No one sings or tells a story like Merle... he will forever live in our hearts because he not only gifted us with song, but he gave us a piece of his soul. He was always true to himself and honest to the rest of us and when you were in his presence you not only knew it, but you felt it. I heard from him via text in 2015. It read "Merry Christmas friend." The last text I received from my friend, Merle read, "Hope you have a great New Year! 2016. Your friend, Merle."

Red Simpson of Bakersfield: "I'm A Truck"

I was playing lead guitar in Tom T. Hall's Band at the World-Famous Palomino Club in North Hollywood, Los Angeles, when Tom called up singer-songwriter the late Red Simpson to sing on stage. For some reason, Red stood like a *deer in the headlight* at the audience for a good 3 to 4 minutes when he belted his infamous song, "I'm A Truck." Well, that got the beer-loving crowd going crazy, and you could see Red get his confidence up after that. I knew he was a good friend of Merle's, who I thought the world of, so after the gig, we were all sitting around with nightclub owner Tommy Thomas, Red, and his agent.

I love California, aka the Golden State, and all the diversity (people and fun places) you can visit, so I enjoyed everything. There's much to do in Los Angeles and its surrounding hot spots. I understand there were even Japanese tours to stop and visit "the Pal." It was a popular venue for booking both country and rock. It would also be the first venue I'd perform at going solo when I started to tour.

The last words I remember Red shouting was "I want to play here, but it will cost them $500.00." His then Agent, Cliffie Stone, gave him a stern look and straight out told him, "Red, you better let me do the talking because I'm pretty sure I could book you for $1,000.00." That is always why I let my managers book my shows because if left up to me, I will agree to any offer being I love to sing in front of an audience. Most artists are kindhearted that way whereas Managers and Agents always have business in mind and getting everyone in the band paid equitably. Cliffie was also a DJ on the radio and an announcer, as well as an author of *Everything You Always Wanted To Know About, Songwriting But Didn't Know Who To Ask.*

Tommy's place was the best-known country music club in Los Angeles and popular entertainers including Merle Haggard, Johnny Cash, Willie Nelson, Mel Tillis, Patsy Cline, Waylon Jennings, Kenny Rogers, and Crystal Gayle, along with many more country and rock artists headlining like Bob Dylan.

Robert Earl Keen

Singer Robert Earl Keen shared with me when I played at the Astrodome in 1974 that as a kid, he was in a school contest to write an essay, "Why I feel Johnny Rodriguez is the best songwriter in the world." He lost and the winner got to meet me.

Shortly while talking, a Keen song came on the jukebox. I explained to him that when I was a kid, I always wanted to travel to Mexico, so I started hitchhiking at 13 to Mexico because we could get drunk if you could reach the bar. It took me 30 minutes to write "Ridin' My Thumb to Mexico." I could relate to it, and I was only 22.

Friends

I would meet many celebrities worldwide, and many of them would become close friends. I could not list them all, but here are a few that come to mind. Singers: Roger Miller, Glenn Campbell, Conway Twitty, Charley Pride, Toby Keith, Moe Bandy, Johnny Lee, James Hand, Hank Williams Jr. Ray Price, Little Anthony, Josh Brolin; Loretta Lynn, Tammy Wynette; Actor: James Garner, Comedian, Minnie Pearl, actresses: Sally Struthers, Terry Moore, singer, and Play Girl Magazine, Bobbi Benton, Little Anthony, Evil "Daredevil" Knievel (stunt performer), Boxer Mike Tyson, Reverend Jesse Jackson, James Garner, Bear Lindsay, Robert Duvall, and more.

Some other celebrities I got the opportunity to know were Anthony Quinn, Glenn Ford, Cliff Robertson, and Terry Moore, the famous actress who played "Little Sheba." I stayed with her in Hollywood and in Malibu. We became close friends. She was married to the late Howard Hughes. There were so many people I got to know in show business, and I ended up knowing the Los Angeles/Hollywood scene pretty good. I also got to fly with her in the Goddess Knight country. That was a real honor and rush seeing the Blue Angels training in Florida.

Also, I drove the first team benefit for the children of America, a lady hired me after seeing me driving a stagecoach. I didn't get hurt, but it turned over on me when it was going too fast. I would have liked to hand that one off, but nope it was on TV News Edition.

Throughout my remarkable career, I have met so many people at various places in time that I think about the memories and miss today... I want to thank these singers and friends who graciously invited me to write with or sing on stage with them. Thank you for giving and sharing great times with me. They include Willie Nelson, Merle Haggard, Buck Owens, Johnny Cash, Waylon Jennings, George Strait, Dennis Quaid, Randy Van Warmer, Dickie Betts, Bobby Whitlock, James Burton, Jerry Kennedy, Steve Cropper, Hargus (pig) Robbins, Jerry Lee Lewis, Bob Moore, Buddy Emmons, Tanya Tucker, Charly McClain, Pete Drake, Johnny Christopher. Crystal Gail, Emmy Lou Harris, Little Anthony, and Chuck Berry. I enjoyed the

Everly Brothers, Bob Dylan, Little Richard, Minnie Pearl, and many others.

California Friends

I met Lisa Loring, "Wednesday" of the Addams Family television series (1964–1966). She and I, along with Antonio Fargas, who played Huggy Bear Brown in *Starsky* and *Hutch*, hung out together. Once, we were all out having a good time with actor-comedian Jim Varney at the Andaz West Hollywood *Hyatt* on Sunset Strip Boulevard, Los Angeles, California. Those were good times with actor-comedian Jim Varney at the Andaz West Hollywood Hyatt on Sunset Strip Boulevard, Los Angeles, California. Those were fun days. I loved hanging out with funny people. R.I.P.

Cartoonist Charles Addams named "Wednesday" after the well-known nursery rhyme, "Wednesday's Child Is Full of Woe." She was obsessed with death on television and wore a collared black baby doll dress. That's funny to me and millions of others. I met Gene Autry too, and I introduced him to George Jones.

I want to thank Don of the Everly Brothers. He lived with a Mexican girl from Texas for over 25 years. They both drove to Nashville as the Garza twins, *Adeleida* and *Adela*. Their brothers are badass boxers. They all remain my friends. May they R.I.P.

My other two California friends are singer/actor Mayf Nutter of Bakersfield, California, Freddie Weller of a band called the Raiders, and Bobby Bigelow from *Little House on the Prairie*. I also met Xavier Hollander, called "The Happy Hooker." What an act for a time when the censors went crazy over such acts.

Nashville Friends

I've been in Nashville for over ten months now and I can't tell you how good it feels to be back getting reacquainted with some old friends. It's been too long, yet it feels as though we can just pick up like old times. And some of my friends' memories are from Printer's Alley, not far from my memory. They include Jim Vest, Jerry Croon, Cliff Parker, Diane Sherrill, Sondra Rucker, "Skull," Willie Raynesford, Ronnie Prophet, Sammi Smith, Waylon Jennings, Mack Vickery, and Earl Clark.

Here's something out of left field... but here it goes. The reason I ask so many questions, I believe is because I think I'm about half Jewish and I mean that in a good way. Now, a Catholic Jew. Go figure! Seriously, in my life if it were not for my Jewish friends and people; I'd probably be dead, now. Thank God for heaven-sent friends.

Sabinal & Texas Natives

Academy Award-winning actor/producer Matthew McConaughey is a Uvalde native who is a respected actor in Hollywood, California and advocates strongly for gun control and safety before the US Senate. He most recently wrote his memoir, *Green Lights*, a very intimate and honest portrayal of his life story. Also, the late Dale Evans, wife of Roy Rogers.

Robert A. Rodriguez is a filmmaker and composer who lives in Texas. The Ayala family of San Antonio, Texas; Little Larry and Jerry Keenan, *Red Dog*. Texan Eva Longoria, Head Coach, Oail Andrew, "Bum" Phillips of the Houston Oilers gave me a cowboy buckle that I proudly wear, "Bum Phillips Charities, Johnny, 2018."

I received the most stunning-looking buckle and award from my longtime cowboy friend, OD Anderson, Director of All Cowboy and Arena Champions Hall of Fame... A World Association of Champions decorated with ruby and turquoise stones with a sign of the cross in the center. It is the most beautiful gold-plated cowboy buckle I've ever seen or received in my life. I wear it with pride in reverence to cowboys around the world, born in the past and in the future under the star-lit skies of the Americas.

Chapter 26 Testimonials

"Bring My Flowers Now (While I'm Livin')"
– Tanya Tucker

In the past, Johnny has been honored and recognized by three U.S. Presidents including George H.W. Bush, and George W. Bush as well as Jimmy Carter. According to April Foley, people were looking around with the accouterments of money and power listening to Opera and Classical music, but George W. Bush while attending Harvard School of business and his college friends were going to the Opera, but George Bush was listening to Johnny Rodriguez's music over and over in his pickup truck. Cited in the Washington Post Company, At Height of Vietnam, and Bush Picks Guard and written by staff writers; George Lardner Jr. and Lis Romano, July 28, 1999.

Johnny Rodriguez, While the Luke, Blakes and FGLs may get the lions' share of publicity at CMA Fest, the backbone of the festival is the veteran . . . artists who connect today's Nashville with its roots. Bobby Bare, Jeannie Seely and T.G Sheppard all turned in nostalgic sets on the fan Fair X concourse, with the appearance of Johnny Rodriguez in a rare treat. Although the 65-year-old Texas singer sported a cast on his right hand that prohibited him from playing guitar, he was in excellent voice during a heartfelt performance on Friday afternoon, offering hits like "Ridin' My Thumb to Mexico" and "You Always Come Back to Hurtin' Me." But it was his beautiful rendition of his 1973 number one hit, "That's The Way Love Goes," that reminded fans how important Rodriguez was to 70s country.
– Rolling Stones Magazine: Joseph Hudak

Congratulations Buddy! During the years we worked together, we produced and recorded some fantastic records. You have proven your talent over and over. I appreciated the opportunity to work with you; you were absolutely a huge bright spot in my career in music and I'll never forget that. I love you!
– Jerry Kennedy, Producer

Johnny, "Charro" you are the epitome of a true country music singer and role model in the Latin community. Your bilingual songs have impacted cowboys and cowgirls in and out of the roping arenas. Bushwacker and I salute you for your contributions honoring our ancestral traditions and paying homage to country music, Norteño, Ranchera, and Mariachi fans around the world. Vaya con dios, mi amigo
– Julio Moreno, Bull Stock Contractor & Owner of Bushwacker

I saw him when I was a kid and became a huge fan. He taught me how to attack a song while singing along with his albums. Nobody sounded like him. Country music is better because of Johnny Rod. Top shelf.
– Toby Keith

Yes, I did have a crush when I was getting started in the music business, or even before when I was in college. Johnny Rodriguez, so cute. I've always been a huge fan of his and his music.
– Reba McEntire

The first time I met Johnny was in Brainerd, Minnesota for a benefit hosted by Steve Hall, aka "Shotgun Red." Mickey's sister, Debbie, and I (Moore & Moore) were also on the show. Johnny not only performed, but he was also a celebrity bartender. His talent and charisma won everyone over. We have traveled to several countries with Johnny doing shows together, and I have worked with him as his booking agent for many years. It's amazing to see how loyal his fans are. I could personally write a book about all our adventures together, but suffice it to say, there will never be another Johnny Rodriguez.
– Terry Moore, Third Coast Talent Agency

The life and career of my friend Johnny Rodriguez is now a book that every country fan will love and want to read. He is one of the true legends in country music, and his story is one of the most unique ones in our business. Do yourself a favor and get it.
– T.G. Sheppard, T.G. Sheppard Enterprises

The Johnny Rodriguez story epitomizes the true rise from obscurity to fame and fortune while opening the musical doors for legions who have had his same hunger. I have booked Johnny for many years and have found that he always gives everything in his personal appearances while sharing his incredible talent with those he loves the most-his loyal and very dedicated fans. Working with Johnny has always been an honor.

– Tracy Pitcox, Promoter, Texas Country Music Disc Jockey Hall of Fame

I have always been a big fan of Johnny Rodriguez. His voice, music, and style of singing are unmatched. When Johnny sings, he makes you feel and believe every word of the song. I enjoy listening to some of the deep cuts that I believe are big hits. Johnny has so many great songs that will continue to influence generations to come. I feel blessed, and I'm thankful to know Johnny and to call him my friend.

– Rodney Collins, Promoter

Johnny's had a huge impact on the Latin community singing bilingually at a time Tejano music was mixing and taking off in the direction of the country music genre. His influence was major to me and to many other musicians. He's a great singer and actor, too. I remember the first time hearing him sing, *Wing Beneath My Wings,* and bringing me to tears. I was sobbing because he touched me so deeply. A piano was accompanying him. I love all his songs, but this one song was so beautiful, and his rendition was delivered pitch perfect that I can't explain what it did to me. It was in Austin, Texas. Besides, being a great singer, Johnny is a loving and kind human being who makes time for anyone anywhere. He has a rare quality that few artists do these days. I love you, *Chingon Badass.*

– Little Joe (Jose Maria De Leon Hernandez)

Johnny Rodriguez is probably one of the most unique voices in country music! I've been listening to him since the '70s and I still enjoy his songs as much today as I did then…Truly one of the Best!

– Mickey Gilley

Johnny's voice is distinctive and is as rich today as it was in his yesteryears. Country music is new and improved because of the likes of Johnny Rodriguez. He arrived in Nashville at the right time and place bringing his unique Latin style and voice; the best of both worlds when we needed him most. He was one of the youngest country singers to take Nashville by storm and become an international superstar. He is a true Champion for country music lovers leaving no man left behind because he has a song for everyone. He's a trailblazer and continues to lead others to success. Johnny's music is timeless...others may try to copycat him, but there is only one Johnny Rodriguez in my book. Congratulations on the Ameripolitan Music Awards, "Master" Award, 2023. You richly deserve it. Love you man.

– Dale Watson

Johnny Rodriguez's singing style is so original that it's difficult for me to guess who might possibly have been his musical influences! Perhaps, his sound is so unique that it can only be traced back to him. He may have blazed a trail that no one else could follow! And now, almost fifty years after Johnny burst into the country music scene with his mile-long string of hit records, he is unbelievably still singing strong those songs in their early keys . . . one of the few artists ever who could make that boast. Let's face it, no matter how much time passes, Johnny Rodriguez is destined to always be a "teenager in song." It's a great honor to attend his shows and call him my friend. I dearly love this sweet and humble guy, and I am his forever fan.

– Jeannie C. Riley, July 23, 2020

Johnny Rodriguez is one of the all-time greatest country singers in my lifetime, His songs and legacy will be remembered by generations of country music fans. He is one of my mentors, an all-around great person, and I am blessed to call him my friend. Love you, my brother.

– Kelly Kenning

Johnny Rodriguez is not only one of my favorite country music singers and songwriters of all time . . . he's, my friend. I think the world of him, and I don't think he knows just how good he is. That's what I love about him . . . his humility. His signature is stylish and unique with his Spanish and I'm one of his biggest fans. Johnny Rocks!

– Moe Bandy

Who didn't have a crush on Johnny Rodriguez? I drove around Nashville listening to his music.

– Leann Womack

I've known Johnny Rodriquez for quite a while now and I don't think I have ever seen him without that incredible smile. I've seen him walk out on the stage in front of thousands of people and throw that smile at them and the show was his! Another gift Johnny has is picking great songs to record and singing for his many fans. People all over the world love Johnny Rodriquez and so do I.

– David Frizzell

I've always felt like Johnny Rodriguez was one of the most underrated artists. Not only is he one of the best ballad singers, but with his uniquely good looks, disarming smile, and command of two languages I always felt like he should have been in movies . . . maybe a modern-day cowboy star! He is one of the most genuine people I know and I'm proud to be his friend.

– Jeannie Seely

My first memory of Johnny Rodriguez is when I recorded his song playing on the radio because I wanted to hear it over and over. I loved his voice, and I loved his music. I was such a huge fan of his and when I saw him in person . . . I thought he was gorgeous. I was absolutely in love with him. Today, I still am a fan of his great music and we're good friends.

– Rhonda Vincent

Johnny is one of the few ones in the music business with "stick and stay." I admire his tenacity and consistency in singing traditional country and bilingual songs from his heart. It's been a pleasure knowing him and his music. I love him like a brother.
– Gene Watson

I think that country singer from Texas, what was his name? . . . oh yeah. Johnny Rodriguez. I think he did a fantastic job on "Something."
– George Harrison

I first met Johnny in the early 1970s when I was playing *King of The Road.* I think he was still working for Tom T. Hall. We became friends and I would invite him up to do a few songs. The crowd loved him. He never lost the magic that was Johnny Rod. He still has that and he's still my friend. Just like those early '70s at the King of The Road."
– Eddy Raven

Johnny Rodriguez is not only a legendary artist . . . he's a kind soul with a heart who has an ear for great songs. His support and encouragement help me stay on course when I lose my way. As a singer-songwriter, I contemplate the wisdom and inspiration he gives me when I need a reference for greatness. His songs have carved out a musical milestone in country music history that is unmatched by any artist who came before or will after. Rodriguez's legacy will never die but will continue to live in the hearts of music lovers everywhere for generations to come. It's a privilege to know the legend, but an honor to know and love the man I call my friend.
– Tony Ramey

Johnny is one of the greatest country music voices of all times and genres. He has one of the most loyal fan bases that any singer and band could hope to have. It's been a privilege and a blast to work with my friend all these years.
– Jody Maphis

Johnny and I were a novelty in the country music scene. He was the first to make country music inclusive where patrons were an expanded audience coming to hear us perform on stage. That was the best feeling to watch the audience wearing a sea of hats to dance and sing along. I don't think my friend ever understood the impact he had on Latino musicians and country music lovers; when Johnny arrived on the Nashville scene our people had arrived and came with him too. He opened the door for musicians to play country music *Rancheras* and he opened the floor for others to dance and watch a show without fear. Country music was no longer exclusive to some. Rodriguez's words ring true. If you know him, he'd be the first to say, "All I Ever Meant To Do Was Sing!"

– Gus Barba

Johnny has always been one of the good ones and is always the same. I'm proud to say that he's not only been a friend from the beginning, but I remain a big fan of his music. I love hearing him sing in Spanish. And he's about the only one I know who still wears the same size and fits into his Wranglers.

– Johnny Lee

I am and have always been a fan of Johnny Rodriguez. In my opinion he is the most original stylist to come out of Nashville since the '70s. I have only made three predictions in my career about singers destined to become superstars. Willie Nelson, Charley Pride, and Johnny Rodriguez.

– Johnny Bush

Johnny Rodriguez is one of the most humble and talented guys I have ever had the privilege to work and hang out with. He's, my brother.

– Joey Rodriguez

It was an honor and a privilege being asked to participate on the Johnny Rodriguez album "Coming Home." Johnny is a humble guy and a great singer and I'm grateful for the opportunity to be a part of his musical career.

– DLG

Johnny symbolizes an artist's ability to create a legacy when he freely accepts his nature and his culture. Doing so allowed his personal and unique qualities to boldly shine. He has genuinely earned the title of an artist because he is courageous to express his creativity and total being to others; quirks and all. He is one of a kind. Thanks for leading the way, buddy.

– Felix Truvere

It was an honor to play and sing with Johnny for 34 years. I first heard *Pass Me By* on the jukebox at Garner Park and bought it for my collection. Never in my wildest dreams did I think I would one day work for him. I have always been blown away with his strong vocal delivery and range. I have been blessed to "take the music to the people," because of Johnny. I will always remember the package concerts with other artists, tv shows, the Opry and fan fair, USO tours, foreign countries, playing for President Bush, plus of all the musicians that have played in the band through the years and many friendships. Thank you, Johnny, for 34 great years.

– Gary Goss

Johnny is one of my biggest influences, one of the greatest to ever sing a song. He's always been an ally to me. We met in Nashville in 1994. I've traveled all over Texas with him as well. He introduces me to his fans and has me sing a few songs every time. Johnny's had a lot of help along the way himself, so he understands the importance of that and pays it forward whenever he can. He even sang "I Couldn't Be Me Without You" when my wife, Kim walked out to meet me under that oak tree on our wedding day. Love you amigo!

– Richie Allbright

* * * * *

Chapter 27: Q & A

Question and Answer . . . Fans Wanna Know

How do you describe yourself?

I am a simple man. I'm positive and happy most of the time. One of the things I will say is I am not materialistic. Things mean nothing to me, but my family means everything.

What is the best part of being a dad?

The discovery of knowing and spending quality time with my loved ones every chance I can get.

When you are totally alone with no one else around and you truly search your heart, what does it reveal.

I meditate in silence and I listen for God and His music.

What is your favorite song to sing when you're at home in Texas?

"Over The Rainbow" by Israel Kamakawiwo'ole

What were your Christmas traditions growing up?

We would build a fire in the backyard. Friends and relatives would come over and gather. We would all make tamales so that we'd have something delicious to unwrap. After everyone went to bed if they did; we would sing both country and mariachi songs. Happy times!

What is your favorite memory?

On one Thanksgiving, we were going through tough times because we were broke, out of work and nobody talked about it. That's when my brothers Vale and Reynaldo took matters into their hands, and without saying a word grabbed their shotguns and headed to the Sabinal River.

My sister was staring out the window and yelled, "Look! The boys are coming." My brothers came back with two turkeys and talked about how they spotted and shot two wild strutting

birds. What was amazing to me…to their credit was that my brothers only had 4 shotgun shells between them.
That day I observed and learned a lot. I learned that my brothers not only talk the talk, but they were men who walk the walk. How tall my brothers stood in all our eyes, but no taller than in our mother's as we feasted on all the fixings. Thanks be to God and my brothers' shooting ability, we had a good Thanksgiving that year. And, even today, I smile thinking about it.

What was your first paying gig?

My football buddies and I would head out to Tarpley, Texas (Hill Country) close to Utopia on Saturday nights where I would lay my hat on a bar for tips and play on stage with the old cowboys' *vaqueros.*

Later, I was playing in Tom T. Band in Nashville when he notified me that a Promoter called his Booking Agency wanting to book me in San Antonio. He said I could use his bus and band. It seemed like a sweet deal for me at the time. I was reluctant to go out on my own, but I took the job anyway.

My first solo gig was at the Farmer's Daughter, in San Antonio. Club owner, Bobbi Barker, paid me $500. It was really something the way the crowd went crazy and there were girls, girls, girls everywhere. That was a good thing . . . it's what guys dream of 'til the reality struck—paying the gas bill.

When was the first time you heard yourself on the radio?

I had just left the studio with Tom T. Hall after talking to the disc jockey, who had promised he would play my song sometime in the night. I was sitting up front with the bus driver on Tom T. Hall's bus, and at 3 a.m. on WSM Radio the DJ had said he might play my record that night. I felt ecstatic when I heard my song come on. Right there and then, I wanted to call someone, but everyone was asleep.

What is your once-in-a-lifetime, biggest thrill of your life?

When I performed at the White House for George H.W. Bush's inauguration. I had never been anywhere like that royal black-tie event. I've travelled before, even abroad, but nothing compares to that feeling of playing for the President of the

United States and the multitude of dignitaries and supporters in attendance. It was the highlight of my life for this South Texas boy to be in the house of a fellow Texan's home. That special moment gave me a deep feeling of pride and honor.
Traveled.

What is your most embarrassing moment?

One Christmas Eve, I was housesitting Randy Willis's home in Austin while he and his three sons were skiing in Colorado. That evening, I thought I'd go outside and relax in the hot tub. I got comfortable in the whirlpool, decided I had enough, and headed back to the house. To my surprise, that's when I discovered I had locked myself out by slamming the door to the patio. I was wearing only my underwear in the chilling air. With no cell phone, I had no choice but to knock on the neighbor's door for help at 11 p.m. A kind elderly woman obliged me to use her phone so I could call a locksmith. She didn't blink an eye. I appreciated her cool demeanor and felt so grateful to her that I autographed my newly released CD, *You Can Say That Again*. Randy had negotiated the record deal with HighTone Records in Oakland, California, and received a case of CDs the day before he flew out. I gave his neighbor the first copy. He later told me he had asked her to keep an eye on me, and I would feed her cats if she left town. Randy would feed her cats when she was out of town.

Did you ever consider another profession besides singing?

Yes, I was always attracted to law enforcement and thought about being a policeman. The Police Commissioner in San Antonio deputized me after a friend, Rick Gipprich introduced me to him after seeing me do an exhibition to help the prisoners exercise. It inspired them but surprised me more. Before I knew it, I was one of the boys in blue.

What is it you are most proud of?

I am most proud of my family and bridging people of all walks of life together through my music. To watch the cowboys and cowgirls smile, sing, and dance to my music in peace without fighting on the dance floor makes me happy.

What do you contribute your success to?

God's grace

What does my album title, *Building Bridges*, mean to me?

It means having resilience of the human spirit to practice effective communication and compassion. The ability to offer hope and inspiration to others, outside of yourself because giving is true happiness. I've learned the value of both giving and receiving and connecting the dots when it comes to building and mending relationships.

What is your favorite quote?

"Whenever there is change and whenever there is uncertainty, there is opportunity." – Mark Cuban

The above quote was my "why" when I was determined to go to Nashville and make something of myself that my family and I could be proud of. I went to Nashville on a prayer and my mother's blessing, along with blind faith I could make it.

How do you think others view you?

Good question. A desperado of sort and a confirmed bachelor. It's true. I love adventure and my freedom. Probably more than the average guy. Remember, Roy Rogers song, "Don't Fence Me In?" Well, no one likes being told what to do, not even children, let alone when they grow up. I'm a bit of a Nomad. I'll be the first to admit this, but deep down inside I will never give up on love. I believe she is out there somewhere waiting for me like Glenn Frey's song, "Lover's Moon," by *The Allnighter*. I'm a bit old-fashioned and a romanticist, but it will take someone special to lasso this cowboy in. She's got to have a pure heart and I'll know her when I meet her. My pal, Johnny Cash's wife, June, wanted to set me up with some nice church girls, but I'm old fashioned that way and want to pick her on my own. Do I look up among the stars and ever make a wish? You bet . . . Someday!

In a nutshell, I mostly consider myself a free spirit, if you will. And I think many people wish they could be as well.

I've just learned in life not to take myself too seriously. There really isn't much that gets to me anymore. I understand that life is for the living and there's no sense sweating the small stuff when there's not much you can do about it anyway. I do my best to live in the present.

I believe a lot of the artists I meet wish they could do the same, and those that hang out with me end up having a good time . . . maybe too much of a good time. I've been told by some wives and management in the music business, that they prefer their husbands and artists (for obvious reasons) not hang out with me. After feeling the sting of it…I get it. It's all about the choices we make in life that we can live with or not that can make or break us. I do miss those friends that I had come to know, admire, and respect and I know some miss me, too.

I have experienced a vicious downward spiral of addictions to alcohol, drugs, gambling, sex, and work; these were all self-sabotaging. Shortly after having COVID-19, though, I awoke, and I'm work in progress as I try to balance my life day to day. It's something I work at every day to relax—I will do this for the rest of my life.

I'm content in my life today because even though I'm slowing down some, I know that my life is just as relevant today as it was throughout my decades of success.

Acknowledgments

There is nothing more powerful than the expression of a song or heartfelt words that's spoken to and from the heart.
– Johnny Rodriguez

My experience living in the public eye has not always been an easy one. I have tried to balance my private life between the two and not lose sight of who I am or forget where I come from. To the many who have been in and out of my life, you are treasured in my heart more than you know. I count my blessings and believe that I am the person I am today because of you.

First and foremost, with all my heart and soul, I want to thank my beloved parents, Andres, and Isabel Rodriguez, for their support and love that sustained me throughout my entire life. Too, I am grateful to them for giving me the tradition and love for the universal language of Spanish and music. Because of their teachings, I built bridges communicating through song with a multitude of people and places around the world.

To my loving and caring daughters, Aubry and Teresa, who are the reason for me living... they are the better half of me. A special mention to my siblings who played a big part in my life and were a continuous source of fun-loving childhood memories, encouragement, and advice. My beloved brothers and sisters include Andres Jr., Vale, Reynaldo, Jesse, Raul, Ricky, Ofelia, Antonia, and Eloisa. The dear ones who are now with our heavenly father, my world changed in a heartbeat when you passed. I cherish your memory in my heart, always and forever.

I also want to acknowledge Debbie McNeely, mother of my daughter, Aubry, for raising an amazing and loving daughter who lights up my life. From the beginning, you've been the best mom in the world to our little girl... with your love, prayers, and our faith and trust in God, we did it! From the day Aubry was born, she was our pride and joy who grew to be our shining star.

Also, a special and heart-felt thanks to Melanie Clark for her friendship and help in preparing my income taxes. Over the years, your expertise and counsel have been invaluable to me, and I am deeply indebted to you. Happy Birthday! She may have been born on April Fool's Day, but the lady is no fool.

I want to thank the excellent work and dedication of the people who work behind the scenes, better known as the Rodriguez A-Team who get 'er done. In this big world of ours no one does anything alone nor is it wise to be The Lone Ranger. It's good to know and have confidence in a team that they've got your back. I've seen a lot of good in the world and I've seen and experienced a lot of despair and heartache. And every now and then I feel lucky when a diamond shines a light on my life, and I see hope at the end of the tunnel. There's nothing like it and it helps me to shine a light back on others, too. I credit my publisher and contributor, Pauline A. Vega, for her efforts guiding me through the publishing process and allowing co-author, Austin Teutsch, and me to put this book together with all the time and freedom necessary. Without her believing in me sharing my story with you, this book would not have been born.

Additionally, the same freedom that we have in this book is the freedom that I feel, presently working with producer-artist and friend, Rick "Reno" Stevens, Lisa Wysocky, and executive producer, Pauline Vega on my album, *Building Bridges: A Beyond the Interview Boxset*, to be released in 2023. I encourage my readers to believe in wonders and have the faith of a child where miracles and blessings are its rewards.

A special thanks to extraordinary photographers: Patrice Ash, Rick Henson, Earl Nottingham, Chas E. Wilkins, "Codak Charlie" Wilkins Photography, Carol Roshkind, Cranston Reid Photography, Ron Losey, Francesco Scavullo, Diane McBride, Ann Straughan, Donna Smith, Frankie Kins, Diane Thede-Casey, Johnny Mack, and the late Shirley Fresh all for capturing amazing photos and videos at my shows.

I would also like to shout out to computer guru Jim Southerd, known as Jimmy the Greek, who came to our rescue more times than I can count and award-winner Reporter Bob Price of KGET-TV 17. Both offered invaluable guidance during times of uncertainty; Your support got me through the book process that few authors seldom make to the finish line.

I want to thank Mary Minter of CMA of Texas for lending her support and expertise to me and all musicians over the years. Your counsel and commitment to excellence and music is commendable and deeply appreciated.

A special shout out to the lady who first wrote my name in the *Sabinal Times* article, "Local Boy Does Good." Her name was Undine Bales; and her sons Gregory and Bill were friends of mine. I was not used to the attention and had never been written about except when I was on a jail docket! But it made me feel good about myself that I was on the right track to take that job with Tom T. Hall's band. This also includes Meghann Garcia, Managing Editor of Uvalde Leader-News of Uvalde, Texas.

To the many supportive team members and fans . . . you know who you are. You gave me support and shared memories and gathered information for my first memoir.

I am grateful to you for your amazing generosity of time, following, and loyalty to me, and the Rodriguez Sound. Each of you contributed and inspired me to bring this book to fruition. Thank you for your support and prayers over all the years. The phenomenal individuals who have kept the "Rodriguez Sound" and brand on social media to this day include: Mary Jane Losey who administers my official website johnnyrodriguezmusic.com; Fan-site Administrators: Ann Straughan (Johnny Rodriguez Official Internet Fan Club), Paulette Sanchez, Mary Esther Rositas (my dear cousin), (Living Legend Johnny Rodriguez Fan Club); Donna Smith and Maureen Czinder-Sherman (Legendary Johnny Rodriguez Fan Club); and the late Shirley Fresh and Patricia Crews (Chasin' Johnny Rodriguez) Patrice Ash and Belinda J. Anderson-Machen (Johnny Rodriguez CMA Hall of Fame Campaign Workers). I would also like to express my deep appreciation to the following Merchandise Representatives: Shanna Pearce Wood (since 2015), Texas; Mary Jane Losey, Colorado; Forrest Davis, Texas; Terry Barber and Nancy Parks, Tennessee; and the late Ellen and Ezra Owens (2003–2009), Oklahoma.

I also appreciate those who read parts of my manuscript from a reader's careful eye. My gratitude goes to Nancy Jo Purdue for her encouragement, prayers, and support.

I have had a lot of help along the way…these people are just a few individuals (more like friends) who I have needed to keep my music going these past 50 years. No one is an island,

and we cannot do it alone. You would be wise to always remember this as I will forever feel grateful to this team for their friendship and loyalty. They deserve the biggest applause you could ever give me.

I thank J.P. Newby Management, Jack D. Johnson, and Bill & Melinda Gates Foundation for their commitment to grants in Music and Arts Productions and Artist and Sculptor Bill Raines.

Booking Agency: Carrie and Terry Moore-Reed of Third Coast Talent Agency in Nashville, Tennessee; and A.A. Clarence Selman. Promoters: Tracy Pitcox of Heart of Texas Country Music Association, Brady, Texas; Dr. Jack Teeler of JMT Productions; Club Owners: Barbara and Tim Worthy, Jean Czajkowski and Kiran Desai (Jen Chidgey) of Stagecoach Ballroom of Dallas Fort Worth, Texas; Mo Jeloudarzadeh Jr. and Mo's Place (Katy, Texas); Tony Talanco of Texas Pride Barbecue of Atkins, Texas. Randy Willis, Rodney & Jennifer Collins and family, The Troubadour and Music City Bar & Grill.

Special Friends who have always been there for me along the way: Kelly Kenning, Bruce Carter (Road Manager), Gary Goss (Former Band Manager), Mike Solee, Jody Maphis, Don and Allen Sowersby, Richie Albright, Alex Fox, Corky Parker, Charles Gammill, Thomas "Twig" and Bethany Phillips, Donald Sweat, Dee Dee Cordova (Prayer Warrior), Kandy Walker and sister, Elizabeth; Happy Shahan, Frances Preston, Gus and Kathy Barba; Terry Cline; and special friend, Mary Bailey; Sabinal childhood friend, the late, Carlos Tovar and Austin, "Hot Shot" Schaefer, and Billy Ray McNair.

In deep appreciation of Record labels and Producers Roy Dea and Jerry Kennedy, Owen Bradley, Decca Records, Rick "Reno" Stevens, ANR Records; Drew Davis, Forrest Davis, Drew and Delaney Davis of Runnin Wild Open Productions; Tom Collins of Capitol Records, David Briggs, Producer-Publisher, and musician (former piano player for Elvis Presley) who influenced my success in my musical career as business associates. These special individuals were there for me with guidance and support, along with many colleagues around the world; Music Conductor, Nelson Riddle; Special Mention to artists who have recorded my songs, including Ronnie Dunn,

Janie Fricke, and Barbara Fairchild and the numerous musicians who sing and keep my music alive in honky tonks everywhere.

TV and Movie People: LKLAC; Jack Johnson; J. Colleen Chappell.

I especially wish to express my gratitude to the attorneys who helped me during my Murder trial that included Alan Brown, Jay Norton, and Adrienne Urruthia, as well as John Lentz. Legal and equal access to the justice system is something I advocate for everyone, the rich and the poor. I feel it better levels the playing field where and when issues arise. Better to have it and not need it than need it and not have it. I'm thankful to God I've had and have access to the best counsel and criminal defense team I could have hoped for throughout my life. I've discovered in life that bad things happen to good people where quantum lessons are learned.

Special thanks to the drivers who were there for me and transported me to the shows on time... I am forever grateful to these friends who drove the distance and ran errands for me many times. They include Kelly Kenning (Keonning) Alex Fox and Eric Fox, Albert Castillo, David Peaches, Mike Solee, Jody Maphis, Allen Sowersby, Kandy Walker, Corky Parker, Kansas Keonning, Cody Deaver, Joey Rodriguez, Rick Gipprish, Cody Johnson, Debbie Lee Winslow, Jimmy Velvet, William Stewart, Juanita Vasquez Ramos, Gus Barba, Shane Mercer, Lanette Grindstead, Sharon Dillingham Rodgers, Cody Preston, Rodney and Ron Collins, George Dickerson, Ronnie McDowell, Sharon Jackson, Javier and Irma Moreno, and Tracy who worked with Ride Support; and the late Steve Harrison and the late, Ezra and Ellen Owens, and late, Curtis Webb who drove my bus, the red and *Silver Eagle*, and Rack Jobbers. And, finally, AI Security (Steve Park of Corpus Christi) and U.S. Marshalls for their unwavering support to this day.

I am grateful for the following friends who have given me a place to rest my head over the years: Kelly Kenning and his dad, Ray Keonning and sons, Tony, Sam, and Gavin who operate a successful franchise business called, *Dairy Queen*. Gus and Kathy Barba, Melanie Clark, Kandy Walker, Randy Willis, Alex Fox, Mike Solee, Jody Maphis, Mando Martinez, Rick Gipprich (retired, Police Officer, San Antonio) Robert and Martha Flores,

Mary Jane Loosey, Roland and wife, Pauline Ortiz of Pipe Creek, Texas, Bubba Estes and wife, Anita. Other friends who opened their homes to me—including Juan Contreras, Alan Chapman, Kandy Walker, who let me stay with her in South Texas in a beautiful oceanside apartment; Austin "Hot Shot" Schaefer and family who let me stay overnight with them when we were kids. Their friendship and support meant a lot to me and my mom.

A special big thanks to all the radio and television stations worldwide for keeping my music alive on the airwaves. Without your music selections and the ability to play my songs, I would not have reached the pinnacle of success and the ears of the fans I care about and love. KKYX and Max Gardner for playing my record first, and Sally Chapman and GM for the continuous years of support. Special tribute: San Antonio Radio icon, the late Bruce Hathaway (Top 10 Radio). Some of those stations include:

Texas: Willie's Roadhouse, DJ Paula Nelson XMRadio Channel 59, Dish network 6059, 94.3 FM, KKYX, WBAP, KLAC, WHN, KXTM; Austin, 94.7 FM, KBSO The Nashville Network and WSM 650, WKDF 103.3, WSIX-FM 97, WPLN-FM; KSSL 107.3 FM, Lubbock, Texas; Spanish: Domingo Live KlllTV3, Rudy Trevino of Corpus Christi, Joe Bielinski "Mayor of Country Music," KTFW Radio, Ft. Worth, Texas; Rudy Trevino "Domingo Live," Telemundo, and Univision stations around the world. Muchas gracias! Buck Owens Production Company, Bakersfield's Best Country, KUZZ (550 AM, KCWR 107.9 FM). Disc Jockeys and Juke Box Operators everywhere. Johnny Rodriguez music station is on Pandora.

I'd like to thank the mentors, colleagues, and musicians (Bakersfield Sound studio musicians of Bakersfield, California) and regional bands everywhere who always gave their support and lent a helping hand to fill in when asked. You are the blood and lifeline that keeps music and musicians alive and thriving. I'd like to acknowledge Buck's son, Johnny Owens and the Bakersfield Sound, and thank Buckeroo Willie Cantu who played drums for Mr. Buck Owens.

There are many people who showed concern and helped me in both my young and adult life and I am thankful…especially all the people in and around Sabinal who hired me as Juan Raul Davis-Rodriguez until I got famous. A special thanks to two of my favorite first-grade teachers, Mrs. Shuddie and Mrs. Wyatt, but to be honest, I loved all my teachers in school.

Lastly, I want to salute the men and women of the United States military as well as our First Responders: veterans, fireman, law enforcement officers, and their families for your service, sacrifice, and support of our great country. You're all heroes to me, and you have my respect. A special recognition to the following Law Enforcement Personnel: Bruce Carter, Dan Hodges, Texas Ranger and great friend of mine, Arturo "Uncle Artie" Rodriguez, Uvalde, Texas; retired FBI/Swat team and Rick Mauity. No one inspires or gives me more pride than those wearing the uniform of our country for American families. May God keep you safe.

Also, I'd like to thank Jack D. Johnson and Clarence Selman who got me to Charter Lakeside Hospital, Memphis, Tennessee (Best thing that ever happened to me!) and my personal physician, Dr. Rad Kothmann, and the other dedicated doctors and nurses who have played a significant role in saving my life, keeping me alive, and in good health and shape. It is not an easy feat, but as the popular saying goes, "*Health is wealth.*"

At the risk of leaving anyone out, I want to say a special thank you to the many who have been there for me in my life. If not for the love of family (numerous special nephews, nieces, and cousins), and the many friends, acquaintances, and colleagues who have contributed to my life in one way or another, this book would not be possible.

Lastly, my book is dedicated to music lovers everywhere, who show up and prove over and over that music matters — that it is albondigas soup for the soul. "I couldn't be me without you."

It's impossible not to exclude someone who has touched me with their encouragement at such an important moment. You have made a difference in my life and are deeply valued even though your name is not mentioned. Including those who doubted me, you motivated me to be more determined to work hard to achieve success. *Gracias!*

Discography

Albums

1973 *Introducing Johnny Rodriguez* (Mercury Records)
1973 *All I Ever Meant to Do Was Sing* (Mercury)
1973 *My Third Album* (Mercury)
1974 *Songs About Ladies and Love* (Mercury)
1974 *Country Classics* (Mercury)
1975 *Just Get Up and Close the Door* (Mercury)
1975 *Love Put a Song in My Heart* (Mercury)
1976 *Greatest Hits* (Mercury)
1976 *Reflecting* (Mercury)
1977 *Practice Makes Perfect* (Mercury)
1977 *Just For You* (Mercury)
1978 *Love Me with All of Your Heart* (Mercury)
1978 *Rodriguez Was Here* (Mercury)
1979 *Sketches* (Mercury)
1979 *Rodriguez* (Epic)
1980 *Through My Eyes* (Epic)
1980 *Gypsy* (Epic)
1981 *After the Rain* (Epic)
1982 *Biggest Hits* (Epic)
1983 *For Every Rose* (Epic)
1984 *Foolin' With Fire* (Epic)
1986 *Full Circle* (Epic)
1988 *Gracias* (Capitol)
1993 *Run for the Border* (Intersound)
1993 *You Can Say That Again*
1995 *Super Hits* (Epic)
1996 *You Can Say That Again* (Hightone)
1996 *Funny Things Happen To Fun Lovin' People* (Paula)
1997 *Hits* (Mercury)
1998 *Johnny Rodriguez* (K-Tel)
1998 At the Trap (Erv Woolsey Company)
2001 *Back-to-Back* (Intercontinental)
2002 *Desperado: His First Twenty Hits* (Mercury)
2004 *Desperado: A Decade of Hits* (Compendia)

2005 *Greatest Hits* (K-Tel)
2005 *Greatest Hits* (Intersound)
2006 *Country Chart-Toppers: Johnny Rodriguez* (Sterling)
2009 *Some of Mine, Some of Theirs and*
2009 *Live From Texas:* (Runnin' Wide Open Productions)
2009 "Some of Mine, Some of Theirs" (Runnin' Wide Open Productions)
2009 "Texas Legends" (Runnin' Wide Open Productions)
2014 *The Definitive Collection* (Hump Head Records)

Singles

1973 "Pass Me By"
1973 "You Always Come Back"
1973 "Ridin' My Thumb to Mexico"
1973 "That's the Way Love Goes"
1973 "Something"
1974 "Dance with Me (Just One More Time)"
1974 "We're Over"
1974 "I Just Can't Get Her Out of My Mind"
1975 "Just Get Up and Close the Door"
1975 "Love Put a Song in My Heart"
1975 "I Couldn't Be Me Without You"
1976 "I Wonder If I Ever Said Goodbye"
1976 "Hillbilly Heart"
1976 "Desperado"
1976 "If Practice Makes Perfect"
1977 "Eres Tu"
1977 "Saving This Love for You"
1977 "We Believe in Happy Endings"
1978 "Cuando Caliente El Sol (Love Me with All of Your Heart)"
1978 "Alibis"
1979 "Down on the Rio Grande"
1979 "Fools for Each Other"
1979 "What'll I Tell Virginia"
1980 "Love Look At Us Now"
1980 "North of the Border"
1980 "I Want You Tonight"

1981 "Trying Not To Love You" 1981 "It's Not The Same Without You" 1981 "Born With The Blues"
1982 "He's Not Entitled To Your Love"
1982 "Foolin'"
1983 "How Could I Love Her So Much"
1983 "Back On Her Mind Again"
1984 "Too Late To Go Home"
1984 "Let's Leave The Lights On Tonight"
1984 "First Time Burned"
1984 "Rose Of My Heart"
1985 "Here I Am Again"
1986 "She Don't Cry Like She Used To"
1986 "I Didn't (Every Chance I Had)"
1988 "I Wanna Wake Up With You"
1988 "You Might Want To Use Me Again"
1988 "No Chance To Dance"
1989 "Back To Stay"
1993 "You Can Say That Again"
1996 "One Bar At A Time"
2009 "Texas Legends" (Runnin' Wide Open Productions)
2013 "You Go Around," *Heroes, Mentors, and Friends* album with Amber Digby

Guest Singles
1979 "I Hate The Way, I Love It," with Charley McClain
1990 "Tomorrow's World," with various artists

Music Videos
1985 "Tears on My Pillow" (Gus Barba, Director)
1990 "Tomorrow's World" (Gustavo Garzon, Director)
1993 "Run For The Border" (Tom Bevins, Director)
1996 "You Can Say That Again" (Unknown Director)
2007 "Rosie's Cantina" (Dr. Ruben Barrera, Director)
2011 "She Beat the Cheat Out of Me" (Dr. Ruben Barrera, Director)

Films/Television
1976 *Nashville Girl* (Movie)
1996 *Down for the Barrio* (Movie)

1974 *Adam 12* (TV Episode, Season 7)
1974 *The Dating Game* (TV Episode)
Mike Douglas – *Moments & Memories* (TV Episode 1961, Guest)
1982 *Hee-Haw* (TV Episodes, 9 appearances)

Accomplishments

- "Most Promising Male Vocalist" Academy of Country Music, 1972
- "Male Vocalist of the Year" Country Music Awards; Nomincc/Prcscnter, 1974
- Performed at Carnegie Hall, 1974
- Performed at Wembley Stadium in London, England, 1974
- Performed throughout the US and overseas (Australia, Canada, France, Germany, Guam, Japan, Monte Carlo, S. Korea, Mexico, Spain, Switzerland) 1974.
- Trendsetter Award "First Mexican American International Country Star," 1976
- Performed for U.S. President George H.W. Bush (inauguration) The White House
- Recognized by U.S. Presidents George W. Bush and Jimmy Carter
- Latin Music Hall of Fame, Hollywood-Chamber of Commerce
- Tejano Music Award, (recipient) 1991
- Terry Music Awards, Branson, MI, 1998
- Charted 14 number-one hits; 4 Top 10-100; Billboard, World Record, Cash Box, and Gavin Report
- Recognized by Arturo Rodriguez, UFW Foundation (Cesar Chavez), 2000
- Member of the Texas Country Music Hall of Fame, Carthage, Texas, 2007
- Institute of Hispanic Culture Pioneer Award in recognition of his accomplishment "First Mexican American Country Music Star" (2010)
- Performed at 100th Anniversary for Wounded Knee, 1990
- Annual Tejano Music Award, 1991
- Terry Music Award in Fort Worth, Texas, 1998
- Pioneer Award from the Institute of Hispanic Culture, 2010

- Inducted into the Texas Country Music Hall of Fame in Carthage, Texas, 2007
- South Texas Music Walk of Fame, 2017
- CMA of Texas, "Living Legend" Award, 2020
- CMA of Texas, "Top of Texas" Award, 2021
- "Legendary Singer-Songwriter" Cowboy & Arena Champions Hall of Fame, 2022
- Ameripolitan "Master" Music Award, 2023, Memphis, Tennessee

About the Authors

©Cranston Reid Photography

Johnny Rodriguez is an American award-winning country music singer, songwriter, and author who pens songs and stories during moments of inspiration. He is also a master guitarist, actor, and Taekwondo Black Belt. Johnny was born Juan Raul Davis-Rodriguez, of Mexican and Irish descent, singing genres in country music, Tex Mex, Rancheros, Tejano, Norteño, and Mariachi.

At age 21, he was one of the youngest country singers to arrive on the Nashville scene, achieving international stardom. In 1972, Johnny recorded his first song, "Pass Me By (If You're Only Passing Through)" with Mercury Records, which rose to Number 9 on the Hot Country Songs list, establishing Rodriguez as the "First Mexican American Country Superstar." That same year, he was voted Most Promising Vocalist by the Academy of Country Music. That Rodriguez Sound infused country in his distinct Spanish style, touching millions across the miles.

In 1973, his debut album, *Introducing Johnny Rodriguez*, reached Number 1. He was also nominated for Male Vocalist of the Year by the Country Music Association. Johnny won the Billboard Trend Setter Award in 1976, propelling him to a national audience. The Number 1 hits continued: "You Always Come Back to Hurting Me," "Riding My Thumb to Mexico," "That's the Way Love Goes," "Just Get Up and Close the Door," "Desperado," "Down on the Rio Grande," and "Foolin'."

According to the Gavin Report, Johnny has charted 14 number-one hits, releasing 35 albums and 45 singles.

Perhaps the most treasured credentials for this favored son of Texas include standing ovations from the Ryman Auditorium to Carnegie Hall and performing at the Presidential Inaugural Ball at the White House for President George H.W. and George W. Bush. He was also recognized by Presidents Jimmy Carter and George W. Bush.

Rodriguez's new album, *Building Bridges: A Beyond the Interview Box Set,* is scheduled for release in 2023. Johnny is a father, grandfather, and godfather who enjoys living on a Texas ranch, the scene of his peaceful life in the hill country.

Austin Teutsch grew up in Jourdanton, Texas where he graduated from Jourdanton High School in 1973. He promptly entered the University of Arkansas in Fayetteville, Arkansas. He has been playing country music since he was 14 years old, slipping in the back doors of some of the roughest honky-tonks and roadhouses in Texas to chase a dream of his own.

He came back to Texas in 1980 and married Martha in 1981. Over the next 35 years, Mr. Teutsch has two wonderful sons—Taylor, 31, and Parker, 26—two best-selling biographies on the lives of Wal-Mart founder Sam Walton and former Texas Congresswoman Barbara Jordan, and many articles in publications around the country.

He has worked on the biographies of Dick York of *Bewitched* fame and Jimmy Nicol, a drummer who played as a Beatle when Ringo Starr was hospitalized in 1964.

Austin states co-writing this book with Johnny Rodriguez has been an amazing journey that he is proud to be a part of. From a small South Texas town to Nashville, Tennessee's capital known as Music City, Rodriguez was a talented young Mexican boy with stars in his eyes and a wagon full of talent, who opened a musical door few thought could ever be opened.

Austin Teutsch has lived in Austin, Texas for 30 years with his wife, Martha, to whom he dedicates the song, "Your Love Put A Song In My Heart."

References

- Duncan, Dayton, and Ken Burns. "Country Music." In *An Illustrated History Based on the Film Series*, by Ken Burns and Dayton Duncan, 2019.

- Holding, Larry and Randy Davis, Reporter Country Weekly Magazine

- League of United Latin American Citizens. "About." Lulac.org.

- Morthland, John. "Johnny on the Spot," Texas Monthly Magazine, December 1, 1998.

- Nevaer, Louis. "Marilyn Monroe's Mexican Origin Story," July 26, 2020.

- Price, Robert E. "The Bakersfield Sound: How a Generation of Okies Revolutionized American Music." www.iuniverse.com, 2015.

- Smith, Mira. "Country Song Round Up," Charlton Publication, May 1975.

- Suttie, Jill. "Greater Good Magazine," January 20, 2015. greatergood.berkeley.edu.

- "46 years ago: The Eagles Release 'Lyin Eyes; Earn a Country Hit," Taste of Country, August 2, 2021.

- Janzen, Rebecca, The Conversation.com. Why the Virgin of Guadalupe Is More Than A Religious Icon to Catholics in Mexico. December 10, 2020. University of South Carolina.

- "Reiko, Jennifer: Pre-show Interview." Taste of Country, December 12, 2018.

www.Rollingstone.com

Made in the USA
Columbia, SC
04 June 2025

58935360R00236